Geopolitical Economy

After US Hegemony,
Globalization and Empire

Radhika Desai

Fernwood Publishing
HALIFAX & WINNIPEG
www.fernwoodpublishing.ca

First published 2013 by Pluto Press
345 Archway Road, London N6 5AA

www.plutobooks.com

Published in Canada by Fernwood Publishing, 32 Oceanvista Lane, Black Point, Nova Scotia,
B0J 1B0 and 748 Broadway Avenue, Winnipeg, Manitoba, R3G 0X3
www.fernwoodpublishing.ca

Fernwood Publishing Company Limited gratefully acknowledges the financial support of the
Government of Canada through the Canada Book Fund and the Canada Council for the Arts,
the Nova Scotia Department of Communities, Culture and Heritage, the Manitoba Department
of Culture, Heritage and Tourism under the Manitoba Publishers Marketing Assistance Program
and the Province of Manitoba, through the Book Publishing Tax Credit, for our publishing
program.

Library and Archives Canada Cataloguing in Publication
Desai, Radhika, 1963-
     Geopolitical economy : after US hegemony, globalization and empire / Radhika Desai.
(The future of world capitalism)
Includes bibliographical references and index.
ISBN 978-1-55266-562-6
     1. Geopolitics--United States--Forecasting. 2. World politics--21st century--Forecasting.
3. Hegemony--United States--History. 4. Globalization--Forecasting. I. Title. II. Series: Future
of world capitalism (Winnipeg, Man.)
JC319.D49 2013   327.101   C2012-907000-9

British Library Cataloguing in Publication Data
A catalogue record for this book is available from the British Library

ISBN 978 0 7453 2993 2 Hardback
ISBN 978 0 7453 2992 5 Paperback (Pluto Press)
ISBN 978 1 55266 562 6 (Fernwood)
ISBN 978 1 8496 4839 4 PDF eBook
ISBN 978 1 8496 4841 7 Kindle eBook
ISBN 978 1 8496 4840 0 EPUB eBook

Library of Congress Cataloging in Publication Data applied for

10 9 8 7 6 5 4 3 2 1

Designed and produced for Pluto Press by Curran Publishing Services, Norwich

Printed and bound by CPI Group (UK) Ltd, Croydon, CR0 4YY

You are not likely to find a better contemporary history of the world's economy than this one. It is hard to put down, but the greater joy is that it undoes myth after myth about neoliberalism's inevitability and the neoclassical abstractions that economic history has little to do with the state any longer. The state and class battles will continue, and had better, argues Professor Desai.
—Jeff Madrick, Editor, *Challenge*

Radhika Desai's book shatters the stale notions that characterise traditional international political economy. Just as the world economy is crumbling before us, she has provided scholars with a fresh, compelling and forceful account of the US's failed efforts to dominate the world order order.
—Professor Ilene Grabel, Josef Korbel School of International Studies, University of Denver, USA

This impressive book powerfully questions the conventional wisdoms of both the right and the left about U.S. hegemony, globalization, and the "new American empire." Professor Desai takes us back to Marx and Engels and forward to Keynes, Polanyi and Brenner to give us a coherent narrative of capitalism's history and its future prospects. The nation-state, it turns out, is not withering away. This is radical scholarship at its best.
—Mel Watkins, professor emeritus of economics and political science, University of Toronto

This is a refreshing book with a punch. Desai not only charts the end of an era in global political economy, she offers us a stimulating framework for understanding the coming multipolar period, one full of promise if only we recognize its key features. Catholic in scope, *Geopolitical Economy* draws on a rich diversity of scholarly traditions to fashion a new outlook on political economy, one which combines the global thrust of capitalist dynamics with what she calls the fundamental materiality of the nation-state. It promises to have a significant impact on scholarship, and I recommend it to anyone interested in comprehending the changing political, economic and social contours of our world.
—Randall Germain, professor of political science, Carleton University, Canada

This is a bold and imaginative book. At a time when many see the United States consolidating its position as the leading imperialist power because of the travails of Europe and Japan, Radhika Desai sees a contrary tendency towards a weakening of U.S. hegemony and the emergence of multipolarity. At a time when the uncertainty surrounding the fate of the Euro makes many see the US dollar as strengthening its position as the most favoured medium of wealth-holding, Desai sees a tendency towards a decline of dollar hegemony. At a time when many, including important voices on the Left, see "globalization" as an irreversible process, Desai argues the need for a re-activation of the development-promoting role of the nation-State. And she argues her case with an analysis of history that has both sweep and rigour. Whether one agrees with her or not, this is a highly stimulating piece of work.

—Prabhat Patnaik, professor emeritus, Department of Economic Studies and Planning, Jawaharlal Nehru University, former chairman of the Kerala State Planning Commission, member of the UN taskforce on the reform of the world financial system.

A penetrating account of the complex interrelations between US hegemony and the transnational sweep of capital. Firmly planted in the long tradition of historical materialist analysis of imperialism, Desai breaks new ground in taking forward some of the most incisive theorisations from this lineage, critically dissecting theories that have for too long assumed that interstate rivalries were a thing of the past.

—Kees van der Pijl, professor emeritus, Department of International Relations, University of Sussex

Radhika Desai's book challenges several widely accepted ideas. The first of that is that hegemony of a nation provides stability to the world economy. The second is that the USA really enjoyed hegemony in any real sense during the second half of the twentieth century. The third is that the kind of globalization favoured by the financial industry and transnational corporations and their client states was a purely economic affair and witnessed the demise of the nation state. In support of her argument she undertakes a detailed biography of the US dollar as a hegemonic currency, showing how insecure that supposed hegemony was. In all this she deploys the Marxist notion of uneven and combined development as a strategic tool. Even if one disagrees with some of the details of the argument, anybody who is interested in understanding today's multipolar, contentious capitalism will have to read this book. I have every confidence that every student of the global economy and polity will greatly benefit by studying this outstanding monograph.

—Amiya Kumar Bagchi, founder-director of the Centre for Studies in Social Sciences, Kolkata and former Reserve Bank Professor at the Centre for Studies in Social Sciences, Calcutta

[This] is a timely work. Radhika Desai offers a critical and vivid analysis of what she aptly calls the geopolitical economy of capitalism which will be attractive as a textbook for international political economy courses at both undergraduate and graduate levels and a thrilling read for readers at large.
—Makoto Itoh, professor emeritus of the University of Tokyo.

Radhika Desai provides a clear-eyed and incisive look at some of the central concerns in the world today. Her main proposition is that a long period of actual or attempted dominance by one power is now effectively over, at least for a time—and this has significant implications for global capitalism's trajectory of "uneven and combined development". This book will persuade and engage you, it will make you think and want to discuss many of these issues further. So it must be read by anyone seeking to make sense of the rapidly changing global environment.
—Jayati Ghosh, professor at the Centre for Economic Studies and Planning, Jawaharlal Nehru University, executive secretary of the International Development Economics Associates (IDEAS)

Geopolitical Economy painstakingly confronts fashionable notions of US hegemony, globalization, and empire with a steady stream of discordant facts. Desai shows that the US was never actually hegemonic, that states were and remain central to capitalism, and that the aims and outcomes of policy have been shaped crucially by capitalism's endogenous crisis tendencies. She resituates the evolution of the global political economy within a new version of the theory of combined and uneven development. Highly recommended.
—Andrew Kliman, professor of economics, Pace University, author of *A Failure of Capitalist Production* (Pluto, 2011)

Radhika Desai has, with her brilliant *Geopolitical Economy*, given us an essential work on global political economy. This volume exquisitely weaves together a critical history of the US dollar, a devastating critique of global hegemony theory, and a rethinking of Marxian and Keynesian ideas about global economic crisis. ... Anyone seeking to understand the future of the global economy will draw wisdom, if not comfort, from this scintillating text.
—Gary Dymski, professor of economics, Leeds University Business School and University of California, Riverside

The Future of World Capitalism
Series editors: Radhika Desai and Alan Freeman

The world is undergoing a major realignment. The 2008 financial crash and ensuing recession, China's unremitting economic advance, and the uprisings in the Middle East, are laying to rest all dreams of an 'American Century'. This key moment in history makes weighty intellectual demands on all who wish to understand and shape the future.

Theoretical debate has been derailed, and critical thinking stifled, by apologetic and superficial ideas with almost no explanatory value, 'globalization' being only the best known. Academic political economy has failed to anticipate the key events now shaping the world, and offers few useful insights on how to react to them.

The Future of World Capitalism series will foster intellectual renewal, restoring the radical heritage that gave us the international labour movement, the women's movement, classical Marxism, and the great revolutions of the twentieth century. It will unite them with new thinking inspired by modern struggles for civil rights, social justice, sustainability, and peace, giving theoretical expression to the voices of change of the twenty-first century.

Drawing on an international set of authors, and a world-wide readership, combining rigour with accessibility and relevance, this series will set a reference standard for critical publishing.

Also available:

The Birth of Capitalism:
A Twenty-First-Century Perspective
Henry Heller

Remaking Scarcity:
From Capitalist Inefficiency to Economic Democracy
Costas Panayotakis

To Live and Die in America:
Class, Power, Health, and Healthcare
Robert Chernomas and Ian Hudson

CONTENTS

For my late grandmother,
Manorama (Kamu) Desai,
who taught me the best things I know.

ACKNOWLEDGEMENTS

The writing of books typically incurs many debts, and one that has taken so long to go from conception to completion is particularly heavily leveraged.

Scholarship is a lot like detective work. You prowl about libraries and plod through books and articles seeking clues. In this search the occasional tip from a reliable source who normally hangs about thoroughfares of scholarship with which you are unfamiliar can save a lot of time and effort. I received important pointers and references from Alain Alcouffe, Robert Bernner, Robert Chernomas, Victoria Chick, Donald Coffin, Thomas Ferguson, Jayati Ghosh, Henry Heller, Bob McKee, Robert Wade and Paul Zarembka.

Here in Winnipeg, I am part of two remarkable intellectual communities. Fletcher Barager, Robert Chernomas, Ian Hudson, Mark Gabbert, Julie Guard, John Loxley, Ardeshir Sepehri, John Seriuex and Seth Widgerson are regular interlocutors and co-conspirators on many themes and schemes. Wayne and Carol Choma, Linda Christian, Yilang Feng, Bob Gowenlock, Henry Heller, Ken Kaltrunyk, Ben Klass, Souske Morimoto, Karen Naylor and Zac Saltis of the Winnipeg Marx Reading Group provided weekly intellectual sustenance in the final year of writing.

In London, where so much of this book was drafted during long sojourns, seminars and conferences at the School of Oriental and Africal Studies (SOAS), the London School of Economics (LSE), University College London (UCL) and the interlinked dialogues and debates they generated gave a broader bottom to my ideas than they might otherwise have had, as did the many conferences I attended, including annual conferences of the Association for Heterodox Economics, Historical Materialism, and the World Association for Political Economy. The rather international set of interlocutors these and related networks created for me includes the late Giovanni Arrighi, Amiya Bagchi, Hasan Bakshi, Riccardo Bellofiore, Michael Brie, Stefan Bulla, Victoria Chick, Peter Fleissner, the late Chris Freeman, the late Peter Gowan, Makoto Itoh, Andrew Kliman,

David Kotz, Costas Lapavitsas, Ronen Palan, Costas Panayotakis, Prabhat Patnaik, Utsa Patnaik, Michael Perelman, Carlota Perez, Kees van der Pijl, Cornelius Renkl, John Ross, Dietmar Rothermund, David Schweikart, Robert Wade, Julian Wells and Jude Woodward.

The Federal Reserve Bank of St Louis gave full electronic access to the Economic Reports of the President, making it easier to use these sprawling texts. The British Library and its vast and efficiently provided resources were invaluable during the very long periods I spent in London without access to the better part of my own library. The library and librarians at the University of Manitoba did much to facilitate my work: Carol Budnick and Mavis Gray, for example, turned up the very interesting information that no subject heading for 'globalization' existed in the Library of Congress catalogue until 1999.

I would like to thank the two anonymous referees who read the text carefully and made many important suggestions for improving the argument and the clarity of the presentation while supporting it enthusiastically. Mark Selden made many helpful comments on the proposal. Kees Van der Pijl always encouraged this project and made suggestions for reorganization which much improved the structure of the book after carefully reading an early draft. Henry Heller read, and critically commented on, a later draft. Ben Klass read many chapters of the penultimate draft, picking out typographical, grammatical and stylistic errors and unclear formulations, leaving a much cleaner text. The Global Political Economy Research Fund came up with a timely pot of money to help with tidying the manuscript for publication, and Yilang Feng helped with its wearisome details meticulously and efficiently. Finally, Victoria Chick's high-precision engagement with many chapters of the text in its penultimate version improved its content, formulations and writing. I remain, of course, responsible for all residual limitations of the book.

Roger van Zwanenberg's characteristic combination of scepticism and enthusiasm is what every writer should enjoy from her publisher. David Shulman, who took over from Roger toward the end, read the typescript carefully and urged many valuable suggestions for improvement. Susan Diane Brophy has provided intelligent and efficient help with running the book series over the past year. Thanks are also due to Susan Curran for an excellent copy-editing job.

Finally I come to three very personal debts. Guido, prince among dogs, supervised the writing of this book from end to end. I cannot recall its writing without thinking of his massive and glossy black form lying curled by my chair, his direct gaze, sonorous sighs and warm cuddles. He insisted on my taking well-timed breaks, whether to throw sticks for him into the Thames, or skate along the frozen Assiniboine so he could take in the crisp Arctic air. As I produced more and more words, Guido's enigmatic demonstration of the superfluity of most of them for a rich and engrossing life continued to give pause.

Alan Freeman's love and support are inseparable from this book. He took over the bulk of household tasks every time the writing reached a critical stage. But he also interrupted the writing with new enthusiasms to which I proved susceptible. So though I cannot say he hastened its writing overall, his intellectual engagement and our animated, and not infrequently heated, discussions and arguments, made it far more interesting to write, and, I hope, to read. He also read the entire manuscript with care and improved it greatly.

The book is dedicated to my late grandmother who brought me up. She lives on in my best impulses in ways I continue to discover. She grew up in a village and had only six years of formal schooling. Her effect on my scholarship is, however, greater than such facts might lead you to imagine. Of these, I want to mention two. Some of my fondest early memories are of her reading me to sleep with stories from the *Mahabharata*. They left me, I have come to realize over the years, with a sense of what makes a good story: while much of it remains ineffable still, this much I have grasped: a good story must contain all the elements that get it moving and propel it to a conclusion. If good scholarship is ultimately about constructing good stories, I like to think the sense of narrative I absorbed from these stories helps make mine more complete and more satisfying. My grandmother also had a profound sense of justice which made her a better exemplar of the liberal values of the professional family she married into than many of its natives. She never exceeded her authority and I witnessed her speak up courageously when powerful others had overstepped theirs. So, if the story told here is judged good, and if its politics gain a wider resonance, a considerable part of the credit will be hers.

Radhika Desai
London
14 July 2012

ABBREVIATIONS

APEC	Asia-Pacific Economic Cooperation
BEA	Bureau of Economic Analysis
BEM	big emerging markets
BIS	Bank of International Settlements
CEA	Council of Economic Advisors
CPI	Consumer Price Index
ERP	Economic Report of the President
FDI	foreign direct investment
FIDC	Federal Deposit Insurance Corporation
FOMC	Federal Open Market Committee
FIRE	finance, insurance and real estate
GATT	General Agreements on Tariffs and Trade
GDP	gross domestic product
GNP	gross national product
GPE	global political economy
GSG	global savings glut
HST	hegemonic stability theory
ICT	information and communication technology
ICU	International Clearing Union
IFIH	international financial intermediation hypothesis
IMF	International Monetary Fund
IPE	international political economy
IPO	initial public offering
IR	international relations
MNCs	multinational corporations
MMM	money market mutual (funds)
MBSs	mortgage-backed securities
NAFTA	North American Free Trade Agreement
NBER	National Bureau of Economic Research
NICs	newly industrializing countries
NIEO	New International Economic Order
OECD	Organisation for Economic Co-operation and Development

OPEC	Organization of Petroleum Exporting Countries
OTC	over the counter
PNAC	Project for a New American Century
QE	quantitative easing
R&D	research and development
SAPs	Structural Adjustment Programmes
S&Ls	savings and loans (institutions)
SDRs	special drawing rights
SIVs	structured investment vehicles
TARP	Troubled Asset Relief Program
TRPF	tendency of the rate of profit to fall
UCD	uneven and combined development
UN	United Nations
UNRRA	United Nations Relief and Rehabilitation Administration
WMD	weapons of mass destruction
WS	world systems (analysis)
WTO	World Trade Organization

1

INTRODUCTION:

WHY GEOPOLITICAL ECONOMY?

The owl of Minerva, Hegel once remarked, takes wing at dusk. Knowledge results from reflection *after* the tumult of the day. This gloomy view may be too sweeping, but it certainly applies to the multipolar world order. Influential figures began hailing it in the wake of the 2008 financial crisis and the Great Recession. The American president of the World Bank spoke of 'a new, fast-evolving multi-polar world economy' (World Bank, 2010). Veteran international financier George Soros predicted that 'the current financial crisis is less likely to cause a global recession than a radical realignment of the global economy, with a relative decline of the US and the rise of China and other countries in the developing world' (2008). However, the multipolar world order was much longer in the making. Developments of this magnitude simply don't happen overnight even in a crisis (though, as we shall see, emerging multipolarity was a decisive factor in causing it), and this has important implications for prevailing understandings of the capitalist world order.

Recent accounts stressed its economic unity: globalization conceived a world unified by markets alone while empire proposed one unified by the world's most powerful – 'hegemonic' or 'imperial' (the terms tended to be used interchangeably) – state. They also assumed either that nation-states were not relevant to explaining the world order (globalization), or that only one, the United States, was (empire). We can call these views cosmopolitan, a term the *Oxford English Dictionary* defines as 'not restricted to any one country or its inhabitants' and 'free from national limitations or attachments'. Neither can explain the multipolar world which is the result of national states playing large and openly acknowledged economic roles to boost growth in the emerging economies, pre-eminently China, fracturing the world economy and undermining the United

1

States's importance in it. This development suggests that the cosmopolitan understandings are not only obsolete, they were never accurate.

Moreover, it was not just in emerging economies that states played important economic roles. The influential *Financial Times* proclaimed that 'The State ... is back' (Wolf, 2009), scrambling to respond to the crises with bailouts and fiscal stimuli after three decades when anti-state and pro-market ideologies – neoliberalism as well as globalization and empire – dominated. In reality, these ideologies notwithstanding, the state had never gone away and the world's economies retained their national distinctiveness, as the Eurozone crisis underlines so starkly. Even in the Anglo-American heartlands of these ideologies, states continued to play important economic roles, only more one-sidedly in favour of the wealthy.

As the acknowledgement of multipolarity upsets more and more received wisdom, *Geopolitical Economy* seeks to lay the foundation of more accurate understandings by advancing three major arguments.

The first and most fundamental argument insists on the materiality of nations. It sees the capitalist world order and its historical evolution as the product of the interaction – conflicting, competing or cooperative – of multiple states. This interaction is governed by the economic role each must play in managing capitalism and its crisis tendencies – chiefly its constrained demand and consequent surfeit of capital – which only grow sharper as capitalism matures. This economic role involves both domestic economic action and international engagement. The geopolitical economy of the capitalist world order this argument yields draws on the intellectual resources of classical political economy up to and including Marx and Engels, the classical theories of imperialism, later critiques – like those of John Maynard Keynes and Karl Polanyi – of neoclassical economics, the developmental state literature and economic history, such as that of Robert Brenner. In it, states' international interaction is seen in terms of the dialectic that the Bolsheviks termed uneven and combined development (UCD). On the one hand, dominant states seek to preserve existing uneven configurations of capitalist development which favour them, including through formal and informal imperialism. On the other, contender states (a term gratefully borrowed from Kees van der Pijl, 2006b) accelerate capitalist, and in some cases such as the USSR, communist, development to contest imperial projects of dominant states. Such hot-house development is called combined development because it combines or compresses many stages into shorter and more intense bursts. Despite the economic, geopolitical, military and ideological power marshalled by dominant states, so far the latter tendency has dominated in UCD – sometimes against great odds and with apparently interminable delays. This politico-economic dialectic, and not the market or capitalism conceived in exclusively economic terms, is responsible for productive capacity spreading ever more widely around the world. By the early twenty-first century it had created the multipolar world in which there were now too many economies that were too substantial for any one of them to even hope to dominate the rest.

This last point is critical: the present crisis marks the end a long phase in the history of the capitalist world order, and of imperialism, the phase characterized by the actual or attempted dominance of single powers. In this phase, cosmopolitan views of the capitalist world order as a single unified world economy in which most states played no economic role served critical ideological functions. They dissimulated the economic roles of the imperial states or disguised them as benevolently 'hegemonic', and they discouraged and forestalled, where possible, those of contender states. Nineteenth-century free trade, under which UK imperial ambitions were advanced, was the first of a succession of such ideologies. It was followed by twentieth-century hegemony stability theory (HST) and, more recently, the much shorter-lived globalization and empire, all of which articulated US attempts at world dominance. Like the imperial projects they articulated, these ideologies were never uncontested. This book builds on the dissenting traditions listed above.

The second argument is that the world dominance of the first industrial capitalist country, the United Kingdom, was inevitable as well as unrepeatable. The further unfolding of UCD, in which the combined development of contender states undermined UK dominance, also ensured that such dominance was no longer possible. US attempts to emulate it, beginning in the early twentieth century, had to be scaled back: eschewing territorial empire the United States confined itself to making the dollar the world's currency and New York its financial centre. Even in this modest form, the US imperial enterprise would fail. Thus, the widespread idea that the United States was (or is) hegemonic is simply false. What is true is that the United States engineered a succession of unstable arrangements through which it pursued its imperial mimesis. The tremendously harmful military and economic actions it entailed have been justly and unflaggingly exposed by generations of critical and progressive writers. This book makes arguments that these US actions were the price of the benefits of US 'hegemony' ring even more hollow than they ever did.

Indeed, ideas about US hegemony – that cluster of theories usually grouped together as HST – were rooted in little more than the United States's mimetic imperial aspirations. HST emerged in the 1970s after the most promising attempt to realize these aspirations – installing a gold-backed dollar as the world's currency at Bretton Woods – had already failed. All versions of HST retrospectively posited a postwar US hegemony clinched by the dollar's world role, supposedly based on the overwhelming economic and financial dominance the United States achieved after the Second World War. However, that dominance was wrought by war and would prove temporary. Internationally, the United States was just one, albeit the largest, among a growing number of states pursuing combined development more powerfully than ever. Domestically, the US economy was a national, not an imperial economy. In these circumstances even the scaled-down US attempts to emulate the United Kingdom's nineteenth-century dominance could only give this sort of single-power dominance a strange afterlife.

Finally, this book tracks the crisis-ridden career of the dollar as the world's money to demonstrate its third major argument: that globalization of the 1990s and empire of the 2000s were ideologies of the two most recent US attempts to maintain that role, not genuine theories. The dollar's world role was problematic from the start, and its mounting troubles led to the closing of the gold window in 1971. Thereafter the dollar continued to be the world's currency, and to plague it with financial troubles. As the dollar lurched from one unstable basis to another, its ability (not to mention suitability) to continue in this role was regularly cast into doubt. As attempts to sustain the dollar's world role, globalization and empire rested on the vast increases in dollar-denominated world financial flows. They were the main element of what came to be known as financialization. It enabled capital to flow into the United States. It flowed into the US stock market under globalization as Federal Reserve chairman Alan Greenspan fed illusions about the US's 'new economy' and 'hidden productivity miracle'. And it flowed into the swelling market for US mortgage-backed securities as Greenspan and his successor Ben Bernanke fed new illusions about the trajectory of house prices and the justified capital flows into the United States under Bush Jr's empire. The financial crisis in which the latter culminated leaves the US administration no viable options to stabilize the dollar's world money role. Arrangements for displacing the dollar in international payments are being proposed and even made – from an expanded role for special drawing rights (SDRs) through barter and swap arrangements for trade financing to regional institutions for reserve pooling. While it is still difficult to tell exactly how long the dollar's already diminished role will linger, and it has certainly been prolonged by the crisis in the Eurozone, its fate is now governed by forces its makers cannot control.

As Figure 1.1 shows, these three arguments of descending generality are placed one inside the other, like Russian *matryoshka* dolls. In the rest of this Introduction I trace my path to geopolitical economy and then discuss why it is politically necessary at the current conjuncture and end with a plan of the book that outlines

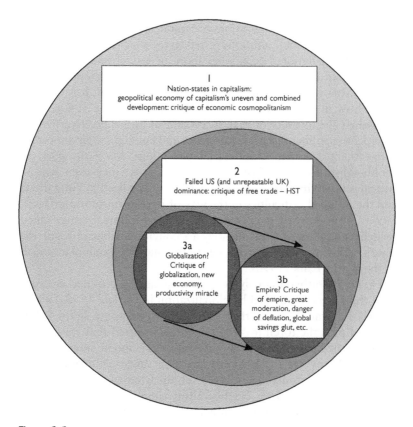

1
Nation-states in capitalism:
geopolitical economy of capitalism's uneven and combined development: critique of economic cosmopolitanism

2
Failed US (and unrepeatable UK)
dominance: critique of free trade – HST

3a
Globalization?
Critique of globalization, new economy, productivity miracle

3b
Empire? Critique of empire, great moderation, danger of deflation, global savings glut, etc.

Figure 1.1

how its three arguments proceed and intertwine through the following chapters.

GETTING TO GEOPOLITICAL ECONOMY

Writing this book was a long intellectual journey. Only towards its end did the expression 'geopolitical economy' suggest itself as an apt description of my approach. In doing so it gave a measure of the length of that journey and marked the intellectual distance it put between the final product and five bodies of thought it emerged from.

During my Indian schooldays, textbooks by some of the country's foremost critical historians and economists introduced me to progressive anti-imperialist/nationalist perspectives on India's economic problems and prospects. At graduate school in Canada, a historical and materialist approach to politics and comparative political economy enabled me to understand national economies as historically distinct configurations of capital, labour and pre-capitalist classes. On these configurations rested states which, in turn, directed and regulated national economies more or less effectively through distinct institutions and practices, as capitalism developed in one country after another, first in Europe and then beyond. It is easy for forget how mainstream such a view was well into the 1980s. That was when the assaults of that succession of anti-state, free market ideologies, neoliberalism, globalization and empire, swept almost all before them. I remained among the exceptions. My early work on neoliberalism swam against the flow of most writing, even writing critical of neoliberalism, to emphasize its intellectual limitations and the political difficulties in the way of its implementation (Desai, 1994b). I noted with satisfaction that when neoliberal policy failed to deliver and neoliberal ideology to convince, admissions of the state's necessary economic role began to issue from high places such as the World Bank (1990).

However, rather than dying a natural death, pro-market, anti-state thinking was rescued by globalization in the late 1990s, which argued that states were ineffectual in a global economy. In the 2000s it would pass the torch to 'empire', which asserted that states were insignificant forces against the imperial or hegemonic power of one of them. Many see the last 30 years as a single neoliberal period with three distinct ideologies. However, the latter two were critically different from the first. Neoliberalism simply sought to provide a better prescription for national economic growth by blaming prevailing statist policies for the slow growth of the 1970s. It was part of what Hobsbawm (1994) called the 'short twentieth century' (from 1914 to 1989), during which the parameters of economic policy remained national. Globalization and empire were, on the other hand, cosmopolitan ideologies. Although, of course, they entailed prescriptions for domestic economic policy, they posed as accounts of world order – indeed, theories of it.

My background and intellectual evolution had inoculated me against globalization's cosmopolitan charms. Posing as a social scientific theory, it had few advocates (but see Ohmae, 1990). It had, instead, plenty of 'realists': politicians like Blair or Clinton and intellectuals like Giddens or Stiglitz argued that globalization was real, powerful and unstoppable. They made globalization as mainstream an assessment of the dynamics of the world order as any. The anti-globalization movement, paradoxically, only added credibility to their arguments by accepting globalization's reality and seeking only to change its form. My views were aligned with the determined band of sceptics (pre-eminently Hirst, Thompson and Bromley, 1996/2009; Wade, 1996b; Weiss, 1998) who meticulously marshalled facts, arguments and statistics to show that every claim made about globalization – on growth, trade, investment, finance, migration, technology, inequality or poverty, and pre-eminently about the irrelevance of the state – was tenuous.

That would have been the end of matter had globalization really been a social-scientific theory amenable to refutation. Instead, the sceptical critique led leading writers on globalization to move it onto new 'transformationalist' terrain (Held et al., 1999). Here, globalization's claims were made radically ambiguous: globalization was not 'the' but only 'a' 'central driving force in the world' which was 'closely associated with, although by no means the sole cause of, a transformation or reconstitution of the powers of the modern nation-state' (Held et al., 1999: 436). It was, moreover, 'an essentially contingent historical process replete with contradictions' whose protagonists made 'no claims about [its] future trajectory' and called instead for 'dynamic and open-ended' analysis. Globalization was 'inscribed with contradictions' and 'significantly shaped by conjunctural factors'. But, for all that, it was 'an idea whose time has come' (Held et al., 1999: 7).

On transformationalist terrain, discourse about globalization could expand without constraints of evidence or logic, and did. As one rare perceptive analyst pointed out, globalization had become at once the *explanandum* and the *explanans*, at once that which required explanation and the explanation itself (Rosenberg, 2000).

Rather than intellectual validity or consistency, the sheer volume of writing that hordes of academics, journalists, policy-wonks and politicians now debating its multiplying minutiae generated on the subject undergirded the diffuse conviction that settled over public discourse in the late 1990s that something called globalization was somehow real. It was amid this stalemate between the validity of the sceptical arguments and the volubility of transformationalist discourse that I realized that the sceptics' powerful case begged an important question: if globalization was not what it was supposed to be, what was it? What occasioned the discourse and gave it strength?

That question set me on the path that led to this book. The late Peter Gowan's *The Global Gamble* (1999a) and Michael Hudson's much earlier work *Super Imperialism* (1972) provided a solid start. In their agential perspective, the constitution and evolution of the world order was the vectoral sum of the actions of powerful states, pre-eminently the United States. They were also dialectical accounts: even the most powerful states could fail to achieve their objects or be prevented from doing so by other states, despite their lesser power. In identifying globalization as a US government, specifically a Clinton government, strategy – 'Washington's Faustian bid for world dominance' as his book's subtitle had it – Gowan was soon followed by others. On leaving office Clinton was hailed as the 'globalization president' (*Foreign Policy in Focus*, 2000) and his successor's 'imperial' presidency led many to contrast the two projects. Giovanni Arrighi, for one, wondered about 'The strange death of the globalization project':

> For all its free-market rhetoric, the Bush Administration was never as enthusiastic as the Clinton Administration about the process of multilateral liberalisation of trade and capital movements that constituted the central institutional aspect of so-called globalization. Indeed, the word 'globalization' has rarely, if ever, cropped up in Bush's speeches. According to a senior presidential aide, the word 'makes him uncomfortable'. Speaking of the December 2002 tariffs on imported steel, under threat of $2.3 billion in retaliatory sanctions, the aide explained that the White House 'thinks what went wrong in the 90s is that we forgot to put American interests first. So globalisation sounds like the creation of a lot of rules that may restrict the president's choices, that dilute American influence.'
> (Arrighi, 2005b: 62; see also Bacevich, 2002: 72–3; Mann, 2004: xvi; Johnson, 2004: 255)

These contrasts also negated transformationalist attempts to portray globalization as decades, if not centuries or millennia, old and give it a long scholarly pedigree. In fact, the word 'globalization' emerged, and writing on it took off, only in the late 1990s (Therborn, 2001; Fine, 2004). That was the moment when, as Chapter 7 shows, the Clinton Administration began to give the word the distinctive cluster of meanings with which it would dominate public discourse in the late 1990s.

Obituaries of globalization began to appear in the early years of the new century, typically connecting the end of globalization to the events of September 11, 2001 (Ferguson, 2005; *Economist*, 2001a). Of course by this time so many scholars had invested so much scholarly credibility in the idea of globalization that writing on it could hardly stop overnight. But it definitely levelled off (Fine, 2004), and there was a distinct new mood. Not only was globalization replaced by empire, claims about globalization became even more qualified, circumspect and ambiguous. Martin Wolf, who had long argued that globalization was not only real and desirable but also more or less inevitable turned, in his *Why Globalization Works* (2004), to making the case that it needed to be given a chance. Globalization had been demoted from unstoppable juggernaut to a delicate plant needing careful nurture.

It was in this context that I set about writing a book about globalization as a US strategy of world dominance. It would fill an important gap in understanding. Hudson's account had ended in the early 1970s. Gowan's also came too early, just a little too early: writing in the immediate aftermath of the Asian financial crisis, he identified it as the apogee of globalization. However, as I would discover, by directing capital flows back into the United States, that crisis only set the stage for an even more spectacular climax, the bursting of the dot-com bubble, whose aftermath determined the economic strategies of Bush Jr's empire. And later writers had just made passing, if to me at least very suggestive, remarks. Moreover, my book was also to set the account of globalization in a systematic theorization of the capitalist world order and its development.

I initially assumed that HST provided that theorization. After all, it focused on the *world* economy, showing how powerful states – the United Kingdom before 1914 and the United States after 1945 – organized its productive expansion. HST's highly erudite and avowedly Marxist world systems (WS) version even stretched the succession of 'hegemonies' back to seventeenth-century Holland and the sixteenth-century Italian city states. So originally I assumed, in line with HST, that the United States had been hegemonic in the 1950s and 1960s. However, further investigation of the historical record undermined such assumptions. And that meant that though HST, including its most elaborate WS version, had been erected precisely to understand the US case, it was anomalous. Worse, the very idea of hegemonies turned out to have originated in the long-standing imperial ambitions of the US political classes themselves.

These realizations deepened and broadened my project. The planned ironic account of globalization could no longer be based on HST but had to take it, and its epigone, 'empire', on in a fuller account of the evolution of the world order and the evolving positions, practices and ideologies of the United States in it. This was just as well, because I could now round out the account by discussing empire too – the credibility it derived from HST and its dangerously contradictory political economy which took financialization to new heights. Given that the literatures on empire and financialization exist in separate silos, this connection was worth emphasizing. Empire's advocates, of course, celebrated it and called on the United States to accept its imperial responsibilities (Ferguson, 2004; Maier, 2006; Ignatieff, 2003) while its realists saw it as a grimly settled and stable reality (Panitch and Gindin, 2004). Even its opponents, while they did expose its contradictions and purposes (Bacevich, 2002; Harvey, 2003; Johnson, 2004; Mann, 2003), mostly concentrated on military aspects and on the question of US deficits. While these were not irrelevant (Arrighi, 2005a, 2005b), financialization was, in my view, critical to understanding globalization, empire and the dollar's world role.

Casting about for a new theoretical framework, I gravitated to UCD. In retrospect, this was fated. UCD had framed the Bolsheviks' understanding of their historic revolution against capitalism and imperialism. It was connected to the contemporaneous classical theories of imperialism and rooted in Marx and Engels. Moreover, it became part of the further unfolding of UCD in the twentieth century. As the strongest form of combined development, communism, whether of the USSR until the 1990s or the People's Republic of China today, would support, and generally widen the opportunities for, other states pursing combined development, capitalist as well as communist, in a broader anti-imperialist configuration. UCD and the classical theories of imperialism were the first theories of modern capitalist international relations, not Wilsonian idealism and the 'realism' which replaced it, as students of international relations (IR) are usually taught. Geopolitical economy takes them as its theoretical point of departure.

I encountered UCD as one does a sophisticated piece of machinery unjustly abandoned at the waterside by those who inherited, but did not comprehend, it. It lay buried under layer upon layer of sedimented misinterpretation and partial appreciation that passing intellectual fads and trends had washed upon it over the decades. Only parts that remained in use stuck out in view. There was its understanding of the Russian Revolution, which some deployed to understand the possibilities of communism in the developing world (e.g. Löwy, 1981). And there was the concept of unevenness, which others used to emphasize the inequalities of capitalism (e.g. Smith, 1990). Both neglected the multiplying instances of combined capitalist development to which their age was witness, and by the 1970s it became the province of largely non-Marxist writers on developmental states (e.g. Deyo, 1987; Wade, 1990; Berger and Dore, 1996; Amsden, 1992; Woo-Cumings, 1999). As I pulled UCD out of this mire, its basis in Marx and Engels's writing was exposed to view. Cleaning it up and overhauling it so it could once again be put it to explanatory work on later twentieth-century and early twenty-first-century developments involved fitting it with carefully chosen modern trappings – Keynes, Polanyi, the largely non-Marxist developmental state literature and Robert Brenner's economic history.

UCD's restored theoretical machinery assumes not only that states play economic roles in domestic political economy and geopolitical economy to manage their capitalisms' contradictions, but also that there is a dialectic between unevenness and combined development. The unfolding of UCD has taken the capitalist world order through distinct historical stages. The phase of UK dominance gave way to the intertwined industrial and imperial competition between the United Kingdom and contender states, chiefly the United States, Germany and Japan, which climaxed in the First World War and birthed the Russian Revolution. In the following phase, actually existing communism was added as a mode of combined development to the usual capitalist forms, and its powerful anti-imperial thrust widened the geopolitico-economic space for combined development, whether capitalist or communist. Seeing both communism and national developmental capitalisms as forms of combined development makes it easier to see why so many critical writers insist that both were the targets of the US cold war: it was more an exercise to maintain capitalism's unevenness than an ideological crusade (Block, 1977: 10; Van der Pijl, 2006a: 14, 30).

The unfolding of UCD is not without effects on the progress of inevitably national class struggles: unevenness tends to empower capitalist and propertied classes particularly in imperial centres, while combined development generally empowers working classes and popular sectors. In the postwar phase of UCD, for instance, Soviet power and prestige not only ensured decolonization and supported combined development in the newly independent states, it facilitated a historic development in the domestic political economies of the advanced industrial powers. The enfranchisement of working classes had already made high unemployment politically intolerable in the early twentieth century, and made states even more involved in economic management. Now, working-class assertion increased wages. Domestic markets widened, providing a timely substitute for the loss of colonial markets. However, once these markets were saturated, the geopolitical economy of the latter twentieth century witnessed the logic of UCD unfolding as a struggle for limited markets which Brenner (1998, 2002, 2006, 2009) reconstructed so vividly.

Moving beyond comparative political economy and forsaking HST for UCD was quickly followed by three other breaks – with international (later global) political economy (IPE), Marxist economics and the emerging Marxist international relations – all for one critical reason: these bodies of thought were all creatures of 'economics'. Let me explain.

Neoclassical economics has been subject to much criticism, not least in the aftermath of the 2008 crisis. But all such criticism is incomplete if it fails to appreciate that the discipline emerged in the late nineteenth century precisely because Marx and Engels's intervention made classical political economy an unsuitable source of legitimacy for capitalism. Indeed, it had been far from ideal even before their intervention, and two fictions had been necessary to make it so: Say's law ruled out gluts in the market, denying the need for colonial markets for excess output, and comparative advantage justified as natural the imperial world division of labour between industrial mother countries and agricultural colonies which emerged out of that need. And just when these were combined in Ricardo's writings, Marx savaged Say's law while questioning comparative advantage in less noticed but equally important ways. He also exposed political economy's contradictions and limitations to turn it into a tool for working classes to justify socialism and anti-imperialism. Now bourgeois thinkers had to devise a brand new way to legitimize capitalism. The result was neoclassical, marginalist equilibrium economics, which reached back over Marx and Engels to Ricardo, and installed Say's law and comparative advantage at its core.

Neoclassical economics rested on two critical substitutions: classical political economy's focus on history, conflict and crises was substituted by equilibrium, and its labour theory of value (as distinct from price) and Marx's discovery of the source of surplus value were substituted by a theory of prices as constituted by subjective preferences in markets. The first substitution created an ahistorical and static 'social science', typically written in simple present tense (political parties do this, inflation does that), in which societies did not change fundamentally, certainly not because they generated crises endogenously. The second substitution focused economics on markets alone, away from production, classes and struggles. Such an economics, separated from other social sciences and privileged in relation to them in a new social-scientific division of labour, no longer required an understanding of politics, law and society. Its capitalism was thus purely economic and economically cosmopolitan for the same reason: states played no economic roles. It was a seamlessly global system whose division into an increasing plurality of states was inconsequential. Such a conception of capitalism might dissimulate capitalism's injustice and anarchy, but only at the expense of understanding it. This 'economics' formed the basis of IPE, Marxist economics and the Marxist international relations that has emerged in recent decades.

IPE pioneers founded the new discipline around 1970 because the separate disciplines of international economics and international politics could not capture the complexity of the mounting international economic difficulties that arose from the travails of the dollar. However, the name could be misleading for anyone who expected the new discipline to reach back to the tradition of classical political economy: this was not possible unless its pioneers were willing to abandon their bourgeois and US-centric (as IPE was and remains) positions and preoccupations. Worse, for all the fanfare about combining international economics with international politics, the higher status of economics within the social-scientific division of labour made IPE more often an exercise in the 'politics of economics'. The latter's biases remained unquestioned, producing, for example, laments about how 'special interests' compromised axiomatically superior free trade and free market arrangements instead of investigations about the intertwined national and class interests at play in trade. The limitations of economics also ensured, as we shall see, that the mainstream of IPE became the credulous audience for a succession of discourses of US power, not least HST, globalization and empire and their more specific accompaniments – the international financial intermediation hypothesis (IFIH), the new economy, the productivity miracle, the danger of deflation, the great moderation and the global savings glut – which issued from influential sources as US governments took ever more unlikely and unstable measures to maintain the dollar's world role.

It might have been expected that Marxism, which had survived the cold war, McCarthyism and other capitalist campaigns against it, at least as a dissenting tradition in the academy if not as a politically relevant force, would contest these discourses. It was, after all, the legatee of classical political economy. But it too failed. Since the early twentieth century more and more Marxists have turned to cultural and philosophical pursuits (Anderson, 1976, 1983), while the small band of those who dealt with Marx's critique of capitalism and political economy were trained as 'economists'. They wheeled the Trojan horse of neoclassical economics into the Marxist citadel and sought to fit Marx's critique of political economy into its methodological framework, despite the fundamental theoretical, methodological and political antagonisms between the two (Clarke, 1991). The resulting 'Marxist economics' ended up rejecting value theory (and thus Marx's account of surplus value) on the basis of alleged inconsistencies and the alleged 'transformation problem' (Kliman, 2007; Freeman, Kliman and Wells, 2004; Desai, 2010a). It also embraced neoclassical theory's purely economic conception of a more or less crisis-free capitalism. Marx's view that capitalism suffered from paucity of demand and the tendency of the rate of profit to fall (TRPF) was discarded (Freeman, 2010). Such Marxist economists wasted no time on the classical theories of imperialism: states played too great a role in them. No wonder then that the most important resource in reconstructing the geopolitical economy of recent decades has been not the work of a Marxist 'economist' but Brenner's Marxist economic history of postwar capitalism.

Finally, when a specifically Marxist strain of international relations (IR) emerged in the 1990s, so completely was it a creature of the purely economic and cosmopolitan account of capitalism that it began by brandishing that account against the dominant state-focused, realist approach in IR (Rosenberg, 1994, see Desai 2010c for a fuller critique). Later scholars of Marxist IR did attempt to give politics and even UCD greater theoretical space (e.g. Teschke, 2003; Van der Pijl, 2006a; Callinicos, 2009). However, as we shall see, they either let the economic cosmopolitan conception in through the theoretical back door and/or emphasized capitalism's unevenness exclusively in an un-dialectical account which left no room for combined development.

While it emerged in engagement with comparative political economy, HST, IPE, Marxist economics and Marxist IR, geopolitical economy lies beyond these five bodies of thought. Unlike comparative political economy, *geo*political economy focuses on the world level. Unlike WS or HST, which one-sidedly privilege dominance, *geopolitical* economy places contestation at its core. Unlike IPE, geo*political* economy reaches back to classical political economy and thence forward to critics of neoclassical economics to foreground states' economic roles. Unlike Marxist economics, geo*political economy* recovers Marx and classical Marxism to insist that capitalism is prone to endogenous crises and that imperialism was one way they were managed historically. And unlike the new Marxist IR, *geopolitical economy* conceives of states playing critical economic roles, both in creating unevenness and in promoting combined development.

The distance I have travelled beyond these bodies of thought does not, however, negate their contribution to my understanding, or that of scholars I frontally criticize in these pages. If anything I appreciate all the more how much, as Marx said of Adam Smith, whom he greatly respected, a scholar's 'contradictions are of significance because they contain problems which it is true he [or she] does not solve, but which he [or she] reveals by contradicting himself [or herself]' (Marx, 1969: 151).

This book is only a beginning. It has faults I already recognize. The foremost is that, ironically for a book challenging the notion of US hegemony, it is embarrassingly US-focused. The contender states whose combined development sealed the fate of US attempts to emulate pre-1914 British world dominance – the proper Hamlets of any full account of capitalism's geopolitical economy – remain largely in the background, only appearing now and again, like Rosencrantz and Guildenstern, 'to swell a progress, start a scene or two' in T. S. Eliot's memorable line. The sheer amount of misunderstanding about the US world role which the book must address means that the fuller parts they deserve will have to await other works building on the ground cleared by *Geopolitical Economy*. Here these numerous cases of combined development take guises and appear at cues that are, I trust, uncontroversial and minimal. Another fault is a greater degree of self-citation than is normally necessary. It is another indication of the length and difficulty of the intellectual journey that ended in this book, in that I found myself writing articles on particularly knotty issues which, while necessary for the book's further progress, were not strictly part of it.

WHY GEOPOLITICAL ECONOMY MATTERS POLITICALLY

Crises teasingly hold out the possibility of dramatic reversals only to be followed by surreal continuity as the old order cadaverously fights back. So far in the current crisis military fight-back appears to be failing. Multipolarity and the shift in the world's centre of gravity to the emerging economies opened the way for the toppling of US-supported dictators in Egypt and Tunisia. Though Western intervention in Libya could not be prevented, it was stalled in Syria. However, there were more worrying signs of continuity in political economy and geopolitical economy. Announcements of the return of the state and of the 'Master', Keynes, which came with initial flurry of bailouts and stimuli were followed by austerity, signalling 'the strange non-death of neoliberalism' (Crouch, 2011).

Governments not only spent billions bailing out corrupt and irresponsible financial institutions, and used their consequently swollen debt burdens as reasons to keep fiscal stimuli small and cut welfare spending back drastically, they also insisted that the private sector must power recovery when in fact it was too enfeebled to do so. All this was done just to assuage financial interests. No greater sign of their continuing hold on political power is necessary than such appeasement when punishment was due. After the bailout repaired their balance sheets, financial institutions, particularly in the United States, seemed to be back to business as usual, entering new arenas of speculation: commodities and emerging markets. This led to calls to regulate commodities trading and capital controls (UNCTAD, 2011). In the United States the banks also poured billions into resisting the implementation of the 2010 Dodd–Frank Wall Street Reform and Consumer Protection Act, which would re-regulate finance and impose, *inter alia*, the 'Volcker rule' that banks under federal deposit insurance be prevented from proprietary trading.

Part of this continuity must be attributed to the lack of widespread mobilization against austerity except where it was particularly acute, as in Greece. After all, wresting worthwhile reforms, let alone revolutions, from crises requires organized parties and movements capable of taking the opportunities that crises proverbially offer.

However, such capability also requires understanding the drift and direction of change and, on the principle that 'in the contradiction lies the hope', the possibilities that fractures in the old order contain. This is what globalization and empire, in whose thrall so much left and progressive thinking still remains, are unable to offer. These cosmopolitan ideologies obscure the possibilities contained in national politics and avoid the complex task of linking them to the possibilities for international solidarity and action, preferring instead to affect a dangerous disdain for the national – treating it as practically synonymous with the chauvinistic – and a politically enervating cosmopolitanism. They also one-sidedly emphasize the strength of the forces of order in self-restricting and ultimately self-defeating ways. In their place, *Geopolitical Economy* shows that the present crisis contains more possibilities for progressive change than the world has seen in at least a generation.

Prima facie, this book shows that the present historical moment is one in which one long chapter – that of the dominance, actual and attempted, of single powers – in the history of imperialism has closed. The world now stands at the cusp of a further deepening of the multipolarity that imperial and would-be imperial powers and their cosmopolitan ideologies – free trade, HST, globalization and empire – have failed to prevent. Of course, imperialism as such has not ended – stronger countries will continue to try to maintain unevenness and resolve the contradictions of their capitalisms at the expense of weaker ones – but neither has combined development. Stronger powers are less likely to have their way in the face of more numerous and stronger contenders and larger populations capable of aspiring to more than bare survival. And while collusion between imperial powers, and between national ruling classes and imperialism, cannot be ruled out, greater competition between a greater number of relatively powerful countries in the world is likely to make both relatively less probable.

Geopolitical Economy also shows, more esoterically, the fracture in the foundations of the power of financial capital, the contradiction in its present condition which not even continuing access to the corridors of power can resolve. For US attempts to keep the dollar as the world's currency have, since 1971, rested on financial contrivances, and these have been at the root of what is known as financialization. Its end leaves US attempts to preserve the dollar's world role with little to conjure with. Financialization was not something that affected all countries more or less evenly and separately, but a US- and dollar-centred phenomenon that undergirded the dollar's career as the world's money. Not only did international, largely dollar-denominated, capital flows collapse in the crisis, they have failed to recover to 2007 levels (Borio and Disyatat, 2011), even though the United States bailed out its banks so fulsomely. Worse, the bailout and the deterioration of the US fiscal position it entailed have only pushed the dollar further down. Though the US dollar went up at particularly acute moments of crisis and though it was considerably buoyed up by the Eurozone crisis, overall it has sustained its downward trend since 2000. Meanwhile, European banks were not so fully bailed out by their more conservative financial authorities and have since suffered 'haircuts' amid the Eurozone crisis. Indeed, the bailouts themselves, and their very different national patterns, have also effectively renationalized financial sectors, fracturing the 'global' financial system that undergirded the dollar in recent decades into its national components.

These developments point to two very important possibilities for the left, which are not currently being pursued precisely because, under the lingering influence of globalization and empire, it is unable to see them. Firstly, there is the possibility of re-regulating finance nationally, because the international structures that sustained each national pattern of financialization have been drastically weakened. And secondly and equally importantly, there is the possibility, and increasingly the reality, of making new international monetary arrangements that no longer rely on the US dollar's dangerously unstable ways of providing international liquidity. In place of the dollar-denominated financialization that for so long strangled the productive sectors and created more inequality than ever before, both within and between countries, such arrangements promise to create a world of more equal, productive and egalitarian, and also more culturally dynamic and environmentally sustainable, societies.

THE PLAN OF THE BOOK

This book deals with ideas, the historical developments that occasioned them and the politically mediated relationships between the two. It cannot therefore treat ideas as eternal, to be discussed first in a 'theoretical' chapter, as is the custom of so much social-scientific writing. Instead the book is organized in a broadly chronological manner, and ideas and developments are interweaved throughout, although Chapters 2 and 5 linger longer over ideas than developments. The book's three arguments, moreover, intertwine in its historical narrative.

The first argument, about the materiality of nations, is taken up mainly in Chapters 2 and 5, which contest free trade and HST respectively, though it also figures in the other chapters, particularly Chapters 7 and 8 in relation to globalization and empire respectively. Chapter 2 proceeds by undermining the idea of the liberal free trade nineteenth century. The leading capitalist power of that era indulged in protection as well as imperialism to achieve and sustain its industrial revolution. The two fictions on which free trade rested – Say's law and comparative advantage – formed no part of sounder understandings. Adam Smith, Hamilton and List, Marx and Engels, the classical theories of imperialism and UCD, and Keynes, Polanyi and writers on the developmental state all underlined the materiality of nations, state roles in capitalism, and capitalism's intimate connection with imperialism, and with state-directed protectionist development, each in their own way. Not only was Smith no advocate of free trade and the 'invisible hand', classical political economy contained a greater appreciation of the importance of states than of the beneficence, let alone inevitability, of free trade.

A novel interpretation of Marx and Engels is critical to making the case for the materiality of nations, and Chapter 2 recovers their theories of crisis from the disdain of most Marxist economics and shows that, contrary to the dominant interpretation, Marx and Engels were neither advocates of free trade nor believers in its centrality to capitalism. Rather, they criticized free trade, understood its ideological functions for imperialism, and conceived of the geopolitical economy of capitalism as 'the relations of producing nations' in an understanding that encompassed combined development *avant la lettre*. They would have needed to have their heads in the clouds to do anything else: after all, they witnessed how, while Britain imposed one-way free trade on her colonies, independent jurisdictions willing and able to assert their policy autonomy, under the influence of policy makers and thinkers like the American Hamilton and the German List, protected and developed their economies to emerge as the United Kingdom's competitors, imperial as well as industrial.

For international competition between capitalist states at this time was as much about colonies as about markets. As such competition heightened international tensions in the decades preceding the First World War, a starburst of predominantly Marxist and Bolshevik theories – the classical theories of imperialism – emerged to explain them. They either traced imperialism to capitalism's contradictions in general, particularly the paucity of demand (Hobson and Luxemburg), or to a new phase of capitalism characterized by 'monopoly capital', 'finance capital', or (a more intense) 'nationalization of economies' (Lenin, Hilferding and Bukharin respectively). UCD systematized the more diffuse Marxist understanding of the world order in conjunction with these theories. Together they responded to the need of the growing working class parties in the Second International to understand the fast-evolving world situation and that of Bolsheviks to forge a political line amid the Russian Revolution.

Meanwhile the turn towards neoclassical economics set the intellectual clock back and, rather than using Marxist tools to criticize it, Marxists sought to adapt Marxism to it. Marxist economics acquired a purely economic understanding of capitalism quite foreign to the Marxist tradition, and left further theoretical advances towards a genuine geopolitical economy to be made by non-Marxist critics of neoclassical economics such as Keynes and Polanyi. Amid the social-scientific division of labour that now came to prevail, the bourgeois discipline of IR, for its part, emerged to take a purely political view of its object, which would ever since sacrifice understanding to legitimizing great power behaviour.

Domestically, Keynes and Polanyi not only underlined states' central role in capitalist societies but also advocated the extension of that role to promote full employment and social protection. Internationally, their overlapping critiques of free trade and the international gold standard rested on acute insights into the geopolitical economy of the world of nation-states that would emerge from the impending end of British supremacy and formal colonialism. Keynes's critique underlay his original proposals at Bretton Woods to create a multilateral currency and a clearing system that would minimize trade imbalances. Such arrangements offered the best chance for productive and egalitarian national economies and international cooperation (Desai, 2009a). They were defeated, however, by a United States intent on emulating the United Kingdom's former world dominance, at least by installing the dollar as the world's currency. Thanks to the Second World War, it was better positioned to attempt it than it had ever been, or would ever be again.

Chapter 3 opens the second argument, which proceeds through the rest of the book, tracing the United States's imperial career up to the Bretton Woods moment. It outlines how the United States's foundational imperial aspirations, which were from the start bound up with economic expansionism, powered its early continental expansion. After it reached the Pacific, the United States briefly and disastrously pursued territory overseas. However, by the early twentieth century, a new corporate elite had reformulated US expansionism into an aspiration to replace the United Kingdom's imperial world role, not by acquiring a territorial empire, which the unfolding of UCD now made impossible, but by making the dollar the world's currency and New York the world's financial centre. It also laid the institutional basis for such emulation by creating the Federal Reserve in 1913.

This recast aspiration determined that the United States would enter the First World War just when its economic bonanza for the United States threatened to end without US entry, and both world wars increased the United States's economic strength relative to the rest of the world. In the inter-war period New York and the dollar did overtake London and sterling in world financial affairs, but only just. Moreover, the United States achieved these aims only in a rather perverse way. For the capital flows on which the dollar's and New York's new importance rested were not the sort of private flows that gave London its prominence before 1914, but intergovernmental flows stemming from US insistence on being repaid for its war loans to its allies, and on the allies' consequent insistence on being paid the infamous reparations by Germany. The unfolding of UCD not only denied the United States a territorial empire but ensured that the world economy was more than ever composed of competing national economies. The governments of these economies had, moreover, become even more important economic actors and their competition had resulted in war. Moreover, war-generated capital flows made their own contribution to the depth of the Great Depression in the United States.

As the Second World War began to pull the United States out of the Great Depression, Henry Luce relaunched the idea of the United States replacing the United Kingdom as the 'managing segment' of the world economy with his famous vision of the 'American century'. The United States deployed the overwhelming economic and financial superiority the war had fashioned for it to determine the shape of the postwar world order at Bretton Woods. Contrary to the widespread view that the United States created benign multilateral institutions of economic governance, it insisted on installing the gold-backed dollar as the world's currency, left the multilateral institutions it could not avoid creating as weak as possible, and rejected Keynes's far more progressive proposals in the most promising attempt yet to realize its mimetic imperial aspiration.

Chapter 4 charts the troubled course of the dollar as the world's currency until Nixon closed the gold window. This *dénouement* was all but inevitable: the unfolding of UCD up to that point had already ensured that the United States was a national, not an imperial, economy, and as such its currency could not stably be the world's currency. And the further unfolding of UCD ensured that its overwhelming postwar economic dominance would soon be eroded. In the 1950s, the US export surplus subjected the world to a 'dollar shortage' which Marshall Plan aid was too small to address. Once Western European economies recovered, made their currencies convertible in 1958 and began competing with the United States, however, there was a dollar glut instead. The dollar now sat on the horns of the 'Triffin dilemma' (Triffin, 1961). Being only a national economy committed to its own expansion (a commitment which an enfranchised working class only strengthened) the United States could not provide liquidity through capital exports (see also Hobsbawm, 2008: 80–91, Arrighi, 2005b: 113–16). Running balance of payments deficits was the only way to provide the world with liquidity, but it was self-defeating, as deficits undermined the dollar's value. Worse, the US economy began to lose competitiveness and acquired that tendency to suck in imports and create trade deficits with growth that dogs it to this day. US imperial aspirations ruled out the sort of vigorous state intervention that would have been necessary to address the problem, confining it to macro-economic policy and a surreptitious industrial policy, military Keynesianism, which was advanced in the guise of defence policy. These could only produce inflationary growth, while military Keynesianism only made the US economy unduly reliant on uncompetitive industries, further undermining the dollar.

To top it all, the recovery of Western Europe and Japan undermined the United States's postwar economic position. The United Kingdom had lost its dominance as the first industrializer to the combined development of its first challengers, and the United States faced even stronger forms of combined development. Communism actually truncated the capitalist world that the United States could attempt to lead, and forced it to foster combined development in its rivals and to support decolonization, allowing former colonies to also pursue combined development. Indeed, the United States failed to create a liberal world economy, the *sine qua non* of its planned emulation of the United Kingdom. Thanks to the threat of communism and the devastation of war, not only did capital controls remain necessary, such liberalism as the postwar world economy could achieve was 'embedded' in statist institutional arrangements, national and international (Ruggie, 1982). Moreover, UCD entered a new phase with the recovery of Western Europe and Japan. It mired the advanced industrial world in the long downturn of 'overcapacity and overproduction' in which they would compete for shares of a stagnant world market (Brenner, 1998).

How these difficulties of the US imperial project were encountered and dealt with by policy makers comes through in the Economic Reports of the President (ERPs) annually presented to Congress under the 1946 Employment Act. It enjoined the US President to '"coordinate and utilize all its plans, functions, and resources" to bring about and maintain maximum production and employment' and report on progress to Congress (Employment Act quoted in ERP, 1948 Midyear: 47). Annual ERPs (semi-annual reports stopped after 1952), produced by the Council of Economic Advisors (CEA), covered the developments of the previous year and were an 'opportunity for national self-examination and self-criticism ... a challenge to the President and the Congress to determine the causes of whatever problems we face in our economic life and to find the solutions to those problems' (ERP, 1947 January: vii). As such, the ERPs constitute the textual nexus where the chief contradictions of the US imperial enterprise at the national and the international level were worked out. The accounts of Chapters 4, 6, 7 and 8 rely on them.

The Triffin dilemma worsened through the 1960s. Creditor governments and central bankers began to demand gold for their dollars. As gold flowed out, the gold pool was created in 1961 to ensure the dollar's cover. It was amid the dollar's mounting difficulties that elements of HST first began to appear. Influential policy intellectuals like Charles Kindleberger began to argue that the erosion of the United States's economic weight, competitive strength or gold reserves did not matter. They had never undergirded the dollar's world role: the depth and sophistication of US financial markets had done so. The dollar's gold peg was at best incidental, whereas the United States's debtor status was its condition: the United States was banker to the world, providing it with critical financial intermediation (Despres, Kindleberger and Salant, 1966; Salant, 1966). This international financial intermediation hypothesis (IFIH) averred that if foreign governments and central bankers did not know this, private holders of dollars did, and they would support the dollar's value.

There is no evidence that the Nixon Administration believed in the IFIH when it closed the gold window in 1971, though Treasury Secretary Connally's statement that 'the dollar may be our currency but it's your problem' was widely taken to mean that the United States has since followed a policy of 'benign neglect' of the dollar's value leaving private confidence to support it. Chapters 6 to 8 show how far this view is from the truth.

Chapter 5 pauses over HST to detail how it was composed and spread thereafter. It recast the US world role in the 1950s and 1960s as 'hegemonic' entirely retrospectively. And it framed the actions the United States now took as attempts to recreate this desirable state of affairs. Amid the gathering declinism of the 1970s, HST's influential originator, Charles Kindleberger, argued that the Great Depression was caused because the United Kingdom was no longer able and the United States was not yet willing to take up the tasks of world economic 'leadership'. The implication was that the economic difficulties of the 1970s resulted from the loss of that leadership, and reviving it would resolve them. This was not a social scientist originating a theory, but an influential US opinion and policy maker giving the United States's formative expansionism, recast by Luce at mid-century, yet another form but with one critical difference: he was doing so after the best attempt the United States could ever hope to make had failed. Unlike free trade, which had disguised the United Kingdom's protectionist industrialization and imperialism in the heyday of its productive dominance, HST emerged only after the erosion of the closest thing to such dominance the United States would enjoy to dissimulate the inherent instability of the successive financial bases the dollar's world role would now rely on. HST took a number of distinct forms, soon dominating IPE and acquiring its WS version. Well into the 1980s the emphasis remained on the exhaustion of US hegemony. Renewalist strands began to emerge in the late 1980s, though they had to wait nearly a decade before the United States's illusory economic strength in the late 1990s and its equally illusory military strength in the early 2000s made it briefly but very widely credible.

Chapter 5 ends with the alternative to HST as an account of the world order: the geopolitical economy of capitalism in the latter half of the twentieth century and the early twenty-first century. It relies on Robert Brenner's history of the long boom and the long downturn (Brenner, 1998, 2002, 2006, 2009). It reveals that the combined development of recovering economies powered the long boom and created the overcapacity and overproduction that was the initial cause of the long downturn. It persisted over the next decades because firms and governments of states with politically enfranchised working classes were unwilling to permit a 'slaughter of capital values' on a scale sufficient to end it. How the United States managed the dollar's world role in these circumstances we see in the chapters that follow.

Chapter 6 covers the period between two major low points in the career of the dollar – 1971 and the end of the George Bush Sr presidency in 1992. The Nixon Administration did not take the breezy IFIH view when it closed the gold window: it was aware that the mercantilism of its actions could spell the end of the dollar's world role. Private confidence signally failed to replace the confidence that foreign governments and central bankers refused to repose in the dollar. The United States soon had to intervene in currency markets to prop it up. The dollar's future remained uncertain until the oil price rise by the Organization of Petroleum Exporting Countries (OPEC) and US success in convincing OPEC governments to deposit oil surpluses in dollar-denominated investments. The massive spurt in international capital flows these petrodollars created was the first of the many financializations – distinct phases of financialization – that would be necessary for the dollar's world role, and the most benign. With sluggish advanced economies not demanding capital, US banks lent to developing and communist countries for productive investment, setting off a spurt of debt-led industrialization on historically low real interest rates. By the late 1970s, however, the dollar headed down again, requiring the United States to cooperate with other major industrial economies in regular G-7 meetings to stabilize exchange rates and maintain growth. However, when the second oil shock hit, this time without any significant increase in capital inflows into the United States, the dollar plunged again. The new Fed chairman, Paul Volcker, allowed interest rates to rise to double digits to shore up the dollar, causing a severe recession. 'Declinism' peaked with President Carter's 'malaise speech' proposing to scale down the US world role and increase competitiveness to help the United States earn its keep.

Reagan's election cast this option into history's dustbin, but his neoliberal, monetarist, supply-side economics proved no solution. Rather, amid high interest rates, the Reagan Administration generated growth through massive fiscal stimuli – large tax cuts, renewed military Keynesianism and a massive programme of subsidies for defence-related research and development (R&D) which might aptly be called military Schumpeterianism. Unprecedented budget deficits resulted and, with the United States's fundamental competitiveness problems remaining unresolved, growth now generated trade deficits.

The dollar remained strong despite the 'twin deficits' because capital flowed into the United States in three ways: in response to Volcker's high interest rates; as debt repayments from the third world thanks to the International Monetary Fund (IMF)'s management of the resulting third world debt crisis to save US and Western banks; and from Japanese financing of US deficits in exchange for access to US markets. These capital inflows constituted a second major burst of dollar-denominated financialization. They sent the dollar so high above its value that manufacturers pressured the government to bring it down and leading policy makers worried about a potentially catastrophic drop. The 1985 Plaza accord organized controlled dollar depreciation. The stock market crash two years later would make it unnecessary.

Reagan's unprecedented fiscal stimulus notwithstanding, the US economy could only absorb so much capital: the rest inflated the stock market bubble that burst in 1987. In its aftermath the policy that would keep new bubbles coming made its first appearance: the new Fed chairman's 'Greenspan put', the provision of extra liquidity to financial markets amid crises. It was widely credited with averting an immediate recession. None of the asset price bubbles that followed (and the biggest were yet to come) could hide the weakness of the US economy for long, and each worsened it significantly.

The lower dollar of the late 1980s and early 1990s briefly indicated the direction that US economic fundamentals could really sustain: higher demand for US exports combined with slower growth limiting imports helped close the US trade deficit briefly in the early 1990s. If imperial aspirations were forsaken in favour of a determined state effort to revive productivity and competitiveness, prosperity was at hand. It was not to be. By the time communism collapsed, the US economy was in the doldrums and the president and party that 'won' the cold war were defeated in an 'It's the economy, stupid!' election.

Chapter 7 traces the strange trajectory of globalization. The Clinton Administration first used 'globalization' in the sense given it by Robert Reich, an early Clinton economic adviser and secretary of labor until 1997. It referred to competitive threats to be countered with a strategy for higher-value production and trade promotion aimed at the 'big emerging markets'. It was soberly productive compared with the heady financial brew Joseph Stiglitz concocted for the second Clinton term. The latter would be backed by the financial interests whose power the Greenspan Fed had increased so much that they dominated US business and the Democratic Party.

They turned plans to revitalize the US economy into a programme for deficit reduction, higher interest rates and, through the 'Reverse Plaza accord' of 1995, a high dollar.

In the mid-1990s, in its third major phase, financialization briefly took a centripetal form, directing capital outwards as the high dollar regime interrupted an incipient manufacturing recovery. And, having suffered near collapse in the third world debt crisis, US and Western financial institutions now lent only short-term funds in the form of securities. They, however, came with their own dangers. These short-term funds were entering markets they knew little about, did not finance productive investment there and were easily spooked into sudden and massive exits. The series of financial crises in third-world countries culminated in the massive 1997–98 East Asian financial crisis. Only thereafter, as money fled home to the United States, did the geopolitical economy of globalization fully compose itself. The US-centred international financial system, which sucked in capital from around the world and poured it into the United States, particularly into the US stock market, was its pivot. 'Globalization' acquired its more familiar meaning of the desirability and inevitability of a unified world economy. It was fully expressed in ERP 1997, when Stiglitz chaired the CEA. In a world where economies remained national and trade was heavily politicized, the report's generalities about openness and interdependence focused on financial openness, particularly on lifting capital controls in third-world countries, ostensibly so they could get better access to capital. In the short period when capital did flow into these economies, it generated little productive investment and much economic mayhem. Thereafter, the effect of freeing capital movements was to allow it to flow into dollar-denominated assets to finance the US deficits and swell US-centred financialization. In the 1990s these flows, particularly of private capital into the US stock market, would be further encouraged by Greenspan's talk of the US new economy and its 'productivity miracle'. The result, the real and intended result of globalization as it came into its own in the late 1990s, was the stock market bubble and associated consumption and investment booms. When the stock market bubble burst in 2000, the main motor of globalization fell silent, though some misidentified 9/11 as the cause (*Economist*, 2001a; Ferguson, 2005).

Chapter 8 shows how empire proved the last and most desperate attempt to maintain the dollar's world role and entailed the greatest increase in international capital flows. The war on terrorism that defined the empire phase was not prompted by 9/11. Those events, whose official interpretation continues, in any case, to be questioned a decade later (MacGregor and Zarembka, 2010), only provided a barely credible excuse for launching a project Bush Jr took office with. But while the military expenditure involved was greater than ever (Stiglitz and Bilmes, 2008), the US economy was less prepared than ever to support it.

An intractable recession followed the stock market decline in 2000. The Fed had become the main manager of the US economy since Clinton's turn to deficit reduction, and the economically illiterate Bush Jr Administration was not about to change that. The Fed recognized that credit-fuelled consumption among upper-income groups, thanks to a housing bubble that had been building since the mid-1990s, was the only source of growth. It now inflated that bubble further in the fourth major financialization as the easiest way to produce the growth figures that would keep foreign funds flowing in to finance the United States's ever-widening deficits, keep growth going and support the dollar. The willingness of the rest of the world to hold dollars now governed the fate of the US economy. A new a series of discourses emerged to explain away the US economy's reliance on rock-bottom interest rates (the danger of 'deflation'), its inability to grow fast (the 'great moderation'), and the manifest obscenity of the world's capital financing consumption predominantly of the rich, in one of the world's richest societies, rather than much-needed developing world investment (the 'global savings glut'). The capital inflows financed the United States's deficits cheaply and expanded the volume of dollar-denominated financial activity on which the dollar's liquidity depended. The bulk of these flows came from the rest of the advanced industrial world, contrary to the 'global savings glut' argument's focus on East Asia (Borio and Disyatat, 2011).

Talk could, of course, postpone the inevitable only so long. By the middle of the decade, growth in the emerging economies, particularly China, was increasing the prices of commodities and capital and putting downward pressure on the dollar. The high interest rates that were now necessary burst the housing bubble, thus ending the consumption-led growth it had supported. It is this shift which also ensured that the great recession would end not just the Bush empire project but the succession of US attempts to dominate the world economy since the early twentieth century, in particular by establishing and maintaining the US dollar as the world's currency.

2

THE MATERIALITY OF NATIONS

Oppositions between politics and economics and between markets and states have critical ideological functions in capitalist society. They emerged in early bourgeois assertion against the aristocracy and also pitted commerce against conquest, peace against war and reason against violence. These oppositions reinforced the view that states play minimal roles in capitalist societies, roles inconsequential to their economic fates. In this view, the plurality of nation-states in the modern capitalist world order can only be explained in terms of culture: they are economically inconsequential (for critiques see Desai, 2009b, 2010c, 2012). Against these ideas, this chapter opens the first argument of this book by underlining the materiality of nation-states.

For the bourgeoisie could not do without the state: not only in the revolutionary transformations that gave birth to capitalism (Marx, 1867/1977; Bagchi, 2005; Heller, 2011), but thereafter. Capitalism contained tendencies to injustice and crisis, and needed state management of their consequences, the more so as capitalism developed. Domestically, the state managed capitalism's economic contradictions and crises, above all those arising from its demand constraint: 'The ultimate reason for all real crises remains the poverty and restricted consumption of the masses' (Marx, 1894/1981: 615). The state also created and managed relationships between capitalist and other propertied classes, including feudal classes, whose economic power persisted well past the emergence of capitalism (Mayer, 1981), and mediated inevitable struggles between propertied classes and working and popular classes. Indeed, working-class political assertion everywhere transformed states into 'strategic battlefields' (Carnoy, 1984: 124) and 'material condensations' of class struggles (Poulantzas, 1978: 145). Internationally, states were also the chief vehicles of national bourgeoisies in engagements that defined the geopolitical economy of capitalism. The early revolutionary bourgeoisie may have affected disdain for imperialism in a register not unlike Saint Simon's: as 'grotesque and funereal', a vainglorious feudal pursuit whose costs, they reckoned, outweighed its benefits (quoted in Semmel, 1993: 40–1). However, the state was already then, deeply imbricated in the geopolitical economy of capitalism's uneven and combined development, with dominant states seeking to maintain unevenness and contender states to challenge it, free trade ideology notwithstanding. Capitalism was not defined by any strict separation of the political from the economic but by the ability of capitalist classes to ensure that their states' resources would be used to pursue the policies they favoured, at home and abroad.

Unsurprisingly then, free trade, the nineteenth-century cosmopolitan ideology that accompanied UK imperial supremacy, was questioned from the beginning. This chapter outlines the history of this questioning, identifying in the process the most weighty and substantial intellectual figures and traditions that underlined instead the materiality of nations in ways essential to geopolitical economy. It begins by contesting two myths that undergird the near-universal idea of a liberal free trade nineteenth century: that the United Kingdom industrialized without protection and that it was anti-imperialist in the nineteenth century. The chapter goes on to show how little support free trade had in classical political economy before Ricardo, let alone among neo-mercantilist thinkers like List and Hamilton. Going on to Marx and Engels, the chapter contests the dominant interpretation that they regarded free trade as essential to capitalism and underlines their canny understanding of the realities of imperialism, combined development and the geopolitical economy of the 'relations of producing nations'. Equally importantly, the chapter recovers the essentials of their understanding of capitalist crises so that the evolution of the state's role in managing them can fully be understood. The classical theories of imperialism and uneven and combined development (UCD), which elaborated, systematized and updated essential Marxist insights into the first theories of capitalist international relations are dealt with next. Finally, after Marxist economics effectively dammed the further flow of such Marxist theorization, attention shifts to two major critics of neoclassical economics, Keynes and Polanyi, who carried further the political economy on which geopolitical economy must rest.

THE LIBERAL NINETEENTH CENTURY?

The role of the state in twentieth-century capitalism is too great to be ignored: working classes demand that it act in their favour and capitalist classes complain of its burdens. However, capitalism before 1914 is almost universally considered liberal, competitive and cosmopolitan, spreading over the world and uniting it through markets alone, with states playing minimal 'night-watchman' roles. This idea rests on two key misunderstandings about the first industrial capitalist country, the United Kingdom: that it developed without much state intervention and that it was, in its mid-nineteenth-century heyday at least, 'anti-imperialist'. These misunderstandings have obstructed our understanding of the state's necessary economic role in capitalism.

UK exceptionalism?

The notion that the nineteenth-century United Kingdom practised free trade is powerful and has been reinforced from many quarters. For example, when Gerschenkron (1962) classically argued that 'late development' typically required state intervention in catch-up industrialization, and that the greater the 'backwardness', the greater would be the state effort required, he implied that first industrial capitalist country did not require or use it. Later this alleged freedom from the statist incubus was held to explain the United Kingdom's relative industrial decline since the late nineteenth century (Hobsbawm, 1968). The first industrial capitalist country, it was further argued, had merely undermined pre-capitalist production everywhere. It had never needed, nor did it subsequently acquire, the institutional capacity for combined development to counter competition from other capitalist manufacturers (Leys, 1989).

However, Ha-Joon Chang, writing in the developmental state tradition, pointed to at least four distinct phases of UK trade policy which were critical for the industrial revolution: the 'sixteenth-century equivalent of modern infant industry promotion strategy' of Henry VII and his successors; Walpole's 1721 reform of mercantile law, which manipulated duties and gave subsidies to promote higher-value industry; industrial promotion throughout the industrial revolution until Britain's technological lead became overwhelming; and finally, the repeal of the Corn Laws. This last, so widely regarded as emblematic of the British commitment to free trade, really constituted 'an act of 'free trade imperialism' intended to 'halt the move of industrialization on the Continent by enlarging the market for agricultural produce and primary materials' (Chang, 2002: 19–22, quoting Charles Kindleberger). Needless to say, once the technological lead was achieved, free trade was the best form of export promotion.

In reality, it was the dominance of the financial and commercial interests of the City of London over industrial ones that lay behind British industrial decline. Though home to the industrial revolution, the British state remained dominated by its original agrarian capitalist class, and its financial and commercial interests were as intimately linked to the state as the industrial capitalists were socially distant from it. The British industrial lead, moreover, made London the world's 'major international commercial and banking centre', and British financial and commercial interests, headquartered in the City of London, came to constitute the 'City–Bank–Treasury nexus' (Ingham, 1984; see also Anderson, 1987). This ensured a policy bias towards maintaining London's world commercial and financial role. The formal commitments that required, namely 'a domestic gold standard – which later unintentionally served the world – free trade and budgetary prudence', hampered the United Kingdom's industrial lead when competition from contender states sharpened. As 'the City's diversion or draining of capital accelerated' (Ingham, 1984: 226), its 'invisible earnings' were supposed to compensate for the industrial damage it did. But they never did. British manufacturing became and remained a victim of these policies up to and including the devastation wrought by Margaret Thatcher in the 1980s (Leys, 1990).

Industry and empire

Even Chang's detailed list of trade policy measures, however, does not include imperial conquest. The empire made an indispensable contribution to the industrial revolution, providing not only raw material and markets but, during industrial take-off, also a monetary contribution so great that without it, 'it is doubtful whether an increasingly food-deficit Britain embroiled in war and its attendant strains, could have transformed its structure ... at the fast pace it actually did to merit the term "industrial revolution"' (Patnaik, 2006: 61). However, an essential element of the notion of a liberal nineteenth century was that its dominant power, the United Kingdom, was 'indifferent' to empire, even 'anti-imperialist'.

As Gallagher and Robinson (1953) showed conclusively long ago, this was hypocritical. In reality, there was 'a fundamental continuity in British expansion throughout the nineteenth century' (Gallagher and Robinson, 1953: 5), 'informally if possible and formally if necessary' (1953: 13). And it was not coincidental: 'British industrialization caused an ever-extending and intensifying development of overseas regions' (1953: 5). While informal empire was also extended, the record of annexation alone was impressive:

> Consider the results of a decade of 'indifference' to empire. Between 1841 and 1851 Great Britain occupied or annexed New Zealand, the Gold Coast, Labuan, Natal, the Punjab, Sind and Hong Kong. In the next twenty years British control was asserted over Berar, Oudh, Lower Burma and Kowloon, over Lagos and the neighbourhood of Sierra Leone, over Basutoland, Griqualand and the Transvaal; and new colonies were established in Queensland and British Columbia.
>
> (Gallagher and Robinson, 1953: 2–3)

It is a testament to the strength ideologies can have that the nineteenth century is still considered liberal.

FREE TRADE AND PROTECTION IN CLASSICAL POLITICAL ECONOMY

That Adam Smith thought colonies were useless, wasteful and expensive (1976, II: 485) is often cited to support the idea of a free-trade nineteenth century, and today's neoliberals with their Adam Smith neckties also trace free trade to him. However, *The Wealth of Nations* is anything but a paean to unfettered capitalism. Rather, it is 'an immanent critique of commercial society', attempting to show that its 'fundamental categories' 'such as capital and labour, would themselves suggest their own critique if they were analysed thoroughly in relation to one another' (Göçmen, 2007: 113; see also Meek, 1977). It is true that Smith opposed 'mercantilism', his term for the various policies absolutist states followed in competing for bullion through export surpluses, colonization and chartered companies (like the East India and Hudson's Bay companies). However, this opposition did not imply endorsement of free trade. Smith objected to mercantilism's focus on long-distance trade, colonization and plunder. In its place, he advocated not free trade but a concentration on domestic trade and division of labour, for him the real source of the 'wealth of nations'. Though generally opposed to the restrictions on trade that capitalists schemed for, Smith justified them when they were in retaliation for other nations' duties and to protect employment (Smith, 1976, I: 489–91), situations which would become more common as more countries industrialized and competed with one another.

Imperialism and mercantilism were fixtures of the geopolitical economy of capitalism in Smith's time. Mercantilists justified colonial arrangements in which mother countries exported higher-value manufactures, and colonies lower-value agricultural products: 'it was ... right that the advantage rest with the metropolis'. If such arrangements were resisted, 'mercantilist nations readily took up violent means to expand and retain their possessions' (Semmel, 1993: 2). Smith attributed colonial domination to 'accidental' European superiority of force, and foresaw a time 'when the inhabitants of all the different quarters of the world may arrive at that equality of courage and force which, by inspiring mutual fear, can alone overawe the injustice of independent nations into some sort of respect for the rights of one another' (1976, II: 141). Though his own perspective implied that colonies were useless and expensive, he also admitted that they appeared attractive markets for 'surplus goods' and that foreign trade would similarly attract surplus capital (1976, I: 394–7).

Two Ricardian fictions

Ricardo is more suitably regarded as the apostle of free trade: he accepted Say's law, which against all evidence ruled out 'general gluts', and justified the imperial division of labour between manufacturing and agricultural (in other words, imperial and colonized) nations through the law of 'comparative advantage', in which welfare was maximized when each country specialized in what it produced most efficiently (Semmel, 1993: 20–1). Both were fictions, and they were connected. It was precisely because, contrary to Say's law, there were regular gluts that the protection of home markets and the establishment and maintenance of colonial divisions of labour became necessary. While the former was simply denied, the latter was justified through comparative advantage. Against such justification, many political economists, such as Malthus and Wakefield, argued that colonies were necessary to settle surplus population, absorb surplus goods and capital, and defuse class tensions, particularly when a three-decade-long depression followed the Napoleonic wars. Kindred diagnoses and prescriptions also lurked in liberal thinkers, whether Bentham or Mill (Semmel, 1993: 23–38). Such insights into capitalism's need for regulation and imperialism, and ambiguities about its benefits, were overpowered by the two Ricardian fictions.

At least in England. Abroad, explicit critiques of free trade became the basis of state policy. As we shall see in the next chapter, the first

US Treasury secretary, Alexander Hamilton, recognized clearly that free trade only reinforced the existing colonial division of labour, and therefore that the United States needed protection to industrialize and produce higher-value goods. Friedrich List, who studied Hamilton's policies and writings on a sojourn in the United States, set out a systematic case for contender states' combined development in his *The National System of Political Economy* (1841/1856), which became influential in Germany at the time. List contrasted the ideological dominance of free trade with the protectionists' practical outlook: 'No branch of political economy presents a greater diversity of views between men of theory and men of practice, than that which treats of international commerce and commercial policy' (1841: 61). As a result, 'in spite of its grave errors, practice has not acquiesced in any reform proposed by theory' while 'theory has not been willing to heed the voice of history or experience, or of government, or of any particular nation' (1841: 65). What was at stake between free trade and protection was 'the education of a nation with a view to its independence' (1841: 64): the cultivation of the investments and skills needed for higher-value production. Free trade also ignored or disfigured lessons of history 'which are opposed to its system; it is under the necessity of denying the effects of the Act of Navigation, of the Treaty of Methuen, of the commercial policy of England in general and of maintaining against all truth that England arrived to wealth and power in spite of that policy, not by it' (1841: 65).

Today's developmental state tradition, which arose to challenge neoliberalism, rightly traces its origin to List and Hamilton (key works in this tradition include Amsden, 1992, 2001, 2007; Hamilton, 1986; White, 1988; Wade, 1990; Chang, 2002; Woo-Cumings, 1999; Reinert, 2007). Their examples would be followed by economic policy makers in more and less successful developing countries. National independence was necessary for the policy autonomy to first resist the United Kingdom's dominance on the domestic market and then challenge it on the world market. No wonder then that the first raft of challenges to the United Kingdom's industrial supremacy occurred after key states were centralized and stabilized around 1870: the US Civil War resulted in the Northern victory, Germany was unified and Japan's Meiji Restoration created a centralized state. And it remains true to this day that in any given hierarchy of rich and poor countries which capitalism's unevenness routinely establishes, 'the more freedom it has to determine its own policies, the faster a developing country will grow'. A combination of planning, protection and state promotion of industry remained the backbone of all successful development and 'the better the institutional system in place, the faster the development' (Amsden, 2007: 153). While such systems could fail, no development was possible without them.

Marx and Engels

Marx and Engels regarded classical political economy up to and including Ricardo as scientific rather than apologetic, and their critique of it noted its achievements as well as contradictions and limitations. Their rejection of Say's law lay at its centre. It is worth quoting in full because its distinction between direct exchange or barter and the circulation of commodities in a money economy like capitalism proved important in later developments.

> Nothing could be more foolish than the dogma that because every sale is a purchase, and every purchase a sale, the circulation of commodities necessarily implies an equilibrium between sales and purchases. ... [I]ts real intention is to show that every seller brings his own buyer to market with him. ... No one can sell unless someone else purchases. *But no one directly needs to purchase just because he has just sold.* Circulation bursts through all the temporal, spatial and personal barriers imposed by the direct exchange of products, and it does this by splitting up the direct identity ... between the exchange of one's own product and the acquisition of someone else's [in barter] into *two antithetical segments of sale and purchase.* ... [I]f the assertion of their external independence ... proceeds to a certain critical point, their unity violently makes itself felt by producing – a crisis.
>
> (Marx, 1867: 208–9, emphasis added)

Expanding the market so that it 'bursts through temporal, spatial and personal barriers' comes at a price: a money economy which, by splitting purchase and sale, contains the kernel of crisis. Capitalism cannot escape these crisis possibilities: privately produced goods must be socially validated through sale, and there is no guarantee that they will be, precisely because money received from the sale of goods need not be spent; it can be hoarded.

Worse, capitalist economies are structured to ensure that it will be. For capitalist production aims at the production of surplus value – the usually greatly positive difference between the value of labour power (wages) and the value which that labour power produces when it is used by the capitalist. Both the value invested in production – what is spent on wages and the materials of production – and the additional value must be realized through sale. Therefore, although surplus value cannot arise without production, 'it is equally impossible for it to arise apart from circulation' (Marx, 1867: 268). But such realization faces systematic obstacles precisely because the monetary equivalent of the surplus can be hoarded by the capitalist, while workers can generate demand only to the extent of their wages. The maximum limit of the capitalist's demand is the original capital invested in labour, raw materials, machinery and infrastructure, while his supply is greater than that. Worse, 'as production advances, the capitalist's demand for labour power, and hence indirectly for necessary means of subsistence, becomes progressively smaller than his demand for means of production' (Marx, 1884/1978: 198).

When capitalists increase demand by investing more, they only increase productive capacity and production, exacerbating the problem of realization. Moreover, widely perceived realization difficulties tend to reduce capitalists' willingness to invest. Exports, furthermore, would 'only shift ... the contradictions to a broader sphere, and give ... them a wider orbit' (Marx, 1884: 544), which was, as we shall see in later chapters on the geopolitical economy of postwar capitalism, precisely what happened. Ultimately, paucity of demand, specifically workers' demand, arising from the extraction of surplus value, remains capitalism's chief contradiction.

> The workers are important for the market as buyers of commodities. But, as sellers of their commodity – labour-power – capitalist society has the tendency to restrict them to their minimum price ... the periods in which capitalist production exerts all its forces regularly show themselves to be periods of over-production; because the limit to the application of the productive powers is not simply the production of value, but also its realization. However, the sale of commodities, the realization of commodity capital, and thus of surplus-value as well, is restricted not by the consumer needs of society in general, but by the consumer needs of a society in which the great majority are always poor and must always remain poor.
>
> (Marx, 1884: 391n)

Money breaks up reciprocity of sale and purchase in barter, and becomes the means to store surplus value not spent on consumption or investment. As such, it is the means through which paucity of demand expresses itself.

Say's law could only be credible to those who, like Say and Ricardo, treated the capitalist economy as effectively a barter economy over which money is merely a 'veil'. However, so critical was Say's law for the legitimacy of capitalism that, after Marx devastated it, it gained a new lease of life in neoclassical, marginalist, equilibrium economics, and Keynes would later have to mount a critique of it in that new form (Sardoni, 1997). In doing so, however, he took Marx's distinction between a monetary and a barter economy as his point of departure (Sardoni, 1997; Dostaler, 2007; Desai, 2010a). For both Marx and Keynes, capitalist crises were rooted in money's critical role as a store of value (Patnaik, 2009a), what Marx called 'money proper' whereas Say, Ricardo and neoclassical economics treated it merely as a means of exchange.

Marx's critique of comparative advantage is as sketchy as his critique of Say's law is thorough. Surviving early plans for *Capital* show that he planned to write about international trade and the world market (Nicolaus, 1973: 53–4), plans which were never realized. However, in his scattered remarks on Ricardo's trade theory, he does note insightfully that 'its only purpose is to support [Ricardo's] theory of value' in which all incomes, including profits, were justified (Marx, 1863/1972: 253). A critique every bit as powerful as that of Say's law is implied, however, in Marx and Engels's more extensive treatment of free trade and protectionism. It also contains broad outlines of a geopolitical economy of capitalism.

There is a widespread tendency to cite Marx and Engels's *The Communist Manifesto* (1848/1967) in support of capitalism's cosmopolitan tendency to create a unified world economy: what better evidence could there be than the word of capitalism's greatest critics? After all, they spoke of the bourgeoisie's 'most revolutionary' part in creating 'a constantly expanding market' and giving 'a cosmopolitan character to production'; in drawing 'from under the feet of industry the national ground on which it stood'; in expanding communications to draw 'all, even the most barbarian, nations into civilization'; in 'battering down all Chinese walls' with the 'heavy artillery' of the 'cheap prices of its commodities'; and in 'creating a world after its own image' (Marx and Engels, 1848: 82–5). But such quotation is partial. Just a few pages down, Marx and Engels spoke of how the bourgeoisie created 'political centralization': 'Independent, or but loosely connected, provinces with separate interests, laws, governments and systems of taxation, became lumped together into *one nation, with one government, one code of laws, one national class-interest, one frontier, one customs-tariff* (1848: 85, emphasis added). They also spoke of workers struggling for 'legislative recognition of particular interests of the workers'; of bourgeoisies pitted against 'the bourgeoisie of foreign countries' (1848: 90); and finally of how, if not 'in substance, yet in form, the struggle of the proletariat with the bourgeoisie is at first a national struggle' (1848: 90). Thus, '[t]he proletariat of each country must ... first of all settle matters with its own bourgeoisie' and achieve political supremacy by 'centralizing all instruments of production in the hands of the state' (1848: 92–3).

Marx and Engels saw more clearly than most that the separation of the economy – civil society – from the state under capitalism was what distinguished it from previous class societies. However, only its full fruition could precipitate a pure and purely economic capitalism and, as Engels put it, 'we shall not let it come to that' (quoted in Mandel, 1978: 68). Not only was this tendency far from fully realized, capitalism's own contradictions and working-class struggles during and since Marx and Engels's time added new obstacles in its way. A purely 'economic' capitalism would not emerge anywhere.

Part 8 of *Capital* Volume I, devoted to 'The so-called primitive accumulation', famously underlines the state's critical role in establishing capitalism by separating workers from their subsistence. However, not only does such primitive accumulation continue into capitalism's maturity (Luxemburg, 1913/2003; Harvey, 2003), it is closely tied to the expansion of the state's role for combined development through 'the colonies, the national debt, the modern tax system, and the system of protection'. The national debt permitted the state to 'meet extraordinary expenses [such as for colonial ventures] without the taxpayers feeling it immediately' while the resulting taxes and wage goods inflation separated more artisans and peasants from their subsistence. The effectiveness of this system of primitive accumulation was further heightened by the 'system of protection, which forms one of its integral parts' (Marx, 1867: 921).

Marx 'pronounced, in principle, in favour of Free Trade' (Engels, 1888/1990: 523) and said that 'the laws of political economy [received] an increased force, a surplus of truth' (Marx, 1847/1976: 290) under it, because he thought at the time that free trade 'hastens the social revolution' by quickening capitalist development (Marx, 1848: 465). He certainly did not accept Ricardian comparative

advantage notions about free trade being mutually beneficial. As
he remarked acerbically: 'If the Free-traders cannot understand
how one nation can grow rich at the expense of another, we need
not wonder, these same gentlemen also refuse to understand how
within one country one class can enrich itself at the expense of
another' (Marx 1848: 464–5). Although the repeal of the Corn
Laws reduced wages, diminishing workers' social position absolutely
and relatively (Marx, 1847: 290), Marx supported free trade in
the hope that it would destroy 'the last remnants of feudalism',
leaving the working class with 'only one enemy left to deal with'.
Moreover, free trade prompted landlords to make 'common cause
with the workers to carry the Ten Hours' Bill, which the latter had
been vainly demanding for 30 years' (Marx, 1848: 457–8). And
when Marx also advocated free trade for Germany, it was because
although German protectionists had claimed that 'their system ...
is ... necessary to begin with social reforms in one's own country',
they had 'abandoned the social question', regarding it as a 'special
question'. They 'never protected small industry, handicraft proper',
he complained, but regarded its decline as 'sad but inevitable', even
necessary (Marx, 1847: 281).

Had protection and reform been combined, as they were at a
later date, we can safely assume that Marx's conditional position
would have changed. For he could see that, in certain circumstances,
protectionism rather than free trade could hasten capitalist
development and destroy feudalism. The 'protective system' was
'nothing but a means of establishing manufacture upon a large scale
in any given country'. Protective duties served the bourgeoisie as
'weapons against feudalism and absolute monarchy, as a means for
the concentration of its own powers for the realization of Free Trade
within the country' (Marx, 1848: 465). And it had uses abroad:

> European states tore each other to pieces to gain the patent of
> protectionism, plundering their own people, indirectly through
> protective duties, directly through export premiums and also
> using it to forcibly uproot ... all industries in the neighbouring
> dependent countries, as for example, England did with the Irish
> woollen manufacture.
>
> (Marx, 1867: 922)

Though for a time after its triumph in England, free trade seemed
to 'verify the most extravagant expectations of prosperity founded
upon that event', things soon changed. In the face of the United

Kingdom's fabulous success, other countries could hardly be expected 'to sit still and to submit to this change, which degraded them to be mere agricultural appendages of England', the 'workshop of the world'. They did not, and protectionism rather than free trade became 'the plan which would soonest bring capitalist society to ... deadlock' (Engels, 1888: 525). Marx made clear how well he understood the rationale of combined or contender development when he sarcastically ventriloquized List, champion of German protectionism:

> We German bourgeois do not want to be exploited by the English bourgeois in the way that you German proletarians are exploited by us and that we exploit one another. We do not want to subject ourselves to the same laws of exchange value as those to which we subject you. We do not want any longer to recognize outside the country the economic laws which we recognise inside the country.
>
> (Marx, 1845/1975: 279–80)

The competition between nationally organized protectionist blocs of capital that replaced the 'world market' created by the United Kingdom's imperial expansion was, Marx clearly said, similar to competition between firms, and just as contradictory. His remarks on the American protectionist Henry Carey are most revealing. Carey attempted to portray capitalist relations in a protected economy as harmonious domestically. He failed to see, however, that this

> ends with *the most complete disharmony of these relations on the grandest terrain where they appear, the world market, and in their grandest development, as the relations of producing nations....* What Carey has not grasped is that these world-market disharmonies are merely the ultimate adequate expressions of the disharmonies which have become fixed as abstract relations within the economic categories or which have a local existence on the smallest scale ... . This contradiction forms the originality of his writings and gives them their significance.
>
> (Marx, 1858/1973: 886–7, emphasis added)

The idea that Marx and Engels thought of imperialism as the 'pioneer of capitalism' (Warren, 1980), serving, for all its apparent brutality, to integrate far-flung corners of the world into the world market and implant capitalist development in them, is unfounded and contravenes their geopolitical economy of 'relations of producing nations'. They saw imperialism instead as a case of 'one nation [growing] rich at the expense of another'. Partisans of the former view point to Marx's famous remarks about how imperialism in India would lay down the 'material premises' of the Indians' emancipation through the development of their productive powers (Marx, 1974: 321). They fail to note that he also argued that only with an end to colonial exploitation either in socialism or in nationalism – when 'in Great Britain itself the now ruling classes shall have been supplanted by the industrial proletariat, or ... the Hindus themselves shall have grown strong enough to throw off the English yoke altogether' – would Indians 'reap the fruits of the new elements of society [thus] scattered among them' (Marx, 1974: 323; see also Habib, 2006: liii–liv).

Marx and Engels's view of imperialism anticipated later and fuller critiques of comparative advantage. It made colonialism 'morally defensible' (Reinert, 2007: 304; Patnaik, 2005; Saul, 1960) on faulty assumptions – of full employment in the trading countries, of all countries being capable of producing all goods – and wrote developmental states out of capitalism's script by assuming that technological innovations were made under free trade. This was particularly lethal:

> by eliminating from economic theory a qualitative understanding of economic change and dynamics, it has created an economic theory that makes it possible for a nation to specialize in being poor. In Ricardian theory the economy is not going anywhere, there is no progress and consequently nothing to emulate.
>
> (Reinert, 2007: 19)

Given that state-directed contender development was precisely about emulation, not to mention leapfrogging, comparative advantage worked to reinforce existing patterns of unevenness ideologically, by ruling out combined development's challenge to the status quo.

Marx and Engels also understood the state's domestic economic role in ways that anticipated later understandings. Engels foresaw that as capitalism socialized production, the contradiction between it and private ownership would sharpen and force capitalists into trusts that would eventually lead 'the official representative of capitalist society – the state – .... to undertake the direction of production' (1880/1989: 318). Competition between capitalists and class struggle would make their own contributions to increasing the economic role of the state. Marx had argued that 'under free competition, the immanent laws of capitalism confront the individual capitalist as a coercive force external to him', and capitalists themselves agitate for regulatory legislation (1867: 381 and n). Moreover, 'Capital ... takes no account of the health and the length of life of the worker unless society forces it to do so', and class struggle moves society to do so when capitalist power is sufficiently weak and working class power correspondingly strong (1867: 409).

IMPERIALISM IN THE MIRROR OF REVOLUTION

The geopolitical economy of capitalism entered a new phase in the late nineteenth century. More and more states played larger economic roles as contender industrialization increased industrial competition between 'producing nations'. The world created and dominated by the singular imperial expansion of the first industrial capitalist country progressively gave way to one shaped by competition between a plurality of industrial nations, as contenders – pre-eminently the United States, Germany and Japan – industrialized. Moreover, the continued availability of easily acquired territories and the intimate connection between industrial success and imperial reach meant that industrial competition also entailed imperial competition, which culminated in the First World War. The period of imperial and industrial competition from 1870 to 1914 is thus best seen as the cusp, a moment of equipoise, between capitalism's imperial origins and its future of international competition and increasing multipolarity.

During this period the distance between the ideological dominance of free trade, thanks to the dominance of financial interests within the UK state, and realities on the ground only widened. Competitive imperialism between industrial states, which resulted in the Boer war, the scramble for Africa, Japan's forays into Manchuria and Korea and the United States's into the Philippines, led to far more violence than the earlier 'expansion of England', which had proceeded by overpowering weaker native resistance and rivals. But ideology remained so distant from these realities that one of the most successful books in the run-up to the First World War was Norman Angell's *The Great Illusion*. It claimed, *inter alia*, that 'a nation's political and economic frontiers do not now necessarily coincide', that 'military power is socially and economically futile, and can have no relation to the prosperity of the people exercising it', and that 'war, even when victorious, can no longer achieve those aims for which peoples strive' (Angell, 1914: vii–viii).

No wonder then that more accurate understandings of the geopolitical economy of the times emerged from politically critical intellectual currents. Marxist leaders of the Second International and Bolshevik leaders of the Russian Revolution produced the works on imperialism – Rudolf Hilferding's *Finance Capital* (1910/1981), Rosa Luxemburg's *The Accumulation of Capital on a World Scale* (1913/2003), Vladimir Lenin's *Imperialism* (1917/1970) and Bukharin's *Imperialism and the World Economy* (1917/2003, but written in 1915) – which today enjoy a classical status. J. A. Hobson's *Imperialism: A study* (1902/1965) preceded the Marxist works and influenced the best known of them: Lenin used Hobson's study 'with all the care that, in [his] opinion, that work deserve[d]' in writing his own widely read pamphlet. Hobson's intellectual antecedents lay in English new liberalism. It rejected free trade to make the 'necessary intellectual adjustment' (Hobsbawm, 1964: 267) to reform capitalism 'piecemeal into a more rational and humane social order in which inequalities of wealth and incomes would be drastically reduced and democratic rights extended and substantiated and in which the still marginalized and alienated working class would be integrated into the political system' (Desai, 1994a: 47; see also Clarke, 1978). We might note that the 'bourgeois Marxist' (Catephores, 1994) Joseph Schumpeter's contemporaneous *Imperialism and Social Classes* (1919/1951) associated capitalism with free trade and imperialism with aristocratic influence. It shared little with works that implicated either capitalism as such, or a new phase of it, centrally in imperialism.

Imperialism and capitalism

Hobson traced imperialism to capitalism's central contradiction – the paucity of consumption demand. Workers' low wages divorced the 'desire to consume' from 'the power to consume' (Hobson, 1902: 87). The resulting demand shortfalls were exacerbated by increases in productivity and production thanks to competition, and constrained demand restricted investment opportunities. Competitive imperialism was inevitable:

> As one nation after another enters the machine economy and adopts advanced industrial methods, it becomes more difficult for its manufacturers, merchants and financiers to dispose profitably of their economic resources, and they are tempted more

and more to use their Governments in order to secure for their particular use some distant undeveloped territory by annexation and protection. .... It is admitted by all business men that the growth of the powers of production in their country exceeds the growth in consumption, that more goods can be produced than can be sold at a profit, and that more capital exists than can find remunerative investment. It is this economic condition of affairs that forms the taproot of Imperialism.

(Hobson, 1902: 80–1)

Hobson, a new liberal, clearly rejected Say's law, but developments that would prevent the majority of Marxists from doing this were already under way. Though national capitalist classes were reliant on the state to address capitalism's contradictions at home and promote their interests against competing capitalist nations abroad, rising working class assertion made them uneasily aware that state intervention opened the possibility that 'national capitalism would serve simply as a stopping point on the road to some type of socialism' (Block, 1977: 9). Classical political economy, even Ricardo's, could no longer legitimize capitalism. It was uncomfortably close to contentious questions of class and distribution even before Marx and Engels's interventions. Neoclassical, marginalist 'economics' now emerged precisely to explore 'the possibilities and limits of state intervention in the regulation of economic relations, including, in particular, the resolution of the labour question', and to ensure that such intervention did not tilt the balance of political forces too far in favour of labour through welfarist intervention (Clarke, 1991: 188).

As Marxists trained in neoclassical economics, beginning with Michael von Tugan Baranowski (1901/2000a, 1901/2000b), began fitting Marx's ideas into the neoclassical marginalist conceptual apparatus, one consequence was to rule out most forms of crises. Given their acceptance of Say's law, paucity of demand was a particular target, and 'underconsumption' has since remained a byword for economic illiteracy in these circles (see Desai, 2010a for a full discussion of the issues).

Rosa Luxemburg challenged this still-nascent tendency, arguing that it relied on a tendentious reading of the reproduction schemas in Volume II of *Capital*. It ignored the plentiful references to crisis in Volume II as well as the aim of the reproduction schemas, which was to show how reproduction might (but typically does not) occur. Taking this to imply a crisis-free capitalism flatly contradicted the account of Volume III 'based on the inherent contradiction between the unlimited expansive capacity of the productive forces and the limited expansive capacity of social consumption under conditions of capitalist distribution' (Luxemburg, 1913/2003: 323).

> [T]he desire to accumulate plus the technical prerequisites of accumulation is not enough in a capitalist economy of commodity production. A further condition is required to ensure that accumulation can in fact proceed and production expand: the effective demand for commodities must also increase. Where is this continually increasing demand to come from which ... forms the basis of reproduction on an ever rising scale?
>
> (Luxemburg, 1913/2003: 104)

For Luxemburg, in a 'pure' capitalist economy under the 'universal and exclusive domination of the capitalist mode of production' (1913/1951: 348–9) consisting only of workers and capitalists, which was the construct under discussion, demand would be chronically inadequate. She clearly saw, following Marx and anticipating Keynes, that inadequate demand would reduce capitalists' 'inducement to invest'. Joan Robinson explained Luxemburg's reasoning:

> What motive have the capitalists for enlarging their stock of real capital? How do they know that there will be demand for the increased output of goods which the new capital will produce, so that they can 'capitalize' their surplus in a profitable form?
>
> (Robinson, 1951: xxix)

Competitively driven increases in productivity and decreases in costs would inevitably lead to generalized overproduction and declines in the rate of profit, and rob capitalists of the inducement to invest unless new markets in non-capitalist societies could be found. (See also Marx, 1858: 417.)

For Luxemburg, demand conditions and investment decisions were linked, and a decision against investing surplus resulted in a hoard. As Prabhat Patnaik notes, this idea linked Marx, through Luxemburg (and, we might add, Hobson), to Keynes and Kalecki. In this lineage, the ever-present possibility of hoards in a monetary economy means that investment could always fail to make up for the paucity of consumption demand. This was the crux of Marx's (and later Keynes's) critique of Say's law. The majority of Marx's followers did not pursue 'this fundamental contribution of Marx any further'. Instead, they pursued 'exclusively the other major theoretical discovery of Marx, namely, the one relating to his theory of surplus value' (Patnaik, 2008: 3–4), although, as we shall see below, not without problems.

While imperialism was the preferred method for states to resolve demand deficits well into the twentieth century, Hobson could clearly see another way: deepening and broadening the home market.

> If the consuming public in this country raises its standard of consumption to keep pace with every rise of productive powers, there could be no excess of goods or capital clamorous to use Imperialism in order to find markets: foreign trade would indeed exist, but there would be no difficulty in exchanging a small surplus of our manufactures for the food and raw material we annually absorbed, and all the savings we made could find employment, if we choose, in home industries.
>
> (Hobson, 1902: 81)

This option would, however, strengthen workers economically and politically, and capitalists would not choose it as long as foreign territories could easily be acquired and held. Only with postwar decolonization would the basis of the greatest working-class gains in capitalism's history, as well as the most dynamic phase of capitalist accumulation before or since, be laid.

To be sure, this option was also ultimately contradictory: Marx had argued that periods of rising wages and working-class consumption would cause a new type of crisis by reducing capitalists' desire to invest by squeezing profitability (1884: 486–7). Kalecki (1943) was more categorical: such a solution to the problem of underconsumption would constitute a level of working-class empowerment unacceptable to capitalists. Under capitalism, therefore, underconsumption would be remedied only partially, and would, as later chapters will show, exacerbate the contradictions of capitalism precisely as Marx foresaw.

But this is to run ahead. As long as imperialism remained the preferred resolution, Luxemburg's view that 'capitalism needs non-capitalist social organizations as the setting for its development' and that 'it proceeds by assimilating the very conditions which alone can ensure its own existence' (1913/2003: 346) remained true. However, the just-emerging Marxist economics subjected this view to some of the most irresponsible critiques in the history of Marxism. While differing on many points, critics like Bukharin and

Grossman, as well as their followers in the later twentieth century, insisted that imperialism 'can and does happen and it does aid capitalist accumulation when it does happen, but it is not required by the logic of capitalism' (Zarembka, 2003: 8; see also Desai, 2010c: 125–30). For them, Luxemburg had taken a morally, but not theoretically, correct stance. Just like a woman.

The new capitalisms and imperialism

In contrast to Hobson and Luxemburg, other Marxists refused to trace imperialism to capitalism's key contradiction. Instead, they traced the intensified and competitive 'new' imperialism to a new historical phase of capitalism in which nationally organized concentrations of capital competed for markets and investment opportunities. These attempts, it is true, suffered from the problem of reinforcing the idea of a free trade, rather than imperialist, nineteenth century (Gallagher and Robinson, 1953: 2). Hilferding, for instance, thought imperialist competition 'revolutionizes the whole world view of the bourgeoisie, which ceases to be peace-loving and humanitarian [sic]. The old free traders believed in free trade not only as the best economic policy but also as the beginning of an era of peace' (1910: 335). However, those who traced imperialism to a new phase of capitalism also pointed to important specificities of contemporary capitalism. The industrialized production of producers' goods in the 'second industrial revolution' had vastly increased capital intensity, and new organizational forms – joint stock companies, monopolies and cartels – emerged to concentrate capital. Finance came to the fore and interacted with productive capital in new ways. Finally, the state came to play an even more prominent economic role through a 'process of 'nationalization' of capital, i.e. the creation of homogenous economic organisms included within state boundaries and sharply opposing each other' (Bukharin, 1917: 81). These were the developments captured by Hilferding's 'finance capital', Lenin's 'monopoly capital' and Bukharin's 'nationalization of capital' in slightly differing ways. However, two problems prevent proper analytical deployment of these works.

The first concerns the relationship of capitalism and war. Lenin's *Imperialism* is the best known of these works, and its contention that inter-imperialist rivalry necessarily meant war has made the relevance of these works for any coherent understanding of the evolution of the capitalist world order doubtful, given the apparent cooperation between major capitalist powers after the Second World War. Not only did much conflict underlie this cooperation, as later chapters show, a proper contextualization of Lenin's claim also puts it in a new light. It was made against Karl Kautsky's (1914/1970) argument that imperial competition could turn into an 'ultra-imperialist' peace. Lenin's opposite contention was made to argue that war made socialism more urgent. However later, as a revolutionary leader, he too came to fear possible collusion between imperial powers isolating his fledgling regime. US President Woodrow Wilson had responded to the Bolshevik anti-imperialist Peace Decrees of October 1917 by proposing in January 1918 that a community of nation-states be set up after the war. Enthusiastic response to this proposal in war-weary Europe, Lenin anticipated, could result in 'a shift "from imperialist war, which brought the people utter misery and the great betrayal of Socialism ... toward an imperialist peace, which will bring the people the greatest deception in the form of nice phrases, semi-reforms, semi-concessions, etc"' (quoted in Mayer, 1964: 161–2). So Lenin too could envisage cooperation rather than conflict between imperial powers. The most important thing about the classical theories of imperialism, therefore, is not what they predict about the outcome of inter-imperial competition, but how they understand its drivers. That arguably remains relevant in any account of the historical evolution of capitalism's geopolitical economy.

The second problem is an anachronistic understanding of 'finance capital'. Writing on late twentieth and early twenty-first century financialization frequently and reverentially refers to Hilferding's concept of finance capital. However, the relationship between production and finance it denoted was the opposite of that in recent financialization. Focused on developments in Germany in particular, 'finance capital' denoted the subjection of finance to industrial expansion in ways Marx had anticipated (Hudson, 2010). Why and how such finance capital turned into its opposite a century later is a question on which this book sheds considerable light here and in later chapters.

Though financial capital is older than industrial capital, Marx anticipated that capitalism's maturation would lead to the 'subordination of interest-bearing capital to the conditions and requirements of modern industry', principally through the 'transformed figure of the borrower': no longer a supplicant in financial straits but a capitalist to whom money is lent 'in the expectation that he ... will use [it] to appropriate unpaid labour' (Marx, 1894: 735). This subordination could be achieved by using 'violence (the State) ... against interest-bearing capital [to effect] a compulsory reduction of interest rates'. However, mature industrial capital would, Marx believed, achieve it much more thoroughly and effectively through 'the creation of a procedure specific to itself – the credit system [which] is its own creation and is itself a form of industrial capital which begins with manufacture and develops further with large scale industry'. When it first emerged, therefore, the credit system took a 'polemical form directed against old-fashioned usurers' (Marx, 1979: 468–9).

Hilferding's *Finance Capital* contrasted the early subordination of industry to finance and the later reversal of this relationship: England exemplified the former and 'the protectionist countries', like Germany and the United States, the latter. Modern bank capital arose from the 'resistance of "productive" capital, i.e. of the profit-earning capitalists ... against the interest-earning capitalists'. To be sure,

> [t]he power of the banks increases and they become founders and eventually rulers of industry, whose profits they seize for themselves as finance capital, just as formerly the old usurer seized, in the form of 'interest', the produce of the peasants and the ground rent of the lord of the manor.
>
> (Hilferding, 1910: 226)

However, the relationship never reverts to pre-capitalist forms. Finance capital drives the expansion of production instead of squeezing it. Earlier banks supplied only short-term commercial credit, as City of London banks still did in England. The continental bank, however, financed production. As such, it had to 'necessarily concern itself with the long-range prospects of the enterprise and the future state of the market'. Its 'momentary interest' became 'an enduring one' and 'the larger the amount of credit supplied and, above all, the larger the proportion of the loan capital turned into fixed capital, the stronger and more abiding will that interest be' (Hilferding, 1910: 95). Such a bank may remain 'the more powerful party' with access to 'capital in its liquid, readily available, form', but it focuses on long-term productive investment (1910: 95).

Banks' involvement in industry, moreover, 'intensifies all the tendencies toward concentration which are already implicit in the technical conditions of the banking system' (1910: 95) and also transforms the relation of capital to the state. Although 'even in England the triumph of *laissez-faire* was far from complete',

the protectionist countries, Germany and the United States ...

became the model states of capitalist development, if one takes as a yardstick the degree of centralization and concentration of capital (that is, the degree of development of cartels and trusts) and of the domination of industry by the banks – in short, the transformation of all capital into finance capital.

(Hilferding, 1910: 305)

For 'finance', 'monopoly' or 'nationalized' capitalisms of this sort, protection was no longer 'a defence against the conquest of the domestic market by foreign industries' but 'a means for the conquest of foreign markets by domestic industry' (1910: 310).

The difference between Hilferding's finance capital and recent financialization, and the transition from the one to the other, can now be clarified. In the United Kingdom, the historical seniority of financial capital and its hold on the UK state had resulted in the contrasting pattern of finance subordinating the interests of industry (Anderson, 1964, 1987; Ingham, 1984; Leys, 1985, 1990). It allowed London to be the world's financial and commercial centre and guarantor of its gold standard, but at the cost of relative industrial decline. Marx's expectation that this pattern was something capitalism would grow out of was fulfilled for the continent. However in the United Kingdom between 1970 and 1914, thanks to its financial and commercial role, undergirded by its colonial empire, the opposite pattern prevailed. And, if this pattern lived on to reappear in spectacularly unstable ways less than a century later, it was because the United States sought vainly to emulate the United Kingdom's financial role. Without an empire, such as the United Kingdom had, operating as one national economy among many others, the United States's attempts at emulation had to fail, as later chapters show. The recent US-centred financialization, in which the UK financial sector played such an important subordinate role, was the apogee of these mimetic attempts. Such financial arrangements have no future in the multipolar world of the twenty-first century.

Uneven and combined development

The classical theories of imperialism were embedded in a wider anti-imperialist understanding of capitalism's geopolitical economy, uneven and combined development. This nascent theory formed the basis of the Bolsheviks' historical understanding of their revolution, the 'revolution against Capital', as Gramsci termed it because it took place in a backward rather than advanced capitalist country. UCD also framed the Bolsheviks' analysis of anti-colonial nationalist movements and the fledgling USSR's 'nationalities' problem (Trotsky, 1969; Mayer, 1964; Suny, 1993, 1998; Martin, 2001).

The first chapter of Trotsky's *The History of the Russian Revolution* is UCD's *locus classicus*. In Trotsky's view, human advancement before capitalism proceeded as backward countries 'assimilat[ed] the material and intellectual advancements of the advanced countries' by repeating the stages through which the advanced society had passed. It was 'provincial and episodic'. Capitalism, by contrast, 'prepares and in a certain sense realises the permanence of man's development' and rules repetition out (Trotsky, 1934: 26). Though unevenness was 'the most general law of the historic process', under capitalism it 'compelled' backward countries 'to make leaps'. Thus, 'a backward country does not take things in the same order' as the advanced. Instead, it exercises the 'privilege of historic backwardness' by 'skipping a whole series of intermediate stages', as Germany and the United States recently had done while the United Kingdom was paying the price for its early lead (1934: 26). Such skipping compressed 'the different stages of the journey' in 'an amalgam of archaic with more contemporary forms' (1934: 27). Such combined development was the distinctive feature of capitalism.

While it was first systematically outlined by Trotsky, readers will have detected the similarity between UCD and Marx and Engels's views on free trade and protection, and their understanding of the world order in terms of 'relations between producing nations' (see also Mehringer, 1978; van der Linden, 2007). Such an understanding also underlies their thinking on the differential development of European countries, particularly on German backwardness against English and French advance, and their analysis of its consequences, whether for philosophy or economic theory (Marx, 1843/1974, Althusser, 1969; Desai, 2012).

What united the Bolshevik understanding of imperialism with UCD was the understanding of capitalist states as nationally organized blocs of capital and of the consequences of differential development. Bukharin, for instance, contended against Kautsky that differences in 'the economic structure of France and Germany, of England and America, of the developed countries in general [and] such countries as Russia' meant that the possibility of 'a world capitalist organisation' was remote (1917: 148). UCD also underlay Lenin's 1916 division of the world into imperialist countries where the class struggle was being waged most intensely; Eastern Europe, where workers had to struggle for national as well as class demands and meaningfully align them; and the 'semi-colonial countries, like China, Persia, Turkey, and all the colonies' where 'bourgeois-democratic movements have either hardly begun, or are far from having been completed', and in which socialists must support national self-determination against imperialism (Lenin, 1916/1942: 54–5).

Postwar developments made UCD and the classical theories of imperialism more, not less, relevant. If capitalist competition did not lead to further world wars, this was substantially because the USSR became part of UCD's further unfolding. As a revolutionary state founded on UCD's understanding of the capitalist world order, it took opposition to imperialism beyond national (capitalist) opposition to imperialism to encompass working-class opposition as well. As such it represented the strongest form of combined development: rather than trying to hasten capitalist development it sought to skip capitalism entirely. That communist China did so too, and survived to rank as the strongest of the so-called BRIC contender countries in the early twenty-first century, is also telling.

The significance of Soviet combined development was not confined to its borders. After its decisive role in the defeat of fascism in the Second World War, the USSR ensured decolonization and supported combined development in newly independent countries, strengthening resistance to imperial pressure among many ex-colonies. The USSR's existence also ensured that combined development, as well as 'full employment' and welfarist policies, had to be tolerated in recovering economies. As Chapter 7 will show, by the time the USSR disintegrated, sufficient combined development had taken place among recovering and developing countries to make the US 'victory' in the cold war pyrrhic.

THE THIRTY YEARS' CRISIS

The First World War is widely seen to have marked a historical caesura – the death of 'liberal capitalism', the gold standard, and British financial and commercial supremacy. By incubating the Russian Revolution, it opened the 'age of extremes' (Hobsbawm, 1994). Its importance as a major rupture in intellectual history is less widely appreciated. Three aspects are relevant here. After 1914, the social-scientific division of labour in which the social sciences studied 'differentiated' spheres of society and one of these, neoclassical economics, was privileged above the rest, became settled reality and exacted its price. The bourgeois discipline of international relations (IR) which now emerged looked resolutely away from its economic drivers to give an exclusively 'political' account of its subject. Second, Marxists outside the USSR, already divided by the war and the Russian Revolution, either neglected political economy entirely or fell increasingly under the influence of 'Marxist economics'. The price here was that the legatees of the most powerful critique of capitalism failed to produce an enduring explanation of the Great Depression.

The First World War's 'fundamental politicodiplomatic realignments' (Mayer, 1964: 368) intertwined domestic mass politics and international relations, political economy and geopolitical economy, class and nation, and capitalism and the nation-state, more closely than ever. On the one hand, capitalist economies became even more national – because of both the war itself, and the political power of working classes and their mobilization for war entrenching mass politics even deeper in the countries of Europe. On the other hand, the Bolshevik Revolution combined resistance to class exploitation and to uneven development for the first time in history. And yet both Marxist and mainstream scholarship became committed to forms of understanding that could not comprehend these intertwinings. Third, therefore, it was left to non-Marxist thinkers such as Keynes and Polanyi to generate understandings of the age of mass national politics and its geopolitical economy.

The new diplomacy and international relations

The bourgeois discipline of IR studiedly ignores the importance of Hobson, the classical theories of imperialism and UCD in understanding the world order. E. H. Carr's still widely read classic, *The Twenty Years' Crisis,* set in stone two myths about IR's origins. He argued, first, that the 'campaign for the popularization of international politics … in the English-speaking countries in the form of an agitation against secret treaties' (1939/1989: 2) forced relations between nations to cease being the preserve of professional soldiers and diplomats and to be publicly debated and open to scholarly inquiry (1939: 2). This was the birth of the IR discipline. However, as Arno Mayer (1964) showed, the transition from elite, secret and annexationist 'old diplomacy' to the 'new diplomacy', which at least promised publicity and democracy at home and anti-colonialism and national self-determination abroad, was the tortured historical work of the war and the Russian Revolution. Wilson's Fourteen Points of January 1918, which dropped imperial conquest from war aims, substituted national liberation and democracy, and called for 'open covenants openly arrived at', were not a response to any British campaigns. Rather they were designed to counter the stunning popularity of the November 1917 Bolshevik publication of Tsarist secret treaties and their Peace Decree among the growing 'progressive coalition' of left and radical forces across Europe ranged against imperialism and war (Mayer, 1959: 265).

Second, Carr's account of the origins of the still-dominant 'realist' approach in IR obscured the true nature of the settlement after the First World War. In Carr's view, after a brief naive flirtation with 'idealist' Wilsonian schemes – pre-eminently the League of Nations – which failed, early IR scholars wisely settled for 'realism', which recognized that the road to hell was paved with good intentions, and stuck to the facts. However, Wilson's 'idealism', as we shall see in greater detail in Chapter 3, was nothing of the sort. Thorstein Veblen saw in the allegedly idealist Covenant only an 'instrument of Realpolitik'. It

> provides for enforcing the peace by recourse to arms and commercial hostilities, but it contemplates no measures for avoiding war by avoiding the status quo out of which the great war arose. The status quo was a status of commercialized nationalism.
>
> (Veblen, 1919)

As the world's largest economy, the United States was preeminent among the commercial nationalists, and the League covenant was 'in an eminent sense America's Covenant'.

Carr defined realism in an astonishingly anodyne fashion: it emphasized 'facts' and 'the analysis of their causes and consequences' in a 'sequence of events which it is powerless to influence or alter'. Realist scholars had to accept 'the irresistible strength of existing forces and the inevitable character of existing tendencies' (Carr, 1939: 10). Conceived as such, it could only have ideological, not intellectual, functions. Realism came into its own after the Second World War. Drained of economic content that might have accounted for the material bases of international conflict or cooperation, and focusing instead on the pursuit of essentialized 'national interests' in an 'anarchic' international system, realism performed yeoman service in malleably justifying the cold war, military build-ups and the international actions of the United States and the advanced capitalist countries where it was headquartered.

'Marxist economics' and the Great Depression

The adaptation of Marxism to neoclassical economics had two critical consequences: crises were written out of Marxism just in time for the Great Crash of 1929, and state action to cope with capitalist crisis tendencies was ruled out just when the Great Depression effectively demanded it in capitalist economies and the tensions of UCD sharpened acutely.

One of the first Marxist economists, the Russian 'legal Marxist', Michael von Tugan-Baranowski, had allowed only one cause of crisis: disproportions between sectors of industry arising from unplanned capitalist production. These Yvgenii Preobrazhensky would later link to the inability of an increasingly monopolistic capitalism to redeploy resources from declining to rising sectors (Howard and King, 1992: 15). Though Tugan-Baranowski's account of crisis was contested by other Marxist economists, his rejection of insufficient consumption demand as a cause of crisis was now set in stone: 'underconsumption' would now be labelled 'counter-revolutionary' and 'reformist' (1992: 17; see also Desai, 2010a). Otto Bauer produced the solitary mathematical model of underconsumption, in which rising accumulation, and therefore productive capacity, systematically outstripped society's (principally workers') consumption capacity (Howard and King, 1992: 18). The pervasive rejection of underconsumption in Marxist economics had momentous consequences: 'Marxist analyses of the Depression proved deficient, and the ultimate reason is similar to that applying in the case of bourgeois economics: they lacked an adequate theory of effective demand' (1992: 19).

With crisis of realization thus ruled out, Marxist economists focused instead on crises of accumulation. For Otto Bauer, crises resulted from overaccumulation, leading to wages outstripping productivity as labour markets tightened and workers' bargaining power improved (Howard and King, 1992: 13). But the major new development was Henryk Grossman's *The Law of Accumulation and the Breakdown of the Capitalist System*, published months before the stock market crashed in 1929. It focused on the tendency of the rate of profit to fall (TRPF) as the chief cause of crisis. This constituted an important departure. Hitherto, though widely appreciated, the TRPF was not considered a source of crisis (Howard and King, 1989: 316). Marx had argued that capitalists were forced to increase their fixed investment to gain cost advantages over competitors. However, these advantages lasted only until competitors made similar investments. For the economy, or sector, as a whole, competition therefore led to a general tendency toward increasing investment and lower profit rates. This tendency could be counteracted by factors such as lower wages or cheaper capital goods, but would prevail in the long run. Grossman was right that the TRPF was an important crisis mechanism; it would play a key role in postwar capitalism, as discussed in later chapters. However, he thought it would lead to a shortage of capital to invest (Howard and King, 1992: 12), whereas Marx had seen it leading to a disincentive to invest, rendering capital surplus and creating an unproductive hoard which could only be invested in speculation, something which Keynes explored in greater detail.

Like 'underconsumption', the TRPF too would be rejected as a cause of crisis by most Marxist economists. Again Tugan-Baranowski originated the rejection by arguing, first, that capitalists would never invest if it decreased their rate of profit, and second, that technical progress, because it made capital goods cheaper, meant that the rate of profit would over time rise (Tugan-Baranowski, 1901/2000b: 91–6). These arguments still persist. The second, accepted by Marx as a potential counter-tendency, is a matter for empirical verification. The first simply overlooks the complex relation between individual capitalists' intentions and the systemic effects of their actions which Marx had carefully outlined:

> No capitalist voluntarily applies a new method of production, no matter how much more productive it might be or how much it might raise the rate of surplus value, if it reduces the rate of profit. But every new method of production of this kind makes commodities cheaper. At first, therefore, he can sell them above their price of production, perhaps above their value. He pockets the difference between their costs of production and the market price of the other commodities, which are produced at higher production costs. This is possible because the average socially necessary labour-time required to produce these latter commodities is greater than the labour-time required with the new method of production. This production procedure is ahead of the social average. But competition makes the new procedure universal and subjects it to the general law. A fall in the profit rate then ensues – firstly perhaps in this sphere of production, and subsequently equalized with the others – *a fall that is completely independent of the capitalists' will.*
>
> (Marx, 1894: 373–4)

The later 'Okishio theorem' (Okishio, 1961) only further entrenched the rejection of the TRPF on this flimsy ground, and led many Marxists to claim that Marx was simply wrong (Kliman, 2007; Freeman, 2010; Desai, 2010a). Very few Marxists within the neoclassical framework sought to demonstrate the TRPF any longer (Shaikh, 1978, was one, though he attempted this within the confines of Marxist economics).

The TRPF would also be rejected by the Keynesian wing of Marxism, pre-eminently Paul Baran and Paul Sweezy, though on the more contingent basis that capitalism had entered a new stage. While the TRPF may have operated under competitive conditions, increasing monopoly removed price pressures (Baran and Sweezy, 1966). This had the interesting implication that profit rates were contingent on prices, therefore the operation of the TRPF was reliant on levels of demand, a point Robert Brenner emphasized in his account of postwar geopolitical economy, as we shall see in Chapter 5.

While the erasure of crises from Marxist economics eliminated the need to understand the need for state intervention and thus the national character of capitalist economies, the history of social democracy until and immediately beyond 1914 put a further obstacle in the way of such understanding. The First World War split the Second International when the majority of social democratic deputies voted for war credits in their parliaments, committing workers to fight other workers, against the movement's own proclaimed internationalism. The internationalist senior leadership saw this as a great betrayal. In reality, however, national perspectives had become entrenched in the social democratic parties of various countries through practices that, for decades, had exploited and widened national spaces for meaningful concessions to working people (Joll, 1974; Schorske, 1983), just as Marx and Engels had clearly foreseen that they could (Desai, 2012: 56). The internationalism of the Second International took little account of this practical nationalism, while condemning those who brought attention to it as revisionists. Matters have more or less remained there. The relationship between the inevitably national struggle for reform and its connection with revolutionary politics and internationalism remains largely unconsidered among Marxists. This is despite the fundamentally national struggles that enabled European working classes' most enduring gains – the welfare state and its extensive postwar development, and macroeconomic management for relatively high levels of employment – and although both were made more urgent by the communist threat. Not burdened by this intellectual and political history, Keynes and Polanyi could and did appreciate the effect of the rise of mass and working-class politics on national economies. Their thought was far more radical than is usually appreciated.

Keynes and Polanyi: internationalism versus imperialism

Keynes's intellectual lineage – principally the English social or new liberalism which encompassed Hobson, the Fabians and Shaw – had moved leftward in response to 'the social question' (Clarke, 1978), and his thought was not only more radical than his stated liberal convictions, but shared similarities with, and drew from, Marx's. Like Marx, Keynes was a moral, political and historical thinker, who criticized the received economic wisdom of his time. Like Marx, his thought centred on a critique of Say's law which, moreover, rested on Marx's crucial distinction between what the simple circulation of commodities (in Keynes's terms a real exchange economy) and a money economy like capitalism, in which money played an independent and disequilibrating role and made crises endogenous to capitalism (Torr, 1980; Sardoni, 1997). As we shall see below, this theoretical radicalism was matched by a political radicalism (Dostaler, 2007; Desai, 2009a; Desai and Freeman, 2009).

While post-Keynesians (Chick, 1983; Davidson, 1991; Tily, 2007) at least acknowledge his theoretical, if not political, radicalism, 'bastard Keynesians', as Joan Robinson called those who claimed Keynes's mantle but sought to render him acceptable to mainstream postwar thinking, elide both. This fate too Keynes shared with Marx: 'Marxists without Marx' (Freeman, 2010) deradicalized his legacy too. In these circumstances, naturally, no synthesis of the two bodies of thought could emerge. Most 'Marxists without Marx' sought to establish their radical credentials instead by dismissing Keynes as a 'mere reformist', while most Keynesians, of course, never read Marx (Further on links between Marx and Keynes, see Patnaik, 2009; Desai, 2009a; Desai and Freeman, 2009).

Keynes replaced neoclassical economics with the macroeconomics that would make full employment – a situation where all available labour was employed (Keynes, 1936/1967: 26) – its goal, and enabled national income accounting as an essential instrument for such a policy. He claimed to be reforming capitalism, but far overshot that goal. According to Keynes, aggregate production and employment levels in a monetary economy, in which investors' expectations play a determining role, are far from assured. Counter-cyclical government intervention is necessary to keep demand for consumption, and by extension for investment, sufficiently high for full employment. This also entails greater egalitarianism. Workers have 'higher propensities to consume' and spend more of their income than capitalists, so high employment levels and egalitarian income distribution would increase consumption demand, pulling investment demand behind it, while the lower consumption propensity and excessive 'liquidity preference' – a preference for liquid money over productive investment – among the rich and capitalists would have the opposite effect.

And Keynes went far beyond demand management. In fact, he had clearly foreseen that, practised on its own, as postwar 'bastard Keynesians' prescribed, it would run aground, as it did (Chick, 1992). And he foresaw a stage when fiscal and monetary stimuli alone would not suffice to increase investment sufficiently. Then

> a somewhat comprehensive socialization of investment will prove the only means of securing an approximation to full employment; though this need not exclude all manner of compromises and of devices by which public authority will co-operate with private initiative.
>
> (Keynes, 1936: 378)

Not only does this entail a 'large extension in the traditional function of government' (1936: 379), it also requires a reduction in the role of entrepreneurs to 'the personal services of the entrepreneur and his assistants' (1936: 213–14), much like skilled workers (Dillard, 1983; Chernomas, 1984). Rentiers – speculators or 'functionless investors' – are of course to be eliminated (Keynes, 1936: 158). Their saving restricts productive investment and stands between society and 'that degree of material well-being to which our technical advancement entitles us'. That degree of material well-being and full employment would be promoted by a low rate of interest to encourage private productive investment, supplemented by government investment when the former fell short of desired amounts. The purpose, over time, would be to contrive to eliminate the interest rentiers earn without any 'genuine sacrifice' only because capital is scarce by increasing it 'until it ceases to be scarce' (1936: 376).

Capital controls – government controls on inward and outward movements of capital and, generally, large sums of money – are critical to maintaining full employment, as is 'a greater measure of national self-sufficiency and economic isolation between countries than existed in 1914'. Keynes was clear that the commercial aggression that disguised itself as free trade had led to war, and that peace would be promoted by bringing 'the producer and the consumer within the ambit of the same national, economic and financial organisation' (Keynes, 1933). Industrial advance made this more, not less, true, and made it easier too. Most modern industrial production could be 'performed in most countries and climates with almost equal efficiency', and its role was, in any case, diminishing in favour of 'houses, personal services and local amenities', which neither yielded the same efficiency gains nor faced the same international competitive pressures in the advanced economies. Although it could cost a little more, 'National self-sufficiency … may be becoming a luxury which we can afford if we happen to want it' (Keynes, 1933). Keynes considered the society these policies would create 'quite compatible with some measure of individualism' (1936: 375–6). This 'measure of individualism' was what he valued about capitalism, and wanted to salvage by 'reforming' it. As he saw it, this required eliminating the *sine qua non* of capitalism: markets, capitalists (as such) and their political power.

From a different starting point, Polanyi also stressed the centrality of states. They had always been necessary to protect society 'against the perils inherent in a self-regulating market system' which treated land, labour and money as commodities – objects produced for sale – although they were not. That was why the spread of markets elicited 'a network of measures and policies … integrated into powerful institutions designed to check the action of the market relative to labour, land and money'. This 'double movement' of markets and social protection was 'deep-seated' (Polanyi, 1944/1985: 76), and nation-states were the fulcrum of social protection even in the nineteenth century when free trade dominated consciousness: 'The world continued to believe in internationalism and interdependence, while acting on the impulses of nationalism and self-sufficiency' (1944: 207).

Keynes's and Polanyi's political economy stressed the essential and increasing economic role of states, not least due to the increasing political assertion of working classes. Their geopolitical economy was embedded in their critique of the gold standard. For Polanyi, free trade and the free capital flows it assumed made central banking necessary as social protection for money, the linchpin of the economic organization of society. Contrary to the Humean ideology of the gold standard, money was token money, not commodity money. And national token monies' relationships to the gold standard and other national monies had to be mediated by central banks to protect them against the harsh verdicts of international markets. For example, the gold standard would require domestic prices to be lowered whenever the national currency came under pressure, thus interfering with the credit system. Central banking overcame this problem.

By centralizing the supply of credit in a country, it was possible to avoid the wholesale dislocation of business and employment involved in deflation, and to organize deflation in such a way as to absorb the shock and spread its burden over the whole country. The bank in its normal function was cushioning the immediate effects of gold withdrawals on the circulation of notes as well as of the diminished circulation of notes on business.

(Polanyi, 1944: 194)

However, as Keynes noted, even with central banking buffers, the gold standard was generally deflationary. It sacrificed economic activity (and price levels) to the preservation of national currencies' gold price during balance of payments difficulties, and threw the burden of adjustment to trade and payments imbalances on debtor countries, 'the weaker and above all the smaller in comparison with the other side of the scales ... the rest of the world'. Such adjustment was 'compulsory for the debtor and voluntary for the creditor', and stimulated exports 'by reducing their international price in terms of imports' (Keynes, 1980: 29), imposing further deprivation on weaker economies.

That the gold standard was thoroughly inappropriate for growing economies was further underlined by its history. Only a series of historical contingencies made it even appear to function 'automatically' from the 1880s to 1914. Fortuitous discoveries of gold expanded liquidity (Keynes, 1963). Capital flowing into the UK imperial economy from its colonies was exported to other countries, creating international liquidity and increasing productive capacity while also ensuring that increased money supply in the relatively small mother country economy was not inflationary (Keynes, 1980: 30). Even so, central banking had reduced the alleged automatism of the gold standard to a mere pretence: it could hardly be otherwise when competing national economies could be expected to resist its deflationary verdicts:

No country adopted [the gold standard] with the slightest intention of linking itself to an international monetary system that would then automatically produce a kind of international economic meritocracy, based on differences in prices and interest rates among the various nations. ... The various governments adopted such economic policies as they deemed would best serve the interest of the ruling classes. They favoured fixed exchange rates when they were expedient and progressive devaluation when it appeared possible. Nor were they afraid to change course whenever they felt it was necessary.

(De Cecco, 1984: 60–1)

The gold standard was already tenuous in its heyday and, after the First World War, both nation and class militated even more strongly against it. With the franchise extended to include at least male workers, a political cost was added to the economic costs of deflation (Eichengreen, 1992). Even the United Kingdom, with its legendary commitment to the gold standard, had, well before the war, begun to avoid the gold standard's 'discipline' and 'adjustment' 'rather than continuing to accept the sacrifice of domestic unemployment' (Block, 1977: 14; Lindert, 1969: 74–5). And the devastations of war and the Great Depression only made nationalist economic policies that much more attractive.

The geopolitical economy embedded in Keynes's and Polanyi's critiques of the gold standard contained the chief elements necessary to understand the further unfolding of UCD in the twentieth century, in particular how the United States's attempt to emulate the United Kingdom's world role would fare. Keynes and Polanyi pointed to the objective fracturing of the imperial order created by the inevitable world dominance of the first industrial power into one of competing national economies of which the United States was only one, albeit the biggest. Keynes's complaint that any country adopting the gold standard in these circumstances would subject itself to the United States's domestic priorities and decisions (Dostaler, 2007: 211) would prove prescient, as Chapter 4 will show. It will also show that a national economy, no matter how large, without colonial surpluses to export, was bound to either fail to provide international liquidity or do so only in unstable and financially dangerous ways. That was why, at Bretton Woods, Keynes called for a world reserve currency multilaterally managed by nation-states, which he called 'bancor'. It would be the best means through which national and international liquidity for world growth and trade could be created and national governments could have control over domestic productive arrangements, particularly to pursue full employment and progressive social policies. As we shall see in the next chapter, these proposals were defeated by US imperial aspirations.

3

THE US IMPERIAL CAREER

Myths have always shrouded imperialisms but also changed in telling ways. By the twentieth century, imperialism had become so illegitimate that when the United States attempted to emulate British dominance, nineteenth-century myths about imperialism's benevolence had to be supplemented with myths about US reluctance. According to the 'myth of the reluctant superpower', the United States was an anti-colonial revolutionary state, originally inwardly directed and isolationist, which accepted its postwar world role only reluctantly (Bacevich, 2002). The kindred myth of US isolationism stated, more specifically, 'that the United States was isolationist until world power was "thrust upon it", first to help Cuba, then twice to save the world for democracy, and finally to prevent the Soviet Union and other Communist regimes from overwhelming the world'; 'that, except for a brief and rapidly dispelled aberration at the turn of the century, America has been anti-imperialist throughout its history'; and that 'a unique combination of economic power, intellectual and practical genius and moral rigor enables America to check the enemies of peace and progress – and build a better world – without erecting an empire in the process' (Williams, 1972: 20). The myth of reluctance was neatly lodged at the heart of hegemonic stability theory (HST) when Kindleberger argued in 1973 that the Great Depression occurred because the United Kingdom was no longer able, and the United States not yet willing, to exercise world 'leadership' between the world wars. He implied that the postwar 'golden age' was the result of the United States finally giving leadership, belatedly, reluctantly and of course altruistically (Kindleberger, 1973).

In reality, as this chapter shows, the United States was expansionist from its beginnings. After its continental expansion came up against rival empires, emerging nation-states and the Pacific, it ventured abroad. However, with most of the world spoken for, whether by empires or nation-states, its colonial gains remained meagre and the United States settled for asserting informal dominance over the Western hemisphere's independent nation-states under the Monroe Doctrine it had proclaimed decades before. Later the Open Door policy extended that doctrine to the world.

By the early twentieth century, as US capitalism became more concentrated and centralized, its powerful corporate capitalist class set a more concrete goal: that of replacing the United Kingdom as the 'managing segment of the world economy' (Parrini, 1969: 13). Since matching the United Kingdom's vast colonial empire was out of the question, the United States focused on replacing London with New York as the world's financial centre, and sterling with the dollar as the world's currency. This aspiration, not any 'isolationist' aversion to involvement in European affairs, now governed US international engagement. During the First World War, the US economy grew by supplying allied powers while other capitalist centres were destroyed and became indebted to the United States. The United States's relative weight in the world economy grew, the dollar overtook sterling as the de facto leading world currency and New York became the world's financial centre, although unlike London before 1914, the funds that flowed through New York were not private but centred on intergovernmental war debts which were ultimately owed to the US government (Hudson, 1972). After the Second World War widened disparities between the United States and its capitalist rivals even more, contrary to HST, the United States used its position not to exercise stable and benevolent 'hegemony', but to ensure that plans for genuinely benign and multilateral forms of international economic and financial governance put forward by John Maynard Keynes and the United States's own Harry Dexter White at Bretton Woods were defeated. Instead, aiming to maximize the dividend from its postwar economic dominance, the United States insisted on making the gold-backed dollar the world's currency and keeping multilateral institutions weak. As the next chapter shows, these arrangements were neither stable nor benign.

This chapter's outline of the US imperial career to 1945 relies on the critical historiography that has brilliantly and passionately exposed the harms of US imperialism – the violence and brutality, the deprivation and poverty, and the racism and disparagement, first on the North American continent and then beyond. However, against that noble tradition's insistence on the similarities between United States's largely informal imperialism and nineteenth-century formal colonialism – 'If it was not old style colonialism, it was not less effective' (Lens, 2003: 4) – I emphasize the differences. The purpose is to throw the limits of US power – indicated by ambiguous terms like 'neo-colonialism', 'empire like no other', 'anti-imperial imperialism' and 'soft power' – into relief.

IMPERIAL REPUBLIC

It is a paradoxical truth that the world's first modern republic, born amid empires, thought of itself 'as an empire at the outset of [its] national existence' (Williams, 1972: 21). The American Revolution was as much a refusal to pay for Britain's imperial wars as a push for westward expansion to create 'an independent empire' (Stedman-Jones, 1970: 66, 64). More than a century before Fredrick Jackson Turner's famous frontier thesis claimed that expansion over 'free land' had defined US history (Turner, 1893/1958) and half a century before the term 'manifest destiny' was coined to assert the same, a prominent Massachusetts statesman proclaimed expansion to be 'the very principle of our institutions' (Edward Everett, quoted in Williams, 1972: 23).

The classical antithesis between republic and empire was rejected by the new republic's leaders. Expansion created 'the largest single domestic market in the world' (Stedman-Jones, 1970: 65) and was politically necessary to prevent 'factions – themselves primarily the result of economic conflicts – from disrupting the fabric of society' (Madison, quoted in Williams, 1972: 22). Official discourse and dominant public opinion in the expanding republic confounded self-preservation and aggression and benevolence and acquisitiveness from the start: the 'great law of self-preservation' for the United States meant expansion. Americans represented 'a higher societal order, carrying progress wherever they went' (Lens, 2003: 2).

US expansion eventually ran into the obstacles that defined its borders. Its northern boundary with British North America was fixed by the war of 1812. A weaker French colonialism to the south-east was dispatched with the Louisiana Purchase. The open frontier westward was secured from the Spanish empire by exploiting the nationalist revolts farther south, concluding the Transcontinental Treaty in 1819 for the purchase of Florida, and setting the boundary with New Spain. For good measure, the Monroe Doctrine that the Western hemisphere was the United States's special sphere of influence was proclaimed in 1823 to claim territory the United States did not yet control. And later the United States fought a new nation-state, Mexico, wresting from it Texas and California in part by encouraging settlers and claiming to protect them.

US territorial expansionism went hand in hand with combined development. Rejecting the colonial division of labour, the republic's first Treasury secretary, Alexander Hamilton, inaugurated the long and 'highly successful' history of US industrial policy. It included protective tariffs, import restrictions and prohibitions, subsidies and tax exemptions for infant industries, bans on innovative machinery exports, and infrastructure investments (Bingham, 1998: 41, 22). Hamilton believed there was 'no purpose to which public money can be more beneficially applied, than to the acquisition of a new and useful branch of industry; no consideration more valuable than a permanent addition to the general stock of productive labor' (quoted in Bingham, 1998: 22). State and local governments joined in the effort, directing their economies and investing in private enterprises: 'They plotted to stimulate economic growth in town meetings and state legislatures, and never questioned whether it was proper for the government to involve itself in economic matters' (Dobbin, 1994: 28).

In the early nineteenth century, however, the latent conflict between north and south put the brakes on growth. The American Revolution had not been 'a triumph of capitalism over a landed aristocracy' as Charles and Mary Beard had argued, but 'a compromise or coalition between men of wealth in the cities and men of wealth on the land' (Lynd, 1970: 53). With southern slave-owning landlords favouring free trade and emerging northern industrial capitalists favouring protection, the Civil War settled that issue as well as the issues of slavery and whether northern-style independent farmers or southern-style slave-owners would expand over new territories (Stedman-Jones, 1970: 65).

THWARTED NEW IMPERIALISM

The northern victory in the Civil War made expansion even more urgent. The emerging industrial economy had already undergone a series of depressions characterized by gluts of commodities and capital. An 'industrialist thesis' – at once underconsumptionist and imperialist – emerged to argue that, with technological advancement, US industry produced more than could be consumed and accumulated more capital than could profitably be invested. Similar surpluses plagued US agriculture. Therefore,

[o]utlets for these increasing 'surpluses' of goods and capital must and can be found abroad, through the channels of commerce; otherwise the development of American industry and agriculture,

with corresponding opportunities for gains and profits, will be slowed down, and brought, perhaps, to an impasse or deadlock which cannot be broken. It is, therefore, a question of commercial expansion or stagnation and decay; world power or economic decline.

(Beard, 1935: 37–8)

This industrialist thesis would also justify the United States's new imperialism after continental expansion reached the Pacific and the frontier closed. As expansion went offshore, the United States partook of the 'partition of the world's total commerce and the distribution of its undeveloped opportunities'. It claimed for 'citizens of the United States ... "their share"', and its extent was 'limited only by the power of American private enterprise and the support which it received from the Government of the United States' (Beard, 1935: 40). The government stopped at little in making and supporting these claims: 'diplomatic representation and pressures, discriminating legislation at home, the resources of official soliciting agents, a subsidized merchant marine, marines and soldiers upon occasion, the coercive force of the Navy, measures short of war, and, ultimately, war' (1935: 43). And while export markets were urgently sought, 'the import of goods – manufactured and agricultural – [was] to be restrained, managed and controlled by elaborate tariff legislation and administrative practices, with sharp discrimination between imports of raw materials and imports of manufactures' (1935: 44). The industrialist thesis, Beard argued, was no mere rational policy: it was 'a statement of alleged fact' – that the United States produced more than it could consume, 'an allegation of possibility' – that the rest of the world could absorb these surpluses, 'a prophecy' – that it would, 'a theological assertion' – that US agencies were veritable forces of God, and an 'interpretation of history' – that this pursuit of economic opportunity around the world was the United States's destiny (1935: 46–7).

Turner's 'frontier thesis' of 1893 would recast this industrialist thesis for a new phase. As three centuries of settler expansion ended,

the demands for a vigorous foreign policy, for an interoceanic canal, for a revival of our power upon the seas, and for the extension of American influence to outlying islands and adjoining countries, [constituted] indications that the movement [of expansion] will continue.

(Turner, 1893: 219)

While the domestic resistance to overseas expansion organized by the Anti-Imperialist League was defeated, and although the depression of the 1890s made expansion more urgent, its prospects were dim. It would have required 'a global challenge to European colonialism and a direct confrontation with anti-colonial movements', a historical reality that disappointed the 'many vocal advocates for colonialism' (Smith, 2003: xvii–xviii). Powerful rival powers already occupied much of Asia and Africa, and Latin American nations could not easily be overrun. British military power also remained superior. Moreover,

> the destructiveness of warfare was escalating in a frightening fashion. In the 1904 fighting between Japan and Russia, battle lines were sometimes forty miles long; single engagements lasted as long as ten days or more; field guns shot four miles distant, and more ammunition was often expended in one day than in the whole Spanish-American War combined.
>
> (Lens, 2003: 196)

While Cuba could be turned into a dependency by giving its people hope for independence from Spain, ruling the much larger Philippines in the teeth of nationalist resistance proved more difficult. As national consciousness rose around the world, so did the cost of colonial control.

The empire's workshop

Informal control was another matter. When first proclaimed, the Monroe Doctrine had an anticipatory quality because the United States did not yet have the power to enforce it. 'It could only attempt to prevent (and that with British help) other imperial powers from subjugating the continent's new nations, formally or informally' (Lens, 2003: 95). By the early twentieth century, however, US naval power grew to rank second only to the United Kingdom's. Now Latin America became the US 'empire's workshop' (Grandin, 2006), where the United States's distinctive 'empire like no other' was forged by 'investing capital, establishing control over crucial raw materials and transit routes, gaining military expertise, and rehearsing many of the ideas that to this day justify American power in the world' (2006: 23). This was the form of US 'empire' that was 'better suited for a world in which rising nationalism was making formal colonialism of the kind European nations practiced unworkable' (2006: 23). It involved economic penetration of weaker countries, backed as necessary by military force. For example, the United States claimed the right to interfere in the affairs of Central and South American states on the grounds that 'the government of a foreign state whose subjects have lent money to another state may interfere to protect the right of bond-holders, if they are endangered by the borrowing state' (Fredrick Jackson Turner, quoted in Stedman-Jones, 1970: 73–4). It is a measure of the opposition to US economic penetration that by the 1920s the United States was involved in 'something akin to perpetual war' in Latin America (Grandin, 2006: 27).

From Monroe to Open Door

The Open Door policy, formally proclaimed in 1899 in relation to China, aimed to persuade rival empires to open their colonies to US commerce, so 'equality with all competing nations in conditions of access to the markets' was realized (quoted in Grandin, 206: 25). Since neither its economic nor military power was as limitless as its expansionist ambition, the United States operated through alliances. Most important, in light of developments to come, was that with the United Kingdom. By this time the two countries had settled disputes pending from the American Revolution and others involving Canada. Cultural and personal interaction increased, and the United Kingdom accepted US protectionism in return for US adherence to the gold standard. US exports to the United Kingdom and UK investment in the United States increased. The United Kingdom also accepted the Monroe Doctrine and agreed to cooperate in 'maintaining the Open Door in Asia' (LaFeber, 1973: 313–17). The United States also allied with Japan against European imperial powers in the 1890s. Though Japan had previously attempted to secure exclusive access to Chinese markets, US officials calculated that it was not strong enough to pose a competitive threat (1973: 312).

The Open Door set the mould for US imperial policy. As William Appleman Williams argued in his classic work, its inevitable failures would punctually lead the United States to military actions and wars (Williams, 1972: 57). The United States assumed that its sheer economic size gave it a 'virtuous omnipotence' (1972: 210): although US exports amounted to only 4–5 per cent of GNP before 1914, by 1910 it was already the world's third largest trader. This was, however, dangerous. Powerful countries like Japan and Germany could react to US overtures with war, and relatively poor countries like China and Cuba could withdraw from the US ambit, provoking US military action. So wars, officially considered failures of policy, were more or less inevitable, as were 'foreign policy crises that would become increasingly severe' (1972: 56–7). This Williams called 'the tragedy of American diplomacy'.

IMPERIAL MIMESIS

The thirty years' crisis of 1914–45 was as momentous in the making of the United States's global ascendancy in the twentieth century as it is ill understood. Two misunderstandings must be dispatched forthwith.

The first is that the United States's overwhelming economic and financial dominance after 1945 – it produced some 50 per cent of world product and owned 70 per cent of its gold reserves – was the inevitable apogee of the productive dynamic of its vast and continent-sized economy. Eric Hobsbawm's view is representative:

By 1913 the USA had already become the largest economy in the world, producing over one third of its industrial output – just under the combined total for Germany, Great Britain and France. In 1929 it produced over 42 per cent of the total world output, as against just under 28 per cent for the three European industrial powers. This is a truly astonishing figure. Concretely, while US steel production rose by about one quarter between 1913 and 1920, steel production in the rest of the world fell by about one third. In short, after the end of the First World War the USA was in many ways as internationally dominant an economy as it once again became after the Second World War. It was the Great Slump which temporarily halted this ascendancy.

(Hobsbawm, 1994: 97)

Hobsbawm pauses over the Great Depression's interruption of US ascent, but notes only in passing how the First World War's destruction diminished other major economies and boosted that of the United States. He does not even mention the even greater differential impact of the Second World War.

The second misunderstanding centres on HST originator Charles Kindleberger's claim that the Great Depression was caused by 'the inability of the British to continue their role of underwriter to the [world economic] system and the reluctance of the United States to take it on' (1986: 11). The problem was not merely that this widely accepted claim modernized the myth of the reluctant superpower. It also underwrote a misinterpretation of US actions in the first half of the twentieth century that was as radical as it was ideologically necessary to obscure the United States's true motivation: to attempt to emulate, however vainly, the United Kingdom's world dominance. Indeed, as the next two chapters make clear, HST was itself a late issue of these ambitions.

Corporate capitalism and the Federal Reserve

A social Darwinist capitalism of robber barons emerged from Civil War profiteering and rapid economic growth thereafter. During it '[t]he Jacksonian notion that government should not interfere on the side of the rich ... [was reformulated]... into the theorem that government had no business interfering on behalf of the downtrodden' (Phillips, 2002: 42–3). This capitalism gave way, in turn, to the United States's second industrial revolution of heavy industry by the end of the century. Its vastly greater capital needs produced the US version of 'finance capital', 'Morganization'. Big finance, more often than not the house of J. P. Morgan, sponsored cartels and mergers to produce industrial behemoths. They formed the basis of the new corporate capitalist class, which reshaped the political economy of US capitalism at the turn of the century.

The politics of the age of reform that stretched from the first failed presidential bid of William Jennings Bryan in 1896 to FDR's New Deal in the 1930s was determined from above by the requirements of this new corporate capitalism, and from below by populist mobilization amid rising inequality, urbanization and industrial concentration. The so-called 'trust question' – how to control giant corporations in the interests of a wider social good – took centre stage. The progressives, the political representatives of the corporate class, managed to ensure that reforms promoted 'the growth of great industrial organizations by deflecting the attack on them into purely moral and ceremonial channels' (Arnold, 1937: 212), and that 'men like Bryan and La Follette, who did not enjoy the confidence of at least large segments of the business community' never came close to the White House (Hofstadter, 1955: 250). Chief among the legislative and institutional legacies that sustained the next phase of US capitalism's development was, as James Livingston (1986) has argued, the Federal Reserve, created in 1913 as the culmination of the movement for banking and monetary reform.

Central or reserve banks in the early twentieth century maintained parity between national token money and gold under the gold standard, and acted as lender of last resort to the country's banks. They had become central to the 'organisation of capital' (Bagehot, 1873/1978) with the industrial revolution. The Bank of England, for example, though originally established in 1694 to finance wars by borrowing from capitalists rather than taxing them, responded to the growing commerce flowing through London by agreeing to 'rediscount' bills already discounted by a small circle of banks in the early nineteenth century, effectively becoming their lender of last resort. It assumed responsibility for converting sterling into gold and thus maintaining its parity when the United Kingdom went back on the gold standard after the Napoleonic wars. Most industrial nations had established central banks to act as lenders of last resort in response to fiscal problems (Shull, 2005: 60), and these took on the second function as countries joined the gold standard.

The United States was an exception, its first two attempts at setting up a central bank having failed. In the first decade of the twentieth century several developments came together to prompt the founding of the Federal Reserve. The United States's dispersed structure of private banks regulated by state governments and typically confined within state boundaries proved inadequate in the 1907 crisis, when J. P. Morgan saved them, but only just (Ahamed, 2009: 52–6). The populist 'free silver' movement posed a threat to the capitalist organization of money and finance, and to US interests abroad. Above all, however, with the increasing international weight of the US economy, US banks, exporters and importers chafed at the international non-acceptance of the US dollar for lack of a central bank (Broz, 1997: 132ff). The *sine qua non* of international acceptance, a central bank, also had other advantages: the 'seignorage' of automatic access to international credit, higher returns for its banks and lower transaction costs for US concerns doing business abroad (1997: 75). These imperatives and incentives were, moreover, inextricably tied with the corporate elite's reformulation of US imperial ambition into a desire to 'build an international commercial system which would allow American business to topple and replace British business interest as the managing component of the world economy' and to 'create new institutional means of performing the politically stabilizing task which Great Britain alone had performed before 1914' (Parrini, 1969: 1).

A central bank could not be created by small-scale social-Darwinist capitalists. It required 'corporate leaders who recognized the difference, or the conflict, between short-term profit-making and long-term political-economic stability and who would act accordingly when necessary' (Livingston, 1986: 228). For the central bank,

even if owned and controlled by private shareholders [as the Fed
remains to this day] .... would, at times, have to restrict credit
when doing so meant forgoing additional profit. At other times,
it would have to extend credit when doing so meant taking on
unwanted risk and/or reducing its profits.

(Shull, 2005: 60)

In return for serving US capitalists' common interest in this way,
the Federal Reserve would get a steady if moderate return on its
capital (Shull, 2005: 60). The new corporate elite understood
that 'the changed circumstances of socio-economic life would give
the state new responsibilities' (Livingston, 1986: 228–9). It also
managed to overcome conflicts between different capitalist interests
such as those between large manufacturing corporations favouring
protection and large banks favouring more trade whose profits
could be repatriated as imports. New legislation such as the Clayton
Antitrust Act of 1916, which freed foreign commerce from anti-trust
legislation, and the Webb–Pomerene Act of 1918, which allowed
US businesses to divide up foreign markets, began a new 'era of
cooperation' in US business (Parrini, 1969: 8). As this new frontier
opened, the newly created Federal Reserve freed 'part of the nation's
domestic bank reserves for the development of foreign trade on a
continuing basis', including by allowing US banks 'to grant credit
for foreign trade where hitherto it had been financed by Sterling bills
on which London earned fees, and to establish branches overseas'
(1969: 22–3). US corporate capital was now ready to engage with
the world on its terms. No sooner was the Fed created than a world
war brought the most promising opportunities for such engagement.

DOMINANCE THROUGH DESTRUCTION

It should be clear by now that the United States was far from
isolationist when the First World War started. Wilson kept the
United States out of the war initially to wait for a stalemate so that it
could step in as arbiter and architect of a US-centred postwar order.
In the meantime, moreover, the war was bringing the United States
out of a depression it had entered in 1913. Its future First World
War allies already purchased 77 per cent of US exports in 1913,
and now generated 'the greatest industrial boom the nation had had
until that time' (Lens, 2003: 253). Large conglomerates benefited
disproportionately, expanding munitions and other exports and
financing them. War also constituted a financial turning point.

From being a chronic debtor whose capitalist development had hitherto relied on absorbing a considerable part of the famed British capital exports, the United States turned into a creditor nation. Between 1914 and 1917, when the United States finally joined the war after the outbreak of the Russian Revolution, US banks, led by Morgan, raised $2.5 billion in secured and unsecured loans to allied governments, which also bought or requisitioned $4 billion of their citizens' assets in the United States for collateral as well as just plain cash (Hudson, 1972: 40). 'And since the British had suspended gold payments and embargoed loans "for undertakings outside the Empire", Wall Street was now the banking center of the world' (Lens, 2003: 252). For good measure, American business also benefited from the withdrawal of British and generally European businesses from Latin America.

The United States finally entered the war neither because of German bombing of commercial ships nor out of any 'idealist' desire to 'make the world safe for democracy', but because the allies could no longer keep up their purchases from US firms. Guaranteeing their borrowing was now beyond even the great J. P. Morgan's means. The US ambassador in London, reporting on the international situation, found it 'most alarming to the financial and industrial outlook of the United States'. British and French inability to keep up orders would surely mean 'a panic in the United States', and he concluded that it was not 'improbable that the only way of maintaining our present preeminent trade position and averting a panic is by declaring war on Germany' (quoted in Lens, 2003: 260). Only by entering the war could the US government guarantee the $3.5 billion the allies owed to US bankers and businesses, and authorize a further $3 billion in loans for continued allied purchases from the United States. So with war and what amounted to a government export credit to the belligerents, US manufacturing went from 35.8 per cent of the world total in 1913, compared with Germany's 14.3 per cent and the United Kingdom's 14.1 per cent, to 42.2 per cent in 1926–29, while the war reduced Germany's and the United Kingdom's shares to 11.6 per cent and 9.4 per cent respectively (League of Nations, 1945: 13).

The massive increase of federal debt could be financed through the Federal Reserve. Its regional Federal Reserve banks became 'intermediaries between the government and the banking community' (Shull, 2005: 64), which not only retailed government securities to their customers but bought them on their own account, so that '[g]overnment paper soon became the principal collateral for

borrowing at the discount window' (Shull, 2005: 64). To encourage
uptake, not only did the regional reserve banks adjust their discount
rates to the below-market rates of Treasury securities,

> [p]referential discount rates were established for borrowing from
> the Reserve Banks to purchase government securities; the securi-
> ties served as collateral for the borrowing. The commercial banks
> borrowing to buy securities earned the interest on the securities
> at the cost of the preferential discount rate.
>
> (Shull, 2005, 64)

All this was justified, of course, in terms of 'the great national
emergency ... [that] made it necessary to suspend the application of
well-recognized principles of economics and finance which usually
govern banking operations in times of peace' (Shull, 2005: 65).

THE UNITED STATES IS WILLING

The admirable but unrealistic Wilsonian idealism to which failure
of the League of Nations after the First World War is usually
traced was, as we have already seen in Chapter 2, mythical: 'it
was not a struggle between an Old Order and a New Order, but
merely a quarrel as to how the Old Order should settle its affairs'
(Hofstadter, 1959: 272). In Wilson's 'moral imperialism', the United
States was destined to be the 'justest, the most progressive, the
most honourable, the most enlightened nation in the world' (quoted
in Williams, 1972: 69) through expansion which, like his friend
Turner, Wilson thought 'a natural and wholesome impulse' (1972:
71). Wilson and his detractors at home differed only over the most
effective way to realize 'the right [of US businesses] to use their
capital and managerial talents everywhere on a basis equal to that
enjoyed by the businessmen of other nations' (Parrini, 1969: 1).

It was essential that the League Covenant provide for states to
act collectively against an aggressor state but contain no 'meaningful
demand for a substantial change in [the] international economic
relations' (Hofstadter, 1959: 269–70) that had bred industrial and
imperial rivalry and war. At Versailles, Wilson, like other capitalist
leaders, focused on politics (Hofstadter, 1959: 270), and it was left
to Keynes (1919/2004) to bring its repressed economics to light.
Europe had been devastated and needed a new approach, including
cancellation of inter-allied debts, loans for reconstruction, and
links with communist Russia. Although Wilson and his successors

rejected this as an option in pursuit of the US aim to emulate British dominance, the objective realities that Keynes recognized ensured that US actions either failed or succeeded only in perverse ways.

Having failed to create a disarmed world subject to its own overwhelming economic power under the League of Nations, the United States pursued other tactics. However, despite the weakness of, and divisions among, European countries and their need for US capital, three underlying developments were unpropitious for the achievement of US aims. These were war and its aftermath; the collapse of London-centred institutional arrangements – including the so-called gold standard and free trade; and the increased legitimacy needs of capitalist states in the face of mass mobilization for war and class conflict at its end. All three pointed 'toward state capitalism and a policy of discrimination in commercial relationships that would allocate world markets politically' (Parrini, 1969: 37). In these circumstances, the United States could use its creditor status to ensure the defeat of the 1916 Paris programme, which 'would have created an exclusive European economic community based on joint development of neutral markets by Allied governments, and an alliance of European state capitalisms against Germany (and, implicitly, against the United States)' (1969: 37). But it could create 'an economic community of interest which [it] would manage, with the Western Europeans and Japan acting as associates with full rights in the system' (1969: 259) only in a rather perverse sense. Whereas 'Britain had reached its economic and financial peak in a period of [more] unified world markets held together by a common gold standard and without the need to face major industrial competition', the United States 'faced a disintegrated world market without a common monetary standard, and major industrial competition' (1969: 101–2).

It could not have been otherwise. The first industrial capitalist country was bound to become the 'managing segment' of the world economy, which was, after all, a creature of its own capitalist expansion. Equally inevitably, contenders eventually industrialized by fracturing that unity, and challenged that industrial, and eventually imperial, supremacy. The peculiar class structure in which financial capital dominated industrial capital in the home of the industrial revolution, and the vast British Empire, extended the United Kingdom's tenure as the world economy's 'managing segment' beyond its industrial supremacy. But that too ended in 1914 after the further unfolding of uneven and combined development (UCD), in particular contender development, including the United States's own, transformed the world order into a plurality of industrial states whose competition resulted in war. These states played even greater economic roles domestically (where their forms of governance would soon include communism) and internationally (including war).

The governmentalization of finance

In this context it is interesting to look at how the United States became the world's creditor, and New York and the dollar came to displace London and sterling. Two interrelated points are relevant. First, until 1914, London was the world's private financial centre, whereas:

> [t]he emergence of the United States as the overwhelming world creditor was at its origin a governmental function. It was not the product of private investment abroad of surpluses earned through foreign trade, nor the result of self-expansion of private overseas investment through reemployment in foreign ventures of earnings and internally generated cash flow. Although such reinvestment of private funds did occur, it was small in comparison with the advances made by the U.S. Government during the war to its allies and after the war for relief and reconstruction.
>
> (Hudson, 1972: 53)

Moreover, as intergovernmental claims mounted as a result of the war, private international financial claims were also wound down by it. Ironically, 'the disenfranchisement of private capital was in large part the result of a war whose motivations stemmed largely from competition of international finance capital' (1972: 63).

Second, the structure of international financial obligations after the war – the 'network of heavy tribute payable from one ally to another' (Keynes, 1919: 281) incurred over an essentially destructive rather than productive enterprise – was historically unprecedented. These obligations, and in particular the allegedly vengeful British and French insistence on German reparations, are widely agreed to have contributed to the rise of Nazism. However, few recognize that the British and French insistence on reparations was, in its turn, rooted in US insistence on repayment of the war debts these countries owed. 'In the history of warfare no ally has requested ... payment for its military support.' Instead, '[t]he provision of arms to allies, by universal custom, had been written off as a war cost' (Hudson, 1972: 50). The United States had originally given the allies to understand this would be so, including through emotional appeals to America's historic links to countries like France. However, after the war ended, the US government claimed it had joined the war not as an ally but as an associate uninterested in territorial gain (1972: 43–4), and insisted on repayment. It facetiously complained that the allies seemed to want to 'make Germany indemnify them for having started the war and to make us indemnify them for not having entered the war sooner' (Norman Davies, assistant Treasury secretary, quoted in Parrini, 1969: 52), and cited public opinion in favour of repayment (Hoff, 1971: 151–3). This insistence explained how '[t]he world financial order grew to rest upon the dominant part in world finance ... played by the government of the United States' (Hudson, 1972: 54). It was also historically important in another way:

> It would be false to say that the United States provoked World War II .... It is true, however, that no act, by whatever nation, contributed more to the genesis of World War II than the intolerable and insupportable burdens which the United States deliberately imposed upon its allies of World War I and, through them, upon Germany.
>
> (Hudson, 1972: 112)

Some US corporate leaders did call for cancellation of these debts, but only partially and because they could see the damage these obligations could do to their own interests abroad. Keynes foresaw most clearly the politico-economic and geopolitico-economic difficulties the US insistence on repayment would create, and pleaded, diplomatically, for a 'general bonfire' of the 'vast paper entanglements' (1919: 283). But the United States refused to permit any such blaze of relief.

After the war, as the US government's Liberty Loan guarantees to wartime export credits ceased, a new pattern of peacetime governmental financial flows emerged. Though US industrial corporations were eager to invest abroad, and Europeans to import capital goods, US banks remained leery of financing this trade. They considered governments a safer bet. And since US middle classes could not be persuaded to buy foreign government obligations, capital mainly flowed out of the United States through banks supplying short-term credit at high interest rates to foreign governments (Parrini, 1969: 75–6). This was despite US corporations' attempts to induce banks to extend long-term credits for capital exports under the 1919 Edge Act, which permitted US banks to establish foreign subsidiaries and engage in banking activities abroad, and to separate their foreign from their domestic risks. In a further twist, the overhang of government debt made such investment unsafe in the eyes of big bankers like Morgan (1969: 99).

The project to make New York the world's financial centre proceeded, as it turned out, in cooperation with the United Kingdom, which wished to channel US finance to Europe through London (1969: 100). US financial capital was divided. Industrially focused banks like the National City Bank favoured displacing London entirely with a system of branch banks specifically to support US trade. Banks like the House of Morgan, already considerably invested in the purely financial activities of the London-centred world financial order, favoured cooperation (1969: 60–3) aimed at 'Americanizing' the British banking system, making it 'an American instrument which has all the elements contained in the systems of other nations' (Jason Neilson of the Mercantile Bank of the Americas, quoted in Parrini, 1969: 63). The victory of the latter was fateful: it ensured that US 'finance capital', which originally resembled Hilferding's continental pattern in which finance pursued productive expansion, would come to resemble more and more the British – City of London – pattern in which financial dominance sidelined or squeezed productive capital. It was in this form, and one, moreover, unconstrained by such discipline as the gold standard imposed on London in its heyday, that it would reach its full flowering in the financial bubbles of the 1990s and particularly the 2000s.

This transition was aided by British financial capital hoping to salvage what it could of its world financial role. This entailed the disastrous operation to put sterling back on the gold standard at its pre-war parity in 1925 by pursuing deflationary policies. The operation was encouraged by the US government. The United States kept interest rates low so as to help push British prices lower, and promised a secret loan for stabilization when the old parity was in sight. US bankers, including the chairman of the Federal Reserve, Benjamin Strong, believed that the stabilization of the pound was in the US interest (Block, 1977: 16), not least because it was

> an opportunity for New York to gain in stature as an international financial center since, under the cooperative arrangements to facilitate the return, New York would for a time maintain its interest rates below London's and so become the more attractive center in which foreigners could borrow.
>
> (Clarke, 1967: 72)

Keynes's critique of the consequences of this decision for British industry and the working class was devastating, all the more for showing that it was unnecessary, and correctly predicting the 1926 General Strike as working classes resisted the resulting downward pressure on wages (Keynes, 1963: 24–70). Although the experiment would be declared a failure in 1931, while it lasted it proved its worth to the United States. While in the early 1920s New York's emerging centrality 'was still somewhat obscured ... because of continued British leadership in the extension of world-wide acceptance credits', when the 1924 Dawes Plan rescheduling German reparations payments in response to the 1923 default was implemented, 'American bankers floated over half the loan. The British took what was left' (Parrini, 1969: 137; Clarke, 1967: 57). When this policy inevitably failed, it was followed by the Young Plan of 1929. Sponsored by the US government, such initiatives provided Wall Street with its main opportunities for international investment in loans to governments.

By the mid-1920s the apex of the US financial system consisted of three parts: banks close to US industry with branches in Latin America and Asia, the House of Morgan's branches in Latin America, and links with the UK and French banks and self-financing US corporations exporting and investing abroad (Parrini, 1969: 122). From then on, US productive investment abroad – whether financed by US banks or by corporations themselves – advanced alongside the United States's complex state–private expansionism (Williams, 1972: 131–2). Though occasionally softened, as in the famous 'good neighbour' policy response to increasing resistance to US expansion in Latin America, and accompanied with rhetoric about US expansion bringing prosperity and reform, the basic pattern of expansion remained the same as it had been before 1914.

In every instance, the key move was the assertion of the policy of the open door. And in each case, the objectives were markets for American industrial exports, raw materials for American factories, and the right to enter directly into the economic life of a country by establishing factories and other enterprises. That economic expansion made it possible to exercise a growing influence on local political and economic decisions, served to provide a base for further penetration, and ultimately took on military significance.

(Williams, 1972: 158)

The Great Depression

The Great Depression was deepest in the United States, and the inter-governmental flow of funds kept going by New York made its own contribution to that depth. Given their sheer volume, debt repayments came to rely on capital flows, rather than trade flows, and a triangular flow of funds developed from the United States to Germany, thence to the European allies and back to the United States (Hudson, 1972: 66). These flows were unsustainable: 'the assets required to underwrite the debt simply did not exist' (1972: 66). Worse, thanks to 'the shortcomings of New York as an international capital market', speculative and irresponsible foreign lending 'became a fad'. 'American underwriting houses pressed foreign governments to borrow more because new bond offerings meant large new commissions', and the US government did little to regulate them (Block, 1977: 20–1). At the same time, the United States sterilized gold inflows – the result of debt repayment as well as flights to safety from Europe – to prevent domestic inflation. This not only kept the gold flowing into the United States but also imposed heavy adjustment burdens on other countries (1977: 21–2) and further exacerbated the insecurity of their loans. It was not a question of whether, only how and when, the flow of funds would break down.

Underlying tensions were exacerbated by differences in growth patterns. Economic policies in Europe remained in the pre-1914 deflationary mode. Meanwhile the United States experienced economic expansion through easy and cheap credit. Low interest rates were partly aimed at helping the United Kingdom stay on the gold standard after 1925 despite its trade deficits, but they also played a critical role in the growth pattern of the 'roaring twenties'. There was 'prodigious and incredible' growth in the United States (Keynes, 1931/1973: 345) as its Fordist productivity revolution transformed cities with motor cars, electricity, movies and telecommunications. In the absence of corresponding wage increases and the transfer payments that would become so important as the economy's 'automatic stabilisers' from the latter twentieth century, demand for goods produced at Fordist productivity levels was sustained by easy consumer credit. The resulting growth did, however, justify much of the rise in the stock market. Eventually, however, its fate became intertwined with that of the international debt bubble.

Low US interest rates kept up US borrowing, as did the repayments that came in, which swelled available credit. However, by 1928–29 funds began to be redirected to the rising stock market, and lending to European governments peaked (Hudson, 1972: 68). As the Fed attempted to contain the bubble in the stock market by raising interest rates, it triggered the stock market crash. It did not cause the Great Depression – the slowdown in investment had already begun in early 1929 (Keynes, 1931: 350). Consumer credit could only go so far in expanding the market. At the same time, the cessation of lending to Europe, which had financed exports, made things worse (Hudson, 1972: 68), making the United States 'a major victim of its own intransigence with regard to the Inter-Ally debt problem' (Hudson, 1972: 69). In the ensuing Great Depression, capital simply stopped flowing abroad altogether (1972: 66–7).

As the United States went into the Great Depression from its Roaring Twenties, it naturally suffered the steepest decline in production among major capitalist countries. This was bad enough for the project of the United States taking over the United Kingdom's world role. Moreover, amid the financial and economic dislocations of the 1930s – the collapse of trade, the tightening of credit, the cessation of international capital flows and exchange rate chaos – all economies withdrew even more into their national shells, seeking security against international trade and financial disruptions through a variety of measures including quantitative restrictions on trade, bilateral clearing arrangements and financial restrictions.

The Roosevelt administration adopted heterodox economic policies – including suspending the domestic gold standard in 1933 followed by devaluing the dollar in terms of gold internationally in 1934, and a programme of government spending – thanks more to Roosevelt's willingness to experiment, particularly after being 'baited into a leftward turn by die-hard conservatives' and the upper classes from which he hailed, than to any Keynesian conviction (Hofstadter, 1959: 327–30). Indeed, contrary to popular impression, the New Deal did not see the creation of a larger domestic market as an alternative to war-induced external expansion. 'Our economic frontiers are no longer coextensive with our territorial frontiers' said William Culbertson (an economic advisor and policy maker to several administrations in the inter-war period), while Cordell Hull stated, more prosaically, in 1938 that 'Only healthy [i.e. US-dominated] international trade will make possible a full and stable domestic economy' (quoted in Williams, 1972: 194). Resistance to US expansion continued to be construed in the United States as dangerous economic nationalism. It seemed to be erupting not only in Latin America but also among rival capitalist powers.

Roosevelt's New Deal recovery remained reliant on government spending. So when the Fed tightened credit in 1937 to slow down what it saw as an overheated economy, and Roosevelt cut his government's spending to curb fiscal deficits, the economy turned down again (Hofstadter, 1959: 335, citing Alvin Hansen). It would not recover until the Second World War spurred an even more spectacular recovery from depression than the First World War had.

European powers remained mired in gold-standard orthodoxy, though their attempt to reinstate the standard through international cooperation at the 1933 London Economic Summit was thankfully scuppered by Roosevelt, because it involved writing off European debts, and interfered with his own plans for expansion of the US economy. The Tripartite Monetary Agreement of 1936 was regarded by Kindleberger in his case for HST as a 'milestone' in international cooperation aimed at keeping economies open. However, it was in fact aimed at making national economic management more effective by stabilizing currencies and discouraging competitive devaluations. In any case, there were no further instalments of international economic cooperation as the world hurtled toward war: no 'international monetary order ... could satisfy both the status quo powers – France, Britain and the United States – and the new imperialist powers that were seeking a redistribution of international resources – Germany, Italy and Japan' (Block, 1977: 30).

The Great Depression brought the US share of world manufacturing down to 32.2 per cent in 1936, from 42.2 per cent in 1926–29 (League of Nations, 1945: 13). Worse, from the US point of view, the gainers were not only European countries but also increasingly assertive Latin American countries and some colonies, such as India. The Depression and European protectionism upset existing trade links, and the international division of labour they sustained, and permitted a degree of autonomous import-substituting industrialization in formal and informal colonies (Rothermund, 1996: 93–9).

SECOND WAR, SECOND CHANCE

As economic, political and military competition sharpened in the late 1930s, US political and business leaders rehearsed the succession of moods that preceded entry into the First World War: protesting neutrality and isolationism while tying their interests to war. A 1939 debate in *Fortune* magazine was revealing:

The participants formally and vigorously rejected entry into the war. But almost everything else they said indicated either that they expected American involvement or that they were still trying with considerable success to avoid facing the fact that the things they did want could not be obtained short of war. No war, they agreed, and then voted 'unanimously' to oppose giving way to Japan's New Order in Asia. No war, they reiterated, and then flatly refused even to discuss the possibility of a more self-contained economy. Overseas economic expansion was mandatory. No war, they repeated, and then agreed that the Philippines had to be defended in order to protect 'the rich resources' of Southeast Asia.

(Williams, 1972: 198)

Moreover, they insisted also that the United States could not continue to function if Europe and Asia were to abolish 'free enterprise'. So the postwar order had to ensure it in 'every country' (1972: 198). From the earliest days of the republic, expansion had remained at the heart of the US vision: while 'enlarged consumer sales at home' were necessary, according to the editors of *Fortune*, so was 'a tremendous expansion of 'foreign trade and foreign investment'. To ensure both, it was important that 'more and more corporation leaders enter the Roosevelt administration and subsequent governments' (1972: 200–1).

Thus Henry Luce's (1941/1999) famous call for an 'American century' simply expressed the consensus among the influential opinion makers, backed by US business. They had kept faith in the prospect of emulating pre-1914 British dominance through inter-war disappointments, and now argued for a 'second chance' (Divine, 1967: 39–40). Until 1941, the United States once again profited from war's economic bonanza while staying out, but in that year Luce laid the ideological groundwork for entry. He exhorted the United States to abandon 'isolationism', enter the war, define its aims and take up its singular challenge. Bringing the early twentieth century corporate leaders' ambition of replacing the United Kingdom as 'the managing segment' of the world economy even closer to what would become HST in the 1970s, Luce recast that ambition as a 'responsibility', and portrayed the US failure to take it up after the First World War as a disaster not to be repeated:

[T]he fundamental trouble with America has been, and is, that whereas their nation became in the 20th Century the most powerful and the most vital nation in the world, nevertheless Americans were unable to accommodate themselves spiritually and practically to that fact. Hence they have failed to play their part as a world power – a failure which has had disastrous consequences for themselves and for all mankind. And the cure is this: to accept wholeheartedly our duty and our opportunity as the most powerful and vital nation in the world and in consequence to exert upon the world the full impact of our influence, for such purposes as we see fit and by such means as we see fit.

(Luce, 1941: 165)

According to Luce, the United Kingdom was not only 'perfectly willing that the United States should assume the role of senior partner', but '[a]mong serious Englishmen, the chief complaint against America … [is] that America has refused to rise to the opportunities of leadership in the world' (1941: 164). The 'golden opportunity' handed America on a 'silver platter' had been squandered in 1919. That must not be repeated. In all this shining bimetallic hypocrisy, Luce got one thing right: his idea of the US world role could be traced to the 'manifold project and magnificent purposes' of the earliest days of American society (1941: 171).

Neil Smith recently noted the 'the abstractness, even vacuity, of [Luce's] geography' – '"Are we going to fight for dear old Danzig or dear old Dong Dong?" Luce mocked. "Are we going to decide the boundaries of Uritainia?"' (Smith, 2003: 18). Smith interpreted this as a vision of informal empire in which foreign geography and places were incidental (2003: 18), in contrast to European formal empires, with their 'attention to local and global geographies'. US informal empire was constructed on 'the more abstract geography of the world market rather than through direct political control of territory'. In it, 'governmental involvement … increasingly focused on establishing broad legal and policy conditions' for its corporations (2003: 19).

Luce's preference for historical over geographical terminology – 'century' rather than 'empire' – did betray something important. However, it was not that in contrast to 'the geographical language of empires [which] suggests a malleable politics', that whereas 'empires rise and fall and are open to challenge', the American century suggested an 'inevitable destiny': 'How does one challenge a century?' (2003: 20). Rather, it betrayed the derogation of the imperial vocation by the time the United States could pursue it, a derogation that, as later chapters reveal, made what the United

States did manage to fashion of its American century progressively more spectral.

Like the First World War, the Second World War also lifted the United States out of depression. However, this time it was the Great Depression, and the boost it gave the US economy was even greater. Nominal US GDP more than doubled, going from $84.7 billion in 1938 to $211.9 billion in 1945, an increase of 250 per cent. Real GDP went from $192.9 billion in 1938 to $355.2 billion in 1945 (ERP, 1970: 177–8). This 184 per cent increase would not be repeated for over 20 years, even though those years included the 'golden age' of capitalist growth. This increase, and the even greater devastation that war wreaked on the rest of the world, laid the basis of that overwhelming economic and financial dominance that the United States took into negotiations over the postwar world order at Bretton Woods. There, contrary to the fairy tales of HST, it did its best to subordinate the paramount question about how to revive the world economy and world trade to its imperial ambition.

BRETTON WOODS: DOMINANCE OVER INTERNATIONALISM

Bretton Woods has become a byword for US 'hegemony', 'altruism' and 'enlightenment' in creating multilateral institutions that stabilized the world economy and enabled the 'golden age' of growth that followed. These institutions are either considered Keynesian or said to rest on the proposals of the Keynesian US representative, Harry Dexter White. In reality, the United States negotiated at Bretton Woods to perpetuate its just-acquired status as the world's overwhelmingly powerful country. Any 'altruism' it evinced rose from its attempts to find export markets especially for capital goods so its war-swollen economy would not shrink to a more reasonable peacetime size. Any 'enlightenment' it displayed, in contrast to its behaviour at Versailles, was due to its realization that when it 'overplayed its position as world creditor' at that conference, it was left in 'awkward possession of questionable debt instruments' (Hudson, 1972: 137–9). US negotiators aimed not at multilateralism of either the Keynes or the White kind, but at the creation of a US-centred regime which opened the world to US economic expansion. And when concessions to multilateralism were necessary, the United States acquired special privileges in the resulting institutions and ensured that they remained too small for effective world economic governance in the decades immediately following.

Most countries' delegates at Bretton Woods thought that 'the attempt to return to the pre-World War I level of international openness was utopian'; rather, 'the increasing necessity of stable domestic economic conditions required a much diminished level of international openness, so that the future called for the development of a system of "national capitalisms" within an international mechanism for stabilising the world economy' (Block, 1977: 30–1). The US position, however, was an open world economy under its tutelage was possible, that its interwar failures were 'not inevitable' and that '[i]f given a second chance, the United States could stabilize an international order with a high level of openness'. It could fill 'Britain's shoes by making the United States the financial center of the world economy' (1977: 30–1).

Keynes, head of the British delegation at Bretton Woods, was the most prominent spokesperson for the former position. His original proposals form the indispensable backdrop against which US actions, at Bretton Woods and beyond, and their consequences, can be judged. Keynes recognized that, in contrast to the nineteenth century's imperial geopolitical economy, the twentieth century's geopolitical economy comprised national capitalisms. In this situation, economic growth could be substantial and necessary trade could be restored but only by creating structures of international economic governance that permitted national governments a great deal of autonomy to pursue economic goals of their choice, including, critically, full employment. With this in mind he proposed an International Clearing Union (ICU) to regulate and facilitate international trade and payments. It featured a built-in bias toward balanced trade, capital controls, creditor/surplus countries' co-responsibility for adjustment to trade and payments imbalances along with debtor/deficit countries, and a multilaterally managed international currency, 'bancor', which was not the currency of any country, to settle residual trade imbalances.

Each country would have an overdraft facility in bancor proportional to its trading needs. Overall debit and credit balances, reflecting nations' surpluses and deficits, would cancel each other out. Capital controls would ensure national governments maintained control over critical levers for economic management such as interest and exchange rates. Balanced trade would be promoted in two main ways. First, creditor and trade-surplus countries would be as responsible for adjustment to imbalances as debtor and deficit countries. By avoiding large and ultimately unsustainable trade imbalances, not only would deflationary adjustment by debtor and deficit countries which could be so ruinous to growth be avoided, but so would the need to accumulate liquidity to finance them. These arrangements would be reinforced, second, by making trade surpluses and reserve accumulation unattractive, as the ICU would charge interest on both credit and debit balances at year-end, and permit bancor to be bought with gold or national currencies, but not sold, so surplus countries could only accumulate bancor balances. A proportion of balances above a certain quota would be transferred at year-end to a reserve fund for making loans for development purposes (Keynes, 1980: 118–19). Finally, national policy priorities would have considerable leeway when facing adjustment. For example, the ICU permitted debtor countries to devalue up to 5 per cent for low debit balances, and only applied harsher penalties for higher ones. Countries with large and persistent credit balances could undertake several measures: expanding domestic credit and demand; appreciating the national currency or increasing wages; reducing tariffs or other barriers to imports; and exporting capital (1980: 120).

Schumpeter enviously complained of Keynes's influential policy advice that it 'was in the first instance always English advice, born of English problems' (Skidelsky, 2000: 293). In so far as Keynes's proposals reflected the United Kingdom's interests at Bretton Woods, it was a United Kingdom that was economically weak, suffering trade and financial deficits (about to get worse with impending decolonization). In this she was representative of an interest far more general in a world destroyed by war and about to emerge from colonialism than that of the United States, with its war-swollen economic and financial means.

At Bretton Woods, Keynes's proposals were 'rejected on political grounds; they were never rejected or disputed on economic grounds' (Tily, 2007: 79). Nor were they defeated by White's, which aimed in only a slightly different way to create an international order in which national economic planning would be possible. Indeed, his proposals were developed in dialogue with Keynes. They became part of the official US negotiating position for a time only because the broad coalition that underlay the Roosevelt Administration included not only traditional Democratic party interests – 'the primarily agricultural South, the urban political machines and representatives of the dominant business and financial interests' – but also 'the newly emergent industrial unions and representatives of Midwestern agrarian progressivism' (Block, 1977: 34), which favoured national economic planning. Finally, there was the added contingency that the idiosyncratic US Treasury secretary, Henry Morgenthau, was tolerant of Keynesians like White.

However, White's and the planners' position was politically precarious. They faced opposition from Congress, the State Department under the expansionist Cordell Hull, and most critically perhaps from New York's international bankers. As the bankers saw it, quite simply and accurately, any plans to eliminate trade and payments imbalances, impose capital controls and provide governments with more or less automatic access to liquidity in case of imbalances, and institute a multilaterally governed world currency would eliminate their critical role in providing governmental finance and, in the process, their right to require (usually deflationary) economic policies as the price of their confidence. It would also expose their investments to risks of inflation under expansionary governments (1977: 53).

Of Keynes's proposals, only capital controls survived in the eventual Bretton Woods system, and that only because they were critical for the recovery of war-devastated capitalist Europe, which was expected to keep it from going communist. The International Monetary Fund (IMF), which was created to aid countries in temporary balance of payments difficulties, not only contained no bias toward balanced trade, it embodied deflationary conditionality at the behest of US international bankers. So it was their accessory rather than their replacement. In any case, it was left too small to be of much use amid the problems of the transition period, when countries needed substantial financial resources to abandon exchange controls. The IMF would only come into its own in the 1980s amid the third world debt crisis. In place of bancor, the United States sought to recreate a version of the gold standard by promising to back the dollar with its great gold holdings. This was merely making a virtue of expediency. As a US senator put it, the gold accumulated in the United States had 'no actual value at all, more than its value for commerce. In putting up a few billions of gold in this great enterprise [the U.S. was] merely attempting to salvage the value of that gold itself' (quoted in Hudson, 1972: 150).

However, even this could not ensure for the dollar the world role sterling had once played. The United States was aware that dollars would be scarce after the war ended, not least because it wanted to run export surpluses and because it would emerge from the war a world creditor. London had to remain a major international capital market to finance trade in Western Europe and between the United Kingdom and its Sterling area. So the United States undertook bilateral negotiations with the United Kingdom with the aim of getting its support for opening up world trade in return for a loan, which would hasten the restoration of an international role for sterling. Practically all elements of these negotiations failed, and with convertibility of sterling and other major currencies not being achieved until 1958, the dollar could be the only international means of payment outside the Sterling area. This was the beginning of the dollar's postwar world role: even in this shrunken form it was troubled from the start, as the next chapter shows.

4

AMBITION AND REALITIES

The notion that the United States was 'hegemonic' between 1945 and 1971 is so widespread that a re-examination of the period is bound to surprise. For hegemony stability theory (HST) and for the US policy makers in whose aspiration to emulate British dominance HST had its origins, the dollar's world role was the benchmark of US hegemony. It was troubled from the start. If that were not enough, in the geopolitical economy of the postwar period, maintaining US economic strength and the dollar's world role pointed in opposite directions.

Postwar combined development was stronger than hitherto. Its strongest form, communism, took vast territories and populations, including China after 1949, out of the capitalist world altogether, removing them from potential US dominance, and supported combined development elsewhere. For its part, the United States was forced to tolerate and even sponsor combined development among recovering capitalist allies. And it had to tolerate it, at least, among the newly independent countries that strong economic nationalisms, Soviet support for decolonization and the United States' own desire to reduce its capitalist rivals' power were bringing into being. Moreover, as former colonies became independent countries, the 'inter-war consensus on the non-applicability of the right to self-determination to colonial peoples' was replaced by a historic 'nominal great-power acceptance – however hypocritical – of a law-bound international system'. Nation-states now enjoyed legal equality under the United Nations (UN) Charter, and aggressive war was prohibited. True, the UN Security Council's five permanent veto-wielding members discounted both provisions (Chandler, 2003: 30). But if hypocrisy be the homage vice pays to virtue, pretension is homage to reality: sovereign equality and non-intervention were necessary pretences because imperialisms were on the defensive. The newly independent countries now had the policy autonomy to pursue combined development if their ruling classes were willing and able.

Not only was the capitalist world that the United States hoped to dominate truncated and fractured into competing national capitalisms, changes in domestic political economy strengthened the possibilities of combined development. Here too the role of the USSR was critical. It had industrialized impressively while the capitalist countries languished in the Great Depression and some went fascist. And the USSR had made the critical difference between victory and defeat against the fascists. So after the war, capitalism's reputation was sunk and capitalist countries had to take some leaves out of the Soviet planning handbook, especially to keep their own working classes, who had been mobilized for war with promises of material equality and prosperity, from the charms of communism. As a result,

> a return to *laissez-faire* and the unreconstructed free market were out of the question. Certain policy objectives – full employment, the containment of communism, the modernization of lagging or declining or ruined economies – had absolute priority and justified the strongest government presence. Even regimes dedicated to economic and political liberalism now could, and had to, run their economies in ways which would once have been rejected as 'socialist'. After all, that is how Britain and even the USA had run their war-economies. The future lay with the 'mixed economy'.
>
> (Hobsbawm, 1994: 272–3)

High working-class expectations made growth critical in capitalist economies: in the decades that followed it came 'to be expected as a normal feature of the world economy. It is easy to forget that this was not the case in earlier periods' (ERP, 1969: 124). In the world of national economies pursuing growth, therefore, liberalism in the international sphere came to be 'embedded' in a social consensus about 'intergovernmental collaboration to facilitate balance-of-payments equilibrium, in an international environment of multilateralism and a domestic context of full employment' (Ruggie, 1982: 392, 396–7). Mass mobilization for war in the advanced capitalist and communist worlds corresponded to popular mobilizations for independence in the decolonizing world. All postwar governments thus had to fulfil higher popular material expectations. Finally, decolonization also made it more or less mandatory in capitalist countries to expand domestic markets through fuller if not full employment, as Hobson had long foreseen.

Its great postwar economic size notwithstanding, the United States was, in an important sense, just one of the national economies. It pursued the new domestic expansionism with gusto: '[i]f the real needs and aspirations of our people are translated into effective demand through constantly growing employment and purchasing power, our markets can absorb a vigorously expanding output' (ERP, 1949: 5). The Employment Act of 1946 explicitly committed the United States to a 'nation-wide program for continuous maximum employment, production and purchasing power' (ERP, January 1947: 25). However, pursuing this sort of national economic expansion as just one among other national economies conflicted with the dollar's world role in two ways.

First, a national economy could not easily provide world liquidity. The United Kingdom had done so by recycling colonial surpluses as capital exports. With no colonies and a commitment to domestic expansion, the United States could spare little capital. The alternative was to incur payments deficits (Lary, 1943; *Economist*, 1943), and the 1950s and 1960s successively demonstrated the two main problems with this. Immediately after the war, US export surpluses limited international liquidity. The cold war had to be launched to get Congress to approve the Marshall Plan. However, its capital export was too limited even to finance US exports at desired levels, let alone to facilitate trade and allied recovery more broadly. Only the increase in US military expenditure for the Korean War set the postwar pattern of liquidity provision through balance-of-payments deficits. Even then, complaints of a dollar shortage persisted despite the communist world and the sterling bloc operating without the dollar.

After other currencies became convertible in 1958, the dollar shortage was replaced by a dollar glut more or less overnight and the famous 'Triffin dilemma' emerged: providing international liquidity through payments deficits undermined confidence in the dollar (Triffin, 1961). This dollar problem escalated rapidly as declining exports joined rising military expenditures abroad in widening payments deficits. Recovering economies regained competitiveness with new technology. Meanwhile, US manufacturers were laden down with older equipment, forced into foreign direct investment (FDI) by rivals' tariff walls, and suffered neglect from their governments. For US governments would not permit themselves a proper industrial policy for fear of appearing illiberal and endangering the dollar's world role, and only pursued one encumbered by its disguise as defence policy. As rivals recovered and gained ground, the US economy and industry lagged behind.

The second conflict was, therefore, that the United States was helpless before this sort of uneven and combined development (UCD). Giving the dollar its world role involved pushing for open markets for goods and capital. This could not be reconciled with openly implementing the sort of industrial policy for higher productivity and competitiveness that its rivals could permit themselves. So US economists, the successors of Hamilton, Carey and the institutionalists, embraced neoclassical economics in a 'relatively sudden shift'. They fell 'fully in love with the market and out of love with control and intervention just as they became successful at practicing the latter' and just when the latter was being applied more extensively around the world. The cold war and McCarthyism were closely bound up with this shift. Economists would now 'narrow their range of beliefs and ... restrict the acceptable ways of expressing them' (Morgan and Rutherford, 1998: 17, 13, 15). The resulting shrinkage of the macro-economic policy toolkit tied the government's hands. Unable to generate productivity increases on a sufficient scale, macro-economic policy could only create inflationary growth, which widened the trade deficit and undermined confidence in the dollar. Counteracting inflation with these policy instruments could restore confidence in the dollar, but only by reducing growth and hastening the diminution of the very basis of US dominance – its relative economic size – as rival national capitalisms grew through unabashed combined development.

After 1958, gold flowed out of the United States as European governments preferred it to inflated dollars, and the United States's once-formidable gold stock was sufficiently depleted by 1961 to require the creation of the gold pool to sustain the dollar's gold backing. As the dollar's difficulties continued to mount over the decade, the first strains of HST appeared to justify and naturalize the dollar's troubled condition. The authors of the international financial intermediation hypothesis (IFIH) lectured foreign governments and central bankers that they should not regard the United States as just another national economy. It was banker to the world; its payments deficits were merely banking liabilities. The IFIH was certainly too brazen to inform the events that immediately followed.

Neophyte US Treasury secretary John Connally's infamous statement that the dollar may be 'our currency but your problem' is generally taken to indicate that something like the IFIH wager worked after 1971: private confidence in the dollar made up for the distrust of foreign governments and central bankers, and 'benign neglect' sufficed to maintain the dollar's value and world role thereafter. But Connally's statement, made before a European delegation, indicated only the mutual exasperation of US and Western European governments, and as Chapters 6 through 8 will show, the IFIH and HST notwithstanding, the world never came to regard the United States as its banker, and the fortunes of the dollar remained tied to the US national economy.

Nothing could have been plainer to the Nixon Administration in 1971. When recession was added to inflation, balance-of-payments deficits, a weakening dollar and the failure of the gold pool in preventing further gold outflows in 1971, the Nixon Administration found that the recession could be

> remedied by more expansive fiscal and monetary measures. But this remedy would have made the other problems worse. It would have stimulated the still lively expectations of continuing or even accelerating inflation and it would have speeded up the flight from the dollar.
>
> (ERP, 1972: 22)

Faced with a choice between the dollar's world role and US economic health, Nixon chose the latter (Calleo, 1982: 30–1).

FROM WORLD WAR TO COLD WAR

Postwar US policy makers did not 'want to go back to the size of economy ... before the war' (ERP, January 1947: 22). More audaciously, however, they also sought to maintain their economy's relative size. As George Kennan, director of the Policy Planning Staff to the Secretary of State, put it bluntly in 1948,

> we have about 50% of the world's wealth but only 6.3% of its population. ... In this situation, we cannot fail to be the object of envy and resentment. Our real task in the coming period is to devise a pattern of relationships which will permit us to *maintain this position of disparity* without positive detriment to our national security.
>
> (Kennan, 1948, emphasis added)

However, that was not to be. It was not for lack of trying.

Managing the national economy

Truman pursued expansion by maintaining high demand through government procurement for consumption, as with the School Lunch programme, and for investment through public works. This strategy marked three critical changes in economic policy. First, it became more tolerant of inflation, assuming that pre-war price levels could never be restored and that growth would stabilize postwar prices (ERP, 1948 Midyear: 11–12). Second, working-class consumption was seen as critical to maintaining high demand. When tight labour markets in the postwar and Korean booms led to 'a greater proportion of workdays [being] lost to work stoppages than in any other comparable periods after 1946' (Brenner, 1998: 53), the administration favoured wage, price and rent controls to put pressure on 'profit margins ... adequate to absorb wage increases without the price increases' and to limit only those 'wage adjustments which would force a break in a price ceiling' while exempting those 'essential to remedy hardship, to correct inequities, or to prevent an actual lowering of living standards' (ERP, Midyear 1948: 7). Finally, it became more tolerant of fiscal deficits, regarding the one expected in 1949 as 'an element of great stability in the present situation'(ERP, Midyear 1949: 1). Spending cuts would amount to the 'defeatist admission that we cannot prevent our economy from running downhill', and end programmes 'vital to the international security and domestic welfare of our people' (ERP, Midyear 1949: 5–6). Instead, further expansionary initiatives were taken. Thus in the immediate postwar years, wages were buoyant, profits very high – 'in excess of the levels needed to furnish incentives and equity funds for industrial expansion', the administration noted with satisfaction (ERP, January 1949: 5) – and credit expanded.

The cold war as export financing

Despite domestic expansionism and exports two and a half times the level of 1929 and triple that of 1940 (Brenner, 1998: 48–9), the US 'position of disparity' in the world economy could not be maintained because the dollar could not provide the liquidity to finance US exports adequately.

The 'key currency plan' had already failed to remedy this problem. Under it, the United States promised the British a loan to help make sterling convertible and restore London's role in financing world trade (made up, of course, mainly of US exports). However, the loan proved too small and the attempt to make sterling convertible ended in disaster (Block, 1977: 52). So US exports had to be financed by countries running down their gold and dollar reserves, through the UN Relief and Rehabilitation Administration (UNRRA) and export–import bank loans.

By 1947 these sources were drying up and the domestic postwar consumer boom was nearing its end. While financing exports became more urgent, the 1946 elections returned a Congress unlikely to approve further loans. Now the Truman Administration concocted the 'red menace' to 'scare the hell out of the country' (Senator Vandenburg, quoted in Freeland, 1972: 89), enunciated the Truman Doctrine of US support for armed resistance to 'subjugation' which launched the cold war, and Congress granted $400 million to prevent left-wing triumphs in Greece and Turkey in 1947.

In this sense the cold war was not the cause of US imperial policy but its effect (Lens, 2003: 349). It combined financing exports with fighting combined development by national capitalisms as well as communism. When such 'totalitarian regimes' threatened 'free peoples', 'America's world economic responsibilities' included aid to countries battling them (Freeland, 1970: 86). The Truman doctrine saw freedom as primarily economic: other freedoms relied on it. All were endangered by restrictions such as trade quotas, licences and planning, which recovering and developing countries favoured. Worse, they could prompt the United States itself 'to use these same devices to fight for markets and for raw materials' (Truman, 1947) in ways incompatible with its imperial ambitions.

Thus, 18 months after the Second World War, the United States was back on a war footing. Since the conflict was dictated by US aspirations for dominance, the United States would remain there even after the cold war ended, through 'humanitarian wars' and the war on terrorism (Bacevich, 2008: 67). Successive foes – fascism, communism, dictatorship and Islamism – would be demonized (2008: 77). A 'highly elastic rationale' for military action by a structurally unaccountable executive would become 'hardwired into the American psyche' and 'airbrush' away the real gory story of the US pursuit of 'national security' (2008: 78).

Anti-communism was simply a part of this broader tilt at obstacles to US imperial objectives. For the influential conservative, W. Y. Elliott, communism constituted

[a] serious reduction of the potential resource base and market opportunities of the West owing to the subtraction of the communist areas from the international economy and their

economic transformation in ways which *reduce their willingness
and ability to complement the industrial economies of the West.*
(Elliott, 1955: 42, emphasis added)

National capitalisms were only slightly less threatening. Indeed:

the struggle against national capitalism and the conflict with
Soviet Communism were linked. First, the threat of national
capitalism was greatest in those countries where the left was
strongest, and it was feared that national capitalism would simply
be a transition to socialism. Second, it was thought that national
capitalist regimes would be vulnerable to political domination –
'Finlandization' – by the Soviet Union because of their tendency
to develop trade and friendship ties to the Soviet Union.
(Block, 1977: 10)

In the cold war atmosphere, Congress also passed the European
Recovery Programme, also known as the Marshall Plan. However,
at $13 billion over four years, it was simply too small to keep
the US economy expanding at desired levels or to meet its other
objective, to keep Europe liberal. European countries continued to
rely on import and exchange controls, thwarting the achievement
of a US-dominated liberal world capitalism which would also be a
market for US exports (Block, 1977: 92).

With the United States running export surpluses, complaints of
a dollar shortage were taken seriously: '[i]n the long run we can sell
to other countries only if we are willing to buy from them, or to
invest our funds abroad' (ERP, January 1947: 30). However, Charles
Kindleberger was already on the path of the IFIH and HST. If the dollar
shortage was undermining liberalism because other countries wanted
to 'preserve for themselves freedom to restrict imports from the United
States' (Kindleberger, 1950: 5–6), the solution was 'a reconstitution
of the international long-term capital market' (1950: 253) such as
existed in London before 1914. It would, of course, now be relocated
to New York and redenominated in dollars. Such arrangements, no
matter how improbable or unstable, would be infinitely preferable to
any genuinely multilateral scheme, such as Keynes's, that did not have
the dollar at its centre.

The birth of military Keynesianism

By the end of the 1940s Truman's expansionism faced new obstacles,
as '[t]he momentum of war-created demand and war-created

purchasing power ... waned' and 'currently generated purchasing power [had] to absorb a full output of goods and services' (ERP, January 1949: 3). Exports could make a contribution only with capital exports, and after the Marshall Plan ended they would decline to the levels US firms invested abroad plus the official capital flows to effect a transition from aid to trade (ERP 1953: 138). By 1949, the United States was in recession as businesses, sceptical of domestic and international demand conditions, stopped expanding capacity while the resulting reduction in the flow of dollars abroad as a result of reduced imports and exports raised the possibility of heightened protectionism in recovering countries (ERP, Midyear 1949: 12).

While Truman's Council of Economic Advisors (CEA), aware that 'a little recession may lead into a big depression', proposed a programme of public works to keep up demand (ERP, July 1949: 11), far more ambitious plans were being made elsewhere. The Treasury proposed to accelerate convertibility, with devaluations if necessary. But going this way incurred the risk that if things went awry, Europe could become even less liberal (Block, 1977: 98). It was the State Department's infamous document NSC-68 that showed the way forward. It proposed rearmament as the most comprehensive solution:

> Domestic rearmament would provide a new means to sustain demand so that the economy would no longer be dependent on maintaining an export surplus. Military aid to Europe would provide a means to continue providing aid to Europe after the expiration of the Marshall plan. And the close integration of European and American military forces would provide a means to prevent Europe as an economic region from closing itself off from the United States.
>
> (US Department of State,1950: 103–4)

NSC-68 was even more alarmist and shrill than the Truman doctrine. Until the Soviet detonation of a nuclear device and the Chinese Revolution, US policy had followed George Kennan's proposal to contain, rather than attempt to roll back, communism. Now NSC-68 portrayed the United States as besieged by threats. Isolationism (always a fiction in any case) would be capitulation, and preventive war morally repugnant. The solution for its author, Paul Nitze, was

massively increased defense spending, with particular emphasis on accelerating the development of a hydrogen bomb; increased security assistance to train and equip the armies of friendly nations; efforts to enhance internal security and intelligence capabilities; and intensification of covert operations aimed at 'fomenting and supporting unrest and revolt' inside the Soviet bloc. [This amounted to] the permanent militarization of US policy.

(Bacevich, 2009: 110)

The 'Nitze doctrine' originated the US practice of transforming 'trivial concerns into serious threats and serious threats into existential ones' (2009: 113). Nitze was one of a new breed of presidential advisors. Whereas Roosevelt's 'Wise Men' represented 'steadiness, prudence and sobriety' (2009: 106), the new breed combined 'a sense of alarm with a demand for immediate action' and saw 'military power as the optimum means to resolve international issues'. They included James Forrestal, the first secretary in the newly created Defense Department (the United States had fought in two world wars without one), a 'pseudorealist, purporting to see the world as it was, yet badly misconceiving the situation' (2009: 107). Their successors would include CIA director George H. W. Bush, whose alarums about deficits in US nuclear capacities making a Soviet first strike possible attempted to thwart détente in the 1970s, and the neoconservatives of the Project for a New American Century (PNAC) who identified post-cold-war threats in the missile programmes of Iran, Iraq and North Korea (2009: 114). Such alarmism was far from militarily effective: the United States lost China, North Korea and Vietnam to communism, and later added failures in Iraq and Afghanistan to its imperial record. The 'gargantuan' and secretive national security apparatus that grew around the Defense Department obstructed, rather than aided, presidential policy making. It also led Eisenhower to warn of the sinister power of the military-industrial complex and Kennedy to be embroiled in the Bay of Pigs fiasco (2009: 89–96).

Rearmament was expected to result in greater economic expansion than the outlays it required, and was 'consistent with maximum continued freedom for domestic capitalists' while also 'eliminat[ing] the danger of a disruptive economic crisis' (Block, 1977: 107). However, Congress only increased military expenditures and aid after the Korean War broke out. Only now could rearmament lay the foundation of the long-term growth strategy known as military Keynesianism.

In the perverse political economy of military Keynesianism, military spending became so important to US growth that lowering it would lead to recession, while investment in this rather uncompetitive sector 'contributed to stagnation in civilian sectors of the American economy' by siphoning away talent and resources (Block, 1977: 122; see also Perelman, 2002: 104) and undermined competitiveness. It also made US capitalism more national in a perverse way: trade liberalization became less urgent while civilian producers protected by high tariffs had 'little incentive ... to pursue technical innovations'. By the late 1950s it reacted to other national capitalisms' high tariff walls by establishing branch plants behind them, further neglecting the domestic productive infrastructure. Rearmament ironically detracted from US imperial ambitions directly by making the US economy more national, and indirectly by making it less competitive (Block, 1977: 122).

Nor did the US economy draw any 'slew of economic benefits' in the form of spin-offs from military R&D: 'had this same research occurred outside of the military industrial complex, the benefits would have been greater' (Perelman, 2002: 103). Moreover, with R&D in civilian industries lagging in the 1950s and 1960s, machinery prices ceased to be attractive relative to labour costs, and this created 'a countermechanization effect' as managements failed to upgrade machinery despite rising wages. This inevitably 'slow[ed] down the growth of industrial productivity in the economy as a whole' (Melman, 1974: 82) and created 'phantom capacity': 'obsolete capital goods [which] give an appearance of a productive potential that does not exist' (Perelman, 2002: 133) because they had become uncompetitive.

Liquidity and liberalization

In addition to financing US exports, liquidity was necessary if West European governments were to liberalize their economies and cope with the inevitable adjustment pressures. Though such liberalization was necessary for the US dollar to play sterling's pre-1914 role, attempts to achieve it in postwar conditions actually pushed the goal further away.

Unable to provide international liquidity in sufficient quantities, the United States would not permit the creation of new sources it could not control. US financial capital had already ensured, as we have seen, that the International Monetary Fund (IMF) 'would work to reinforce the traditional discipline of the gold standard', and the United States now subjected the IMF's financing to stricter controls, blocked Marshall Aid recipients from resorting to IMF loans and increased the conditionality of its aid programmes (Block, 1977: 113). But autonomous Western European governments only reacted to such moves with less, not more, liberalism. Moreover, as long as they maintained exchange controls, US government encouragement to New York banks to make 'credit available to foreign countries to ease their payments difficulties' (1977: 114) so that New York would more closely resemble pre-1914 London came to nought. The only private investment to flow to Europe was foreign direct investment (FDI) designed to circumvent trade restrictions. Official flows of capital, as first Marshall Aid then military aid, remained necessary to finance trade.

Truman's two terms included the postwar and Korean War booms. Looking back over the period, Truman's last ERP gave an imperial gloss to the dollar shortage. The problem it connoted was not only that other countries did not have enough dollars to purchase US exports: these countries were also 'confronted with an inability to achieve a high and varied enough level of trade with one another' (ERP, 1953: 136). The problem was to be resolved by tackling 'underlying resource and production problems' in 'economically advanced countries' suffering from the 'heavy drain of two world wars and the need to assume a new defense program' prematurely, and in countries suffering from underdevelopment. Initiatives like the Point Four programme for developing countries and the Schuman Plan to create the European Coal and Steel Community would encourage 'improved volume and efficiency [of production] abroad'. Combined with 'increased United States foreign investment, and reduced trade barriers', such programmes 'should gradually enable the world to earn the dollars it needs to pay for its imports from the dollar area' (ERP, 1953: 151). The United States had 'the most to gain by maintaining a predominantly free world and the most to lose if the balance of strength should shift over to totalitarianism' (1953: 138). Increased production and efficiency elsewhere would soon, however, create new problems for the United States.

CONVERTIBILITY AND THE TRIFFIN DILEMMA

It is often forgotten that the fabled growth of the golden age took place primarily in the recovering economies, national capitalisms which, along with the supranational institutions that would become the European Union, constituted a relatively closed economic bloc which the United States had to tolerate. National capitalisms not only thwarted US imperial ambitions directly through their illiberalism, they also undermined them by eroding the United States's competitive position and its weight in the world economy. US FDI was, ironically, central to the latter process. For it was 'the very nature of the so-called "multi-national" corporation (which in nine cases out of ten is in reality an American corporation) [to diffuse] American technology on a world scale, thus equalizing technological levels' (Mandel, 1969: 12–14). The United States began to record its first postwar declines in exports in 1958 and 1959 (ERP, 1959: 124) while imports remained steady and even increased in early 1959 (ERP, 1960: 29).

To this process, the Eisenhower Administration made its own contribution. Its fiscal and monetary policies were noticeably more conservative. Aiming for 'long-term economic growth rather than ... an immediate upward thrust to economic activity' (ERP 1955: iv), Eisenhower interrupted the Korean War boom with a mild recession and responded to a second recession in 1957 with only a mild stimulus. Modest economic growth in the middle and late 1950s widened the spread between United States and the recovering economies' economic performance and hastened currency convertibility. Often portrayed as the pinnacle of US hegemonic achievement which restored a liberal world economy, currency convertibility inaugurated a new phase in the troubles of the dollar. It turned the 'dollar shortage' into a 'dollar glut', as Western European countries could now use their own currencies in more international payments, and set the United States on the path to the closing of the gold window. All this without making Europe more liberal.

With convertibility, measures in place to relieve the dollar shortage contributed to the dollar glut. Military expenditure and aid which, Eisenhower's parting comments about the dangers of the 'military-industrial complex' notwithstanding, had remained central to US growth and exports (ERP, 1955: 121), were chief among those measures. Incentives for foreign investment, such as lower taxes on foreign income and tax deferrals (1955: 53–5), also contributed as convertibility encouraged previously reluctant investors to take the plunge. 'So the United States continued to pump dollars abroad on both capital and government account, and the result was a larger deficit' (Block, 1977: 136). And a larger dollar glut.

The dollar glut would now also be exacerbated by the deteriorating US trade position. The Eisenhower Administration's approach to it laid the basis of the sustained attack on US labour in the decades to come. The administration admitted that 'steady recovery and growth in the productive capacity of other countries' had played a role, as had reduced transport costs, so that some 'new international cost and price disparities may now have developed to the advantage of these other countries'. However, it insisted that much of the change was caused by 'intensified production and export efforts by other countries on the basis of previously existing cost differences' (ERP, 1960: 31): to wit, the historically higher wages of US workers. They could 'earn real wages ... between two and three times higher than real wages in Western Europe, and between four and five times higher than real wages in Japan' only as long as the United States enjoyed a productivity monopoly of the sort Britain did in the nineteenth century (Mandel, 1969: 12). However, with imperial ambition preventing the pursuit of interventionist industrial policy, at least in civilian industries, the United States could not retain its productivity advantages. Instead, Eisenhower appointed a Commission for Foreign Economic Policy 'to clear the channels of trade, to foster foreign investment, and to provide technical aid to underdeveloped nations' (ERP, 1955: 52). In keeping with US imperial ambition, it recommended dealing with the competitive threat by *reducing* tariffs and trade restrictions (1955: 52) on the grounds that imports would push more dollars abroad and prevent trade deficit countries from restricting US exports (ERP, 1958: 48).

As the United States tried to foster growth merely through macro-economic management in circumstances of declining competitiveness, it could only worsen the problem and undermine the dollar's world role. While higher domestic costs and declining competitiveness braked investment growth, demand stimuli could not increase investment. They only induced inflationary growth which sucked in imports and led to further deteriorations in the trade and payments balances, and put pressure on the dollar. This logic would work with a vengeance under the Kennedy and Johnson administrations' more aggressive growth policies. Under the more prudent Eisenhower, however, the 1957–58 recession was met with only mild stimulus, and the administration took comfort that more and more US workers worked 'in industries and occupations that are not readily affected by moderate economic declines' and that income declines 'are offset ... by supplementary payments' (ERP, 1959: iv).

As exports declined, the postwar link between exports and capital outflows to finance them was broken (1959: 131). Short-term capital now flowed abroad to escape the interest-rate ceiling imposed since 1933 by Regulation Q and take advantage of higher West European interest rates (ERP, 1961: iv). The Eisenhower

Administration responded to the resulting deterioration in the balance of payments by launching an export promotion programme, attempting to control the foreign exchange costs of US military spending and stepping up exhortations to other countries to lower trade barriers (1961: 39). For the rest, however, it hoped that lower inflation and higher growth would halt short-term capital outflows as well as FDI (1961: 44). These outflows exacerbated the dollar glut.

The dollar glut was the symptom of the 'Triffin dilemma'. Robert Triffin explained to Congress in October 1959, when the dollar's problems were just beginning, that the dollar was bound to be undermined 'more and more dangerously as time goes by'. The dollar's world role was dependent on the United States's willingness to allow its 'net reserve position to deteriorate, by letting ... short term liabilities grow persistently and indefinitely at a faster pace than ... gold assets' (Triffin, 1961: 8–9). This endangered world monetary arrangements by creating a mismatch between the dollar's real and gold values. However, eliminating US deficits would dry out international liquidity while putting a 'heavy handicap on sound policies for economic growth and stability', effectively preventing expansionary policy, in the United States. Triffin did not mention capital exports: they were just an impossibility for any country in a world hungry for growth. They would have been possible only if the US national economy had productivity advantages on a scale that enabled sufficient capital exports to finance world trade. How long it could sustain such advantages in the highly competitive postwar world is another question. The other option, liquidity provision through deficits, would be subject to the Triffin dilemma unless the US economy became so large, relative to the rest of the world, that its deficits would be large enough to supply the world with liquidity but small enough, relative to its own GDP, as to cause no concern for the dollar's value. How monstrously competitive or large such a US economy would have to be in a world of other producers of no mean competitive advantages or size, and how it could counter contender challenges from them, boggles the mind. No wonder then that Triffin echoed Keynes broadly, arguing that the only solution to this dilemma was a bar on the use of national currencies as monetary reserves by other countries, and 'the internationalization of the foreign exchange component of world monetary reserves' (Triffin, 1961: 8–9). A decade and a half after US *force majeure* overruled Keynes's proposals at Bretton Woods, economic realities reasserted their essential correctness.

THE CONFIDENCE GAME

There had already been a run on the dollar during the Kennedy–Nixon election campaign. After convertibility there was initially an increase in private dollar holdings in Europe but this was soon reversed, with monetary tightening there and easing in the United States. To this outflow from the dollar was added another, as US investors, no longer deterred by inconvertibility, were attracted to 'higher-yielding foreign Treasury bills' (ERP, 1961: 112). Despite the run, and Triffin's warnings, the new Kennedy Administration assumed office proclaiming that 'the maintenance of its established gold value' was essential to the 'strategic role of the dollar' and 'the stability and efficiency of the present system of international payments' (ERP, 1962: 148). The dollar's career henceforth became even more turbulent, as the Kennedy–Johnson governments resorted to policies which sought to stave off, and theories which sought to obscure, the inexorable realization of Triffin's warnings.

As gold flowed abroad, Kennedy's assurance that 'the full strength of our total gold stock and other international reserves stands behind the value of the dollar for use if needed' (ERP, 1962: 149) failed to calm markets. US gold reserves, at $24 billion, or 70 per cent of the world's monetary gold in 1949, were down to $17.7 billion or 40 per cent of the 'free world's' monetary gold in 1961 (1962: 148, 151). They were not enough to instil confidence in the dollar's value, and the gold pool was organized that year to put the gold reserves of the United Kingdom, the six Common Market countries and Switzerland behind the dollar (Hudson, 1972: 300). This would sustain the dollar–gold link for a further seven years.

Rather than concede that the gold pool reflected US inability to sustain the gold-backed dollar's world role, the Kennedy Administration saw it as a confidence-building measure. This was part of its radical new interpretation of the dollar's woes. Since payments deficits had not caused concern until 1958, it claimed, the dollar's value rested on one thing alone: confidence. '[A]s long as foreign holders of dollars are confident that the gold value of the currency will be maintained' (ERP, 1962: 152), deficits would not lead to gold outflows. Beyond that, there was, in any case, 'no conceivable liquidity position which can withstand general loss of confidence' (1962: 153).

The Kennedy Administration admitted practically all of the dollar's real difficulties: European convertibility 'removed an important barrier to international capital flows'; the European

Economic Community (EEC) became 'a large, rapidly growing, tariff-free market in Europe, holding out much the same investment opportunities as the tariff-free internal market of the United States'; the United States acquired long-term foreign military and aid commitments; US rivals improved their competitive position 'mainly by the remarkable advances in output and productivity in those countries' while inflation eroded US competitiveness. It even admitted two other key facts. First that, since 'gold and foreign exchange reserves of many European countries had been rebuilt from their depleted postwar levels[,] U.S. payments deficits were no longer needed for this purpose' and so '[l]arge and continuing deficits cannot be financed indefinitely because foreigners ... will not be willing to let [large liquid dollar] balances grow without limit'. Second, it acknowledged that US 'Intercontinental ballistic missiles and restoration of political stability in Western Europe reduced the special attractions of the United States as a haven for funds and as a location for capital investment' (ERP, 1962: 154–5). But addressing these tangible difficulties remained less important than pursuing that elusive object, confidence.

Disgruntled governments and central bankers were now informed that the dollar's world role gave the United States 'a special world banking function'. Foreign public and private holders, the Kennedy Administration further asserted, trusted the dollar as 'a means of payment and a store of value', never mind the surprise, let alone the fury, of the authorities whose practical distrust could be measured in gold outflows. They had acquired their dollars 'in much the same way that individual depositors hold balances in commercial banks'. And like a bank, there was a critical difference between its liquidity and its solvency. The dollar's international role might require the Treasury 'to sell gold on demand to foreign governments and monetary authorities at a fixed price', and the gold pool would take care of that (1962: 147). Meanwhile, the world should not doubt the dollar's international position. After all, the administration argued, US non-gold assets abroad showed that

> [t]he Nation is not 'living beyond its means'; rather, its means are steadily increasing. At the end of 1960, the U.S. Government owned foreign assets totalling $21 billion, in addition to its gold holdings of $18 billion; and U.S. citizens owned another $50 billion in assets abroad.
>
> (ERP, 1962: 150)

These US claims on foreigners, it claimed, gave 'basic long-run strength to the dollar' even though some of the claims were private and long term and could not be 'quickly mobilized' (1962: 150).

All this brassy ingenuity could not, however, conjure up the required confidence in the dollar. Only a slew of rather old-fashioned measures did, and that too temporarily: the gold pool, the previous and current administrations' measures to reduce the payments deficit, and the Treasury's intervention in international exchange markets to stabilize the dollar for 'the first time in a generation' (1962: 153). The Kennedy measures to reduce the payments deficit included eliminating tax incentives for US investment in other advanced countries, as well as generally discouraging investment of capital abroad and encouraging inward investment through an 'interest equalization tax', cooperation with other central banks to avoid large differentials in short-term interest rates, measures to combat speculative flows, and advance repayments of long-term debt owed to the US government. They also increased domestic military procurement and the proportion of foreign aid spent in the United States and sought allied contributions to military expenditures abroad (1962: 13–16).

However, protection or restrictions on foreign aid and military expenditures, which would be very effective in reducing the payments deficits but would curtail the United States's role in the world, were not to be countenanced. Rather,

> the required adjustment is that the United States must pay for overseas military commitments, grants and investments to a greater extent by an export surplus earned in stiff world competition, and to a lesser extent by selling gold and accumulating liquid liabilities to foreigners.
>
> (ERP, 1962: 155)

Not only was nothing to be done to help the United States face 'stiff world competition', further trade liberalization, which in the absence of such measures was guaranteed to worsen the US trade balance, was pursued as a measure to reduce the payments deficits. Congressional authorization was sought to pursue a new trade agreement with the Common Market (which eventually became the Kennedy round of General Agreement on Tariffs and Trade (GATT) negotiations), a new export insurance programme was established, and foreign travel to the United States was encouraged (1962: 13–14).

THE CAMELOT ECONOMY

Growth promotion was, however, to be the chief measure to restore confidence in the dollar. More than any others, the Kennedy–Johnson administrations attempted to finance imperial activities on the back of a national economy by turbo-charging growth. But their efforts only exposed the futility of this venture.

Decrying the modest growth record of the Eisenhower Administration, the Kennedy Administration saw growth as the panacea for many ills. It would permit the United States to 'meet heavy obligations abroad for the security and development of the free world, without continued depletion of our gold reserves or excessive accumulation of short-term dollar liabilities to foreigners'. It would increase exports, 'a task of the highest priority' (ERP, 1962: 10). And it was a means of 'maintaining the external value of the dollar and bringing our international accounts into balance' which also promoted 'basic national objectives' (1962: 148).

It started off well enough. Kennedy assumed office amid a cyclical upturn. When, two years into expansionary policies, the results fell short of expectations, Kennedy's advisers came up with a 'new economics', prescribing more, not less, fiscal stimulus. The expected budget deficit could not be addressed by tax increases. These would exert a 'fiscal drag' on growth and prevent the very recovery necessary to balance the budget (Calleo, 1982: 13). Rather, tax cuts would close the gap between actual output and that which could be expected at full employment when the economy was no longer in recession. This 'full employment budget' conjured 'hypothetical revenues with actual expenditures' and derived a 'phantom surplus' (1962: 13). Greater stimulus would increase growth and revenues to turn the phantom surplus into a real one (1962: 13).

The real achievement of the new economics was the inflation and fiscal deficits that would now plague the United States (Calleo, 1982: 14). The high growth record of the Kennedy–Johnson years was, instead, the result of an old-fashioned employers' counter-attack on labour, most ferocious where the competition was sharpest, as in autos and steel. It resulted in 'a fundamental shift in the balance of class power and in the character of management–labour relations' which would establish 'the pattern which persists right up to the present' (Brenner, 1998: 58). From here on, the traditionally high-wage US economy would be transformed into an increasingly low-wage one to increase profits. These, ironically, would not be translated into increased investment and higher productivity precisely because intensified work was now the chief means of increasing productivity, an inherently limited strategy, while lower wages dimmed the demand outlook. Not surprisingly, capital flowed abroad 50 per cent faster than the increase in domestic investment during the early 1960s (1998: 62).

With neither its rhetoric nor its measures closing the payments deficits, and thus restoring confidence in the dollar, the Kennedy Administration faced an impasse. Its top confidence-building strategy, growth promotion, not only failed, but also sharply exposed the tension between national economic growth and restoring the balance of payments and thus the dollar's world role:

> These two goals seem to be incompatible. Each attempt to stifle inflation completely, to re-establish a very stable currency, can only be ensured by deflationary policies which create unemployment—and probably unemployment on a considerable scale. Each attempt to create full employment and to quicken the rate of growth inevitably increases inflation and with it the general loss of power of the currency.
>
> (Mandel, 1969: 9)

This was what Triffin had warned about. Essentially, reducing US payments deficits to restore confidence in the dollar involved reducing its deficit-fuelled international role. Precisely because the United States was a national economy and not the world's bank, the dollar could not enjoy both confidence and its world role.

MOUNTING DIFFICULTIES

The end of the growth spurt of the early 1960s and the beginning of the Vietnam War in 1964 took the dollar's difficulties to a new level. International dollar liabilities began to exceed US gold stocks. Gold flowed out but so did more dollars, multiplying claims on the remaining US gold. Lyndon Johnson stated matter-of-factly that 'so long as we remain heavily engaged in Southeast Asia, we will have a balance of payments problem' (ERP, 1967: 7). His implication was that foreign central banks, US firms and individuals and punters in the growing Eurodollar market (see below) could be expected to keep accumulating depreciating dollars to bear the burden of war. All would prove reluctant.

Telling them that that there was no 'over-all tendency for the United States to "live beyond its means"' was not enough. Nor was underlining that the US 'exports of goods and services [still] exceed its imports [and the] deficit ... arises from the fact that the United States transfers abroad – through military expenditures, foreign assistance, and private capital movements – a sum ... larger than the surplus' (ERP, 1964: 122). Nor yet was pointing out that the deficit did not reflect a 'reduction in net worth', since US assets were growing faster than US liabilities, and that the US was suffering only from 'a loss of liquidity in the form of a reduction in gold reserves and a build-up of liquid liabilities to foreigners' (1964: 122). As far as the world was concerned, these were precisely the problems.

Moreover, dollar outflows unconnected with trade increased even more. These included FDI, lending abroad and outward portfolio investment, unrecorded transactions and foreign borrowing in US capital markets 'taking advantage of the relatively low long-term interest rates, the efficient floatation facilities, and the ready avail-ability of capital in our markets' (ERP, 1964: 125). These flows constituted the so-called Eurodollar market, in which dollars were banked, held and used abroad in transactions between non-US parties. It had originated in the communist bloc's desire to park its dollars in Europe, rather than in the United States where they could be confiscated. However, now it grew mainly because of the highly regulated US banking sector which drove US investors to it (ERP, 1975: 212–14) and because European central banks availed themselves of it to earn interest on their depreciating dollar holdings. However, contrary to Hirsch and Oppenheimer (1976), who classically understood the growth of the Eurodollar market as the natural and inevitable behaviour of highly liquid private capital, first trickling and then gushing out of inevitably leaky and futile government attempts to contain it, it too was the result of government action, in this case, the United Kingdom's as well as the United States's. The financial interests that dominated the UK state used these flows to re-establish London as a major financial centre after the war, an enterprise in which US banks participated and US governments colluded (Ingham, 1984: 51–4).

The Johnson government engaged in 'special transactions' to reduce gold outflows and the deficit: persuading European and Japanese governments to repay war and Marshall Plan debts early, buy more US military supplies, make advance payments on them, hold their surplus dollars in non-convertible US Treasury bills and, not least, agree to a de facto embargo on US gold sales well before the closing of the gold window (ERP, 1964: 126). Such measures only increased dissatisfaction among European governments and central bankers. They complained that deficit financing for the war meant that surplus dollars added to their monetary base, thus exporting US inflation to their economies. The surplus dollars also permitted a 'cost-free takeover of Europe's economy' by US corporations while leaving Europeans, who were pressured not to cash their dollars for gold, holding much lower-yielding US Treasury bonds (Hudson, 1972: 295-6). Although Korean War debts had also been monetized, the Vietnam War was occurring at a time when dollar liquidity was dispensable. So foreign central banks demanded gold instead, and they now demanded an end to the deficits themselves.

THE INTERNATIONAL FINANCIAL INTERMEDIATION HYPOTHESIS (IFIH)

It was around this time that new and inventively perverse ways to persuade the world to stop worrying and start loving US dollars and deficits appeared. Like isolated strains of the larger symphonic work we hear when the orchestra is warming up before a performance, these were the first strains of what would compose itself as HST in the 1970s. While there were a number of other arguments (e.g. Roosa, 1970; Krause, 1970), one of the earliest and most elaborate was the international financial intermediation hypothesis (IFIH).

The Kennedy Administration had already flirted with the idea that, rather than another national economy whose currency did not inspire confidence, the United States was the world's banker whose liabilities were being miscalled deficits. Now three economists with 'influence in official Washington' wrote an article in the *Economist* on the 'prime current issue of international payments', and put forward the IFIH. It had to be 'taken into account even by those who baulk at some of the conclusions' (*Economist*, 1966). Stanford economist Emile Despres, MIT economic historian Charles Kindleberger, and the Brookings Institution's Walter S. Salant (hereinafter DKS), all of whom had been highly placed officials in government through the war and postwar ventures like the Marshall Plan, made three arguments.

From world's debtor to world's banker

First, 'to the extent that [US] loans to foreigners are offset by foreigners putting their own money into liquid dollar assets, [the US] has supplied financial intermediary services ... [by] lending mostly at long and intermediate terms and borrowing short'. Like a bank, the

United States, and New York in particular, was simply being 'paid to give up liquidity' (Despres et al., 1966: 527). 'The United States is no more in deficit when it lends long and borrows short than is a bank is when it makes a loan and enters a deposit on its books' (1966: 527). The idea that the US current account deficit amounted to 'borrowing short' when foreign 'lenders' had no choice but to 'lend', or in other words hold valueless dollars, was not the only presumptuous inversion. Complaints about the 'cost-free takeover of the European economy' were not valid, DKS claimed, because Europeans had a 'higher liquidity preference'. So they held 'liquid dollar assets' while needing the long-term funds US multinationals invested there. US financial intermediation, a 'trade in liquidity which is profitable to both sides' (1966: 526), made this exchange possible. Moreover,

> Europeans [including here US firms in Europe] borrow from the United States, and Americans are willing to pay higher prices for European assets than European investors will, partly because capital is more readily available in the United States than in Europe but mainly because liquidity preference in Europe is higher and because capital markets in Europe are much less well organised, more monopolistically controlled and just plain smaller than in the United States.
>
> (Despres et al., 1966: 527)

Not only did DKS add the insult of European liquidity preference and inability to finance their own long-term investments to the injury of their holding decreasingly valuable dollars, they made a virtue of US monetary laxity. US deficits, they argued further, needed no correction. Thanks to increased Eurodollar holdings, they accounted for only a fraction of total financial flows, and curbing them could 'cripple European growth' (1966: 527). Another argument, soon to become a staple of writing on international money and finance, was that financial flows could not be regulated effectively. '[M]oney is fungible. Costless to store and to transport, it is the easiest commodity to arbitrage in time and in space.' Funds prevented from taking one route would take another and '[t]hese leaks in the dam will increase as time passes, and the present system of discriminatory controls will become unworkable in the long run' (1966: 527). Finally, their vision of the United States as the world's bank meant seeing the world not as a collection of national economies but as a single economy: 'If financial authorities calculated a balance of payments for New York vis-à-vis the interior of the United States, they would impose restrictions on New York's bank loans to the interior and on its purchases of new issues' (1966: 527).

Europeans were hardly likely to agree that they were unproductive hoarders, that their forced Eurodollar holdings were the reason why US deficits need not be corrected, that capital flows could not be controlled when the problem was the United States's gushing issue of them, or that Europe was New York's hinterland. Knowing this, DKS made sure to point out that their reinterpretation of the dollar's world role did not rely on European agreement. If Europeans 'unwisely' choose to convert dollars into gold and refused to lift capital restrictions, gold could simply be demonetized, restoring 'a true reserve-currency system'. It would require 'cool heads in the United States' but would result in 'a strong international monetary mechanism resting on credit, with gold occupying, at most, a subordinate position' (1966: 528–9).

Private confidence versus public recalcitrance

DKS argued, second, that only 'government officials, central bankers, academic economists and journalists lacked confidence in the dollar' because of 'their failure to understand the implications of [the United States's] intermediary functions' (1966: 526). In fact, deficits were a sign of private confidence in the dollar, signalled by 'increases in private holdings of liquid dollar assets', thanks to European liquidity preference and to increasing transactions 'as a partial offset to debts in dollars and for other purposes'. These were being miscalled US deficits (1966: 528). Private speculation against the dollar was invariably prompted by governments that did not understand that

> [t]o prevent a bank from pursuing unsound policies – if it really tends to do so – it is not necessary to allow a run on it. Depositors could have their say in less destructive ways, e.g. through participating in the management of the bank of last resort or through agreement on the scale of the financial intermediation.
> (Despres et al., 1966: 527)

While every bank relied on confidence, which could be lost, the United States stood to lose it only as a result of the irrationality of foreign governments and central bankers:

The remedy is to have a lender of last resort to cope with the

effects [of irrational actors] or, better, to educate them or, if neither is possible [and neither was], to make the alternative asset (which, against the dollar, is gold) less attractive or less available.
(Despres et al., 1966: 527)

If it ain't broke ...

Finally, creating alternative multilaterally managed sources of world liquidity was akin to 'destroy[ing] an efficient system of providing internal and external liquidity – the US-based and dollar-denominated international capital market – and substitut[ing] for it one or another contrived device of limited flexibility' (1966: 528). 'The international private capital market ... provides both external liquidity to a country, and the kinds of assets and liabilities that private savers and borrowers want and cannot get at home' (1966: 526).

DKS claimed to be internationalist; the United States would 'preserve the international capital market and thereby protect the rate of world economic growth even without European cooperation' (1966: 529). The *Economist*, however, called them new American nationalists: it argued that the United States could not be compared to a bank since banks did not operate without a lender of last resort, and international credit had to be better organized. As Triffin pointed out at the time, DKS's arguments assumed that all participation in the system was voluntary, although 'the initiative certainly lies far more with the American investor [and, one might add, the US government] than with the autonomous desire of Europeans to raise long-term funds in the United States' (Triffin, quoted in Hudson, 1972: 323). The analysis might apply to private international transactions, but it 'was inapplicable to the international financial transactions of the 1960s and 1970s ... in light of the substantial role played by government transactions – and hence, [by] diplomatic arm-twisting' (Hudson, 1972: 325). Indeed, DKS's arguments constituted something of a Say's law for international finance: 'All surplus funds thrown off by U.S. direct investment abroad and war-related spending created their own demand[,] which expressed itself in the form of increased foreign holdings of U.S. Treasury securities.' In reality, 'it was irrelevant to assert that Europe "wanted" or "chose" to hold short-term claims on the U.S. Treasury, simply on the ground that it did in fact hold such claims.' (1972: 323).

When first broached in the mid-1960s by the Johnson Administration and DKS alike, the demonetization of gold was considered dangerous for the Atlantic alliance (Block, 1977: 196).

However, the dollar's problems worsened in 1967 as funds flowed out of the United States thanks to the Middle East crisis, the intensification of the Vietnam War, the UK devaluation and the speculation accompanying the United Kingdom's liquidation of its assets in the United States (ERP, 1968: 163). To conserve gold, the Johnson Administration suspended the dollar's domestic convertibility: it was necessary to determine neither 'prudent monetary policy' nor the dollar's value: 'the value derives from our productive economy' and only made 'some foreigners question whether all of our gold is really available to guarantee our commitment to sell gold at the $35 price' (1968: 17).

As matters worsened, the United States secretly pressured European authorities not to demand gold at all, and a leak about this prompted further speculation against the dollar. By June 1967 France withdrew from active participation in the gold pool, and its 9 per cent contribution had to be covered by the United States just when the UK devaluation increased gold sales. At the Frankfurt gold pool meeting it was agreed that members be billed for their gold losses only at month-end, providing immediate relief to the United States. But three other US proposals failed: that gold-rich Australia and Canada join; that a system of differential pricing for governments, industrial users and speculators be instituted; and that 'gold deposit certificates', involving elaborate double counting of gold stocks, be created so gold outflows would not be deemed to diminish US stocks while it was gradually demonetizing gold. The meeting's announcement that the gold price of the dollar would be defended temporarily halted speculation, but news of the United States's failed proposals put further pressure on the dollar (Hudson, 1972: 302–5). In the ensuing panic in Congress, some suggested suspending further gold sales to France until it paid off its First World War debts, while others suggested that the US embargo gold more generally (1972: 305).

SPECIAL DRAWING RIGHTS (SDRS): A FOILED PLAN B

With the gold-backed dollar under such pressure, the United States now made an interesting attempt to salvage its aim of being the controller of the world's money. The Kennedy Administration had launched an effort to halt 'speculative movements of short term capital' (ERP, 1962: 15), which were typically directed against the dollar, in cooperation with the Organisation for Economic Co-operation and Development (OECD) and the Bank of

International Settlements (BIS). This involved creating or increasing other, non-dollar forms of international liquidity, which was also justified by invoking the near impossibility that when 'the U. S. Deficit is eliminated – or gives way to a surplus – world reserves will probably rise too slowly (or even contract)' (ERP, 1964: 142).

Gold was ruled out. Having insisted at Bretton Woods on placing its gold hoard at the centre of world monetary arrangements, the United States resorted to Keynes's arguments against gold now that its hoard was so depleted. Historical contingencies underlay the gold standard's apparent success (ERP, 1968: 180), and it could not be relied on to provide liquidity in a fast-growing world economy even though the 'gold-exchange standard' economized on gold. Growing private and industrial demand for it meant that 'the world cannot count on any sustained increase in monetary gold reserves in the long run' (1968: 181). Simply increasing the price of gold would only be a 'one-shot' write-up of the nominal value of the reserves, delivering windfalls for gold producers (pre-eminently the USSR) while penalizing others. Of course, the United States discussed neither dealing with the payments imbalances that led to the need for greater liquidity to finance them, as Keynes would have done, nor acquiring other countries' currencies. That would give them a piece of the world role the United States wished to reserve for the dollar.

So the United States proposed increasing international liquidity through the IMF. Although its capacity to lend for temporary deficits had recently been strengthened by 'a network of short term credit facilities among central banks and by the development of the General Agreements to Borrow which enlist[ed] additional resources from major industrial nations', reserves remained the main means for correcting payments deficits. So 'a reserve asset universally acceptable as a supplement to gold and dollars that can be created in the amount needed to meet the desired expansion of world reserves' was called for. A plan for special drawing rights (SDR) to be issued by the IMF was agreed on in Rio de Janeiro in September 1967 (ERP, 1968: 17).

Since SDRs and Keynes's bancor are often likened to each other, it is important to understand the critical difference. It is true that, with the trade and payments imbalance shoe now on the other foot, the United States sounded more and more Keynesian. To its objections to gold, the United States now added advocacy of surplus-country adjustment, which it had refused when it boasted huge trade surpluses. Now, it appeared that there was 'no *a priori* case for assigning a greater share of the responsibility to either deficit or surplus countries' (ERP, 1966: 154), and that some countries' surpluses merely reflected other countries' deficits. The United States also warned that competitive reserve building to provide for future trade deficits would be domestically deflationary and disrupt trade and capital flows (ERP, 1968: 179). But there was a critical imperial continuity: the United States would control SDRs almost as completely as dollars. Unlike bancor, which were to be issued by the genuinely multilateral International Clearing Union, SDRs would be issued by the IMF, in which the United States effectively wielded a veto.

No wonder the Europeans insisted that there was no need for them, or even for greater liquidity. The only need was to curb the United States's growing deficit (Hudson, 1972: 296). Although they reluctantly agreed to create SDRs in 1967, the Europeans ensured that the first allocation remained small and their role insignificant.

THE DOLLAR IN THE LAST DITCH

For a while creditor governments and central bankers, only too keenly aware of the massive financial disorder US repudiation of its obligations would entail, remained committed to the gold pool, but matters came to a head in March 1968, when the United States was unable to meet its own commitments to it because it was legally required to provide 25 per cent gold cover for Federal Reserve currency. Though legislation repealing that requirement was rammed through Congress, panic closed the London gold market and the gold pool countries met to announce its demise. The price of gold moved freely upwards. Johnson announced that he would not stand for re-election and would not escalate the war in Vietnam. It looked to one US observer that 'The European financiers are forcing peace on us. For the first time in American history, our European creditors have forced the resignation of an American President' (quoted in Hudson, 1972: 307).

Even after March 1968, European authorities agreed not to demand gold and 'to cease supplying gold to the private market' (ERP, 1969: 16) to prevent an increase in the dollar price of gold, which 'would have offered a ransom payment to speculators' (1969: 15). The Johnson Administration in return reiterated its commitment to close the deficits (1969: 14), and thanks to temporary factors and a slew of restrains on capital movements – the Interest Equalization Tax, the direct investment control programme and the

Fed's programme of voluntary restraint on foreign lending (1969: 15), it succeeded that year.

But underlying problems remained. The Johnson Administration remained committed to the war, high military expenditures and domestic expansionism. And the main contradictions of the US world role were in full bloom as Johnson left office. Internationally, US earnings capacity remained considerably lower than was necessary for its imperial ambitions, particularly providing the world with dollar liquidity. Despite the longest uninterrupted expansion in the postwar period and an accompanying stunning rise in its share of world trade thanks to the Kennedy Round of GATT negotiations, US foreign earnings could not keep up with its imperial burden. Domestically, economic expansion in a relative liberal economy clashed with maintaining the dollar's value. Inevitably, expansion brought in imports more than it stimulated exports. This problematic configuration, in which expansion undermined confidence, was what Johnson bequeathed Nixon.

'Our currency, your problem'?

With Nixon, inflation concerns took centre-stage: it argued that the Johnson Administration had failed to match increased US military outlays with cuts elsewhere, and thus fuelled inflation (ERP, 1970: 5). A 'new realism' of fiscal and monetary restraint was necessary. It would make 'slowing pains' – reductions in growth and profits – inevitable (ERP, 1970: 6), but also halt the 'the deterioration in our trade balance' (1970: 9) as imports declined. Over the next year, import controls and reductions in military expenditure of $11.4 billion in real terms, or 18 per cent down from the 1968 peak, helped limit deficits (ERP, 1971: 42).

The Kennedy–Johnson economic illusionism about confidence and being the world's banker was replaced by plainer discourse: since '[o]ur export sales, our investment return, and the inflow of investment from abroad are not large enough to finance our imports, our new investments abroad, and our net Government overseas expenditures' and since 'the difference ... is financed partly by sales of gold and partly by increased foreign holdings of short-term dollar investments by foreign businesses, banks, individuals and governments' (ERP, 1968: 12) which constituted claims on a declining gold stock, the US liquidity position had come under threat. The situation was grave enough to require action 'directly on the key international flows' that contributed to that deficit. (1968: 14). The Interest Equalization Tax had been in place since 1963, and the new administration made what had been voluntary restraints on foreign investment mandatory, further restrained foreign lending by US banks and financial institutions, and called on surplus countries to reduce their surpluses (1968: 15). The Nixon Administration clearly kept its distance from the IFIH interpretation of the dollar's problems and prospects.

This was so even though, in the peculiar circumstances of Nixon's first year, European official influence, which kept US policies, if not always its discourse, real, was temporarily neutralized. The Official Settlements Account – 'the change in our holdings of international reserve assets less the change in liquid and certain non-liquid claims on the United States by foreign official institutions such as central banks or finance ministries' (ERP, 1970: 126), or in other words the balance between US gold holdings and claims of foreign financial authorities on them – had a record surplus in the first half of 1969, while there was a record deficit on the liquidity balance – 'the change in our holdings of international reserve assets less the change in the liquid liabilities to all foreigners, official and private' (1970: 126), or the balance between US gold holdings and all private and public claims on them.

This reversal between the official settlements balance and the liquidity balance had occurred because US commercial banks, unable to attract enough capital because of Regulation Q interest rate ceilings, had increased borrowings on the Eurodollar market. As this drove interest rates up, it attracted funds from other, non-American, sources, which demanded dollars from foreign central banks, producing both the surplus on official settlements and the deficit on the liquidity balance. Long-term capital outflows also increased as restrictions on US FDI led US corporations to borrow abroad (1970: 130). While continental European governments attempted to restrict private funds from flowing into Eurodollar markets, the US government did not.

> [A] circular flow of U.S. funds [arose] ... in which dollars moved from the United States to the Euro-dollar market and back again through the foreign branches of U.S. banks. This flow involved both an increase in U.S. residents' claims on foreign institutions ... and an increase in liquid liabilities to foreign branches of U.S. banks.
>
> (ERP, 1970: 129–30)

If the official settlements balance was in surplus, neutralizing official pressures on the dollar, the liquidity balance, which could affect private confidence in the dollar, had 'lost much of its significance' (ERP, 1971: 145) because the sheer volume of private short-term claims on the United States had made them effectively inconvertible into gold and because gold outflows were dammed with European cooperation.

Even in this context, where it appeared that the IFIH wager about private confidence in the dollar was being won, the Nixon Administration went only so far as to claim that '[r]ather than the quantity of dollars flowing into foreign hands, it is the difference between this amount and the amount they want to hold, given existing conditions, that would be a true indicator of disequilibrium' (1971: 149). But the administration was also aware that the difference could be negative. It recognized that

> [t]he present situation, in which we maintain an official settlements surplus only because of large-scale foreign borrowing by U.S. corporations and banks at high interest rates, creates a feeling of some uneasiness here and abroad, and observers generally regard the present structure of the U.S. international accounts as abnormal and temporary.
>
> (ERP, 1970: 141)

And indeed, in 1971 there was a sudden exit from the dollar (ERP, 1974: 144). It was 'the cumulation of successive and mutually reinforcing layers of evidence and analysis'. The most fundamental was the inability of the United States 'to finance its entire set of external policy commitments – on mutual security, on trade, on development aid, on capital mobility – except through the steady issuance of liquid dollar obligations' throughout the 1960s. This disequilibrium was now demanding recognition and was beginning to prevail over biases against the devaluing of the world's only source of liquidity. A second view was that 'the poor wage–price–productivity performance of the US economy between 1965 and 1969' required corrective devaluation. Finally, there was 'the belief that developments in the conduct of monetary policy here and abroad (and hence in relative short-term interest rates) would induce large outflows of short-term capital from the United States to Europe' (ERP, 1972: 144–5).

Like its predecessor, the Nixon Administration also saw the second of the three problems – of solvency, productivity and credibility – as the key to resolving them all, though it pursued different policies to do so. However, it remained confined to macro-economic policy, and soon faced the essential conflict between using these policies to increase growth and imperial obligation. As long as the dollar's gold value had to be maintained, expansive fiscal and monetary measures to remedy '[a] rate of expansion and a level of employment less favourable than policy had projected' could not be taken for fear of stimulating 'the still lively expectations of continuing or even accelerating inflation [which] would have speeded up the flight from the dollar' (ERP, 1972: 22). This contradiction, rather than any breezy IFIH wager on private confidence holding up the unbacked dollar, led to the closing of the gold window on August 15, 1971. Only now would HST retrospectively recast the troubled decades reviewed in this chapter as an era of US hegemony and a stable dollar. I review it and its influence in the next chapter and outline the alternative geopolitical economy of postwar capitalism before returning to the dollar's post-1971 tribulations in Chapter 6.

5

THE RETROSPECTION OF HEGEMONY STABILITY THEORY

Free trade served to justify the United Kingdom's world role, and in a sense hegemonic stability theory (HST) played a similar role for US attempts to emulate it. However, HST was also quite different from free trade. After all, the US imperial project was an epigone of the British original. It had had to lower its sights to making the dollar the world's currency and New York its financial centre. Success repeatedly eluded the realization of even these scaled-down ambitions. Chief among the resulting differences was that unlike free trade, HST did not emerge at the apogee of US productive power to articulate and legitimize its geopolitico-economic practices. Although the United States had long been expansionist, although it began aspiring to emulate the United Kingdom's world role explicitly in the early twentieth century, and although the Second World War positioned it as favourably to realize its aspiration as it would ever be, HST did not emerge until after its postwar attempt to realize its ambitions had failed.

As we have seen, the first strands of HST – pre-eminently the international financial intermediation hypothesis (IFIH) – emerged amid the mounting difficulties of that attempt, specifically of keeping the gold-backed dollar as the world's money, and it appeared as a full-fledged theory, retrospectively dignifying the US desire to replace the United Kingdom as the world's leading power with the theory of hegemony, only after the closing of the gold window in August 1971. HST was born amid the gloom of 'declinism', when the United States's relative weight in world production was cut from half to about a quarter by the recovery of Western Europe and Japan, its vaunted gold reserves were drained, defeat in Vietnam was impending, the dollar's future world role was uncertain, trade tensions with cold war allies had heightened, and developing countries' international assertion was voluble.

HST is correctly traced to Charles Kindleberger. He argued in *The World in Depression* (1973) that the world economy needed leadership from its most powerful country: its absence in the inter-war period had led to the Great Depression. The implication was that its proper exercise, as by the United States in the 1950s and 1960s, resulted in the 'golden age' of prosperity and growth and its decline was the cause of the economic turbulence of the 1970s. Kindleberger had been building and refining his arguments – of which the IFIH reviewed in the last chapter was an important part – for at least a decade by then.

Not just the timing of HST but also its content differed considerably from free trade theory. Free trade delegitimized combined development and obscured the utility of imperialism through its two key fictions, Say's law and comparative advantage. Between them, they occluded states' economic roles, whether in domestic political economy or in the geopolitical economy of uneven and combined development (UCD). However, by the late twentieth century, states' economic roles – whether in regulating capitalist competition through *inter alia* central banking, or class struggles through welfare measures – were so prominent that they could hardly be denied. So HST could not obscure imperialism, only dignify it as 'hegemony' or leadership, and it could write combined development out of the geopolitical economy's script only by envisaging a world capitalism regulated by such hegemony or leadership so complete as to render other states' economic roles ineffective, unnecessary or undesirable.

Second, the idea of US hegemony was retrospective at least two senses. Not only was the United States's alleged hegemony identified and theorized only after it had admittedly run into trouble; like the early twentieth-century US corporate elite and later Luce and the second-chancers, HST looked to the United Kingdom's nineteenth-century example as the model for the US world role. And world systems (WS), of course, went farther back to sixteenth-century Holland and fifteenth-century Italy.

Third, HST was also, in a critical sense, prospective and performative. More than anything else, the spread of the idea of US hegemony ensured that fresh US attempts to undergird the dollar's world role would not be seen for what they were – malign and dangerously unstable arrangements to postpone the inevitable – but would be interpreted as a way of recreating a coveted and benign condition that in fact never existed.

Fourth, not only was HST never the discourse of the most

competitive nation-state as free trade had once been, even its resemblance to free trade after 1870, when the United Kingdom had lost competitiveness, was only superficial. Then the United Kingdom had exported the capital it drew from its colonies as the way to provide international liquidity. Bereft of colonies, the United States could never replicate these arrangements, and its liquidity provision through deficits would first drain its gold reserves and later, as we see in the following chapters, rest on a series of dangerously unstable financial arrangements.

In what follows, the main forms of HST are discussed first, followed by a discussion of the declinism amid which HST emerged and the brief but unconvincing burst of renewalism in the late 1980s. HST's credibility would have evaporated thereafter but for globalization and empire, which briefly but spectacularly simulated US economic dominance on the basis of financializations centred on the stock market (globalization) and housing bubbles (empire). The chapter ends by briefly outlining the recent development of a Marxist strand in international relations (IR) that emerged in the 1990s, and the limitations that prevented it from contesting HST, and later globalization and empire, before going on to outline this book's alternative account of postwar geopolitical economy, which relies on Robert Brenner's economic history of postwar capitalism.

VARIETIES OF HST

HST and its forerunner, the IFIH, emerged from the same influential and policy circles as the ambition to emulate the United Kingdom's world role and its updates such as the 'second chance' and the 'American century'. Of course, HST's chief originator, Kindleberger, preferred to point to a more intellectually respectable origin. That, interestingly, was Francois Perroux's conservative, and we might say very European, critique of neoclassical economics through his concept of regional poles of development and his associated discussion of economic dominance. For him, '[o]ne country, form or person dominated another when the other had to take account of what the first entity did, but the first could equally ignore the second' (Kindleberger, 1981: 243). Since Perroux's ideas were also influential with the other end of HST's political spectrum, WS, via Fernand Braudel's ambitious economic history of world capitalism, they bear some consideration here.

Elaborated in the late 1940s to understand 'the asymmetric

effects exercised by the United States on world trade' (Perroux, 1988: 82), the idea of dominance originally applied to firms. In simplified neoclassical models, 'goods and services exchanged are homogeneous and perfectly and indefinitely divisible'. They 'move without resistance or friction within one industry or from one industry to another, under the influence of an alteration in the level of their remuneration'. Nothing hinders their fluid movement to points where advantages are maximized (Perroux, 1950: 190–1). Such models could not explain how firms became dominant. In reality, 'goods and services are not homogeneous'. Their 'indivisibility derives from numerous psychological, technical, and institutional causes, and … viscosities hinder the movement of all factors and products'. In this real world, firms that 'bring to life desires which yesterday were latent and are today effective, because they have found the consumption good, the durable good, the production good or process for which people were dimly hoping' (1950: 191) can become dominant.

National dominance, like firm dominance, rested on 'the interrelations that exist between a network of free exchanges and a network of unequal forces' (1950: 199–200). In the twentieth century the most relevant type of dominant economy was not an occupying economy, a mother economy in a colonial system or a 'totalitarian economy' in its relations with satellite economies (1950: 201), but 'the dominant economy which exerts its domination effect through operations compatible with the logic of the firm, of the price system in a regime of workable competition, and of the market considered as a network of exchange between relatively independent centers of calculation' (1950: 202). The United States was such an economy, and exerted domination through its bargaining power, size and the nature of its activities (1950: 203).

Perroux's distinction 'between the economic causes of domination effects' and 'the historical circumstances extending or intensifying' domination (1950: 203) applied to United States's war-wrought economic dominance and the rest of the world's, particularly Europe's, attempt to cope with it. That dominance came with the responsibility to rectify such internal problems as would otherwise reverberate through the system. These included the United States's responsibility to try to balance trade (1950: 203) and to address three kinds of instability that plagued US capitalism and affected the world: its tendency to make huge investments through its big businesses, which subject it to cyclical disturbances, its speculative character, and its subjection to 'the constant criticism of capitalism

... at the very time when it finds itself with no new frontiers and without the resources of a mass immigration' (1950: 203–4).

For Perroux, dominance was not something to be celebrated or recommended. And it was anything but inevitable or permanent: 'in a dynamic economy, invention and innovation, either technical, economic, political, or social, are always at work, [and] it is evident that the opportunities for shifting, halting, or reversing the domination effect are innumerable' (1950: 206). Clearly Perroux looked forward to the day Europe would take them up.

In Kindleberger's hands this 'peculiarly French idea, with strong overtones of resentment at alleged domination by the United States in fields of foreign exchange, trade policy, multinational enterprise and the like' (Kindleberger, 1981: 243), was turned into a concept of leadership, a necessary and relatively benign feature of the world capitalist economy. And Perroux's critique of liberal neoclassical notions became the basis of the idea that dominance – or leadership – was the precondition of a liberal, or in our terms a cosmopolitan, world economy.

Kindleberger

The World in Depression argued that the Great Depression had been caused by 'the inability of the British to continue their role of underwriter to the [international economic and monetary] system and the reluctance of the United States to take it on until 1936' (1973: 28). Kindleberger was cautious: he was providing only 'an', not 'the' explanation of the Great Depression (1973: 291); he was using the term 'leadership' not to invoke the 'overtones of der Fuhrer and il Duce' but to refer to 'the provision of the public good of responsibility, rather than exploitation of followers or the private good of prestige' (1973: 307); and he was avoiding potentially inflammatory words like 'imperialism' or even 'hegemony', preferring to speak of 'leading countries' and their 'responsibilities'. And well he might. He was seeking to rehabilitate imperialism in an age defined by its illegitimacy.

Kindleberger put a benign gloss on the United Kingdom's world role so that similarly flattering light could be cast on the United States's position. However, this also meant that he obscured the critical difference that formal empire and its surpluses made to the discharge of the United Kingdom's 'responsibilities', particularly international liquidity provision through capital exports. He did not discuss the congenital difficulties of the dollar's world role or the relatively meagre capital exports under the Marshall Plan. Some obvious differences – such as the United Kingdom's more liberal economy – were explained away as 'born of cultural lag and the free trade tradition of Adam Smith' (Kindleberger, 1986: 291).

The idea of leadership rode on an essentially Perrovian explanation of the Great Depression. A political account of the Depression was necessary, Kindleberger argued, because solely economic explanations could only apply when there were a multitude of actors, none of whom was important or weighty enough to affect outcomes. For Kindleberger, such secular economic processes could not explain events in an asymmetrical 'world system of a few actors (countries)'. Moreover, following Perroux, who had declared that liberalism 'no longer appears as a natural order, but as a rule of the game defined and usually observed' (Perroux, 1950: 206), Kindleberger made the very possibility of economic processes having free play in the form of a liberal economy depend on the leading country defining the rules of the game. Liberal policies were not easily accepted or generalized – the temptations of protection and free-riding always beckoned – and required enforcement by a power able to benefit from them as well as ensure their long-term beneficence for other countries. So a leading country was one that was

> prepared, consciously or unconsciously, under some system of rules that it has internalized, to set standards of conduct for other countries and to seek to get others to follow them, to take an undue share of the burdens of the system, and in particular, to take on its support in adversity by accepting its redundant commodities, maintaining a flow of investment capital, and discounting its paper.
>
> (Kindleberger, 1986: 11)

In the absence of leadership, unbridled pursuit of national interest caused the Great Depression. 'When every country turned to protect its national private interest, the world public interest went down the drain' (Kindleberger, 1973: 292). Against Keynes's and Polanyi's or even Perroux's idea of a world of national economies, Kindleberger counterposed the idea of a world economy unified by a single leading economy pursuing a single 'public interest'. He disguised the US imperial ambitions in the drag of the world's public interest. He used the myth of isolationism cleverly to make the reluctant and 'nationalist' United States the culprit-in-chief in the interwar period, all the better to make the case for its allegedly necessary and benevolent postwar leadership (Kindleberger, 1986: 297).

Kindleberger's conception of the leading power's responsibilities shifted with the changing fortunes of the US world role. In 1973, to the 'world's banker' conception of the IFIH, Kindleberger added a central banking function, 'discounting in crisis', effectively being a 'lender of last resort' and 'maintaining a relatively open market for distressed [sic] goods', in essence urging the Nixon Administration away from its mercantilism. In the 1986 edition of *The World in Depression*, acknowledging the United States's further loss of primacy which, as we shall see in Chapter 6, forced it to coordinate exchange rate and macroeconomic policies through annual rounds of G-7 meetings, he added two more functions, 'policing a relatively stable system of exchange rates' and 'ensuring the coordination of macroeconomic policies' (1986: 289).

Perhaps because dissimulating US imperial ambition, not to mention its futility, was more important than scientific rigour, Kindleberger was not too particular about when the United States's hegemony ended. It might have come with 'say, the Interest Equalization Tax in 1963 or perhaps the abandonment of the gold pool in 1968, the slamming down of the gold window in 1971, or the adoption of floating exchange rates in 1973' (1986: 11), or yet, as he put it in an even earlier article, with the balance of payments troubles of the United States in 1960 or when currencies became convertible in 1958 (Kindleberger, 1961, referred to in Kindleberger, 1981). He did not comment on the foreshortening of the period of alleged US hegemony the earlier dates implied.

In 1973 Kindleberger foresaw three unstable outcomes – the United States in a leadership position but unwilling to provide it, Europe competing for leadership but unable to provide it, and each vetoing the other's proposals for stabilization – which were to be avoided, and three stable ones – restoration of US leadership, European leadership, and 'an effective session of economic sovereignty to international institutions'. While the attractions of the last could hardly be denied, Kindleberger consigned it to the realm of the improbable, and did not elaborate on its aims or form. In 1986 he extended to Japan and even 'some unsuspected third country such as Brazil' the possibility of being a leading country.

International political economy

Kindleberger was a major pioneer of international political economy (IPE), and had been developing the ideas that would eventually combine in HST for some considerable time when the new discipline was founded circa 1970. Although it is not clear exactly how, an implicit idea of US hegemony and its passing came to be written into IPE's founding self-understanding. A key pioneer, Susan Strange, chose her words carefully when she said in an article widely regarded as a sort of manifesto for the new field that 'the pressures which a fast growing international economy is exerting on a more rigid international political system' required greater exploration of 'the middle ground between politics and economics'. The resulting 'theory of international economic relations' was necessary if the international relations discipline was to avoid 'a damaging loss of contact and consistency with the real world of policy-making' (Strange, 1970: 310–11). Strange's intellectual call to arms would forever ensure that, in the mainstream of IPE, economics would remain privileged and 'rigid' politics be conceived as the system that had to adapt to dynamic economic changes. And it ensured that IPE would take HST's basic proposition – that the 1950s and 1960s had been a haven of stability – for granted, overlooking the tumultuous events set in train by the attempt to force the world to accept the gold-backed dollar as the international currency, and its unravelling.

Thus IPE's remit was to comprehend the changes set in train by the largely regrettable passing of an age of 'stability' and, given that the answer to this 'Really Big Question' was dominated for decades by HST (Cohen, 2008: 13), the referent of this mythical 'stability' was US 'hegemony'. The retrospective labelling of the 1950s and 1960s as an age of US hegemony would also successfully obscure its true character as an age of national economies and combined development, which made the dollar's world role impossible. No wonder IPE became the theoretical mirror of the US imperial career, faddishly accepting the new discourses of US power – not just HST but globalization, empire and their various subordinate discourses – that issued successively from US government sources, as the following chapters detail. Leading IPE scholars were predominantly US-based (Strange was the rare exception, an Englishwoman, and the traditional separation of IPE into 'American' and 'British' schools seemed designed to give it a less provincial image, much like the baseball 'World Series'). IPE's leading scholars reflected US concerns, and since many of them were, or aspired to be, influential in high US policy-making circles, also sported blind spots convenient to the discourses of US power. That within the broad terms of these discourses there was considerable debate and controversy gave IPE the appearance of being a more serious intellectual enterprise than it appears to be on closer scrutiny.

Key pioneers simply saw states losing control over economic processes and the private sphere (see e.g. Vernon, 1971) much as economic cosmopolitan ideologies always had. This was also important at a time when US imperial ambitions ran afoul of resistance from official sources and the IFIH and HST sought to conceive of US hegemony as relying on private actors – multinational corporations (MNCs) and financial institutions. Later the widespread acceptance of this idea made it all the easier for globalization discourse in the 1990s to convert IPE into global political economy (GPE). By contrast, realist and neorealist scholars who entered IPE from realist international relations emphasized the state. Their adaptation of realism to HST involved giving up only classical realism's assumption of an anarchic international political system, instead seeing the United States as the chief suppressor of anarchy in the postwar period. Although it was labelled 'mercantilist', this neorealist wing of HST never sought to understand and theorize developmental states or combined development and their potential for challenging the power of dominant states. They were potentially lethal to HST, something that IPE took for granted: 'A liberal international economy requires a power to manage and stabilize the system' (Gilpin, 1975: 40).

In another sector of IPE, HST shaded into the idea of international regimes. For some the leading country would facilitate, and if necessary enforce, a set of rules and norms by the enlightened, even altruistic, deployment of its power to create stable international regimes. Others used the idea that the US-led system of rules and norms had broken down to explore new patterns of cooperation that emerged, and argued that the decline of US hegemony was not accompanied by evidence of increasing anarchy. Institutionalists like Keohane (1984/2005), for instance, emphasized the importance of cooperation against the realist emphasis on conflict. The idea of a number of functionally separate and discrete 'international regimes' – 'principles, norms, rules and decision-making procedures around which actor expectations converge in a given issue area' (Krasner, 1983: 1) – also emerged to rival that of a single overarching 'hegemony'.

Mainstream HST focused on the UK analogy, which was deployed with considerable sophistication. Important differences were noted, including the truncation of the capitalist world economy thanks to communism, the United States's lack of a formal empire and the much greater military burden shouldered by the United States, which explained the short duration of US hegemony. Krasner saw US limitations in providing the stable basis for an expanding liberal trading system raising fundamental questions about HST itself (1976) while Gilpin saw the unique role of the modern multinational corporation as deeply problematic for the US economy and hegemony (1975). There were rare flashes of greater ambition: 'The modern world economy has evolved through the emergence of great national economies that have successively become dominant .... Every economic system rests on a particular political order; its nature cannot be understood aside from politics' (Gilpin, 1975: 40). However such ambition would be realized only in world systems.

World systems analysis

Marxists operated on the fringes of IPE. They did not, of course, return to political economy, Marx and Engels's own tradition, international or otherwise. Their access to it was barred, thanks to the bifurcation of postwar Western Marxism into a broad mainstream preoccupied with philosophical, cultural and lately sociological pursuits, and a smaller number of 'Marxist economists', creatures of neoclassical economics. Members of the former wing did however produce, for instance, an original account of international class formation which had critical implications for HST (Van der Pijl, 1984), and accounts of HST as a largely cultural phenomenon based on a certain interpretation of the concept of hegemony put forward by the Italian Marxist Antonio Gramsci (Cox, 1996). However, the world system (WS) account of HST, which through the work of Fernand Braudel can also be traced to François Perroux, added to the credibility of HST by giving an avowedly (and we might say idiosyncratically) Marxist account of it. WS scholars were able, thanks to their erudition, to give HST a weight and grandeur beyond anything its originators could have managed. WS's claims and contradictions are worth pausing over.

Like Braudel's contemporaneous history of capitalism (1992) on which it drew, Immanuel Wallerstein's theorization of world capitalism rested on a core axiom: the capitalist world system, unlike previous ones like world empires, was not a single state. That 'peculiarity ... [was] the secret of its strength' (Wallerstein, 1974: 348). The opposed logics of market and state combined economic unity with political division. There was more than a whiff of the 'oriental despotism', not to mention the neoliberal, argument here: 'world empires were ... archaic formations representing the triumphs of the political over the economic .... [W]herever there was an empire, the underlying world economy was unable to develop [;] … its career was stunted' (Braudel, 1992, Vol. 3: 54).

While WS analysts claimed not to see capitalism's dynamic as entirely 'economic', they did separate capitalism from states, whose territories could not contain it: in their conception capitalism necessarily overspilled state boundaries. Since 'economic factors operate within an arena larger than that which any political entity can totally control', capitalists have 'a freedom of maneuver that is structurally based' (Wallerstein, 1974: 348). This is what gives capitalism its dynamism. By contrast states' roles were seen as essentially conservative. Their institutional apparatus and cultures served merely to 'protect disparities that have arisen within the world-system, and as an ideological mask and justification for the maintenance of these disparities' (1974: 349).

In a world system of a 'multitude of political entities', 'it cannot be the case that all these entities are equally strong' for then they could block 'the effective operation of transnational economic entities'. Nor can it be that 'no state machinery is strong'; for that would leave capitalist classes with 'no mechanism to protect their interests, for guaranteeing their property rights, assuring various monopolies, spreading losses among the larger population, etc.' (1974: 354-5). The one state machinery that did have that strength was the hegemonic state. Clearly, there is no combined development here. Only hegemonic states could shape the world system, famously divided into the core, semi-periphery and periphery. Although hegemonic states could replace one another, and states could at least in some rare instances reposition themselves from one rung to another, how these things happened was not discussed.

As a critical scholar, Wallerstein saw hegemony in terms of interests rather than altruism or leadership. That leadership was productive and was exercised over a liberal world economy. Involving 'more than core status', it

> may be defined as a situation wherein the products of a given core state are produced so efficiently that they are by and large competitive even in other core states, and therefore the given core state will be the primary beneficiary of a maximally free world market. Obviously, to take advantage of this productive superiority, such a state must be strong enough to prevent or minimize the erection of internal and external political barriers to the free flow of the factors of production; and to preserve their advantage, once ensconced, the dominant economic forces find

it helpful to encourage certain intellectual and cultural thrusts, movements, and ideologies.

(Wallerstein, 1980: 38)

Hegemonies were by their nature rare and fleeting: 'to date only Holland, Great Britain and the United States have been hegemonic powers in the capitalist world economy, and each held the position for a relatively brief period' (Wallerstein, 1974: 38). The summit also marked the beginning of decline, not because the hegemonic state lost strength but because others gained. Hegemony had a 'marvellously simple' pattern:

Marked superiority in agro-industrial productive efficiency leads to dominance of the spheres of commercial distribution of world trade, with correlative profits accruing both from being the entrepôt of much of world trade and from controlling the 'invisibles' – transport, communications, and insurance. Commercial primacy leads in turn to control of the financial sectors of banking (exchange, deposit and credit) and of investment (direct and portfolio). ... [T]he *loss* of advantage seems to be in the same order (from productive to commercial to financial), and also largely successive. It follows that there is probably only a short moment in time when a given core power can manifest *simultaneously* productive, commercial and financial superiority *over all other core powers*. This momentary summit is what we call hegemony.

(Wallerstein, 1974: 38–9)

Giovanni Arrighi's later *The Long Twentieth Century* (1994) attempted to shed light on the transition between hegemonies which typically took place through financial expansions, something that Wallerstein had left largely unexplored. Drawing on 'the second and third volumes of Fernand Braudel's trilogy *Capitalism and Civilization*', published a few years after Wallerstein's *The Modern World System*, Arrighi constructed an 'interpretative scheme' in which the prominence of finance capital (presumably the opposite of Hilferding's continental model, the UK model of short-term investment) 'is not a particular stage of world capitalism [but] a recurrent phenomenon which has ... signalled the transition from one regime of accumulation on a world scale to another. [Financial expansions] are integral to the destruction of "old" regimes and the simultaneous creation of "new" ones' (1994: ix–x).

Arrighi's hegemonies began with material expansions rooted in regimes combining specific technologies, skills, resources and trans-regional linkages, and ended in an 'autumn' in which the abstract, deracinated, deterritorialized and fluid logic of finance transmitted capital to the core of a successor regime. Arrighi also added, as Braudel had done, an earlier hegemony – that of the Italian city-states – to Wallerstein's three.

The erudition of WS accounts of these hegemonies can hardly be replicated here. Nor can the rich debates that ensued when other Marxists criticized them for stretching the definition of capitalism too far, historically and conceptually. Following Braudel, WS scholars defined capitalism by its financial '"non-specialized" top-layer [which makes] "large-scale profits" [because it] "monopolizes" the most profitable lines of business' and 'has the flexibility needed to switch its investments continually from the lines of business that face diminishing returns to the lines that do not' (Arrighi, 1994: 8). More generally, rather than capitalist organization of production, they focused on market relations as the *differentia specifica* of capitalism. For their critics, this did not accord with Marx's emphasis (e.g. Brenner, 1977; Laclau, 1977; Banaji, 1977) and stretched the history of capitalism back too far. The debate proved complex. Brenner, who had earlier insisted on dating the origin of capitalism to the capitalist organization of English agriculture, later questioned this (2001). Heller traced earlier 'experiments in capitalism' in Italy, Germany and France, where capitalist production emerged but its further development was 'arrested or limited' because capitalist states could not be consolidated, in Italy because the power of merchant capital was too strong, and in Germany and France because the feudal classes prevailed (2011: 52). However, as a form of HST, the problems with WS lie elsewhere.

Two problems are particularly important, one conceptual, the other empirical. Conceptually, while an indifference to the nature of the activity through which it was accumulated certainly defined capital – Arrighi privileged the purer 'pecuniary' rationality of British over the merely 'technological' rationality of German capitalism (1994: 267–9) – a fundamental ambiguity remained. If that was so, why were hegemonies' expansive phases productive and declining ones financial? Why did material expansion have to resume after the decline of any hegemony? Why couldn't financial expansion continue indefinitely? WS assumed these things happened but never explained them, for to do so would have involved stressing the centrality of production to capitalism against the theorists' commercial or financial understanding of it. Empirically, though WS analysis emerged precisely to explain 'the reality of world political developments after the Second World War – US hegemony, the growing role of transnational corporations, the creation of a "socialist bloc", the Sino–Soviet split, and the emergence of a "Third World" collective presence in the political arena' (Wallerstein, 1991: 591), the US case, the primary referent, remained embarrassingly anomalous. By their own account, in its decline it seemed to be absorbing capital at an appreciable rate, rather than exporting it as their model of successive hegemonies required.

Arrighi also introduced another US anomaly. He had once portrayed the United States as more powerful in the twentieth century world than the United Kingdom was at the high noon of its empire in the nineteenth (1978: 148), suggesting that the logic of successive hegemonies was getting stronger. But by 1994, he was ruminating about the anomalous possibility that, unlike previous hegemonic powers, the United States might be able to stave off economic and hegemonic decline indefinitely by deploying its military might to overcome its economic weakness and establish a 'truly global world empire' (Arrighi, 1994: 355). And by 2005, he was arguing not only that the United States was attempting to do just that, but that the project of forming 'a US-centred world government' to bring to an end the dynamism of the world capitalist system had been 'integral to US hegemony from the start' (Arrighi, 2005b: 83–4). The aim reached a peak in

> the new imperialism of the Project for a New American Century [whose failure] probably marks the inglorious end of the sixty-year long struggle of the United States to become the organizing centre of a world state. The struggle changed the world but even in its most triumphant moments, the US never succeeded in its endeavour.
>
> (Arrighi, 2005b: 115)

The United States, it now turned out, had never been engaged in hegemony, but in a project of world dominance of a rather different sort. What did this imply for the entire edifice theorizing capitalism as a succession of hegemonies, when it had been erected to explain and theorize the now illusory US 'hegemony'? What did it imply, indeed, for the WS conception of capitalism itself, as characterized not by world empires but hegemonies? Arrighi did not say.

FROM DECLINISM TO RENEWALISM

HST emerged amid the multiplying difficulties of the United States's and the dollar's world roles – *inter alia* the diminution of the United States's economic weight in the world economy, withdrawal from Vietnam, US–Soviet detente and Sino–US normalization, and the United States's need to share power with the European Community/European Union and Japan in a 'trilateral' exercise of power in world governance – and the mood of decline they engendered. One writer now pronounced the United States an 'ordinary power': the *Pax Americana* was a thing of the past and the United States was now 'only first among equals'. It could not take up special responsibilities on behalf of the world, whether military or economic (Rosecrance, 1976: 11). In *After Hegemony* (1984), the institutionalist Robert Keohane used the idea of US hegemonic decline as the basis of an appreciation of the possibilities of cooperation in the international system: it had been apparent even under US hegemony but would become more so as it waned. But it was Paul Kennedy's *Rise and Fall of Great Powers* (1987) – the work of a historian, not an IPE scholar – that most focused debate. His diagnosis of the US condition was 'imperial overstretch': 'decision-makers in Washington must face the awkward and enduring fact that the sum total of the United States' global interests and obligations is nowadays far larger than the country's power to defend them all simultaneously' (1987: 665–6). Published when the US deficit was burgeoning under Reagan, Kennedy's arguments became the target of the renewalism that emerged at the time.

Renewalism rode on US and Western triumphalism at the fall of the Berlin Wall and claims that the Reagan presidency had revitalized the United States economically although as we shall see in the next chapter, the condition of the US economy remained dire. So renewalism never revised HST's declinist verdict systematically. What it did was to revise and redefine the very idea of hegemony to fit the still implausible, indeed worsening, US case by using even more qualified notions of power than HST, like 'soft power' (Nye, 1990) and 'structural power' (Strange, 1987).

Strange deemed the usual indicators of hegemony 'either irrelevant (monetary reserves, trade as a proportion of GNP) or imprecise (share of world trade, share of world GNP, production of raw materials or manufactures)'. Instead she claimed that hegemony was about 'control over outcomes [which] can only be inferred from historical evidence, a more difficult task' (1987: 554). The indicators of hegemony no longer had to include liberal institutions of world economic governance: unlike the United Kingdom's world role in the nineteenth century, a liberal world economy could be neither the goal nor the outcome of the US-centred world economy (1987: 563). US power, moreover, was not 'relational power' – 'the power of A to get B to do something it would not do otherwise' – but 'structural power', 'the power to choose and shape the structures of the global political economy within which other states, their political institutions and (not least) their professional people have to operate' (1987: 564). It resided in the interrelated structures of security, production, finance and credit, and knowledge, and US power was unequalled 'across all four structures' (1987: 571). While it had in recent times used structural power 'in ways that are destructive of international order and cooperation', creating 'world economic instability and continuing crisis', rectification was still up to the United States: 'A necessary condition, therefore, for greater stability and cooperation lies within the United States, rather than in the institutions and mechanisms of international cooperation' (1987: 554). For Strange, the loss of US hegemony was a myth.

Writing in *Foreign Affairs*, Samuel Huntington creatively suggested that declinist writers' chief function was 'preventing what they are predicting' (1988: 96). While the most recent decline scare was 'triggered by budget and trade deficits and the seeming competitive and financial threat from Japan' (1988: 95), there had been others; in '1957 and 1958 as a result of Soviet missile launches and the Sputnik'; in the late 1960s when 'President Nixon and his national security adviser ... announc[ed] the end of the bipolar world ... [with] ... a "pentagon of power" ... coming into existence'; in 1973 when oil prices rose dramatically; and later, with the '[t]he U.S. defeat in Vietnam, Watergate, the expansion of Soviet power in Angola, Mozambique, Yemen, Ethiopia, Nicaragua and eventually Afghanistan and the continued development of Soviet nuclear forces that rendered U.S. strategic forces increasingly vulnerable' (1988: 94–5). Such scares overlooked contrary evidence. US trade and budget deficits might be problems, as was US consumerism, but they were being rectified. If there was a relative decline of the United States, it had already happened in the late 1960s, and since then the United States's relative share of world production had stabilized at about 23 per cent of the world economy.

According to Huntington, declinists overlooked three important things. First, US strength was 'peculiarly multidimensional', encompassing 'population size and education, natural resources, economic development, social cohesion, political stability, military strength, ideological appeal, diplomatic alliances, technological achievement'. There was, second, the United States's 'structural position in world politics', geographically distant from areas of world conflict and historically untainted by imperialism, its attractively anti-statist philosophy, its involvement in 'a historically uniquely diversified network of alliances' and in having a sense, stronger in the past than more recently, of 'identification with universal international institutions' (1988: 91). Finally, there was 'no alternative hegemonic power, with one possible exception, that seem[ed] likely to emerge in the coming century' (1988: 91). The exception was, for Huntington as for so many others at the time, Japan.

If Huntington argued that declinism averted what it predicted, Joseph Nye feared that it could be a self-fulfilling prophecy, leading to 'the very weakening of American power [it is] supposed to avert. Withdrawal from international commitments might reduce American influence overseas without necessarily strengthening the domestic economy' (1990: 4). US power was not declining: it was being misrecognized. Nye distinguished between 'command power' which rested on carrots and sticks, and 'indirect' or 'co-optive' power:

> Parents of teenagers know that if they have structured their children's beliefs and preferences, their power will be greater and will last longer than if they had relied only on active control. Similarly, political leaders and philosophers have long understood the power that comes from setting the agenda and determining the framework of a debate. The ability to establish preferences tends to be associated with intangible power resources such as culture, ideology and institutions. This dimension can be thought of as soft power.
>
> (Nye, 1990: 31–2)

Nye's reduction of hegemony to the management of juveniles was probably the pinnacle of renewalist sophistry. No wonder many remained immune to its charms. If the 'renewalist side ... was given a particular fillip by the Persian Gulf conflict of 1990–1991', if 'the conflict tended to create a mood of optimism in the United States, confirming for many the correctness of ... renewalists', if it led Nye to claim that 'the action over Iraq has shown' that 'where America leads, others follow – this year, next year and for the following generation.' Cooper, Higgott and Nossal (1991: 391–2) argued that the actual record of the number of countries who were willing to follow the US lead in the war demonstrated that 'the United States had far fewer genuine followers in the Gulf conflict than conventional wisdom would have it'. The Bush administration's military approach was 'not a vision that made enough sense to friends and allies that they were prompted to join the United States wholeheartedly in a military venture' (1991: 408).

The debate between declinism and renewalism was hard to resolve. Huntington complained that declinism did not have 'testable propositions involving independent and dependent variables', only

> an impressionistic picture of economic decline, mixing refer-
> ences to economic trends and performance (economic growth,
> productivity), educational data (test scores, length of school
> year), fiscal matters (deficits), science and technology (Research
> and Development expenditures, output of engineers), interna-
> tional trade and capital flows, savings and investment and other
> matters.
>
> (Huntington, 1988: 77)

How this counted in favour of the renewalists who relied on vague notions like 'structural power', 'multidimensional power' and 'soft power' is anyone's guess.

Renewalism triumphed only as the twentieth century ended. By this time it was more a mood than even the pretence at theory it had been in the 1980s, and it focused more or less exclusively on growth rates. Robert Keohane, who had so far stuck to his view that US hegemony had declined, now revised his position. Although:

> economic growth has been much faster in China, India and
> other rapidly developing countries than in the United States,
> both of America's then rivals, Europe and Japan, have grown
> more slowly. By the turn of the millennium, the United States
> had achieved a preponderance of military capabilities that was
> unrivalled in modern history, and had extended its economic
> advantage over other advanced industrialized states.
>
> (Keohane, 2005: x)

However, writing on the eve of the 2008 financial crisis, Benjamin Cohen was far less circumspect:

Indeed, during the final years of the twentieth century America's lead seemed, if anything, to be widening again, reinforced by the collapse of the Soviet empire, which left the United States as the world's last remaining superpower. Over the course of the 1990s, the U.S. economy enjoyed its longest peacetime expansion in history, avoiding the high unemployment that plagued continental Europe, the stagnation that dragged down Japan after the bursting of its bubble economy, and the financial crisis that devastated emerging markets from East Asia to Latin America. At the dawn of the new millennium, America's economic primacy was once again unquestioned. Now more than one source was predicting more of the same, perhaps even a 'Second American Century'. ... If no longer Gulliver among the Lilliputians, the United States had clearly reclaimed its position as number one. The ageing hegemon had gained a new lease on life.

(Cohen, 2008: 77)

This mood ensured that the series of discourses – not only globalization and later empire but also their component strands, from new economy to the global savings glut – that attempted to justify, rationalize and naturalize the widening imbalances and the financializations on which the US growth record, and the dollar's value, now rested would be all the more credible. They are discussed in the chapters that follow.

COSMOPOLITAN MARXISM

So firmly had neoclassical economics' cosmopolitan conception of capitalism lodged itself among the majority of Marxists – with Marxist economists accepting it and Marxist non-economists taking their word for it – that it constituted the ground from which the work that inaugurated recent Marxist IR criticized the centrality of the state in realist IR (Rosenberg, 1994). Justin Rosenberg remained susceptible to an all too neat separation of the political and the economic in capitalism, which simply defied the historical reality of states' central and increasing economic roles in capitalist societies, not to mention its centrality in the writings of Marx and Engels. Benno Teschke's 'dynamic account of the co-development of capitalism, the modern state and the modern states-system' (2003: 40) recognized states' economic roles in countering capitalist development elsewhere by devising 'counterstrategies of reproduction to defend their position in an international environment which put them at an economic and coercive disadvantage' (2003: 265). However, such counter-strategies, effectively contender development, while important for capitalist modernization, had no significance for mature capitalism. Teschke's discussion steered clear of UCD and would allow a geopolitical economy of capitalist modernization but not one of capitalism. Nor did it have a place for communist combined development and its historic role in the geopolitical economy of the twentieth century. (For fuller critiques of both these writers, see Desai, 2010c.)

Kees van der Pijl's studies of the pivotal transatlantic relationship and its tensions in world affairs (1984) became the basis of a novel and historically rich conception of capitalism's geopolitical economy. At its heart lay a contrast – akin to Gerschenkron's distinction between early and late development, and more recent contrasts between 'Anglo-Saxon' and other capitalisms (e.g. Dore, 2000) – between capitalism's 'Lockean heartland' and a succession of 'contender states' which challenged its supremacy. The Lockean heartland was 'a networked social and geo-economic structure comprising a number of (originally English-speaking) states and a regulatory infrastructure which supervised 'a wider space organised on a shared principle of the sovereignty of property and contract, and hence, of capital' (van der Pijl, 2006a: 13). By contrast, 'contender states' constituted rival apparatuses of 'wealth creation within their separate jurisdictions, at best harnessing the resources of satellites' (2006a: 13) which could hothouse capitalist development. There was a 'structural incompatibility' between their territorial bases and the 'nomadic' (Palan, 2003) predilections of heartland capital. When contender states matched the development of the heartland, their ruling classes desired integration into it. However, the processes it involved endangered their political power, producing a dialectical tension.

There are two main problems with van der Pijl's account. The 'Lockean heartland' constitutes an essentially economistic and cosmopolitan conception of capitalism which cannot be sustained because, as we have seen, development in the United States and the United Kingdom was essentially no different from that of the contender states. If the two have come to be dominated by 'nomadic' finance (rather than Hilferding's finance capital), this was, in the UK case, the product of the United Kingdom's particular class configuration, and in the US case, rooted in its desire to emulate the United Kingdom's world role. Second, though van der Pijl claimed not to presume eventual integration of the contenders into the heartland, pointing to resistance by the European Union and China (Van der Pijl 2006a: 14), the notion of a Lockean heartland that is structurally superior requires it. It must remain uncontained and be superior to contender forms. The heartland's 'double strategy' – 'first, trying to dominate, penetrate and integrate peripheral societies; and second, waging *wars of dispossession* against entrenched state classes' (2006a: 14) – must ultimately triumph. If the geopolitical economy of this book is correct, the final hour of the Lockean heartland, which had rested in recent decades only on a series of unstable financializations, was struck by the 2008 financial crisis.

Alex Callinicos recently returned to the classical theories of imperialism for insights into

> the real asymmetries of power between the United States and the other leading capitalist states [and the] significant conflicts of interest that exist among them (and indeed other states such as Russia and China) that are likely, in the context of the continuing 'long downturn', to give rise to geopolitical struggles.
>
> (Callinicos, 2007: 536)

He began with a question Ellen Wood posed: why 'the political form of global capitalism is not a global state but a global system of multiple territorial states' (Wood, 2006: 26, quoted in Callinicos 2009: 78). Callinicos sought an answer in Lenin's *Imperialism* and more generally in UCD, which would explain geopolitical competition in terms of capitalism's increasing unevenness in the age of 'finance capital'. However, Callinicos conceived UCD in more or less exclusively economic terms: 'the dynamic process of capitalist development [which] continually alters the distribution of these disparities and thereby shifts the balance of power among states' (2009: 65). Though UCD may not be 'the *sole* force sustaining the system of territorial states' – 'the formation of collective, mainly national identities' was another – it remained 'the source of a powerful centrifugal drive that helps keep states multiple' (2009: 92). In this conception, not only were nation-states reduced to the status of exclusively cultural entities, rather than also being economic agents, unevenness was emphasized at the expense of combined development.

Callinicos's conception derives from a particular interpretation of Marx's understanding of competition. It is true that Marx described the introduction of cost-reducing innovation by a 'first mover' who initially enjoyed extra profits. However, as we saw in Chapter 2, in Marx's view, this situation is *necessarily* temporary, lasting only until competition generalizes the new technology across the sector (Marx, 1894: 373–4). So by this analogy, while unevenness can be produced, it would also be undermined by combined development. But Callinicos focused on the possibility that the first mover would accumulate advantage. The innovative firm

> *may* use the additional profit it has already made to make further productivity-enhancing investment that once again put it ahead of the game, so it gains more technological rents that both compensate it for any fall in the average rate of profit and provide it with the resources to continue the same pattern. The result may be a self-reinforcing process that gives rise to privileged concentrations of high-productivity capital.
>
> (Callinicos, 2009: 89, emphasis added)

Though such competition contained possibilities for both 'equalization and differentiation', Callinicos nowhere discussed the former possibility and its geopolitco-economic equivalent, combined development, let alone the state's role in imperialism. Indeed, he failed to specify agency: firms are the agents in capitalist competition, but states as nationally organized blocs of capitalism rate little more mention than a discussion of some apparently randomly selected instances of national competitive advantage and disadvantage in the final chapter. Although he also referred to different kinds of economic activities and their differential returns (2009: 90), states play no role in determining their international distribution.

Worse, detached from their role in creating and managing capitalist economies, nation-states emerge in Callinicos's account as creatures of realist international relations. While he considered it important to set 'the strategies, calculations and interactions of state managers in the context of the crisis tendencies and class conflicts constitutive of capitalism at any stage in its development' (2007: 542–3) and while this would certainly have come closer to the sort of geopolitical economy we need, in fact the two remain quite separate. His discussions of the 'classical imperialism' of 1879–1914, 'superpower imperialism' of 1945–91 and post-cold-war imperialism are largely economistic, while in his discussion of states' actions he considers it necessary to 'take into account the strategies, calculations and interactions of rival political elites in the state system' and believes that there is 'necessarily, a realist moment in any Marxist analysis of international relations and conjunctures'

(2007: 542). This comes uncomfortably close to what Rosenberg rightly dismissed as accounts of 'the diplomatic interchange between pre-constituted states' (1994: 135).

BRENNER'S GEOPOLITICAL ECONOMY OF POSTWAR CAPITALISM

Chapter 2 outlined the chief ideas we need to conceptualize the geopolitical economy of capitalism up to the early twentieth century. What we now need are corresponding ideas that can help reconstruct that of postwar capitalism. For this we must go beyond accounts of postwar capitalism that take no account of states' economic roles. This includes most Marxist economics but also other Marxist writing focusing on economic trends alone or, like Callinicos, rightly intuiting the need for a geopolitical economy but failing to take account of the relation between capitalist economies and their states through a sufficiently systematic account of capitalist crisis and class struggles.

There are some other Marxist accounts of postwar capitalism, including its growth slowdown since circa 1970, which do give states a role, but they focus on the domestic political economy of particular countries or on the common elements in a number of them. The regulation school, for example, attributed the golden age to the massive productivity increases that came with the Fordist organization of production, and its end to its inability to yield further productivity increases (Lipietz, 1992). Others attributed the end to increased labour militancy eroding profits (Glyn, 2006). What is needed, in addition to a proper political economy that theorizes states' roles in terms of capitalist crises and class struggles, is an account of the drivers of international competition and UCD. Robert Brenner's historical account (1998, 2003, 2006, 2009) of the 'long boom' and the 'long downturn' comes closest to fulfilling the requirements of such a geopolitical economy of postwar capitalism. The gaps it leaves – it remains innocent, for instance, of US motives in emulating UK world dominance by maintaining the dollar's world role, and treats the United States as simply one among the main competing economies, and an unfortunate one at that – are filled from other sources, not least the ERPs, in this book.

Brenner treats world capitalism as a system of competing national capitalisms to explain its 'global turbulence' since the mid-1960s. He takes the key elements of the political economy of the biggest postwar national capitalisms – their productive dynamics, states' roles in managing their contradictions, and the resulting modification of their dynamics – to compose the geopolitical economy of their mutual competition and the resulting redistributions of productive and political power between them. For instance, the 'long downturn' is conceived as being caused by the overcapacity and overproduction that came to characterize world capitalism with the recovery, through what this book calls combined development, of Western Europe and Japan, and then prolonged by the unwillingness of governments to force 'what Marx called a "slaughtering of capital values"' (Brenner, 1998: 157) on their own economies.

Brenner's account has elicited criticism for taking the triad of the United States, Germany and Japan as a stand-in for world capitalism (*Historical Materialism*, 1999). However, his focus is on the main sources of tension and dynamism within the system. The newly industrializing countries (NICs) and emerging economies enter the dynamic at historical moments when they become significant. He has also been criticized for focusing on manufacturing alone (Arrighi, 2003), but that is as good a proxy for value production as it is possible to get within existing national income accounts data, and Brenner displays a keener sense of the sources of value than do his critics (Desai and Freeman, 2011). Moreover, his accounts of the stock market and housing bubbles (Brenner, 2002, 2009) rate among the most comprehensive and reliable, not least for taking into account the critical role of government policy in both.

There are two key crisis mechanisms at the core of Brenner's account which explain the actions of firms, states and other relevant actors: the paucity of demand and the tendency of the rate of profit to fall (TRPF). It is true that he provides no theoretical discussion of the first and declares in favour of Marxist economics' dismissal of the second (Brenner, 1998: 12n). However, not only is the reliance on Marxist economics' theoretical dismissal of the TRPF quite incidental to Brenner's essentially historical argument, ironically he re-establishes the TRPF in his historical account: falling profits are central to his account of the long downturn. Moreover he links them to the paucity of demand. In Brenner's account falling profits are traced to

> the tendency of producers to develop the productive forces and increase economic productiveness by means of the installation of increasingly cheap and effective methods of production, without regard for existing investments and their requirements for realization, with the result that *aggregate profitability is squeezed by reduced prices* in the face of downwardly inflexible costs.
>
> (Brenner, 1998: 23–4, emphasis added)

In these circumstances, competition – investment to increase productivity, cost-cutting and later price-cutting to expand market share – leaves 'the cost-cutters' rate of profit … the same as before [while] … the higher cost firms' rates of profit are reduced'. The result is 'an aggregate reduction in the rate of profit in the line'. Such overcapacity and overproduction are premised on paucity of demand: they can be said to exist

> in the sense that – *there is insufficient demand* to allow the higher cost forms to maintain their former rates of profit; they have been obliged to cease using some of their means of production and can make use of the rest only by lowering their price and thus their profitability.
>
> (Brenner, 1998: 25–6, emphasis added)

Moreover, 'the slowed growth of demand that is the unavoidable expression of the reduced growth of investment and of wages that inevitably result from falling profit rates makes it increasingly difficult to reallocate to new lines' (1998: 33). Though Brenner focuses on the overcapacity and overproduction in the system as a whole, he also shows that the United States suffered from it most acutely. As we have seen in the last chapter, with the narrowing of the policy toolkit to macro-economic policy supplemented by military Keynesianism, US industry suffered from 'phantom' industrial capacity and lost competitiveness to a much greater extent than rival capitalist economies.

Brenner's account also permits us to see that the historical specificity of postwar capitalism's geopolitical economy in comparison with the period before 1914 lay in how the insufficiency of demand was handled. Whereas, as we saw in Chapter 2, before 1914 it was resolved chiefly through imperialism, in the postwar period expansion of domestic demand played a greater role: favourable demand conditions created by Keynesian welfare states 'must have helped endow these economies with greater stability than in the past' (1998: 91), something which, as we saw in the last chapter, US economic managers were also mindful of. In postwar capitalism, competition for colonies was replaced by competition among industrial countries for new as well as each others' markets. This competition also had its peculiar geopolitical economy.

Since domestic demand expanded in all major capitalist states, it did not explain why the long boom's growth was concentrated in the recovering economies while the United States stagnated in the

1950s and enjoyed only a brief and highly inflationary boom in the 1960s.

> Where the autonomous growth of demand did operate power-fully to augment investment and growth, it appears to have done so, paradoxically, less within national boundaries than across them. German and Japanese manufacturers derived much of their dynamism by means of appropriating large segments of the fast-growing world market from the United States and the United Kingdom. This redistribution of market share ... gave a powerful boost to their investment and output, while detracting somewhat from the growth prospects of the United States and the United Kingdom. The resulting pattern of development was extremely uneven, but it made for a boom of historic proportions.
>
> (Brenner, 1998: 91)

Not surprisingly, precisely the two economies that followed more liberal policies – the United States in pursuit of its imperial ambitions and the United Kingdom, thanks to the dominance of financial interests in the British state – lost market shares.

While Brenner does not refer to UCD – whether the US imperial enterprise or the specificities of European, Japanese or any other form of combined development – his account carefully describes the main forms of postwar international competition, including the competitive refusal of governments to permit the requisite 'slaughter of capital values' in their own economies, which resulted in the progressive weakening of the productive dynamic of capitalism across the system. What the account in this book demonstrates in addition is that international competition had this effect in substantial part as a result of the US imperial enterprise which, by not permitting more aggressive forms of protection in the United States, laid US industry open to such erosion.

We have seen that US exports began to decline in the late 1950s and the first trade deficits emerged a decade later. By then, competition began to affect profitability by 'forcing down prices of goods in relation to their costs' throughout the capitalist world, and:

> [t]he same processes of cost- and price-cutting that enabled some to improve their shares of world trade could undermine the ability of others, not only to attract investment funds, but to realize their investments at their former rates of return,

threatening profitability not only in particular economies but in the advanced capitalist world as a whole.

(Brenner, 1998: 92)

This problem was compounded further by the entrance of new competitors through combined development of the NICs in the absence of major new sources of demand growth.

While the rising cost of raw materials in the 1960s, a result of rising third world commodity prices, affected US firms' profitability, so did 'the inability of output prices to keep up with the growth of capital stock prices' (Brenner, 1998: 136), because of the increased German and Japanese shares of the world market.

> Their competitors found themselves facing lowered prices for their output with the same production costs as before. Some had to withdraw. Others, to hold on to their markets, had little choice but to accept significantly reduced profit shares, output–capital ratios, and profit rates since they could not raise prices above costs as much as they had previously. ... Overcapacity and overproduction leading to falling aggregate profitability was the result.

(Brenner, 1998: 93)

If the long downturn was caused by 'the failure of the decline in profitability, precipitated by the over-capacity and over-production that resulted from the intensification of international competition from around 1965 to set off the standard processes of adjustment' (Brenner, 1998: 147), it persisted because 'the *further* strategies individual capitalists found it best to adopt to restore their own profits, like the initial ones, continued to bring about an insufficiency of exit and too much entry, exacerbating the initial problem of manufacturing over-capacity and over-production' (1998: 147). Such 'insufficient exit' was caused by firms' 'intangible assets' (1998: 147) and by 'barriers against their entering new lines'. Critically, however, it happened because '[w]ith the growth of profits – and thus of investment and wages – suppressed, *aggregate demand grew more slowly*' (1998: 148, emphasis added).

Governments too were implicated in the problem of insufficiency of exit and too much entry. Among major industrial countries, only the UK Thatcher government permitted a historic 25 per cent contraction in the country's manufacturing sector. The US and other governments, which, by the 1990s also included the UK government, pursued 'Keynesian' policies, increasing both public and private debt, thus fuelling what we know as financialization, to 'cut recessions short' (Brenner, 1998: 151). Western European and Japanese governments, however, also intervened more directly to support productivity and competitiveness while the US and UK governments relied more heavily on private debt expansion. Over the long downturn, after each recession, unemployment remained higher and growth rates lower than after the previous ones.

> Had it not been for the *unprecedented expansion of both public and private debt in response to these recessions*, the world economy could not easily have avoided a depression. Yet the same expansion of credit which ensured a modicum of stability also held back recovery. For, by cutting recessions short – and more generally making possible the survival of those high-cost, low-profit firms which perpetuated over-capacity and over-production, and prevented the average rate of profit from recovering – the subsidy to demand through Keynesian debt creation prolonged the downturn. *Keynesianism made the downturn both milder and longer.*
>
> (Brenner, 1998: 150–1, emphasis added)

If the governments of the advanced industrial world contributed to the problem of insufficient exit, those of the NICs and later the emerging economies, which directed their domestic capitalist (and in the case of China, communist) development and entered the world market for manufactures, contributed to 'too much entry'.

In the neoliberal decades, demand management to ease recessions in the United States took the perverse forms of tax cuts, expansions in government spending (Reagan's renewed military Keynesianism) and later credit-fuelled consumption based on rising asset values in the stock market and housing bubbles of the 1990s and 2000s (credit Keynesianism). Of course, this fiscal and credit stimulus in the United States also furnished demand for competitors and contenders. This series of credit expansions to stimulate growth had to extend ever farther down the social scale, eventually reaching the hapless 'sub-prime' borrowers. This laid the basis of the now infamous 'sub-prime' crisis a few years later. This was the central irony of neoliberalism: the deflation and restriction of consumption demand it imposed on the world economy as a whole forced it into perverse forms of demand expansion which soon came up against their own limitations, most spectacularly in the present crisis.

However, in the 1970s neoliberalism and its successors, globalization and empire, were still some way off. Faced with overproduction and overcapacity, national governments and manufacturers of the industrial world, including critically the United States, where manufacturing interests would remain politically powerful at least until the 1990s, first strove to fend off their worst consequences, if necessary through open mercantilism. That this included the United States betrayed the depth of the crisis of the US imperial project, whose *sine qua non* was a liberal world economy. This is where the next chapter begins.

6

RENEWAL?

The sternest critics of US imperialism regard the closing of the gold window with a certain grudging admiration. The result – variously labelled the 'Dollar Wall Street regime' (Gowan, 1991a) or the US Treasury bill standard (Hudson, 1972) – they believe, left the United States 'still overwhelmingly dominant' and no longer 'constrained by rules' such as the gold–dollar peg. After 1971 dollar dominance became a 'fact which regularly reproduce[d] itself' (Gowan, 1999a: 30, 33, 36). The United States could adopt something like a policy of 'benign neglect' toward the dollar's value because private actors had confidence in it and irate foreign governments and central bankers faced three equally unacceptable options: maintain existing parities and accept US debt depreciation and inflation; allow further dollar depreciation and reduce their competitiveness; or accumulate paper dollar reserves and finance US debt indefinitely. This was 'hegemony on the cheap' (Calleo, 1982: 119). The international financial intermediation hypothesis (IFIH) wager was won. The United States had insouciantly made itself the world's banker.

However, Nixon and his Treasury secretary Connally – a lawyer who admitted he 'knew nothing about finance' (Gowa, 1983: 156) – were anything but insouciant about breaking the dollar–gold link, though the possibility had been canvassed for some time and had come to seem inevitable over the previous two years. Instead, they carefully delayed it until it appeared the only course open to the United States for fear that 'governments of major foreign countries would be less cooperative after a suspension "unprovoked" by an exchange crisis' (1983: 80, quoting a Federal Reserve Board report). Nor did US policy makers subscribe to the IFIH when they closed the gold window. They believed themselves to be addressing the roots of the dollar's troubles – the United States's loss of competitiveness and the burden of overseas expenses, themselves results of attempts to realize imperial ambitions. The Nixon Administration complained that 'Western Europe and Japan were exploiting the United States, penetrating American markets with underpriced exports while simultaneously restricting entry to their domestic markets', and that 'the postwar international monetary system constrained the United States from altering its exchange rates in a way that it constrained no other country' (1983: 156). This was especially egregious because, imperial ambitions notwithstanding, the US economy had remained quite domestically focused: a traded goods sector of 9 per cent of GDP simply did not justify the imposition of deflation, as opposed to devaluation (1983: 65).

Nixon and his wily secretary of state, Henry Kissinger, as well as later administrations, remained committed, however, to some form of US dominance despite diminished strength at home and increased resistance abroad, and they attempted to pursue it. Vainly, as it turned out. Over the next decades, dollar dominance remained far from a 'fact which regularly reproduce[d] itself'. It was not even a case of a series of 'blundering gambles' that somehow managed to contrive such reproduction (Gowan, 1999a: 39). Rather, as this chapter's discussion of developments between 1971 and the US 'victory' in the cold war makes clear, nothing could be farther from an accurate description of the fate of the dollar. The dollar's world role, now unconstrained by its link to gold but also unsupported by it, remained dependent on the fate of the US national economy, whose loss of competitiveness would never be rectified as long as the United States pursued its imperial ambitions and forsook industrial policy. So the dollar lurched from crisis to crisis, each solved by a new equally, if not more, unstable and short-lived financial stratagem.

Over these decades, US allies were increasingly called on to share the burdens of the US world role. If this was 'hegemony on the cheap', it was not because the United States managed to pay little for it, but because of the diminished resources with which it now had to attempt it. Either cooperation from the West Europeans and Japanese was not forthcoming, as in the 1970s, or as with Japanese financing of US deficits in the 1980s, it exacted a price: access to US markets and the further erosion of US manufacturing. The US determination to continue its imperial pursuit would falter at least once, under Carter. So by the end of the period reviewed in this chapter, with the US economy having suffered two more decades of neglect, the closing of the gold window still seemed to former Fed chairman Paul Volcker 'a defeat':

> The inflationary pressures that helped bring down the system ... plagued the country for a decade or more. The monetary system

has not been put back together in a way that really seems to satisfy anyone. And somehow we are still complaining about military, aid and trade burdens.

(Volcker and Gyohten, 1992: 80)

NIXON'S INSOUCIANCE?

The closing of the gold window, which effected immediate dollar devaluation, was part of a mercantilist new economic policy (NEP) which also included wage, price and rent freezes, import surcharges and tax cuts to stimulate the economy (ERP, 1972: 3). It sought to 'raise exports relative to imports' while avoiding 'either... depressing the American economy or imposing controls on foreign trade' except temporarily and to pressure other powers to liberalize trade (1972: 28). In the face of competition, 'US manufacturers, strongly supported by the state, had launched a sustained counter-attack' to achieve dollar devaluation and keep US workers' wage gains below those of competing countries while their productivity increased' (Brenner, 1998: 158).

Benign neglect?

Free market economists celebrated US monetary policy's new freedom after August 1971 and predicted that efficient currency markets would now value the dollar accurately. The Nixon Administration was less confident. Almost immediately after August 15, 1971, it was in negotiations with the Europeans over new exchange rate parities and a more 'symmetrical' international monetary system, with the latter negotiations being formalized in the Committee of 20 in July 1972. The Europeans had originally proposed devaluing the dollar against gold, and after August 1971 they opposed floating in favour of a benchmark that was an 'objective one, or at least a multinational one which did not bear the stamp of any single country' (ERP, 1972: 160), reviving elements of Keynes's bancor.

Round one appeared to have gone to the United States as the December 18 Smithsonian Agreement resulted in an effective dollar devaluation 'favorable to the US competitive position' (1972: 29). The United States also wanted short and long-term trade liberalization, and sought to entice the Europeans into it by agreeing to propose a $38.00/oz price of gold to Congress when 'a related set of short-term trade measures is available for congressional scrutiny' (1972: 142). With devaluation achieved, the Federal Reserve loosening money supply, and temporary wage and price controls being lifted, the Nixon Administration expected the trade deficit to close and US firms to reap the benefits of increased investment abroad.

However, it found that the US payments deficit was not amenable to rectification by devaluation. Too high a proportion of US expenditures abroad – such as on defence or oil – were price inelastic. Dollar depreciation only inflated their value. Second, in the new openly mercantilist world, European governments were chafing under the compulsion to support the dollar to prevent excessive appreciation of their own currencies. The Committee of 20 negotiations for 'redesigning the international monetary system on a new and more symmetrical basis' (Williamson, 1977: xi) were already blighted by Nixon's mercantilist insistence that they be part of a 'single package' along with trade and military relations (ERP, 1973: 7). So the Europeans made a radical move, announcing the creation of the 'Snake', a joint floating of European currencies, in March 1973. European central banks also announced that 'they would no longer purchase unwanted dollars. This terminated the system of quasi-automatic European central bank credit to the U.S. Treasury' (Hudson, 1977/2005: 60).

By summer, with the Europeans dumping the dollar (ERP, 1974: 186), it sank to depths the United States considered intolerable. Not only did private holders' confidence fail to compensate, they proved fickle and speculated against the dollar. On July 18 the United States, having accused the Europeans of 'dirty floating' because they intervened in foreign exchange markets after August 15, was forced into intervention itself. It had to negotiate with European authorities to arrange bilateral currency swaps so that speculation could be discouraged by 'the possibility that the U.S. authorities would buy as many dollars (or sell as many foreign currencies) as would be necessary to prevent a further decline' (1974: 186). When initial efforts failed, additional bilateral swap facilities of $6.25 billion had to be announced, bringing to $18 billion the resources that could be mobilized for the operation, though in the end only $250 million was required to bring the dollar up 4 per cent (1974: 187). This intervention was not the end of matters, however.

The unaffordable luxury of the cold war

Nixon had already de-escalated the war in Vietnam, made history by visiting China in 1971, and initiated détente and the first Strategic Arms Limitation Treaty (SALT I) with the USSR, swapping anti-communism for pragmatism as the principle of US foreign policy. These moves also had an economic counterpart: trade with the communist bloc.

The Europeans had long maintained commerce with the Eastern bloc and, as monetary and trade tensions with the United States grew, West Germany initiated its *Ostpolitik* in the mid-1960s in pursuit of a conception of an 'independent European growth pole in the Atlantic economy' (van der Pijl, 2006a: 228). And as downward pressure on the dollar continued, anti-communism became a luxury the United States could ill afford. Now, amid food price inflation, the United States deployed its 'agri-power' to conclude, in mercantile fashion, a three-year $750 million grain export deal with the USSR. While this helped to close the US trade deficit in 1973 (ERP, 1974: 189–91), the United States had also hoped that the USSR would pay for the grain in gold. But it got borrowed Eurodollars instead – 'precisely those surplus dollars with which the United States had flooded Europe and Japan for so many years', making the historic deal 'equivalent to domestic sales' (Hudson, 1977/2005: 71). In a further reversal of cold war relations, the grain deal with the USSR was accompanied by embargoes on exports of agricultural commodities to Europe even as exports to the USSR exacerbated food price inflation. Western Europe and Japan could no longer rely on US agricultural supply, adding further impetus to wider autarkic tendencies.

Third world assertion

The fracturing of the world economy as a result of overcapacity and overproduction now extended beyond the advanced industrial world as the world economy entered a new phase in the 1970s. Hitherto 'the combination of gold, private investment and military power enabled industrial lead nations to dominate the world economy', while too many of the others 'pursued relatively laissez-faire policies and could not or did not assert their own economic interests' (Hudson, 1977/2005: 236). Now, however, old landed and commercial elites, with vested interests in colonial (read 'liberal') patterns of trade and production, and in support of the United States and ex-imperial powers who had long made development less than a success, were being pushed aside by socialist and/or protectionist regimes. Even the more repressive among these worked 'to broaden their economic base' simply because not doing so threatened 'the tenure of any regime unable to pull its nation out of rural poverty, no matter how great its domestic repression or foreign support' (1977: 243).

'Statism and intergovernmental planning ... spread to all nations', reducing the power of the formerly imperial rich countries (1977: 236). Assertive developing country governments attempted to keep the gains of trade at home, and decreased the value of international investment by wielding the threat of nationalization. The political assertion of these governments on the world stage would soon lead to demands for a new international economic order (NIEO).

If this were not enough, Vietnam was beginning to show that military force was no longer as effective as it once seemed. In this context,

> American policy-makers face a highly complex problem: how to maintain both the unity of the world capitalist market and the supremacy of the declining US economy. Maintenance of supremacy through mercantilist methods tends to undermine the unity of the world market; respect for free trade assures mainte-nance of that unity, but at the price of a loss of economic influence for US capitalism that could eventually become ruinous and lead to the extirpation of the most obvious advantages the Americans draw from the present order: supremacy of the dollar, control of international monetary and financial mechanisms, and so on.
>
> (Parboni, 1981: 23)

US imperial ambition had never faced less propitious circumstances.

Opening the black gold window

The dollar would have resumed its decline after the effects of the market intervention in 1973 wore off but for the quadrupling of oil prices by OPEC a few months later. Oil-importing countries now had four times as many reasons to hold dollars and, since the oil trade remained denominated in dollars and oil prices remained well above their pre-1973 levels, the sizeable oil trade has remained an important prop for the dollar's world role since.

The immediate impact on the US dollar was, however, even more robust. After the oil price rise, OPEC countries agreed with the United States to hold oil surpluses in US dollars and Eurodollar deposits, and international capital flows sustained the first and, until the mid-1990s, the highest and most substantial of the increases that would characterize the decades of US- and dollar-centred financialization. OPEC petrodollars arrived in US and European banks which, given the sluggish demand for capital in the advanced industrial world with the onset of the long downturn, resorted to lending them (to earn the interest they would have to pay the depositors) in official or officially guaranteed loans to developing and Eastern European countries. These flows dwarfed Marshall Aid flows even in real terms (Hopenhayn and Vanoli, 2006) and set off a spurt of debt-led industrialization which promised to eat further into the US weight in the world economy.

So dramatically did these events turn the dollar's fortunes around, and so hard did they strike against its oil-importing rivals, that some argued that the US government had engineered them (Oppenheim, 1976) 'to exercise what George Kennan called "veto" power over military and industrial developments in Japan and Germany' (Kanburi and Mansur, 1994: 317). However, the oil price hike itself was probably simply prompted by the declining dollar. Certainly the Yom Kippur War had complicated political alignments, marking a deep rift between the United States and European countries, which blocked US supply lines to Israel and sought to come to terms with OPEC while the United States was profoundly isolated from the Arab countries.

The agreement with OPEC countries thereafter to deposit oil surpluses earned from the United States's oil-dependent rivals into American banks (Kanburi and Mansur, 1994: 317) was, however, another matter. While Kissinger's Machiavellian diplomacy was probably involved, more decisively, the United States scuttled alternative plans for holding oil surpluses. A proposed IMF 'oil facility' was kept deliberately small (Kanburi and Mansur, 1994; Hudson, 1977: 100); European plans to provide OPEC countries with inflation-protected bonds in payment for oil were sidelined; and the prospect of OPEC countries buying productive assets in advanced countries met with hostility (Hudson, 1977: 108–20).

The Nixon Administration lifted recently imposed capital controls – the Interest Equalization Tax, restrictions on US foreign direct investment (FDI) abroad, and limitations on foreign lending by US financial institutions to facilitate the new financial arrangements with OPEC (ERP, 1974: 200). Substantial sums were involved, with total oil revenues of the region between 1973 and 1988 estimated at $2.5 trillion, and the surplus (exports minus imports and private capital transfers) at $354 billion in 1981 (Kanburi and Mansur, 1994: 318). It is also important to note, given the tendency to point to the size of the Eurodollar market as a mark of private confidence in the dollar along the lines of the IFIH, that before petrodollars, the Eurodollar market was valued at $110.8 billion in 1971 and reached $147.5 billion in 1972, whereas petrodollars swelled it to $215.7 billion (ERP, 1975: 215) the following year.

These developments also scuppered the Committee of 20 negotiations. Although smaller and trade-dependent European countries, now buffeted by the oil shock, needed an agreement even more, the United States needed it even less. In contrast to innocuous explanations in terms of diffuse benefits and concentrated costs (Hirsch, 1973), John Williamson's history of the C-20 deliberations was more revealing. Though averse to criticizing the United States, he noted 'the financial advantage to the United States of an inconvertible dollar standard' (Williamson, 1977: 172), and conceded that the United States definitely exhibited 'a certain ambivalence as regards her anxiety to see an agreed reform achieved'. This was not, Williamson argued, the same as saying that 'reform was unattainable because of a tenacious US defence of a vested financial interest' (1977: 172), but many would not have split so fine a hair. After the agreement with OPEC, 'the United States believed that she could live without discomfort without a reform' (1977: 176). Not only did OPEC oil surpluses deposited in US and European banks provide support for the dollar internationally, so did the expectation that 'a major share of the additional OPEC revenues would eventually be reinvested in the United States'. This 'prompted a strong movement of short-term funds into the dollar and out of the major European currencies and the yen', leading them to fall 20 per cent from their 1973 peaks and prompting their central bankers to intervene to support them (ERP, 1975: 203).

When the recession of 1974 wiped out even the trade surplus caused by the depreciating dollar in 1973, the Nixon Administration declared the resulting payments deficits inconsequential. This was not because private investors' confidence had replaced foreign governments' and central bankers' truculence in determining the dollar's value, as the IFIH expected. The two most important indicators of the US payments positions before 1971 had been the official reserve transactions balance, which went negative when foreign central banks accumulated dollars, typically through currency interventions, and the broader liquidity balance, which went negative when public and private holdings abroad increased. However, after 1971 they no longer put pressure on the dollar because foreign central banks were no longer required to intervene in currency markets to maintain their currencies at a certain value and were no longer obliged to accept dollars from private holders. And petrodollars added a new element: 'a large negative shift in the U.S. official reserve transactions balance can now result on account of the preference of the oil-exporting countries for placing their funds in the United States' (ERP, 1975: 212). Just as the dollars European governments were forced to hold before 1971 signified a higher European 'liquidity preference' in the IFIH, eliminating alternatives for recycling petro-dollars now became the 'preference of the oil-exporting countries for placing their funds in the United States'. The irony was that central banks and governments were not replaced by private holders in supporting the dollar but by a new set of official sources abroad. The days of this comfortable arrangement were, however, numbered.

Before going on, we should note that while the dollar was supported internationally, the increase in dollar liquidity proved problematic for economic governance domestically. The Federal Reserve was already finding it harder to control money supply in the early 1970s because its assumption that small changes in interest rates would suffice to regulate money supply no longer obtained. Competition in retail banking had increased as non-bank institutions began to offer bank-like services (Calleo, 1982: 145; Shull, 2005: 129–32; various ERPs from 1975 onwards). Demand for credit had already become inelastic to interest rates and 'supply determined' (Wojnilower, 1980: 277) because of increased competition between credit suppliers. This became even sharper with the influx of petrodollars. Domestic and foreign borrowing took quantum leaps between 1973 and 1975 (ERP, 1975: 70–1). Floating rate loans and financial futures were developed to reduce risk to banks, which often lent at rates lower than their deposit rates. As we shall see, these developments would increase inflation in the short run and prompt the deregulation that would feed into later bouts of financialization in the long run.

CARTER'S COOPERATION

By the end of 1974, the dollar had returned to its March 1973, post-Snake, value because European oil import restrictions and conservation measures reduced the petrodollar surpluses. Gerald Ford took office after Nixon's ignominious exit in August 1974 and began to deal with the 'severe recession' (ERP, 1975: 3) with a combination of historically unprecedented tax reductions and continuing social expenditures. The recovery beginning in the third quarter of 1975 relied, however, on an employers' offensive, reducing real wage growth amid high unemployment, the low dollar increasing US exports and easy credit from banks. Indeed, easy credit briefly transformed US industrial finance. Hitherto debt had played a small role in it and interest payments were only 1 per cent of profits between 1950 and 1965. They jumped to '11 per cent between 1965 and 1973, as profitability fell sharply' and the reduction in interest rates between 1973 and 1979 increased them to 15 per cent (Brenner, 1998: 160).

The pressure such fiscal and monetary expansionism put on the dollar now had to be dealt with by coordinating economic policies with other countries, and the first G-6 (soon to become G-7, including Canada) summit took place in Rambouillet in November 1975. It opened the most cooperative phase in US economic policy making. The Ford Administration recognized that '[i]f domestic policy objectives are to be achieved efficiently in an interdependent world, economic changes and policy goals in other countries must be given explicit consideration, precisely because they affect the path of any national economy, *even the largest*' (ERP, 1976: 137, emphasis added). But, while necessary, such coordination was far from sufficient. Despite Ford's efforts to create 'a growth-oriented business climate' (ERP, 1977: 110), and 'despite the fact that replacement needs have been cumulating for some years and a general recognition that a return to sustained full-employment levels in most countries presupposes a shift of resources toward investment' (1977: 109), private investment demand failed to revive, and not just in the United States.

When revenues did not increase sufficiently to offset the tax cuts and increased social expenditures, the Ford government responded by limiting tax cuts and expenditures, interrupting the recovery in the middle of 1976. Jimmy Carter took office, blaming Ford for failing to cope with the 'dilemma [of] … how to deal with continued inflationary pressure without diminishing private investment incentives' (ERP, 1977: 119), and pursued expansion more one-sidedly by reducing taxes and increasing expenditures. Growth resumed, but combined with the difficulties the Federal Reserve was having in controlling money supply, it was highly inflationary. The G-7 summits had already dented any assumption of unchallenged US dominance, and this US growth pattern became the contentious issue at them.

Although Carter maintained certain imperial pretences – 'As the strongest economy in the world, the United States has unique responsibilities to improve the international economic climate' (ERP, 1978: 6) – he did attempt 'with serious conviction to solve the problem of the American economy in a cooperative spirit' (Parboni, 1986: 9) at G-7 summits. He proposed to restore '[g]eneral world equilibrium ... not by dragging everyone down to Europe's recession [due in part to its greater fiscal and monetary conservatism], but by having everyone join the United States in expansion' (Calleo, 1982: 126). This was a promising vision. For, in addition to its cooperative attitude, which included deepening détente, the administration took the view that '[t]he main impetus [for growth] must clearly come from internal demand' (ERP, 1976: 134) while also looking to 'a world-wide extension of Keynesian demand-management principles, such as the Brandt Commission proposals to eliminate the bottleneck that the low purchasing-power of developing countries presented within the world economy' (Parboni, 1986: 9). By identifying the demand bottleneck both domestically and in the developing world, this vision contained a far more productive and expansionary future for the world economy than the one it would suffer from the 1980s onwards as countries competed for limited market shares amid the lengthening long downturn.

The weakening US economy was already handicapping Carter's own ability to realize that future. His administration's expansionism generated stronger pressures on the dollar because of a new problem:

> Throughout the postwar period the growth of U.S. imports tended to be greater in relation to domestic growth than the growth of exports in relation to growth abroad. Until 1975 a rough balance between import and export growth was maintained by the fact that growth abroad tended to exceed U.S. growth. From 1975 through 1978, however, growth in the United States surpassed the average growth abroad. As a result, the current account of the United States shifted sharply. In 1977, a year in which U.S. economic growth exceeded that of its trading partners by about 1½ percentage points, the U.S. current account shifted by almost $20 billion, from a surplus of $4.3 billion to a deficit of $15.3 billion.
>
> (ERP, 1979: 146)

The tendency of the US economy to increase its trade and current account deficits with growth was already well established, and now it was being exacerbated by differentials in growth rates between the United States and other major capitalist economies. US governments of the 1980s onwards, rather than rectifying this situation, would simply exercise the United States's 'seigniorage' privilege of giving in to it. The US economy would either grow by expanding trade and current account deficits, or it would not grow. However, these privileges were precisely the sore point, and maintaining them would only get harder and more complicated.

Viewing the dollar's consequent slide as 'excessively rapid and disorderly' (ERP, 1978: 22, 155), Carter initially attempted to curb it through a National Energy Act, trade promotion and fiscal and monetary retrenchment (ERP, 1979: 155). When this did not work and brought pressure from the G-7 for deflationary adjustment, Carter resisted, justifying US deficits by seeing them as 'an acceptable position for the United States and, given the continuing OPEC surplus, even a desirable one from a global standpoint' (ERP, 1978: 107).

But he would not be allowed to do so for long. The Bonn Summit of 1978 marked a 'turning point'. The Carter Administration had to promise to make curbing inflation 'the top priority of economic policy' and pledge drastic action to reduce the trade deficit, particularly a reduction in oil imports (ERP, 1979: 142), in return for a dollar support package comprising $30 billion and a joint intervention programme with Germany, Japan and Switzerland. It also included 'a little publicized decision to replenish US international reserves by issuing $6 billion of Treasury bonds denominated in German marks, Swiss francs and Japanese yen', essentially an admission that 'to run the international monetary system the dollar was not enough: it had to be flanked by other currencies' (Parboni, 1986: 9).

More trouble was in the offing: by the time the November 1978 support package had its effect, interest rates began to tighten around the world and OPEC announced a doubling of the oil price. Unlike the previous oil price hike, which had proved such a bonanza for the dollar, this one only added to US inflation because the OPEC countries were now spending most of their surpluses. International pressure to do something about the depreciating dollar mounted. Until the beginning of 1979 the Carter Administration could still take the view that the problem was more fundamental – the failure of productivity to rise (ERP, 1979: 6) – and attempt to deal with that rather than resort to the 'unfair' option of trying to 'wring inflation out of our economic system by pursuing policies designed to bring about a recession' (1979: 7). However, soon it would soon have no other choice.

Deepening malaise

Economic options were not the only ones that were narrowing. Although postwar US militarism was bipartisan, hitherto the

Republicans, epitomized by Eisenhower, had been more cautious. Defeat in the Vietnam War changed this pattern in the 1970s. The Nixon presidency represented a 'power shift' (Schrag, 1975, citing Kirkpatrick Sale) to 'the "cowboys" of the Southern tier'. Nixon sought to work within US power's increasingly apparent limits, both economic and military, by pursuing détente and deescalating in Vietnam on the advice of his 'realist' wise man, Henry Kissinger. Democratic Eastern Establishment militarism, meanwhile, was 'simply unprepared for more limited national possibilities':

> Its influence ... always depended on the apparent success of its management which, in turn depended on the growth and confidence of the country.... Once this ... was seriously challenged (in Vietnam, in the emergence of the Third World, and through a variety of forces, natural, cultural and political), the Establishment's confidence began to go.
>
> (Schrag, 1975: 58)

New voices deemed the cold war too expensive, military force an 'inept' instrument of foreign policy, the 'balance of terror' with the USSR impossible, and the USSR a status quo power. They complained that the cold war's 'endless hot wars ...in the third world made the US very unpopular there' (Gershman, 1980: 16–18). They urged equanimity 'towards changes in the world which previously would have been considered injurious to American security'; 'benign neglect ... towards international military involvements'; active assistance to 'forces of change which we had opposed during the period of containment'; an end to assistance to repressive regimes; acceptance of the cultural relativism of human rights; and sympathy for global trends toward equality (1980: 18). George Kennan himself was one of these voices, arguing that the best course for the United States was to 'follow a policy of minding its own business to the extent that it can' (quoted in Gershman, 1980: 16).

By the late 1970s restoring 'some semblance of legitimacy and authority under a wholly new and more limited set of conditions' had become urgent. No US politician had hitherto 'been able to talk about those things'; no language was available which was 'not founded on premises of growth and expansion' (Schrag, 1975: 58). In a break with Democratic militarism, Carter had accepted the new Nixon–Ford–Kissinger foreign policy reorientation and, amidst the second oil shock triggered by the Iranian revolution, he attempted to bring Americans to terms with their declining economic situation.

In July 1979, after meeting at Camp David with 'business and labor, teachers and preachers, governors, mayors, and private citizens', Carter gave a televised speech in which he urged Americans to live within their means, give up their 'mistaken idea of freedom, the right to grasp for ourselves some advantage over others' (quoted in Bacevich, 2008: 34), and particularly to reduce their consumption of oil.

Shock therapy

Volcker's interest rate shock was part of this diminution of US power. Having suffered the US export of inflation, Germany and Japan were understandably wary of Carter's hopeful economic expansionism and preferred to combat inflation and press the United States to reciprocate. Moreover, the very different responses of oil importers and exporters to the second oil shock tipped the balance decisively toward inflation control. As oil-importing countries reacted with monetary restraint rather than laxity, and as rising OPEC imports diminished the flow of petrodollars, oil importers now had to pay 'the "OPEC oil tax" largely in current goods and services rather than IOUs' (ERP, 1979: 146). The reduction in trade imbalances also added the pressure on the US dollar, which since 1971 had relied on them for its value and world role. As 1979 unfolded, 'genuine panic' threatened. Gold shot up and the dollar nose-dived as European and Arab holders dumped it, raising fears of 'catastrophic liquidation of the dollar's role as reserve currency, and even of a general stampede away from paper money'. In the face of this 'European–Arab revolt against further dollar depreciation' (Calleo, 1982: 146–7), the Carter Administration appointed Volcker as Fed chairman in the summer of 1979. Only his inflation-busting reputation would pacify markets and other governments. Two other developments also contributed to the steep increase in interest rates that followed.

First, US multinational and financial capital, reliant on the dollar's world role, 'joined the ranks of opponents of US "fiscal irrespon-sibility"' (Brenner, 1998: 180). Postwar US governments had long protected multinational and financial sector interests, for instance by compensating them for restrictions on capital movements in the late 1960s 'by neglecting to regulate the Eurodollar market'. And since the 1970s financial capital had benefited from recycling oil surpluses and the elimination of capital controls that this necessitated. US manufacturing interests, meanwhile, had been able to rely on expan-sionary fiscal and monetary policy. Now, however, the two interests were opposed, and manufacturing capital was the weaker of the two: 'with profitability failing to recover and wages stagnating in the face of rising inflation, enthusiasm for traditional demand-side policies was waning, while the political clout of its most fervent advocates, namely the labour movement, was rapidly evaporating' (1998: 180–1). Second, demand management alone was incapable of delivering non-inflationary expansion or reviving manufacturing competitiveness, and was probably becoming unbearable for capital itself as dollars were losing their value. Indeed, the whole direction financialization had taken since the recycling of OPEC oil surpluses in dollars began had to be reversed in the new circumstances. It had resulted in virtually free capital being lent to developing and communist countries, financing their industrialization and combined development and supporting their international assertion.

> With liquidity apparently capable of infinite expansion, countries deemed credit-worthy no longer had any external check on foreign spending. Several countries, in fact, while running large current-account deficits, nevertheless greatly increased their official monetary reserves by borrowing from the Eurodollar market. Under such circumstances, a balance-of-payments deficit no longer provided, in itself, an automatic check to domestic inflation. Countries in deficit could borrow indefinitely from the magic liquidity machine.
>
> (Calleo, 1982: 138)

Rampant liquidity expansion increased competition between lender banks and tilted the balance of power in favour of borrowers. The developing world's share of world manufacturing went from 7.6 per cent in 1970 to 10.2 per cent in 1980, and that of the socialist countries from 21.3 per cent to 26.6 per cent, while that of the developed world declined correspondingly from 71.1 per cent to 63.2 per cent. It was now time to tilt the balance back to favour lenders.

When it came, the Volcker shock represented 'a major shift in [the Fed's] technique for implementing monetary policy' (ERP, 1980: 54). Whereas before the 1970s small changes in the Federal funds rate had produced desired changes in the money supply, they no longer seemed to do so. The problem lay neither in Fed chairman Arthur Burns's competence nor in Keynesianism, as some alleged, but was caused by structural changes in banking. Credit had already become supply driven before petrodollar flows and increased competition for borrowers amid the long downturn expanded credit. 'Monetary restraint now works more through changes in interest rates that influence a borrower's willingness to incur debt, and less through changes in a borrower's ability to obtain credit' (1980: 31). So there was little the Fed could do, in the short run at least (that is, outside increased financial regulation), to control inflation other than to 'supply [only] the volume of bank reserves consistent with desired rates of monetary growth' and permit interest rates to vary [that is, rise] as necessary with those monetary growth rates' (1980: 54). The result were the legendary double-digit interest rates which did, however, wring inflation out of the economy and dramatically reverse the dollar's downward plunge, especially by drastically increasing developing countries' repayments, as the low and even negative real interest rates of the mid-1970s turned massively positive.

REAGAN'S RESTORATION?

The November 1980 election took place after the Soviets entered Afghanistan and the hostage crisis in Iran began. Ronald Reagan exploited both events to the hilt and, connecting them with Carter's malaise speech, dismissed him as a declinist. Carter's later U-turn on that message made him look even weaker. The new neoliberal president promised to reverse 'the debilitating trends of the past' through a 'fundamental reorientation of the role of the Federal Government in our economy' and to create 'more jobs, more opportunity, and more freedom for all Americans', leading 'to recovery in 1982 and sustained, noninflationary growth' thereafter (ERP, 1982: 3). His 'supply-side economics' prescribed tax cuts, deregulation, wage cuts and restrictions on trade union power to increase competitiveness. The argument was brutally simple: 'Slow growth in productivity only hampers a country's international competitiveness if it is not offset by correspondingly slow growth in real wages' (ERP, 1983: 53). The erosion of US workers' historically higher living standards in the face of international competition had already begun in the late 1950s and speeded up in the 1960s. It was about to accelerate even more: real wages and salaries excluding benefits fell at 1 per cent annually between 1979 and 1990. 'At no time previously in the twentieth century had real wage growth been anywhere near so low for anywhere near so long' (Brenner, 1998: 191–2).

Reagan's programme is remembered for its ideology, for bringing down communism and reviving the US economy, world power and the dollar's world role. In reality, its ideology was never applied consistently, communism in Europe collapsed for internal reasons, and Reagan's economic policy, the last serious effort to restore US industrial supremacy through a combination of an assault on labour, deregulation and a new, military, form of developmental state, failed. That failure made US 'victory' in the cold war a pyrrhic one and put its world role into doubt. However, it did sustain a new bout of financialization. It was qualitatively different from that of the 1970s and formed a prelude to those under globalization and empire.

Reagan's capitalist coalition

Reagan radically changed party political alignments, winning Southern Democrats permanently to the Republicans and north-eastern 'Reagan Democrats' to him personally. Though an economic shift from the north-eastern 'rust-belt' to the south-western 'sun-belt' occurred, the Reagan coalition united both elements, which explains much of his administration's 'pragmatism'. The 'protectionist' faction based in 'old industries long tied to the GOP [Republican Party], like textiles or steel' looked to Reagan for 'political and economic Alka-Seltzer: Relief from imports, from labor, from hated government regulators, and, perhaps, from endlessly menacing Communists'. The 'multinational' faction was more ambitious, funding think-tanks and policy research in a larger effort to reunite the world under US leadership, economic, political and military (Ferguson, 1995: 244–5) and supporting large military investments so that 'the three great economic areas (the Pacific Basin, the Americas and Western Europe) would develop into a single multinational market' (1995: 245). This capitalist coalition was still substantially industrial, not financial. Indeed, financial capital then represented by investment houses liked neither Reagan's deficits nor his administration's free market enthusiasm for repealing the Glass–Steagall Act, from which they were bound to lose to depository commercial banks which could bring their much greater financial muscle to financial markets (1995: 292, 258).

Anti-communism or controlling oil?

The revival of militarism under Reagan is generally regarded as anti-communist in its aims and credited with the demise of communism. The reality is otherwise. During the 1970s, as the Democratic Party seemed to capitulate to declinism consonant with the civil rights, youth, feminist and working-class critique of 'classical liberalism', cold warriors influenced by the political theorist Leo Strauss (Heilbrunn, 2008) and Zionist liberals opposed to the emerging left critique of Israel and support for the Palestinian cause struck out on their own. By the 1980s they had gravitated to the Republicans in a new intellectual formation, neoconservatism (Gershman, 1980).

As part of his recantation of his malaise speech after the Soviets entered Afghanistan, Carter had enunciated the Carter doctrine: that the United States would use military force to defend its interests in the Persian Gulf region. It set US foreign policy on a new direction, and neoconservative influence over the Republicans, and from the 1990s onwards over the Democrats too, ensured that successive presidents would now equate access to oil, not anti-communism, with the sacrosanct 'American way of life', and seek to 'to assert explicit military preponderance' over the Middle East (Bacevich, 2009: 51). Not only was US security policy no longer focused on communism, though the neoconservatives were not averse to claiming credit when communism collapsed, neither Reagan's 'Star Wars' against the 'evil empire', which was really an industrial policy, nor his support for the mujahedeen in Afghanistan caused the Soviet collapse. It was a 'revolution from above' conducted by a leadership no longer confident of, or identified with, communism's purpose (Kotz, 1997).

As Reagan cut taxes and increased military expenditures, making private and military profligacy the touchstones of good economic and military policy respectively, he capped them with 'two decidedly radical propositions' in his 1983 Star Wars speech: that 'Americans could be truly safe only if the United States enjoyed something akin to permanent global military supremacy' and that 'military power offered an antidote to the uncertainties and anxieties of living in a world not run entirely in accordance to American preferences' (Bacevich, 2009: 41). For all that, the Reagan Administration was not 'the Camelot of the Conservatives' (Mann, 2004: 112 ff). Reagan became enthusiastic about arms reduction in his second term under international pressure to reduce US budget deficits, much to the neoconservatives' dismay (Heilbrunn, 2008: 163–4). Worse, the anti-communist crusade boomeranged badly when Reagan forced supporters of the Nicaraguan contras to go underground and then abandoned them to their fate when the 'Iran-Contra' affair was uncovered. These anti-communists faced public scrutiny and humiliation alone.

Recharged military Keynesianism and military Schumpeterianism

Upon assuming office, Reagan revived military Keynesianism, which defeat in Vietnam had interrupted, and became 'the greatest Keynesian in history' (Brenner, 1998: 190). This fiscal expansionism was followed by monetary easing beginning in mid-1982 when Volcker capitulated to manufacturers' opposition to high interest rates citing a mysterious decline in money's velocity – the largest since the Fed began keeping data in 1959 (ERP, 1983: 21) – which had nipped recovery in the bud and a now required 'somewhat greater growth in the monetary aggregates than initially intended' (1983: 21–2).

Thanks to the tendency of the US economy to suck in imports as it grew, Reagan's stimulus began to widen the US trade deficit, bailing out 'not just the US, but also the Japanese and German, economies from the recession of 1979–82' in a new geopolitical economy. It would keep 'the whole system turning over during the 1980s' (Brenner, 1998: 151) but could not 'restart dynamic capital accumulation' because 'over-capacity and over-production ... continued to be a heavily zero-sum struggle for oversupplied manufacturing markets'. Manufacturing profitability could not recover in the G-7 as a whole: the United States's main rivals could not improve profitability 'except at the expense of the United States and vice versa' (1998: 183). This last point was critical. The main centres of capitalist accumulation could grow only at each other's expense because, by interrupting the rise in the developing world's share of the world economy, and therefore its capacity to consume, the Volcker shock had strangled the potentially most buoyant source of demand in the world.

The new pattern of expanding trade deficits made the United States the world's demand 'locomotive', systematically consuming more than it produced and paying for the difference in dollars whose value, when high, rested on unstable bases and, when low, put the future of the dollar's world role in doubt. Import penetration reached new heights as US corporations outsourced production and imports came to include high-technology products. Military Keynesianism had long been accompanied by the practice of channelling research and development (R&D) subsidies to industry in what we might call military Schumpeterianism. It now grew to unprecedented levels as 'the last hope for [US] ruling groups to recover world industrial leadership, and to bring the reluctant European partners back into the US orbit by subordinating them on the military, industrial and commercial planes' (Parboni, 1986: 13).

Governments across the industrial world began to adopt policies to help national firms graduate to higher-technology and higher-value goods, as competition from low-cost manufacturers of lower-value goods intensified in the 1960s (Freeman, 1974). In the United States too, although developmental and industrial policy traditions had long ago been sacrificed to imperial ambition, the recession of 1979–82 increased debate about industrial policy. However, internationalist fractions opposed policies that could result in trade retaliation against the more competitive exports, including services, and a Brookings Institution study even claimed that there was no competitive threat (Lawrence, 1984), even though US exports had held up through the 1970 only because of devaluations. The counter-offensive was so effective that even Democratic candidate Walter Mondale, who raised the issue of competitiveness in the 1984 presidential elections, refused to countenance an active industrial policy with its practices of 'picking winners'.

Contrary to the view that this sealed the fate of US industrial policy (Graham, 1992), there was in fact a great expansion of the US developmental state in the decades that followed. However, given the imperial imperative of dissimulating all state promotion of industry, further reinforced by the Republicans' free market ideology, it was 'hidden':

> [l]ike the purloined letter, the hidden developmental state is hidden in plain view ... rendered invisible by the success of market fundamentalist ideology ... [because] there is simply no conceptual space for the idea that government plays a critical role in maintaining and expanding the private sector's dynamism.
>
> (Block, 2008: 15)

These initiatives

> created a decentralized system through which public agencies would, in fact, invest in potential winners. Some of these initiatives simply facilitated the privatization of publicly funded intellectual property, but others significantly expanded the government's role in directing technological change.
>
> (Block, 2008: 11)

In addition to Reagan's Star Wars programme – that is, the Strategic Defense Initiative – a further 'spectacular program of subsidies' was launched for defence-related production (Ferguson,

1995: 248), including initiatives in computing, semiconductors and biotechnology (Block, 2008: 181–2). Defense Department initiatives such as the Defense Advanced Research Projects Agency (DARPA), and NASA, and the National Institutes of Health critically shaped US high-technology industry. Like the famous Japanese Ministry of International Trade and Industry (MITI), these outfits worked by 'targeting and subsidizing specific technologies, forming industrial cartels, parcelling out research tasks to various companies, subsidizing movements down the "experience curve," and functioning as major purchasing agents' (Reich and Rohatyn, 1984: 6).

Military Schumpeterianism in the 1960s had put US spending on R&D at more than twice the combined total for Germany, France, the United Kingdom and Japan as a share of gross national product (GNP) (ERP, 1989: 226). It had dipped thereafter, but Reagan's massive increases in defence spending contributed a third of total spending on R&D, and brought US R&D spending to the same proportion of GNP as Japan and West Germany, though the civilian proportions in the latter countries remained, of course, higher (1989: 226, see particularly chart 6.4). These programmes importantly expanded the domestic market for certain industries, particularly aerospace, fabricated metals and electronics. 'Overall, the projected $1 trillion military expenditure for 1985–87 [was] expected to have an economic impact comparable to that of the Vietnam War at its height, claiming an equal proportion of national durable goods output (13%)' (Davis, 1986: 55). No major industrial giant was left untouched.

As in the 1950s, the substitution of defence for industrial policy was justified in terms of its 'spin-off' effects for US industry as a whole. It had its detractors then, and according to some at least, things had only gone downhill from there. Not only were there bottlenecks to commercial application resulting in even fewer spin-offs than before, the culture of military contracts with its 'sense of indifference to cost and quality' made these projects difficult to integrate with a firm's normal commercial operations (Reich and Rohatyn, 1984: 7).

Japan's dollars

Reagan's legendary twin deficits – fiscal and current account – had to be financed by capital inflows, and the dollar's international role was critical. Its opposite movements before and after the 1985 Plaza accord reveal the main contradictions of the Reagan programme. Before the accord, the dollar rose strongly despite the widening deficits. Though interest rates remained historically high even after they were eased in 1982, they were not the reason for the dollar's ascent as tight monetary policies elsewhere kept the interest rate differential with the United States minimal. Rather, the dollar rose due to capital inflows caused by 'fears about the financial, political and military stability of the world' (to which Reagan's industrial policy substitute, the second cold war, made the single largest contribution), left-wing governments in Europe which unsettled investors (Parboni, 1986: 10–11), and post-Volcker shock capital flows from the third world, which began as the IMF stepped in to resolve the third-world debt crisis in favour of US banks by imposing structural adjustment programmes (SAPs) on debtor nations, resulting in debt repayment at the new higher interest rates.

The combination of the strong dollar and widening deficits was the pivot of the geopolitical economy of the early 1980s and the Reagan Administration sought to normalize both. Market intervention to ease the dollar was ruled out: 'there is no conclusive evidence that official intervention in the past has achieved its purpose'. In any case, the rising dollar reflected 'economic fundamentals' (ERP, 1982: 172–3). The trade deficit had been the focus of previous administrations' concern, and the Reagan Administration, for its part, certainly hoped that the expenditure the deficits were financing would revive US industry. Growth could initially be expected to strengthen import demand, and 'the effects of this revitalization on U.S. exports will take more time'. So the deficits 'simply reflect[ed] the adjustment process at work' (1982: 179–80).

These generalities apart, however, the presence of old and declining sectors of US industry in the Reagan coalition made him the 'the most protectionist president in recent memory' (Reich and Rohatyn, 1984: 6), but without overt protectionism or devaluation which could justify retaliation. Calls for both were fended off by pointing to the 'temporary factors' – dollar appreciation, loss of third world markets and higher growth than in US trading partners – causing the trade deficit (1984: 43). Instead, a whole range of sectors – 'Automobiles, steel, specialty steel, textiles, apparel' – were protected through 'voluntary' restraints: 'Of course, there is nothing voluntary about these restrictions. We simply threaten exporting nations with far worse restrictions unless they agree' (1984: 6).

More generally, trade deficits were seen as nothing to worry about. For one thing, since 'global current account imbalances *must* add up to zero', if each country tried to achieve a trade surplus 'strong deflationary forces would be set in motion' (1984: 179–80). For another, the trade deficit was a 'narrow concept', covering only goods. The current account, which included trade in services and investment income, 'better indicate[d] the country's international payments position' (1984: 179). Never mind that it too was in deficit. The real question was 'how current account deficits are financed'. A country's international payments position should arouse concern only when a current account deficit was accompanied by 'a persistent depreciation of its currency in the exchange markets' (1984: 179), indicating difficulties in financing it. A 'current account deficit that is comfortably financed' by capital inflows was no cause for concern: 'If foreigners purchase more U.S. real and financial assets in the United States – land, buildings, equities, and bonds – then the United States can afford to import more goods and services from abroad' (1984: 181). (Of course, with US resistance to foreign acquisition of US real and productive assets, foreign holders were largely confined to holding dollar-denominated paper.)

US growth in these years contrasted sharply with the deflationary effects of high interest rates on other countries, and the administration claimed it 'would 'lead the world out of recession' (ERP, 1984: 42). So a critical question was how comfortable, in fact, was the financing of the deficits on which the fiscally stimulated Reagan recovery relied? The answer lies in the singular pattern of trade and financial flows of the early 1980s. For during these years, the Japanese effectively bought access to US markets by financing the US deficits on which the Reagan recovery relied. No wonder the administration made a special effort to normalize Japanese imports. The US trade deficit was, it claimed, the counterpart of OPEC surpluses in general and Japan's deficits on the oil account in particular: 'Japan, with few natural resources, incurs huge deficits in its trade in primary products, especially oil, ... [which it] ... makes up for ... by running surpluses in its trade with other regions'. So 'looking at Japanese–U.S. trade in isolation is misleading' (ERP, 1983: 56).

A 'debt-based subsidy to demand ... had been keeping the world economy turning over in the face of manufacturing over-capacity and over-production' since the 1970s (Brenner, 1998: 181). Now it was redirected, decisively and massively, away from the rest of the world, and towards the United States itself. That was the real meaning of the notion that the United States was the world's 'demand locomotive'. The United States now became the sinkhole for the world's capital and goods, and it would remain so, with the exception of an all-too-brief period under George Bush Sr. This phenomenon would finance successively the Reagan boom, the 'globalization' boom and finally, the considerably less than booming growth of the Bush Jr presidency. While the Japanese acquired privileged access to US markets by financing US deficits, the developing world was shut out. Its higher-value exports faced protection, so that the massive export drive it had to launch to pay off its inflated post-Volcker shock debt was confined to lower-value products.

Thanks to this sort of recovery, the hitherto positive US net asset position abroad was reversed in 1985 (ERP, 1989: 131) and arguments attempting to naturalize this – that this was all right because US assets abroad generated more income than foreign-owned assets (largely low-yielding US securities) in the United States – now began to appear. They would remain central to the discourses, which, over the next decades, attempted to quell doubts about the dollar's capacity to retain its world role.

The flagrant contradiction between Reagan's professed aim of reducing government spending, not least because it 'crowded out' private investment, and the fiscal deficit was also papered over. The administration admitted that reducing the budget deficit would 'lower real interest rates and thus allow the investment sector to share more fully in the recovery that is now taking place primarily in the government and consumer sectors', and that it would lower the dollar and help exports. However, there were also 'costs to reducing the budget deficit, whether by reducing government expenditure or by raising taxes' (ERP, 1984: 62), and in any case, the high dollar made up for the fiscal deficit. It kept inflation low, 'dampened the rise in the real interest rate' and 'reduced the degree of crowding out of investment' (1984: 56).

U-turn at the Plaza Hotel

When prominent US businesspeople and business associations, naturally backed by labour, campaigned for further protection, particularly against Japanese imports, and for dollar depreciation, the Reagan Administration 'flatly rejected' their petitions, while Fed chairman Paul Volcker 'told them that there was nothing they could do, without a change of fiscal policy or the Treasury's intervention policy, that would not jeopardize the goal of reducing inflation'. A more responsive Congress now proceeded on two tracks, threatening to legislate a requirement for market intervention to lower the dollar, and attacking the administration's trade policy. In effect, it held 'trade policy hostage ... to a change in the administration's international monetary policy' (Henning, 1994: 279–80). Reagan's capitulation on devaluation also marked an interesting turn: whereas hitherto devaluation was 'the therapy for the declining US economy', by the 1980s it had become 'a device to stop protectionism' (Parboni, 1986: 14), particularly against Japan.

The high dollar was part of the price for Japan's financing of the deficit, and devaluation would upset this arrangement. However, by 1985 US deficits had overshot the point where the dollar's ascent could still be considered sustainable, and Japan's interest in a high dollar was tempered. Earlier that year, central bankers sold $11 billion and in March the dollar peaked. Fears that it could crash catastrophically remained. Such a crash would lead to further recession-inducing hikes in interest rates. Many central bankers shared these worries, as did Volcker:

We have reached a rather uncertain equilibrium with a large budget deficit and a large current account deficit, both financed in large part by borrowing overseas. Two elements in the triad, the budget deficit and a large current account deficit, are not easily changed, but the third, the capital inflow, can shift very quickly if confidence in the dollar should diminish ... [because of] fear of the re-emergence of U.S. inflation or a shift in the preferences of fickle investors.

(Volcker in 1984, quoted in Volcker and Gyohten, 1992: 239)

And so the United States, the United Kingdom, France, Germany and Japan agreed at the Plaza Hotel in New York in November 1985 to coordinate a fall in the US dollar by assuring the market that 'if the dollar fell too quickly the central banks of the major countries would be ready to buy dollars' (Parboni, 1986: 12–13).

With the dollar headed down, the necessary price for this international cooperation was a US agreement to decrease government spending. It would wind down the fiscally stimulated US recovery while the other four countries committed themselves to expansionary policies to stimulate growth and demand for US and developing-country exports (ERP, 1986: 53).

By the end of 1985 the dollar had fallen by 25 per cent from its peak earlier in the year, and it fell by another 40 per cent a year later. Whereas Reagan's military Keynesianism and Schumpeterianism had failed to revive US industry and competitiveness, the declining dollar now stepped in, boosting exports, as it had done in the 1970s. By the end of 1986 'real gross national product (GNP) growth began to exceed domestic demand growth, as – for the first time in 7 years – the foreign trade sector contributed on a sustained basis to economic growth in the United States' (ERP, 1988: 23). Hitherto high growth in personal consumption, housing and government expenditures slowed while that in net exports, business fixed investment, and inventories, hitherto lagging, accelerated (1988: 24).

As dollar devaluation sharpened competition for market shares between major capitalist countries, the old pattern of European and Japanese central banks supporting the dollar, the United States talking it down and all agreeing to fix mutual currency values in accordance with 'economic fundamentals', reappeared, and was affirmed in the 1987 Louvre accord. Although the decline of the dollar would begin to narrow the US deficit, and a recession would even close it briefly in 1990, in 1987 it remained wide enough that, combined with the still high budget deficit, it put pressure on the dollar. The Fed, as part of the policy of managing a controlled decline, was forced to support it with higher interest rates. These triggered the 1987 stock market crash.

The crash and the put

The stock market ascent of the early 1980s was the first of the major postwar financial bubbles that would hit the US and world economies, and it represented a new political and geopolitical economy. Observers blamed the stock market crash of 1987 *inter alia* on the psychology of traders, technological changes and investors' herd behaviour. But the real question was why and how the bubble had formed in the first place. The answer lay in the form of the Reagan recovery and its interaction with the torrents of capital that flowed in. They would set the mould for the decades to come.

Though Reagan's budget deficits had powered the 'longest peacetime expansion in history', they had failed to revive US industry. Instead they produced a cyclical upturn and an 'explosion of "overconsumption" by the better-paid strata' (Grahl, 1988: 28). Growth was concentrated in services, with their low-wage and low-productivity jobs, and in the increasingly speculative financial sector. The rich enjoyed tax cuts four times larger than those of the Kennedy–Johnson years as a percentage of GDP (Davis, 1986: 47). The government's assault on labour and high unemployment, meanwhile, put pressure on wages. Such rising income inequality generated a new pattern of consumption, as old Fordist mass markets were replaced by post-Fordist niche markets. Working-class consumption now relied more and more on developing world imports expanded and cheapened by SAPs and the strong dollar. The middle and upper classes relied on a high-cost, high-technology market for higher-value, increasingly customized goods and services – whether designer clothing or luxury cars and homes.

US industry had failed to revive, and the capital inflows that financed the US twin deficits (the trade deficit had already reached a historically unprecedented 3 per cent in the early 1980s) crowded into the United States's expanded FIRE (finance, insurance and real estate) sector. Capital flowed in from Japan, of course, but also from elsewhere. In the early 1980s one European country after another had lifted capital controls, and financial deregulation was getting into its stride, particularly with the Thatcherite Big Bang in the City of London, which permitted all banks to participate in securities activity and establish offshore banking facilities. In the United States too, a certain limited deregulation had occurred on the initiative of investment banks and non-bank financial institutions – pension, mutual and trust funds – when they breached the spirit, if not the letter, of the Glass–Steagall separation of commercial and investment banking by entering the market for credit by 'issuing deposit-like instruments and offering bank-like services' (ERP, 1981: 108). This increased securities activity at the expense of ordinary bank loans, and corporate borrowers also increasingly bypassed banks to meet their needs for finance in the commercial paper market.

Although until Alan Greenspan became Fed chairman, government-initiated deregulation would remain confined to rearguard action to update Depression-era regulation for the age of high nominal (and now real) interest rates, a bias toward de- rather than re-regulation and rising competition in the sector was evident. For instance, in a 1980 Act, Congress removed all interest rate ceilings for term deposits and erased many distinctions between different types of depository institutions. Foreign banks began to move into US markets, increasing their share of US business loans from 4 per cent in 1972 to 9 per cent in 1979 (1981: 109). By the 1980s, with institutional investors increasingly mobilizing savings, not only did the difference between saving and speculation become moot, the size of the funds that were being moved increased volatility in financial markets and it was further magnified as large institutional investors took cues from one another, multiplying the speed and extent of any movement in financial markets. Their 'herd' behaviour lay at the root of the severity of the stock market crash in October 1987.

In a major reorientation of the US economy, not only did the FIRE sector grow, non-financial corporations became increasingly financialized. This development blurred the distinction between manufacturing firms and financial firms so that an independent manufacturing interest of the sort that successfully pressed for dollar devaluation in 1985 would soon cease to exist. While employment in the FIRE sector grew only marginally during the 1980s, its share of GDP would go from about 16 or 17 per cent in 1980 to 23 per cent in 2000 and even higher thereafter, and their share of profits, though more volatile, went from 15 per cent in 1980 to about 45 per cent in 2000 (Krippner, 2005: 178–9). A 'merger mania' now occurred, and financial conglomerates – 'diversified, super-holding-companies, dominated by speculative financial strategies (and abetted by new electronic technologies of centralized control)' – eclipsed the older Fordist and 'Slonian' vertically integrated mass-production corporation (Davis, 1986: 56). Now, with even established industrial giants disinclined to invest productively and finding themselves in greater need of liquidity, whether they were prey or predator in the merger mania, more and more non-financial firms began to invest in the financial sector themselves (Davis, 1986; Krippner, 2005).

The stock market bubble was inflated as an intrinsic part of this pattern of financial and financialized growth and the crash was not unforeseen (Rohatyn, 1987a, 1987b). Though the Reagan administration extolled the booming stock market as a 'thriving venture capital market [that] is financing a new American revolution of entrepreneurship and technological change' (ERP 1985: 5), private business investment growth was much lower than in previous decades (Brenner, 1998: 193).

After 1985, the coordinated decline in the dollar's value required the US government to support it through higher interest rates which were, widely and correctly we might add, expected to lead to recession (Evans, 1988). As the dollar continued to decline into 1987, the Fed tightened monetary policy again (ERP, 1988: 30) and triggered the decline in stock values that ended in the crash. While 'sheer panic' may have played a role once the sell-off began, it was a result of 'fundamental factors, such as rising interest rates, overvaluation of the market, and the large trade and budget deficits' (ERP, 1988: 40), which increased expectations of higher interest rates in the future (1988: 42).

When, contrary to widespread expectation, the crash did not lead to a recession, the administration attributed it to the gains having been very recently made (1988: 40, 42). Another popular explanation is that it was because Alan Greenspan, who had become Fed chairman just weeks before the October 19 crash, provided prompt liquidity. The 'Greenspan put' – lowering the Federal funds rate, effectively pumping liquidity back into the market so that its speculative career would resume – became a fixture in the succession of financial crises that followed, and constituted the keystone of the policy structure of moral hazard that would swell the size of financial markets from this point onwards. Whether it avoided a recession is doubtful, mainly because the stock market was unconnected with productive investment or employment growth.

After the crash, as after the series of financial crises to come, the issue of regulation arose. It was settled in favour of deregulation, as it would continue to be until 2008. In 1987, the overriding imperative was, as Ronald Reagan put it in his remarks on the 1988 Economic Report to Congress in January, to

> maintain the confidence of foreigners and our citizens alike in the ability of the United States to generate profitable investment opportunities and to follow responsible economic policies. The vitality of free and open markets, full of opportunity and promise, is the best foundation for investment.
>
> (ERP, 1988: 10)

Between 1985 and 1987, the stock market bubble had helped keep the dollar attractive on its way down so that US deficits would continue to be financed. After 1987, the Greenspan put pushed the dollar lower and soon necessitated even higher interest rates to prevent it from going lower still. Questions about the dollar's suitability as the world's money arose again, and accelerated European monetary integration.

Renewal?

If this record is anything to go by, the tenuousness of the case for renewalism, reviewed in the last chapter, should be clear. A number of points can be made. First, while powerful backers pushed in an imperial direction, Reagan did not set out to renew US world leadership. When he took office, his attention was concentrated on national economic problems and concerns about competitive decline (ERP, 1982: 3–10). He claimed to administer his free market medicine on the US economy – the 'most important contribution any country can make to world development is to pursue sound economic policies at home' (ERP, 1983: 167), based on a 'belief in the superiority of market solutions to economic problems and an emphasis on private economic activity as the engine of noninflationary growth' (1983: 167) – while actually administering military Keynesianism and Schumpeterianism, which was cut short by the Plaza accord. Only in his last ERP of January 1989, when the momentum of change in the USSR and the communist bloc generally left little doubt 'which of these systems will emerge triumphant' (ERP, 1989: 4) did Reagan lay claim to world leadership:

> When I took office 8 years ago there was widespread doubt concerning the ability and resolve of the United States to maintain its economic and political leadership of the Free World. Political events abroad seemed to demonstrate the impotence of American power, while economic events at home raised concerns about the vitality of our system.
>
> (ERP, 1989: 3)

And even while claiming credit for the impending collapse of communism, the Reagan Administration had to admit that '[t]he successful recovery of the war-torn economies and the entry of many newly industrializing and developing nations into the international arena have meant a revision in the role of the U.S. economy in the world' (1989: 105).

Reagan left neither the US economy nor the dollar's world role in a state justifying renewalism. Even on its way down, the dollar necessitated interest rate increases to hold up its value. Budget deficits were only driving it lower, as were the current account deficits, and unlike in the past, with interest rates already high, they could only be reversed by increases in growth and demand abroad so great as to overcome US competitive weakness, or by recession. Thus arguments that continuing 'U.S. current account deficits [were] financing a U.S. spending spree that [would] end in the painful curtailment of future consumption in order to service the debt' could not easily be denied, especially as 'relatively low U.S. savings and investment rates suggest that much of the inflow of foreign capital is instead being diverted to current consumption' (1989: 128).

Finally, the United States's new net debtor position meant that confidence about the US international position could only come from comparing the United States with developing countries. Unlike them, 'the ability of U.S. citizens and the U.S. Government to maintain their contractual obligations is not a concern'. The United States had 'the largest aggregate wealth in the world, and its creation of new wealth remains strong'. While some feared that 'its current financial position increases the temptation for U.S. policymakers to induce an inflation, reducing the real value to foreigners of their dollar-denominated claims' and others that it 'erodes U.S. leadership in the world economy', neither was *a necessary consequence* of a net debtor position' (ERP, 1989, 107, emphasis added). The incoming George Bush Sr. Administration could only hope that its policies of 'noninflationary growth' would somehow maintain the United States's and the dollar's world position. They would not.

THE DISPENSABLE NATION AT THE END OF HISTORY

The Reagan Administration offset the gloomy economic realities it had to outline in its last Economic Report with upbeat predictions of 3.2 and 3.3 per cent annual growth into the early 1990s (ERP, 1989: 284). Growth actually averaged 2 per cent for the years 1990–93, with a recession and 0 per cent growth in 1991. Bush was ideologically a Reagan clone, but was forced to pursue policies that reduced growth, like cutting the government deficit and increasing the savings rate, to prevent the dollar sliding further while hoping the lower dollar would boost exports.

The recession of 1990–91 was blamed on oil price increases following Iraq's invasion of Kuwait and the US-led Gulf War. However, though prices declined fairly quickly thereafter and the recession was short, recovery remained anaemic. The Bush Sr. Administration blamed this on the high interest rates necessary to support the dollar in early 1988. Though they were eased again in late 1989, reduced government expenditures and the 'lagged effects' of the tight monetary policy (ERP, 1990: 55), combined with the increased demand for capital elsewhere, particularly in Eastern Europe transitioning from communism, were blamed for slower growth worldwide. Anaemic and jobless though the recovery was, it widened the trade deficit, which the low dollar made it harder to finance.

Concerns about US productivity and competitiveness also surged as it became evident that over previous decades the United States had become 'an exporter of primary products, agricultural goods and basic commodities' and 'not only [were] manufactured consumer products imported but capital goods [were] as well' (Adams, 1992: 157). Though the economy was technically out of recession by 1991, experientially it did not seem so. This was despite the Fed cutting interest rates 22 times between 1989 and the end of 1991 (Woodward, 2000: 91) and despite the 'peace dividend' allowing reductions in the military budget. Indeed, the Bush Sr Administration clocked up the worst growth record of any postwar president, and '[f]or the first time since Carter arguments that the United States economy faced structural crisis and secular decline became plausible to the average man and woman in – sometimes literally – the street' (Ferguson, 1995: 282). So much for Reagan 'making America great again'.

The Bush Administration took one major policy initiative – financial deregulation – but it was stymied. We saw earlier how investment banks took advantage of the Glass–Steagall restrictions on commercial banks by poaching on their territory, and as commercial banks began to strain at their leashes, the Reagan Administration's deregulatory zeal was extended to the financial sector. The *Report of the Task Group on the Reform of Financial Services* (US Task Group, 1984; see also ERP, 1984), chaired by then Vice-President George H. W. Bush, recommended the repeal of Glass–Steagall as part of an ambitious series of deregulatory proposals which even included the privatization of deposit insurance. However, the proposals went nowhere under Volcker's chairmanship of the Fed. Only after this known opponent of deregulation was not reappointed, and replaced instead with Alan Greenspan in 1987, could the first attempt to repeal Glass–Steagall be made in 1988. It failed amid legislative wrangles (Hendrickson, 2001: 862).

While Chapter 8 details the attempts that continued to be made to repeal Glass–Steagall over the next decade until success was achieved in 1999, we may note here that the Bush Administration's efforts became dogged by the outbreak of the Savings and Loans crisis during his first year in office. Concerns about safety and soundness dampened enthusiastic arguments about increasing efficiency and competitiveness, and Bush Sr left office merely reiterating the need for financial deregulation.

The Bush Administration attempted to put a brave face on its distressing economic record. The recession of 1990–91 was a 'temporary interruption in America's economic growth [which] does not signal a decline in the basic long-term vitality of the U.S. economy' (ERP, 1991: 3) whose carefully enumerated signs were low inflation, export growth, job creation in parts of the United States, and productivity increases. However, these few signs only underlined the dismal economic realities, and the administration's denial of declinism lacked conviction:

In short, the declinists are wrong on the facts. America still has the largest and strongest economy in the world. It is neither de-industrializing, nor losing some overall economic competition with other countries. Although it can improve its competitive position in specific industries, America still enjoys the highest standard of living of the major industrialized countries. But again, the declinists and the authors of this *Report* agree on one point: The Nation cannot take continued economic growth for granted.

(ERP, 1993: 23)

At the end of the cold war, it was not clear whether the United States was the 'sole superpower' or the 'dispensable power'. Triumphalism about market reforms in Eastern Europe, Russia and China was countermanded by the narrowing of economic options at home. Some asked whether striving for primacy was 'worth the candle' any more (Jervis, 1993). American minds were concentrated by the debility of their economy – 'It's the economy, stupid!' as Clinton's campaign manager James Carville memorably put it – and conservative commentator, Edward Luttwak, announced that cold war geopolitical competition had been replaced by the much harder game of 'geoeconomics' (1993). Even neoconservative renewalist-in-chief Samuel Huntington was reduced to shrill calls to keep primacy a US goal while finding ways to overcome the primarily economic obstacles to it. This particularly involved preventing 'Japan from exploiting the openness of the American economy' and inducing it 'to open its own economy further to foreign goods, investment and participation', and taking measures to 'renew [US] economic health: reducing its federal deficit, increasing savings and investment, increasing productivity, promoting research and development, improving its educational system' (Huntington, 1993: 81).

Neoconservatives in the administration did, however, score one fateful policy victory. They ensured that although recession at home and dispensability abroad forced George Bush Sr to fight the first post-cold-war war, the Gulf War, with predominantly Saudi financing and a rag-tag 'coalition of the willing' (Cooper et al., 1991), as we saw in Chapter 5, US security policy would remain as militarily aggressive as ever. The draft Defence Policy Guidance of 1992 reiterated the aims of keeping the United States 'the predominant outside power' in the Middle East so as to preserve 'US and Western access to the region's oil', of ensuring that no hostile power could dominate East Asia and Western Europe, regions 'whose resources would, under consolidated control, be sufficient to generate global power' and of actively blocking the emergence of any possible competitor to US power (Mann, 2004: 210).

It was a march stolen on events. Coming amid a recession and running directly counter to calls in Congress for a 'peace dividend', the draft naturally created a furore. Though the final version was toned down, Paul Wolfowitz, one of the two alleged authors (the other being Zalmay Khalilzad: Mann, 2004: 209), thought the losses minimal. Congressional concerns notwithstanding, the United States never retreated from its established military positions even after the cold war (Mann, 2004: 214). Neither the Clinton nor the Obama Democratic administrations, themselves creatures of a Democratic Party which had accommodated to Reagan's transformation of the electoral landscape as we shall see in the next chapters, were immune to neoconservative influence, even though each took office at times that required a radical rethink of US imperial ambitions.

7

GLOBALIZATION?

The 'roaring nineties' were truly remarkable for the United States. After stagnating, or growing only under fiscal stimulus, for the better part of the two decades since 1973, the economy recovered momentum, apparently powered by a 'new economy'. It turned received truths on their heads. Inflation and unemployment declined together, the stock market rose unstoppably, and its 'wealth effects' sustained unprecedented levels of credit-fuelled consumption- and investment-led growth under the deft monetary management of the chairman of the Federal Reserve, 'maestro' Alan Greenspan. Clinton's last economic report (ERP, 2001), finished just before the inauguration of George Bush Jr in January 2001, was effectively a primer on the 'new economy' it was bequeathing the nation – its creation, performance and wondrous results. However, although it was de rigueur for a departing administration to be upbeat, the report struck a sombre note: the still very new 'new economy' had come to a spectacular end when the stock market crashed the previous year. As this chapter will make clear, it was also the end of 'globalization'.

By contrast ERP, 2000 had struck an epic note. Though it used the expression 'new economy' just once, it celebrated the ongoing 'record-breaking expansion' that had restored US economic vitality. The administration's three-pronged strategy of 'maintaining fiscal discipline, investing in people and technologies, and opening international markets' had led, it claimed, to

> a 20-million-job increase in payroll employment since January 1993, the lowest unemployment rate since 1969, the lowest core inflation rate since 1965, the lowest poverty rate since 1979, rising productivity, significant gains all across the income distribution, and a Federal budget in surplus for 2 years in a row after nearly three decades of deficits. The current economic

expansion, already the longest peacetime expansion on record, is on the threshold of becoming the longest ever. The mood of optimism that prevailed at the dawn of the 20th century prevails today as well.

(ERP, 2000: 21)

This US economy roaring on all cylinders briefly became the model and motor of the geopolitical economy of 'globalization'. If the 'United States ... have never before been as affluent as today... [n]or has economic globalization – the worldwide integration of national economies through trade, capital flows, and operational linkages among firms – ever before been as broad or as deep' (2000: 199). Globalization was driven by technology and the United States was the world's technological leader. Under the 'globalization president' (*Foreign Policy in Focus*, 2000: 19) the United States led globalization's most characteristic processes – foreign investment and trade in services and finance. That it was also 'by far the largest recipient of net capital inflows in the world, amounting to more than $200 billion in 1998' (ERP, 2000: 206) was mentioned only in another context but it was hardly coincidental, as we shall see.

This chapter uncovers how globalization emerged as a strategy during the Clinton Administration and briefly made US imperial ambition appear closer to realization than at any time since 1971. It was a more tortuous process than the contrasts between Clinton's economic emphasis and multilateralism and Bush's stress on militarism and unilateral international action, reviewed in Chapter 1, would lead us to imagine. And it turns out to involve the fate of the domestic economy far more centrally.

The first Clinton campaign used the term 'globalization' to express anxiety about the competitive challenges that the United States faced. Its economic guru, Robert Reich, proposed to overcome them by improving the productive economy through increased state spending on, and investment in, the country's human capital (Reich, 1991) and by increasing trade with the 'big emerging markets' (BEMs) (Rothkopf, 1998). It was the closest thing to a civilian industrial strategy a president would take office on in recent memory. Only after Clinton took office did this meaning turn into its diametric opposite, the meaning given to the term by Joseph Stiglitz as chairman of the CEA in the years spanning Clinton's 1996 re-election bid. This was the one so credulously reproduced by scholars and journalists worldwide. In it, globalization denoted secular processes of increasing trade and other flows, especially capital flows, which states could no longer control. This change coincided with the moment the 'new economy' emerged as its critical domestic counterpart.

A powerful undertow of interests and events – particularly the financial sector's critical role in getting Clinton elected (Ferguson, 1995: 298–305) – led to this switch. The policies that Stiglitzian globalization entailed made the US economy 'deeply distorted and unstable', with 'unprecedentedly high levels of public and household debt, a deep structural balance of payments deficit and a business cycle dependent on asset price bubbles'. It was also 'deeply dependent upon Wall Street financial markets' ability to maintain huge inward flows of finance from all over the world' (Gowan, 1999a: 123). There were three key turning points: campaign spending promises were forsaken for deficit reduction even before Clinton's inauguration in January 1993; the so-called 'Reverse Plaza accord' of 1995 dramatically reversed the decade-long decline of the dollar; and the Federal Reserve under Alan Greenspan raised interest rates, citing inflationary threats as manufacturing activity became brisker. He would leave them at a relatively high plateau until the end of 1999 except for a quarter-point increase.

These changes brutally interrupted the first manufacturing revival to take sustained hold in the United States, thanks to the lower dollar, in the long downturn. Now the US economy turned once again towards finance, in particular credit-fuelled consumption and the credit-fuelled investment that would massively misallocate capital before the decade ended. Reasonable doubts about this pattern of growth were quelled by claims that the resulting ascent of the stock market signified a 'new economy' defying received economic wisdom. The non-accelerating inflation rate of unemployment (NAIRU) had fallen, it was argued, as inflation and unemployment went down together, whereas hitherto they had either risen together, as in the 1970s, or moved in opposite directions, as in the 1960s and 1980s. The Fed chairman encouraged the stock market's gravity-defying upward movement in speech after speech asserting that there was a 'hidden productivity miracle' that justified it. They drowned, as they were meant to, his solitary and perfunctory warning about 'irrational exuberance' in December 1996. Indeed, financial markets were celebrated for their efficiency, heedless of the decade's many financial crises, including the massive the 1998 East Asian crisis. With government spending and deficits already ruled out as economic policy options by promises of fiscal rectitude to bond markets, they were now criticized for 'crowding out' private investment. The Fed and the bond markets became the arbiters of the US economy's fate in a way they had never before been.

The next section examines the origins of the three critical policy shifts and is followed by a discussion of the changes in globalization's meaning by Clinton's second term. The following outline of the configuration of the US economy and its relationship with the rest of the world economy is divided into two: the period between 1995 and 1997/8 when the Asian crisis erupted and the one after. It was the latter that constituted, briefly and spectacularly, that distinctive geopolitical economy of globalization in its fullest form, under which the world appeared willing, indeed eager, to pour money into the United States and, even better, into the US stock market, buoyed by the new economy rhetoric and Greenspan's easy money practices. The final section covers stock market collapse that began in the spring of 2000, and assesses the 'globalization' attempt at realizing US imperial ambitions.

CLINTON'S CHOICES

In the early 1990s, deflationary policies were everywhere limiting market expansion and exacerbating overcapacity. Each major part of the world economy could grow only at the expense of others in a zero-sum game of export-led growth:

> [L]ocal expansions typically occurred by way of a kind of hydraulic dynamic, in which one leading economy or group of them took advantage of reduced exchange rates to undertake manufacturing-led, export oriented expansions, but heavily at the expense of others with correspondingly increased exchange rates.
> (Brenner, 2009: 13)

George H. W. Bush lost the 1992 elections thanks to the parlous state of the economy. He also appeared to have lost business support. Greenspan, the Reagan appointee to the Fed chairmanship reappointed by Bush as a man of declared free market convictions, had reduced interest rates throughout the latter's presidency but refused to reduce them further ahead of the elections despite more or less open pleas from the president (Woodward, 2000: 91, 94). Technically the decision of an 'independent' central banker, it likely reflected business alienation from Bush.

So badly did the US economy malinger that not only did a

pro-business third presidential candidate, Ross Perot, become the most successful of the postwar period, he did so by dusting off forgotten US traditions of combined development and industrial policy and breaking 'publicly with the free trade orthodoxy that had dominated American public policy since the New Deal' (Ferguson, 1995: 307). Perot's mercantilism amounted, of course, to renouncing imperial ambitions and the dollar's world role. Clinton, meanwhile, represented a Democratic Party that had adjusted to the Reagan electoral revolution and decided 'to compete with the Republicans for funds' (1995: 292), rather than challenging Reaganomics and building up its traditional social base behind a better, more progressive social programme. During the 1980s, the 'New Democratic' tendency, ostensibly pledged to a 'third way' between Reaganite neoliberalism and traditional Democratic liberalism (Hale, 1995), came to dominate the party. In fact, however, '[a]mid much flatulent oratory ... the entire spectrum of respectable discussion in the party lurched to the right' (Ferguson, 1995: 292).

This shift attracted increasing sections of business to the Democrats: whereas in 1984 they included only urban real estate interests reliant on federal subsidies for mass transit and infrastructure and financial interests concerned about how their privileges might be affected by the repeal of the Glass–Steagall Act that Reagan threatened, in 1988 they were joined by high-technology and other firms anxious about Japanese competition and in 1992 by interests which, 'like the mainline multinationals that dominated the Bush coalition ... support[ed] an open world economy' but unlike them had 'some direct crucial tie that links them closely to the American state'. Ferguson counted among these backers aircraft companies, investment banks and the oil and gas, transportation and tobacco sectors (1995: 299). This business coalition was 'prepared to countenance a cautious public rejection of laissez faire because they need the American state to work'. They could not 'simply go somewhere else if the relative decline of the United States in the current world economy continue[d] unabated' (1995: 300). It was also clear, however, that this coalition stopped considerably short of the sort of compromise of US imperial ambitions that was implied by a robust industrial policy of the Ross Perot variety. Reich's strategy, necessary to win elections at a time when the competitiveness issue was so prominently highlighted by Perot's candidacy, tamely focused on investment in education and skills.

So in 1992 the Republican free-market incumbent lost against two other business candidates with programmes of more or less state intervention and managed trade in an election that revolved around economic survival, not US world leadership. The winner promised to improve competitiveness – 'we must compete, not retreat' (ERP, 1994: 205) – through 'a high-wage strategy' complete with 'trade policies that will promote trade and foster more-open markets both at home and abroad; and domestic policies that will help American companies remain the world's productivity and technological leaders, and American workers remain the most skilled and productive in the world' (ERP, 1994: 206).

In the new post-cold-war geopolitical economy, this strategy took cognizance of how competition had 'reduced U.S. leverage in substantial ways'. Worse the 'implicit price tag' of the Pax Americana under which '[i]f a country depended on the United States for security protection, it dealt with the United States on trade and commercial matters' no longer applied: 'Now the lesser "need" to deal with the United States hurts efforts to fashion international consensus or gain ground in bilateral trade discussions' (Rothkopf, 1998). In these circumstances US trade had to focus on 'new markets of great size and promise', in particular ten BEMs, mostly Asian. Their share of US exports had nearly doubled from 9 per cent in 1972 to 17 per cent in 1992, making the United States's trade with Asia 50 per cent greater than that with Europe (ERP, 1994: 211).

Clinton's new trade initiatives included a National Export Strategy, the North American Free Trade Agreement (NAFTA) with the United States's largest and third largest trading partners and a renewed focus on the Asia-Pacific Economic Cooperation (APEC) economies which accounted for more than half of all US trade not counting Canada and Mexico, 76 per cent more than US–EU trade. Explicitly recognizing that 'as long as the Asian countries grow faster than the United States, they will become more important in our trade while we will become less important in theirs' and therefore 'past trade strategies based on threats of market closure are liable to become less and less effective', the administration concluded that a multilateral approach was necessary. To this end, it redoubled efforts in the Uruguay Round talks (ERP, 1995: 3) which would lead to the creation of the World Trade Organization (WTO). Finally, a US–Japanese Framework for a New Economic Partnership was agreed. By the early 1990s Japan was eager to neither export to the United States nor finance its deficit, and the partnership only committed Japan to increase imports and the United States to decrease deficits

(1995: 232). At the end of his first two years in office Clinton could boast about having 'opened up more new trade opportunities in just 2 years than in any similar period in a generation' (1995: 3).

Deficit reduction

While Clinton moved energetically on the trade front, the other prong of his Reichian strategy, investing in improving productivity in the US economy and among its workers, was jettisoned even before his inauguration. Deficit cutting became his topmost priority instead and increased taxes, legislation prohibiting spending increases not matched by revenue increases and other measures brought the federal deficit under control by 1998. The apocryphal story of this turnaround features an idealistic president facing up to economic realities. When the departing Bush Administration published dismal estimates of government debt, Clinton's economic advisers explained to him that markets would react badly if strong and clear moves to cut the deficit were not made. To this Clinton is supposed to have responded in a 'half whisper', 'You mean to tell me that the success of the program and my reelection hinges on the Federal Reserve and a bunch of fucking bond traders?' (Woodward, 1994: 84).

However, well before this meeting Greenspan had impressed the urgency of deficit reduction on the president-elect, dangling the carrot that it would free up capital for private investment and growth, brandishing the stick that without a credible deficit reduction plan the bond markets would demand higher returns (1994: 84), and making the barely veiled threat that the Fed would not lower interest rates without such a plan. And even before the meeting with Greenspan, deficit-averse investment bankers had backed Clinton's campaign, and Robert Rubin, formerly of Goldman Sachs, was appointed to the administration (Ferguson, 1995: 276–81).

Deficit reduction was naturally couched in terms of the interests of the economy as a whole and manufacturing in particular. Clinton allegedly faced a 'double bind'. Deficits may generate stronger domestic expansion but the resulting increases in federal debt risks higher interest rates which would eventually choke off any recovery while also reducing the capital available for private investment. Reagan's record was instructive. Given low US savings rates, Reagan's large budget deficits were financed by capital imports. Though they 'limit[ed] the rise of real U.S. interest rates ... *maintaining* the Nation's comparatively meager investment rate' if not increasing it (ERP, 1994: 27), they also increased the current account deficit, made the United States the world's greatest debtor and pushed interest rates and the dollar up, 'handicapping' parts of US industry (1994: 29). Deficit reduction, by contrast, would help reduce the trade deficit by improving the price competitiveness of US exports, partially offsetting 'the contractionary impact of spending cuts and tax increases on domestic demand' (1994: 83). Furthermore, it was expected to permit looser monetary policy at the Fed, lowering bond yields, increasing stock values, and reducing inflation risk (1994: 82–4). Thus, not only was Clinton's already-timid competitiveness strategy beaten back, the government was now not even to wield the instruments of fiscal policy. The Fed and the 'bunch of fucking bond traders' were truly in charge.

The double bind became orthodoxy, interestingly redescribing the problem that Bush had faced and Clinton's Reichian programme proposed to solve. Given the overcapacity and overproduction that plagued the industrial world, and given that Reagan's programme had failed to revive US industry, inflation-free growth was not possible. Bush had to be content with low inflation and low growth. Although Reich's programme had helped Clinton win the 1992 election, powerful Wall Street interests had no intention of permitting its implementation. Though the administration claimed to be concerned about 'three deficits' – the trade and budget deficits and the 'shortage of funds for public investment in critical national needs like education and training, transportation facilities, and environmental infrastructure' (ERP, 1994: 29) – Clinton's initial budget contained a derisory $30 billion of new spending (Ferguson, 1995: 276–81).

In the new language and understanding that accompanied it, the turn to deficit reduction was now portrayed as a new strategy for growth and the administration claimed early success. With the $50 billion decline in the Federal deficit and the legislation of a credible budget reduction strategy, the financial markets 'brought forward' the benefits of deficit reduction with 'the dramatic decline' in long-term interest rates (ERP, 1994: 78). In claiming, however, that it had 'sparked an investment-driven economic expansion that has created more private sector jobs during the last year than were created during the previous four' (1994: 4) and created strong inflation-free growth not seen in 'more than a generation' (1994: 19), the administration was taking credit for the strong manufacturing and export performance that resulted instead from the low interest rates and the low dollar. These two growth props were the next to go.

Keeping ahead of inflation

As inflation fears re-emerged with growth in 1994, the Fed began the series of hikes that would double the interest rate from 3 per cent to a peak of 6 per cent in April 1995. After some reductions amid the Mexican crisis a year later, rates remained at over 5 per cent for the rest of the decade, high enough to interrupt the ongoing manufacturing revival and shunt the US economy back to the financialized track of the 1980s from which it had been temporarily diverted by the low dollar.

The manufacturing revival had gestated in the post-Plaza low-dollar years (Brenner, 1998: 202–3), and in the early Clinton years it stood at the cusp of a 'break beyond stagnation' (Brenner, 2009: 19). However, by then the Fed had become almost hysterically intolerant of inflation. Citing Milton Friedman's complaint that the Fed always raised interest rates too late, Greenspan insisted that 'the Fed needed to be ahead of the game' (Woodward, 2000: 115) and increase interest rates at inflation's mere prospect. When Greenspan began raising rates in 1994, the administration thought inflation 'modest and stable' (ERP, 1995: 19). Greenspan insisted, however, that reduced growth now would avoid a recession later, and Wall Street insiders in Clinton's cabinet managed his irritation at the interest rate increases in a mid-term Congressional election year by telling him that the recession being avoided was scheduled for his own re-election year. They warned, for good measure, that he could not afford to be perceived as anti-Wall Street (Woodward, 1994: 330).

Greenspan's increases in short-term interest rates coincided with increases in long-term rates on government bonds across the G-7 countries as Japan turned from a major supplier of capital to a major consumer, and the reunified Germany and the transition economies also increased demand for capital. The rate hikes provoked the Mexican financial crisis as 1994 ended. By the end of January 1995, a US government bailout became necessary because, amid already slowing growth, US exports to Mexico had collapsed and US investment, so much of which had poured in after the inauguration of NAFTA a year earlier, was threatened. The crisis and the bailout marked an important change in the nature of international financial flows, and were signs of things to come.

The petrodollar lending spree of the 1970s ended in the debt crisis and reverse capital flows of the 1980s. With investment prospects in the industrial world still remaining low, capital flows to the developing world had to resume, but they did so in a new form.

Rather than loans which exposed lending institutions to the risk of default directly, they took securitized forms of investments in the capital markets of emerging countries that had been persuaded to lift capital controls under Clinton's BEM 'globalization' initiative. However, such flows were short term and could not ensure 'comparable increases in direct investment necessary to sustain economic growth' and back the capital flows (Rohatyn, 1994). Moreover, operating with insufficient knowledge of the markets, investors made speculative, and potentially destabilizing, investments through hedge funds and derivatives, creating new risks. Such flows 'were themselves a reflection of the basic fact that so much of the world economy had become too fragile and risky for long-term commitment of funds by the rentiers of the core economies' (Gowan, 1999a: 118). In Mexico, as in so many other developing countries, such short-term investment only blew up asset bubbles even though there was ample scope for productive investment.

Greenspan reduced interest rates during the Mexican crisis, claiming to see evidence of a greater-than-expected economic slowdown that indicated he might have 'overshot' his efforts to effect a 'soft landing' – an economic slowdown without a recession (Woodward, 2000: 149). This did not last, however, and by January 1996 the Federal funds rate stood at a historically high 5.2 per cent (given low inflation), where it would remain until 1999.

The reverse Plaza Accord

With interest rates rising, those concerned about US industrial and trade performance had to take satisfaction that they could have been higher still. In 1995, moreover, just when the US manufacturing revival reached a critical stage, its main driver, the low dollar, was sacrificed in the 'reverse Plaza accord' (Brenner, 2009: 19).

The Plaza accord is regarded as a mutual agreement that Western Europe and Japan would act as markets for US industry, and the 'reverse Plaza accord', as its reciprocation in the pop version of the 'hydraulic dynamic' of low-exchange-rate powered local expansions that were the only form of growth the long downturn permitted. But that implies more mutual cooperation than there actually was. We have already seen how the Plaza accord was prompted by a combination of US manufacturers' pressure and shared anxiety about a potentially catastrophic fall in the dollar's value. Its reversal too had more esoteric causes.

Thanks to the difficulties of the European Exchange Rate Mechanism (ERM), the dollar had already risen in the early

1990s. The Clinton campaign supported its rise against European currencies, but supported devaluation against the yen. Although Japan's share of the US trade deficit had diminished after 1985, it was still the United States's biggest bilateral trade deficit (quite apart from the large proportion of Japanese re-exports in the US trade deficit with other East Asian countries whose currencies were pegged to the dollar after the Plaza Accord). However, instead of devaluation against the yen, the Clinton Administration delivered the reverse Plaza accord.

The administration's explanation was bland: the United States was growing faster than its main rivals, and the dollar had depreciated 'beyond what many viewed as justified by economic fundamentals'. So G–7 finance ministers and central bank governors 'called for an orderly reversal' of this decline, which was conducted through German and Japanese interest rate reduction and 'concerted currency market intervention' (ERP, 1996: 255). However, the turnaround was so complete and so harmful to US manufacturing and exports that more esoteric explanations had to emerge. One tells of negotiations between the Treasury and the Japanese Ministry of Finance to engineer yen appreciation, during which the latter warned 'that Japan was on the brink of a major bank crisis – one that could directly threaten the American economy'. With Japanese funds retuning home, 'American interest rates would likely soar, precipitating a severe recession in the midst of Clinton's re-election campaign' (Judis, 1996: 23-4). The recent Mexican experience having made Treasury secretary Rubin and his deputy Summers receptive to this warning, the result was instead a dollar appreciation.

However this account was simply a melodramatic rendering of duller compulsions. Not only did the investment bankers in Clinton's coalition favour a higher dollar, Japan, which had been a major capital exporter in the 1980s, was now an importer of long-term capital. 'Japanese companies needed every bit of cash they could lay their hands on to keep production lines running at home, while their bankers, groaning under a mountain of bad debts, could ill-afford more spending sprees abroad' (Murphy, 1996: 287). And, by early 1995, with lower US interest rates in the aftermath of the Mexican bailout, 'the Japanese abandoned the market for long-term American government securities' (Murphy, 1996: 287). In these circumstances a rising dollar was a *sine qua non* for attracting capital from other quarters to the United States, to finance its various deficits – trade, budget and savings, the 'third deficit'.

Why the combination of high interest rates and the high dollar did not stifle growth, we shall see in the next section. Suffice it to say that growth remained sluggish in Clinton's first term, and when it picked up, it was distinctly Reaganesque. Non-traded sectors like construction and retail prospered at the expense of manufacturing, consumption at the expense of investment, imports at the expense of exports, and finance took 'center-stage'. This 'truly major shift' amounted to

> the de facto abandonment of any real attempt on the part of the US to stand up to ever more powerful competition from East Asia, ultimately centered in China, and its all out embrace instead of integrated international production by way of supply chains, foreign direct investment and the re-location of industry to lower wage venues, not least China, and the penetration by the US financial services 'industry' of every nook and cranny of the world economy.
>
> (Brenner, 2009: 19)

The high dollar was the last of the three building blocks of the predominantly financial geopolitical economy of globalization as a distinctive US economic strategy. The stage was now set for a shift from Reich's original and anxiety-laden meaning of globalization to Stiglitz's altogether more euphoric one. In it, the purpose of portraying globalization as a secular economic process was dual: to secure other governments' compliance with this US strategy and to ensure that such compliance was dissimulated as an adaptation to allegedly secular unstoppable and irreversible processes rather than compliance with US wishes. In this it was similar to other cosmopolitan ideologies like free trade and hegemonic stability theory (HST).

FROM REICHIAN GLOBALIZATION TO STIGLITZIAN GLOBALIZATION

Though Reich served as secretary of labour until 1997, his view of globalization was jettisoned by the administration's three fateful choices long before that, and globalization's new meaning, so widely adopted by journalists and scholars as to become arguably the most prolific academic industry ever, was most fully articulated in ERP, 1997. It appeared a couple of months after Clinton's re-election. Joseph Stiglitz was CEA chairman.

In place of his growth and competitiveness strategy, deficit reduction was justified as the administration's overriding goal, the keystone of a comprehensive programme to 'secure the expansion and spur long-term economic growth ... reverse the trend toward rising inequality ... reduce Federal borrowing and shrink the trade deficit ... invest more in both private and public capital ... [a]nd bolster our human resources' (ERP, 1994: 30). Clinton's choices also turned trade promotion from a means to revive US competitiveness to its opposite. Bereft of the domestic investment it required, the new multilateral trade thrust could only leave US industry defenceless against intensifying competition. The Clinton Administration had been exceptionally energetic on the trade front early on, notably reviving the stalled GATT negotiations that created the WTO effective 1 January 1995, reduced tariffs, brought in new entrants, particularly developing countries, and expanded its scope to sectors – agriculture, trade in services, particularly financial services, and intellectual property rights – in which the United States was not only the leading exporter but whose importance to US trade was growing. Under globalization's new meaning, the WTO briefly became its flagship institution – allegedly supranational and global as opposed to the merely international and multilateral GATT, it was regarded as an indicator of things to come – before its first round of negotiations, the Doha Development Round, got bogged down in political wrangles only a few years later. It should have been anticipated. Even in 1995 the Clinton Administration stressed the limits of its globalism and supranationalism, if only to allay fears about the WTO diminishing US sovereignty (ERP, 1995: 213).

The economy Clinton built

In Clinton's re-election year, the administration could boast of inflation-free growth that looked 'set to continue for the foreseeable future' (ERP, 1996: 42) provided two developments obtained. The first was 'a forward-looking response of financial markets ... decreas[ing] long term interest rates in anticipation of the deficit reduction' in a way that stimulated investment to offset fiscal contraction and support recovery (1996: 71). Second, it hoped for 'an accommodative monetary policy [which] can validate the market's response and reinforce its positive effects on short-run growth' (1996: 69). Having cancelled most of its planned investments in the productive economy and labour force, and subjected industry to the high dollar, all the administration could do for the productive economy under the new dispensation was wait for the bond markets and the Fed to lower bond yields and interest rates respectively.

The Clinton Administration now revived Reaganite nonchalance about the trade and current account deficits, and topped it with a measure of self-congratulation. The US economy's habit of sucking in imports as it grew was no longer a disease to be cured, not even a condition to be accepted, but a symptom of economic health: since the trade deficit increased with growth and decreased with economic weakness, '[a]n increasing trade deficit is therefore usually the result of a strong economy, not the cause of a weak one' (1996: 252). For all its free-market enthusiasms, the Reagan Administration's horizons remained national, and it paid at least lip service to reducing the trade and current account deficits. Now they became parameters of economic policy making in a new economically cosmopolitan discourse. The United States's

> ability to borrow overseas ... had become critical in maintaining domestic investment and growth over the last 15 years. Had the United States been forced to run a balanced current account, interest rates would have been higher, and investment and economic growth lower.
>
> (ERP, 1996: 258)

Trade policy could only 'have a substantial impact on the sectoral and geographic composition of trade'. It could not significantly change the trade balance, which was 'determined by larger macroeconomic factors', particularly the 'imbalance between national saving and national investment', which did not 'necessarily indicate poor economic performance' (1996: 250–1). This was just as well because the low savings rate, inherited from the Reagan era, was not entirely amenable to policy: 'anything that might strengthen incentives to save by raising the return to saving would also reduce the amount of saving required to meet a future wealth or consumption target' (1996: 259). Ergo, 'continued reduction of the Federal budget deficit is the most effective tool for reducing our external deficit' (1996: 259). The rhetoric of the administration now tamely reflected the Federal Reserve's and the bond markets' capture of the government's agenda.

Hegemony through globalization

ERP, 1997 sought to define 'the legacy this administration hopes to leave' by laying out a 'new vision' (ERP, 1997: 17–19), and the critical chapter on the United States and the world economy, now titled 'American leadership in the emerging global economy', challenged the notion of the post-cold-war dispensability of the United States by reviving HST themes of US leadership. Globalization provided the overarching framework for this revival.

A left-of-centre economist who questioned free market dogma, at least in its extreme versions (Stiglitz et al., 1989), Stiglitz had moved over to the 'third way' social democracy associated with European social democratic leaders like Blair and Schroeder, and intellectuals like British 'third way' guru Anthony Giddens (1994). They claimed to combine 'philosophic conservatism' and left-wing values to make pro-market views social democratic by softening their anti-state elements. This was especially useful to justify intervention in favour of capital. Emphasizing 'the important, but limited, role of government', they believed that 'unfettered markets often did not work well, but that government was not always able to correct the limitations of markets' (Stiglitz, 2001). We must surmise that the ERP, 1997's vision of globalization was a creature of the Clinton Administration: unlike Reich, neither Stiglitz, the chairman of the CEA, not its other two members, had written anything about globalization before this. Stiglitz's books on the theme would come later (pre-eminently Stiglitz, 2002).

According to ERP, 1997, globalization was an unmitigated good, and an arena for the exercise of US leadership as well as its product. Parroting Kindleberger, the ERP spoke of the United States's 'tragic mistake of retreating from international engagement' after the First World War, and how this mistake was rectified after the Second World War, when the United States 'led an economic partnership [sic]' with other advanced industrial countries and assisted decolonization and development (ERP, 1997: 235). It was now time to renew US leadership once again for a new era. The cold war had ended, parts of the developing world had industrialized, particularly East and South-East Asia, and there was 'increased globalization'. The last referred not just to technologically driven increases in trade facilitated by the evolution of international institutions, particularly the WTO, but also, critically, 'increasing openness of developing economies' to trade and investment flows not least because of structural adjustment policies (1997: 237–48). ERP, 1997's vision was not so social democratic as to condemn the moral and human disaster of structural adjustment. Instead, SAPs counted as an essential preparation for globalization.

While some might have believed that US leadership was no longer necessary in the post-cold-war era, the ERP asserted that 'the United States and other countries continue to benefit from U.S. leadership in international economic policy' (1997: 235–6). And if that could sound too altruistic to domestic audiences, ERP, 1997 assured them that '[a] cornerstone of this Administration's economic policies has been to position the United States to benefit from ... global changes' (1997: 248).

Though globalization is so widely regarded as being about trade, it was firmly subordinated to finance in ERP, 1997. '[D]efenders of free trade' were doing it a

> disservice by promoting it as a way to create more jobs or to reduce bilateral trade deficits. Jobs, the unemployment rate, and the overall balance of payments are ultimately a consequence of macroeconomic policies, not of trade barriers. ... In a full-employment economy, trade has more impact on the distribution of jobs than on the quantity of jobs.
>
> (ERP, 1997: 21)

ERP, 1997 did not elaborate on the impact trade had on an economy with unemployment, or poor forms of employment, like the US economy. But perhaps that did not matter. Trade was no longer of much importance, and certainly export promotion was not.

The chronicler of the early Clintonian BEM trade promotion strategy could not explain the demise of trade promotion in the Clinton Administration better than by attributing it to the untimely death of commerce secretary Ron Brown, misguided attacks from Congress and the fact that some BEMs 'such as Indonesia, Korea, China, and Mexico [had] become even more economically vulnerable and/or politically sensitive' (Rothkopf, 1998) after 1997. In reality, trade promotion was a victim of the administration's changed perspective, in which the trade deficit was 'financing a surge in U.S. investment, particularly in business equipment' and could therefore be expected to 'generate the resources necessary to repay our net borrowing from the rest of the world' (ERP, 1997: 252).

Capital flows therefore trumped trade. And this included not just those that financed the US current account deficit but also foreign direct investment (FDI). It had trade advantages. US FDI outflows increased US exports 'both as inputs to foreign production and as consumer goods to supply foreign demand', providing 'U.S. companies a toehold in foreign markets from which they can further expand sales' including through 'investment in distribution and other essential services' and intra-firm trade which 'can be an efficient means of international trade, particularly when problems of imperfect information exist' (ERP, 1997).

Just as ERP, 1997's general remarks on the benefits of trade (and there were predictably plenty about the virtues of the WTO) were directed at allaying fears about the trade deficit, and indeed seeing its inestimable virtues for the US economy, so its remarks about free capital flows were really a way of justifying critical capital inflows into the United States. The general argument that globalization would be mutually beneficial for all participating countries rested on the most trite Panglossian notions of mainstream neoclassical economics – 'Virtually all economists agree that international trade and economic integration raise the living standards of U.S. residents overall, while also increasing economic well-being in other countries.' But a more specific argument underlay it: 'Capital goes to those who are best able to make productive use of it, and the suppliers of that capital receive a higher return, for a given level of risk, than they could get elsewhere' (1997: 252).

Like HST, globalization in ERP, 1997 was not purely economic: governments played a central role in the domestic economy 'to increase economic growth, raise living standards, protect the environment, and enhance security in all its dimensions. Moreover, the market, if left to itself, will tend to underproduce public goods ... [and] this creates a rationale for government action to provide public goods.' And just as in HST, so in ERP, 1997, the government of the leading economy played a central role in providing 'international public goods' (1997: 266). So while globalization's vaunted multilateralism gave it a benign and participatory look, its real purpose was to make a virtue of the reality of diminished US power and to veil the leading role the United States nevertheless sought to play in making sure that 'global' rules and institutions complemented its peculiar geopolitical economy.

War as public good

ERP, 1997 did not, of course, discuss military matters. It did however include a discussion of economic warfare, which framed the discussion of globalization more generally. For globalization required 'an international environment in which nations act peacefully and respect international order', and the United States had, throughout the twentieth century, 'led world efforts to create such an environment', in which '[b]esides military and diplomatic efforts, [it] has also employed economic means'. Chief among these were economic sanctions, and although some considered them 'a somewhat blunt instrument', they were 'one available tool to use against countries that threaten international stability'. Sanctions were not only an 'economic means to achieve peace and order ... particularly when the situation calls for something stronger than diplomatic protest, but less strong than military engagement', but also 'public goods [which] are generally more effective when more nations participate in imposing them' (ERP, 1997: 275–6).

This understanding applied verbatim to the full spectrum of warfare, not just economic, waged by the globalizing Clinton Administration to protect the US- and Wall-Street-centred 'global' economy. Its wars were labelled 'humanitarian interventions', and festooned with banners of democracy and human rights. Though 'multilateral' and 'economic' globalization and 'unilateral' and 'militarist' empire are easily contrasted, Clinton was merely carrying out the post-cold-war military vision laid out in the neoconservative Defence Policy Guidance of 1992.

By 1997, the neoconservatives had organized themselves around the Project for a New American Century (PNAC) to press for a 'neo-Reaganite foreign policy' (Kristol and Kagan, 1996), involving increased defence spending, strengthened alliances and challenges to hostile regimes, and generally 'preserving and extending an international order friendly to our security, our prosperity, and our principles' (PNAC, 2006). The Democrats had failed to come up with 'any clear alternative vision of American Strategy that would forswear the 1992 [DPG] vision', and secretary of state Madeleine Albright's view of 'America's role in the world ... was not substantially different from the idea of the United States as lone superpower' (Mann, 2004: 214–15).

The Clinton Administration opened its military account with the disastrous 'Black Hawk down' intervention in Somalia in 1993, where US forces encountered joint armed and civilian resistance for the first time. Thereafter, the administration 'distanced itself from the United Nations and the concept of collective security', and 'conducted a large-scale massive military intervention in Kosovo without UN approval' (2004: 214–15) to ensure that European powers, particularly Germany, did not act independently in the post-cold-war world. Its actual victims were mere collateral damage (Gowan, 1999b). In this sense, the globalization discourse, which allocated to the United States the 'responsibility' of securing the allegedly universally beneficent globalization worldwide, was also a self-issued exemption from observing international protocols.

The Clinton Administration also foreshadowed the Bush Jr Administration's obsession with Iraq. With US troops permanently stationed in Saudi Arabia after the war in Iraq in 1991, the 'dual containment' of Iran and Iraq was pursued in a radically different way. After the experience in Somalia, troop commitments were largely avoided. Containing Iran meant isolating it economically and diplomatically, while containing Iraq meant, in addition to such economic warfare, whose victims were if anything even more numerous, maintaining draconian sanctions and an unrelenting and deadly bombing campaign (Ali, 2000: 6–7).

The bombing campaign in Iraq was simply a more forceful way of achieving the same globalization objectives. When it seemed only to entrench Saddam Hussein in power, and as neoconservatives urged full-scale military invasion (Abrams et al., 1998), Clinton signed into law the Iraq Liberation Act, which committed the US government to regime change in Iraq in the name of democracy and human rights, and because of the danger posed by the weapons of mass destruction Iraq was supposedly amassing. Already under the 'globalization president', therefore,

Americans became used to wars conducted in their name, requiring no sacrifice and even delivering prosperity without the hard slog of improving competitiveness. Securing the American way of life and freedom, essentially to consume, and consume gas apparently without limit, seemed to depend on wars in distant places fought with sophisticated technology which brought recalcitrant natives and dictators to heel.

(Bacevich, 2008: 58)

Under Clinton, therefore, the neoconservative view that Hussein was 'an affront to American hegemony in the Gulf' and his removal 'the necessary corrective' (2008: 58) was already accepted. Bush Jr would only need the cue of 9/11 to launch his war in Iraq, this time with troop commitments.

Having reviewed the shift in globalization's meaning in Clinton's second term, we are now ready to examine how the actual and very distinctive geopolitical economy of globalization emerged. Until the reverse Plaza accord, growth had been powered by an industrial revival based on the declining dollar. When growth picked up after 1995, it took on a distinctly financial and global pattern, and had two distinct phases. In the first, while capital flowed into the US stock market, it also flowed to various emerging economies. The second phase began in the aftermath of the 1997 Asian crisis. In it money flowed primarily into the United States and to its stock markets, and became critical to the much-misunderstood new economy.

CENTRIFUGAL FINANCE

The expansion of securitized forms of international lending in the 1990s had already caused currency crises in Sweden and the United Kingdom in the early 1990s. The activity and scope of these forms of lending were increased by the Clinton Administration's globalization drive to lift capital controls around the world, especially in the BEMs. However, the financial institutions investing in these financial markets were unfamiliar with them, and the short-termism of portfolio investment meant the investments were unlikely to be productive. All they could do was blow asset bubbles, and the Asian crisis erupted when the reverse Plaza accord belatedly decimated the exports of emerging economies that had pegged their currencies to the dollar.

Dominant explanations that focused on the nature of the affected economies – their unreformed financial systems, 'crony capitalism' and 'unsound fundamentals' – were not very credible. Private lenders and the International Monetary Fund (IMF) had considered these economies creditworthy even after the Thai devaluation of June 1997. And whatever their faults, the structures of the economies had not changed in the run-up to the crisis. In fact, the sheer rapidity with which it engulfed very different economies like Thailand, Indonesia and South Korea indicated that the crisis had little to do with fundamentals or facts (Bagchi, 1998: 1038). Investors simply knew little about the mainsprings of growth in the region, ignored the effect of the one thing they knew about, the rising dollar, and

> ignored their own prudential limits on lending to companies with high debt/equity ratios, because everyone else was ignoring the limits and they each wanted to win business. International bankers have a powerful incentive to follow the herd, because the banker who does not make money where others are making it risks being seen as incompetent but does not suffer by making losses when everyone else is making losses too.
>
> (Wade and Veneroso, 1998a: 9)

This competitive logic had been at work in other crises, and would remain busy over many more crises right up to the big one in 2008.

Only after the Thai devaluation drew attention to the belated effects of the rising dollar, and hedge funds reacted by selling the region's currencies indiscriminately, did institutional investors act, as a herd, recalling old loans and cancelling new ones, creating a massive liquidity crisis while collapsing currencies inflated the debt (Gowan, 1999a: 103). The Clinton Administration's first response aimed to keep open these economies, and others that the crisis might prompt to turn inward, particularly to capital flows:

> It is important for their economic well-being, as well as our own, that they continue along the path toward an outward-oriented market system, on which they had until recently been making such astonishing progress. This will require difficult macro-economic and structural adjustments on their part, including reducing their dependence on foreign borrowing.
>
> (ERP, 1998: 41)

Since this would mean turning these countries' trade deficits into surpluses which would 'inevitably lead to an increase in U.S. bilateral trade deficits', it was important to remember that 'such deficits are not the proper gauge of the success or failure of U.S. trade policy' (1998: 41).

Japanese bailout proposals, which would have better preserved developmental states in affected economies, were successfully scuppered. The US and IMF bailouts instead attempted further 'free market transformation of economic systems that are best described as state-assisted capitalist formations' (Bello, 1998: 434), and gave US corporations opportunities to 'acquire assets at rock bottom prices' (Chandrashekhar, 2007), as US capital in particular sought to buy up distressed Asian companies. So effective did these US actions in pursuit of globalization seem that at least one writer on developmental states in the twentieth century, Bruce Cumings, announced the end of 'late' (that is, contender) development as a potential challenge to US economic and political dominance. In the grandiose narrative he now fashioned, having undone fascism and communism, the United States was now 'eroding, if not erasing, a formidable alternative system, the Japan–Korea model of state-directed neo-mercantilism – one undermined and made vulnerable by its inclusion in the post-war regional order' (Cumings, 1998).

While this was certainly the most impressive exercise of US power the world had seen in some time, Cumings's judgement would turn out to be premature. Though Peter Gowan also considered the transformation of 'the internal social relations of production' (1999a: 108) in the countries hit by crisis by the United States and the IMF a success, he did not lose sight of the contradictions. It was true that international financial liberalization increased 'the leverage of the American state over international economic affairs' and its 'political freedom to manipulate the world economy for US economic advantage'. But it had also 'ended by deeply distorting the US economy itself, making it far more vulnerable than ever before to forces it cannot fully control' (1999a: 123). The pattern of US power and actions after the crisis was

> ultimately an unsustainable one, if for no other reason than because the US economy depends not only upon constantly reproduced international monetary and financial turbulence. … Washington finds itself in a vicious contradiction: the US domestic economy depends upon Wall Street which depends upon chaotic instabilities in 'emerging market' financial systems; but at the same time the US domestic economy depends upon growing 'emerging market' economies able to absorb US products and generate high streams of profits for US companies operating within them.
>
> (Gowan, 1999a: 124)

This pattern was, in fact, not sustained. US dependence on emerging economies' growth more or less ended with the Asian crisis, and a new financial dependence emerged. The crisis, as Gowan also noted,

> provided a welcome boost for the US financial market and through them for the US domestic economy. Huge funds could be expected to flood into the US financial markets, cheapening the costs of credit there, boosting the stock market and boosting domestic economic growth.
>
> (Gowan, 1999a: 104–5)

And they did. After 1997, capital flows bypassed emerging-economy financial markets and went directly into the upward-moving US bond and stock markets. Although the US stock market slumped sharply at the outbreak of the Asian crisis, with the Dow plunging 554 points on October 27, it rebounded the next day, and 'the S&P 500 index and the Dow finish[ed] 1997 near their highs for the year' (ERP, 1998: 54). With this financial recovery, the Clinton Administration coyly admitted that the Asian crisis would 'allow continued growth and job creation with a more moderate outlook for interest rates' in the United States (1998: 19). And the impending widening of the US trade deficit would have another welcome effect: 'aggressive competition from foreign producers is likely to restrain domestic inflation' (1998: 86).

CENTRIPETAL FINANCE

The US stock market had been climbing since about 1982, having bounced back from the crash of 1987 thanks to the first 'Greenspan put', and its rise up to 1995 was largely justified 'by a corresponding rise in corporate profits'. Thereafter, however, it began 'climbing skyward without a ladder' (Brenner, 2009: 21). This long bull run created its own momentum, of course, but 'what actually drove equities to take flight was, almost certainly, a sudden sharp fall in the cost of borrowing, both short and long term' (2009: 21). While the Fed kept short-term interest rates at the historically high level of about 5 per cent, international borrowing became cheaper when the reverse Plaza accord prompted a reduction in German and especially Japanese interest rates. Investors borrowed yen cheaply, converted them into dollars and invested the proceeds in the stock market and in US government debt, in what became known as the 'carry trade'. The latter investment led, moreover, to 'a stunning twenty-three per cent decline in the long term cost of borrowing over the course of 1995' (2009: 21).

Greenspan and Treasury secretary Robert Rubin were aware that the continuing ascent of the US stock market after 1995 was out of whack with industrial data (Woodward, 2000). However, they were also aware that it had become the real engine of growth by fuelling consumption and investment. Rather than reining the stock market in, Greenspan encouraged its ascent. His famous 'irrational exuberance' speech on December 5, 1996 is normally taken as a warning that the rise in stock prices was undue. It was neither intended to, nor did it, affect investor behaviour. '[N]othing he said before or after indicates that he actually took his own message to heart' (Fleckenstein, 2008: 42). Indeed, everything he said before and after that 'warning' actually belied it, and justified rising stock prices. Feeding unrealistic hopes about the information and communications technology (ICT) sector representing an economic transformation as thoroughgoing as electricity or the internal combustion engine, and an economic boom to match the ones they created – a 'once in a century acceleration of innovation' and 'veritable shifts in the tectonic plates of technology' (Fleckenstein, 2008: 81–4) – Greenspan began to advance the view that a new economy was emerging, and a 'productivity miracle' ongoing which the data did not reveal. In riding on it, the stock market was riding on so much hot air.

A hidden productivity miracle?

Greenspan advanced his novel thesis in the August 1995 Federal Open Market Committee (FOMC) meeting, with several distinct assertions. First, allaying concerns that the stock valuation of companies exceeded their assets, he argued that 'intellectual services [like R&D] have historically tended to be written off as expenses in income statements', but in 'an economy in which the value added is increasingly software, telecommunications technologies, and various means of conveying value to people without the transference of a physical good', there was 'increasing evidence that we probably are expensing items that really should be capitalized'. In the United States's ICT-dominated economy, 'the ratio of stock market value to book value is much higher than one … in certain industries it is a huge multiple', only because 'an increasing amount of capital expenditures in the classic sense is being misclassified as expenses'. Second, he claimed that 'there has been a shift toward increasingly conceptual and impalpable value added and that actual GDP in constant dollars [as opposed to nominal] is becoming progressively less visible'. Finally, this meant that the rising stock market

> is basically telling us that there has indeed been an acceleration of productivity if one properly incorporates in output that which the markets value as output. If in effect there has been a failure to capture all the output that has been occurring, we will indeed show productivity growth that is too low. It is hard to imagine that productivity is moving up only around 1 percent under the new weighting basis with profit margins moving the way they are and with the widespread business restructuring that is occurring. I think the difficulty is not in productivity; I think it is at the Department of Commerce.
>
> (FOMC, 1995: 6)

By making the first point, Greenspan was simply preferring to question the data rather than investor behaviour, with accounting rules no half-decent accountant would accept. His aim was to deny that there was a stock market bubble. The related points about hidden production and productivity bear some discussion, however.

For the US data, which did not reveal the production and productivity growth Greenspan wanted to see, was already geared to capture precisely the sort of thing that Greenspan claimed was happening. The Bureau of Economic Analysis (BEA) had been making 'quality' or 'hedonic' adjustments to the value of increasing numbers of products since the mid-1980s in calculating real (as opposed to nominal) US GDP (Wasshausen and Moulton, 2006). The idea was that if the price of a product went up but it also improved in quality, the deemed value of the improvement in quality must be factored in calculating the 'real', inflation-adjusted, price. When this was done, rather than being lower than the nominal price, as was usual, the real price could be, indeed usually was, higher. As such adjustments were applied to more and more products, they increased estimates of real production and reduced those of inflation. Whatever the merits of this procedure, two things must be noted for our purposes. First, critics pointed out that hedonic adjustments were never made downward for deterioration in quality, as was frequently experienced, for instance, in the increasingly important service sector. Second, since no other countries (except the United Kingdom to a small extent: see Islam, 2002) make such adjustments, US real GDP and productivity growth are exaggerated in relation to that of other countries to the extent that those techniques are applied. (This is a point of no mean relevance to arguments about HST which, while granting that the United States's economic weight in the world economy slid from about half to about a quarter between 1945 and the early 1970s, rely on pointing out that it subsequently remained steady until very recently.)

Statisticians joke that there is no datum that will not confess if sufficiently tortured, but the data remained tight-lipped on production and productivity increases despite energetic 'hedonic' ministrations. The quality-adjusted data on productivity showed, first, that increases in productivity in the 1990s, particularly from 1995 to 2000, were hardly 'miraculous'. They fell well short of those of the Kennedy–Johnson and Nixon–Ford years and were only slightly above those of the Reagan–Bush years (Pollin, 2000: 29) and under the average for the century (Henwood, 2005: 48). They justified neither the rising stock market nor the hype about a new ICT revolution, even at their face value. And there were reasons to question that value. Robert Solow had stated his paradox that 'we can see the computer age everywhere but in the productivity statistics' in 1987 (Uchitelle, 2000), and Robert Gordon concluded that 'the productivity revival [of the late 1990s] appears to have occurred primarily within the production of computer hardware, peripherals, and telecommunications equipment, with substantial spillover to the 12 percent of the economy involved in manufacturing durable goods', leaving the rest of the economy dry despite much investment (Gordon, 2000: 50). Not only was this finding confirmed in subsequent debate, it was also agreed that 'computer-using industries like finance, insurance, and real estate (FIRE) and services have continued to lag in productivity growth. Reconciliation of massive high-tech investment and relatively slow productivity growth in service industries remains an important task for proponents of the new economy position' (Jorgensen and Stiroh, 2000: 3).

This finding of some productivity growth in manufacturing was questioned precisely because of the role of quality adjustments in the data. For these adjustments were applied most frequently to ICT products, overstating growth in their output and productivity:

> Between 1990 and the 2000 tech peak, nominal sales of computers rose 78% – but since prices fell by 94%, real [i.e. hedonically adjusted] computer sales rose 1,783%. Computer sales accounted for 1% of nominal GDP growth over the same 10 years – and 12% of real growth.
>
> (Henwood, 2005: 52)

US manufacturing productivity growth was entirely accounted for by this 'adjusted' growth, since there was 'no acceleration in productivity growth in manufacturing outside high tech; in fact, if anything, productivity growth in low- and medium-tech slowed during the 1990s' (Henwood, 2005: 53–4; see also ERP, 2000: 80–3). In an article comparing US and European productivity performance, Gordon found that '[i]n ICT-producing industries there was an acceleration [of productivity growth] after 1995 of 1.9 percent per year in the U.S. and a similar 1.6 percent per year in Europe'. However, though he pointed to the role of quality adjustments in overstating productivity in the retail sector (see below), he did not draw the obvious implication that, contrary to the rhetoric of the US new economy, US performance was worse than the European if the hedonic adjustment, which the latter did not make, was taken into account (Gordon, 2004).

Productivity is notoriously difficult to measure, and estimates of ICT's contribution to productivity growth relied on assuming 'that the annual contribution [to the economy as a whole] equals the economy's average rate of profit – otherwise businesses would not invest in them', because investors are 'well-informed and rational' (Henwood, 2005: 58–9). This assumption was particularly problematic for ICT manufacturing because there were:

> [e]xtraordinary levels of investment in plant, equipment, and software in the late 1990s spurred by easy access to finance, lacking justification in the rate of return, and obsessively focused on information technology [:] it also exacerbated industrial over-capacity, while extending its scope deep into the heart of the high technology sector. Between 1995 and 2000, industrial capacity in information technology quintupled, accounting by itself for roughly half of the quadrupling of industrial capacity that took place in the manufacturing sector as a whole, which also smashed all records.
>
> (Brenner, 2009: 31)

Brenner was concerned about the effect of this massive misallocation of capital on profitability, which declined thanks to overcapacity, but it also inflated productivity measures, because a firm that has purchased new equipment is automatically assumed to have experienced productivity growth due to that investment, no matter what the real causes of the productivity growth are, let alone whether the investment might have decreased productivity – for instance because it necessitated more support, training and so on (Sichel, 1997). But even such questionable assumptions failed to turn up the necessary evidence.

While computer-using industries, overwhelmingly service industries, were clocking decreases in productivity (Triplett, 1999) as a whole, 'mundane wholesale and retail trade' registered the most significant increases in productivity outside ICT manufacturing (Glyn, 2006: 133–4, citing Nordhaus, 2002). However, ICT made a 'barely positive and statistically insignificant' contribution to productivity growth in this sector (MGI, 2001: 4). Instead, productivity grew thanks to 'organizational improvements, the advantages of large scale Big Box stores, and the shift to higher value goods associated with the growth in the number of high-income consumers' (Glyn, 2006: 135–6). Since such productivity increases in retailing were distinctive to the US economy, they were, Gordon cautioned, likely to be the results of hedonic adjustments. Given that a substantial part of the retail sector sold ICT products whose value was adjusted hedonically, and given that retail productivity was measured by the value of goods sold per employee, US methods of measuring productivity would inflate productivity figures: 'While there has been substantial discussion of the role of hedonic price indexes in improving the measured productivity performance of the U.S. manufacturing sector, I am unaware of any similar comments about the potential for noncomparability in retailing productivity' (Gordon, 2004: 12). Finally, statistics about increasing productivity tended to assume that measures of hours worked were reliable, at a time when employees up and down the pay scales were putting in more unrecorded hours than ever before (Henwood, 2005: 67).

In sum, neither the production nor the use of ICT was leading to significant increases in productivity, let alone miraculous ones justifying the stock market's ascent, even though the data was more biased toward finding it to be so than many economists considered acceptable. Intuitive as the idea of great productivity increases might be for those who believed they were living through an era of great technological change, systematic observations failed to confirm it. Indeed, some even questioned whether the ICT age was one of great technological change, pointing out how earlier inventions, from the telegraph (Standage, 1998) to indoor plumbing (Mokyr and Stein, 1997) improved lives and productivity far more dramatically than ICT, and that quality improvement in earlier ages – as with cars in the first decades of the twentieth century – had been greater than the last period (Triplett, 1999).

Doug Henwood drove home how fictitious productivity increases were in both manufacturing and retail by asking 'where these apparent gains are ending up'. The productivity growth from 1997 to 2000 was supposed to be double that of the previous three-year period, but wage growth peaked in 1998, slowing thereafter, and corporate profitability peaked the year before. In addition, some of the profits of the boom years were turning out to be 'accounting fictions'. 'If faster productivity growth doesn't show up in wages or profits, it's hard to imagine where it's gone, or why it really matters, *except maybe to justify the greatest bull market in history and to build capitalism's brand identity*' (Henwood, 2005: 56, emphasis added).

None of this is to say ICT was not transforming life, and even economies. Gordon pointed to a fundamental aspect of computers as a technology, that they were less important in increasing productivity than in increasing control. A critical reason for new computer investments was

> the need to protect market share against competitors ... computers are used extensively to provide information aimed at taking customers, profits, or capital gains away from other companies. This is a zero-sum game involving redistribution of wealth rather than the increase of wealth, yet each individual firm has a strong incentive to make computer investments that, if they do not snatch wealth away from someone else, at least act as a defensive blockade against a hostile attack.
>
> (Gordon, 2000: 69)

In addition to enabling firms to fight for market shares in the zero-sum game the long downturn necessitated, computers could also increase control over inventories and employees, and financial institutions were able to determine the distribution of income and wealth. Jeff Madrick mused, more optimistically, that those looking to ICT to yield productivity increases were barking up the wrong tree. It might be that it was leading to

> a high-technology version of a crafts economy, based on worker skills, thinking, and inventiveness, rather than on the muscle of large-scale factories and distribution networks ... [which] ... may simply not be able to remove human beings from the production process as rapidly as the old standardized economy of the mass production age.
>
> (Madrick, 1998)

A new economy?

Having dismissed the data with his claims about a 'hidden productivity miracle' and assured investors that they were not being irrationally exuberant at all, Greenspan now told them the bull market had put the US economy in a 'virtuous cycle':

> Evidence of accelerated productivity has been bolstering expectations of future corporate earnings, thereby fuelling still further increases in equity values, and the improvements in productivity have been helping to reduce inflation. In the context of subdued price increases and generally supportive credit conditions, rising equity values have provided impetus to spending and, in turn, the

expansion of output, employment, and productivity-enhancing capital investment.

(Greenspan, 1998)

The 'maestro' was conducting this new enchanted 'Goldilocks' economy to which the old rules could no longer be applied (at least until the bears returned home, which they would just two years later). The new economy boasted a low 'misery index' – the sum of inflation and unemployment rates, perpetual ICT-powered productivity growth, capital inflows, investment growth, and superior growth performance compared with the rest of the world.

For all his talk about productivity in the real economy, Greenspan knew that the stock market ascent was the key. He feigned a rather erudite ignorance when uncomfortable questions arose, claiming to be unable to define money, to tell if there was a bubble in the stock market, or to see signs of an imminent recession (Fleckenstein, 2008: 109), while keeping up the rhetoric about productivity and the new economy to keep the stock market rising. And with the Greenspan put remaining on the table, it did so confidently. In December 1998, Jerry Jordan of the Cleveland Fed warned of how 'newsletters, advisory letters, talking heads on CNBC and so on [were] saying that there is no risk that the stock market is going to go down because if it even started down, the Fed would ease policy to prop it back up', and that 'more and more people [were] coming to that belief and acting on it' (quoted in Fleckenstein, 2008: 60).

Greenspan's smoke and mirrors about the new economy and the hidden productivity miracle drove not just the stock market's rise but also a giant investment boom, which resulted in 'massive over-investment in the aggregate' and 'a stunning mis-direction of capital among industrial lines' (Brenner, 1998: 30) towards ICT. Three things were interesting in this connection. First, the stock market bubble was not just a case of overshooting an economic boom. Instead, 'the causal chain was reversed. The New Economy boom materialized as a direct manifestation of the bubble in the stock market by way of its wealth effect, even in the face of declining returns on investment' (1998: 24).

Second, although the infamous initial public offerings (IPOs) by start-ups without assets or sales in the dot-com bubble did raise equity (though whether this led to productive investment is another question), the stock market boom and the investment boom were not directly connected: 'net issuance of equity was actually negative in the late 1990s'. Postwar US corporations had been largely self-financing, and in the late 1990s they turned not to the stock market but banks:

> gross equity issues were more than offset by share repurchases and merger-based stock retirements at other firms, so that debt, not equity, served as the major source of business financing during the investment boom. Business debt rose steadily throughout this period, with net issuance of long-term corporate bonds and short-term commercial paper playing especially important roles.
>
> (ERP, 2003: 39)

Of course, share repurchases and retirements also boosted the value of the stocks that remained in the market, and were meant to do so in a corporate culture that measured executive performance by through stock prices.

Finally, this investment boom reduced profits not just because it increased competition but also for two other reasons. Higher corporate indebtedness reduced profits after payment of interest even more (Brenner, 2009: 34), and the misdirection of capital decreased rates of return and profit.

The famous wealth effect of this stock market boom was therefore ironic:

> US businesses and wealthy households were able to gain access to virtually unlimited funds... at the very time that firms' profitability was ceasing to rise and turning downward – not least as a consequence of the same ascent of the dollar that was helping share prices upward – and the economy was implicitly threatened with slowdown.
>
> (Brenner, 2009: 23)

Given that this sort of US growth formed the main pole of world growth during these years, former Fed chairman Paul Volcker summed matters up rather well when he said in May 1999 that 'The fate of the world economy is now totally dependent on the growth of the U.S. economy, which is dependent on the stock market, whose growth is dependent on about 50 stocks, half of which have never reported earnings' (quoted in Fleckenstein, 2008: 67).

In the absence of productivity gains, three other factors kept inflation figures low, appearing to abolish the traditional trade-off between inflation and unemployment and bringing the 'misery index' to its lowest level since 1968 (ERP, 1996: 3). First, official estimates of inflation were reduced not just through hedonic adjustments but also through changes in calculations of the consumer price index (CPI) on the recommendations of the 1995 Advisory Commission to Study the Consumer Price Index, or the Boskin Commission.

Second, while returns to capital remained very high thanks to high short-term interest rates in the United States and the rising stock market, and higher-income households enjoyed a consumption boom based on the 'wealth effect', returns to labour actually declined. The allegedly booming new economy notwithstanding, average wages for non-supervisory workers and the earnings of the lowest 10 per cent of wage earners 'not only remain[ed] well below those of the Nixon–Ford and Carter Administrations, but [were] actually lower even than those of the Reagan–Bush years', and the ratio of the top and bottom 10 per cent of wage earners increased sharply even compared with the preceding Republican era (Pollin, 2000: 35). Greenspan himself acknowledged that 'a heightened sense of job insecurity and, as a consequence, subdued wages' were helping keep inflation low in his testimony to Congress in July 1997 (quoted in Pollin, 2000: 39). And for him, this situation clearly provided just another lever against inflation: he moved to dampen economic growth by increasing interest rates at the slightest hint of labour-market tightening.

Finally, cheap imports from the developing world suffering income deflation under SAPs since the 1980s had been contributing to low inflation for a long time, and in the latter 1990s distress sales from East Asian economies played a special part.

Clinton's CEA was initially cautious about the claims about a new economy. Under Stiglitz, it had explored the possibility that 'the minimum sustainable unemployment rate or so-called NAIRU (Non-Accelerating-Inflation Rate of Unemployment) has declined' (ERP, 1996: 53), but attributed the decline not to any new economy but to structural changes, not all welcome – 'increased domestic and international competition, a decline in unionization, and increased concern about job security' as well as lower frictional unemployment as the workforce aged – which 'restrained increases in wages and prices' (1996: 53). To these it later added 'delayed alignment of workers' real wage expectations with productivity growth' (ERP, 1997: 48). And under Janet Yellen, the CEA added slowly rising 'costs of providing workers with nonwage compensation (such as health insurance)' (ERP, 1998: 58) as another factor of low inflation, and concluded that the NAIRU might indeed have declined to 5.3 per cent (ERP, 1999: 24).

By 1998, when the issue of the new economy could no longer be ignored, moreover, Yellen's CEA undertook a full discussion. It explicitly rejected the possibility that there was a 'new paradigm' justifying suspension of the old rules, and took a strong anti-inflationary line. While the economy had changed with increased competition, greater exposure to trade, deregulation, and greater efficiency, while output and innovation had increased, and while labour markets had become more flexible and worker anxiety had increased with decreased unionization and greater use of temporary and contingent employees, other questions, such as whether just-in-time inventories had dampened business cycles, had to be investigated further. Naturally the CEA took some credit on behalf of the government, and pointed to the contribution of the changed public sector: social security was geared to help welfare recipients re-enter the labour force, there had been post-cold-war reductions in defence outlays, government had been reinvented to make it more efficient, and of course the deficit was eliminated. However, the report continued sternly: 'Not all of these changes represent unalloyed boons.' It was impossible to quantify the effects of any of these changes precisely, and any productivity increase would have to be 'very large to reverse the post-1973 productivity slowdown to any significant degree'. Even if many of the allegedly new factors turned out to be significant,

> it may imply not that a new model of the economy is needed, but rather that certain key parameters of the current model, such as the NAIRU or trend productivity growth, have changed. Hence one cannot declare with any certainty that the old rules no longer apply.
>
> (ERP, 1998: 63)

However, with the subordination of fiscal policy to the judgement of the Fed and the bond markets, government voices were no match for the powerful Fed chairman in public discourse.

As the 'longest postwar economic expansion' continued, however, the CEA, now under a new chairman, fell in behind the Fed on the new economy. As discussed at the beginning of this chapter, ERP, 2000 hailed the United States as the world's largest and richest economy at the turn of the century, with an 'astounding' economic performance and still-strong 'record-breaking expansion' (ERP, 2000: 21–2). Like the postwar Golden Age, it claimed, the current expansion rested on 'the three pillars':

fiscal discipline to help reduce interest rates and spur business investment; investing in education, health care, and science and technology to meet the challenges of the 21st century; and opening foreign markets so that American workers have a fair chance to compete abroad.

(ERP, 2000: 3)

Driven by technology, especially ICT, increased competition, a well-educated workforce, and pro-investment policies and deficit reduction, the expansion proved the 'gloomy outlook' and 'diminished expectations' of the two previous decades misguided. Despite having clocked 107 months free of recession, the economy was still going strong and, moreover, producing equitable growth (2000: 28). This claim rested *inter alia* on the problematic 'real', 'deflated' figures for earnings, and on family rather than individual earnings, in an economy where more family members were working more hours. Although technology, competition, trade and so on normally increased inequality,

> [b]etween 1993 and 1998, real average household incomes have grown by between 9.9 and 11.7 percent for every quintile of the income distribution, and the median African American household has seen a 15 percent increase in real income. Between 1993 and 1998, family incomes in the lowest quintile rose at a 2.7 percent annual rate, slightly faster than the 2.4 percent rate recorded by the top quintile.
>
> (ERP, 2000: 27)

This showed, the report opined, that '*rapid growth in an open economy can occur without worsening inequality*', and that 'it is time to reappraise the inevitability of the allegedly adverse impacts of technology and trade' (2000: 39).

ERP, 2000's discussion of 'Opportunity and challenge in the global economy' focused on furthering globalization – including through Chinese accession into the WTO, and reforming the financial structures of the crisis-hit economies to keep them open while managing crises better. The latter meant rectifying the 'low levels of usable reserves [which] created vulnerability to a sudden turn in confidence that ultimately became self-perpetuating' (2000: 226). Larger reserves abroad, which had to be held in liquid dollar-denominated assets, would mean, of course, that capital would keep flowing into the US economy as the 'record-breaking expansion' took US current account deficits to record-breaking highs. Of course, such reserve holding would be taken to reflect the desire (rather than the compulsion) of foreigners to acquire US assets, which in turn reflected confidence in the US economy and its financial structures, in time-honoured HST tradition (2000: 232).

ERP, 2000 compared GDP growth in the United States and the rest of the world, and drew the convenient conclusion that '[a] strong economy raises demand for imports and is generally associated with high demand for investment'. Since 1998 the US growth had remained steady while growth elsewhere had declined, and the US trade deficit had expanded from 1 per cent of GDP in the mid-1990s to 3 per cent:

> The dramatic difference between U.S. and foreign growth appears to be the primary cause of the increase in the deficit, as demand grew more rapidly for all products, including imports, in the United States than elsewhere. From the perspective of capital flows, expected returns on investment have been relatively attractive in the United States. As a result, the United States has absorbed substantial net inflows of capital.
>
> (ERP, 2000: 232)

And expected returns in the United States were higher because productivity was higher (2000: 234).

ERP, 2000 was not without some caution. Over-optimism could still be at play in the stock market rise (2000: 68–71), and while better inventory management, the shift to less volatile services, and fiscal and monetary stabilization had moderated business cycles in the postwar period, and though productivity and inflation trends were going in the right direction, it was 'premature to declare the business cycle dead' (2000: 79). However, the Report considered it likely that economic performance had become 'less of the roller-coaster ride that characterized the 1970s and early 1980s (not to mention earlier decades)' because fiscal discipline freed up capital for 'investment in education, business, and technology, spurring faster growth'. And it congratulated the Fed for 'a systematic policy that fosters price stability and long-term growth' (2000: 79). The expansion would be sustained because, unlike previous expansions in which productivity growth slowed as the expansion matured, the current expansion exhibited a 'pattern of strong productivity growth at a mature stage of the cycle' and because core inflation remained stable (2000: 34–7). ERP, 2000 spoke a couple of months too soon.

THE GEOPOLITICAL ECONOMY OF GLOBALIZATION

Not only was the stock markets' rise after 1995 not justified either by rising productivity or any new economy, it was leading (though not directly) to a massive misallocation of investment. It would lower, not raise, profit rates. Whereas normally stock markets rise because of investment, in the enchanted new economy, it was the other way around. It was only a matter of time before declining profits brought investors back to reality, which they did in the spring of 2000 when the stock market first dived.

Greenspan did not react immediately with his famous put. Having decreased interest rates slightly after the Asian crisis from their post-1995 high plateau, the Fed had actually begun to raise them in mid-1999, chiefly because the expansion, driven by misallocated investment and consumption though it was, had finally begun to increase real compensation, indicating a tightening labour market and the possibility of inflation (FOMC, 1999). Rates continued to go up until they reached 6.5 per cent in May 2000. When stock markets took their first dive in March, Greenspan was still more concerned about labour markets than about capital markets, and raised rates once again, this time by 0.5 per cent, in May. It was only after the markets opened 2001 with a couple of days of steep falls that Greenspan cut rates by 0.5 per cent, claiming to detect signs of weakness in the economy (Fleckenstein, 2008: 112), although in reality the economy had started to slow in the spring of 2000. However, the Greenspan put had now lost its magic. Though markets initially put on an impressive rally in response, it could not last. Over the next year, practically all the gains of the previous five years on the NASDAQ were wiped out. 'As one economist wryly noted, "What it means is that, with the benefit of hindsight, the late 1990s never happened." So much for the New Economy' (Brenner, 2009: 34–5).

Clinton's last economic report was written after the stock market bubble had burst. It was to have been a primer on and paean to the new economy, which was supposed to be Clinton's economic legacy. But it had to conclude soberly that

it would be a grave error to assume that the economy has been so transformed that the basic rules of economics no longer apply. The potential for faster growth exists, but demand cannot run ahead of supply without the danger of rising inflation. The economy also remains susceptible to cyclical fluctuations. Indeed, the rewards of the New Economy are associated with increased risk, since the economy depends more heavily than before on financial markets, which remain volatile.

(ERP, 2001: 24)

While most analysts of 'globalization' tend to focus on its effects on national capitalisms and on developing countries everywhere, whether approvingly or critically, its connection with developments in the US economy through capital inflows has tended to be ignored. The Clinton Administration's push for market liberalization, particularly financial market liberalization, the steep differential between historically high short-term interest rates in the United States and low international long-term rates, the high-dollar policy and Greenspan's fairy tales about the hidden productivity miracle and the new economy, not to mention 'hedonic adjustments' which inflated real national income and productivity figures, kept these funds flowing in. The US-dominated world financial structure essentially acted like a giant vacuum cleaner, sucking up capital from the rest of the world and pouring it into the US economy.

Capital inflows into the United States, which had previously peaked in the mid-1980s and declined after the stock market crash of 1987, had started to rise again in the mid-1990s. In 1998 they amounted to $200 billion, or 7 per cent of GDP, whereas they had averaged 1 per cent through the 1950s and 1960s, and peaked at about 4 per cent in the mid-1980s (ERP, 2000: 205–6). And after 1997, the nature of the assets demanded changed. Whereas foreign holdings of the dollar after the 1995 'reverse Plaza accord' had swelled the stock market bubble mostly indirectly, with foreign official and private purchases of US government securities, the Asian financial crisis led to a massive liquidation of reserves among Asian governments trying to support their currencies. But the loss of these flows was more than compensated for by private investors flocking to the upwardly vaulting US stock market, and

by the end of the decade, rocketing purchases of US financial assets by foreign investors were playing an indispensable part in allowing stock prices to reach historic highs and the bubble to live a longer life, amplifying still further the spectacular ascent of US investment and consumption.

(Brenner, 2009: 31)

The geopolitical economy of globalization rested on these capital inflows 'covering the exploding US current account deficit, keeping the dollar ascending, and preventing long term interest rates from rising even as the boom continued, so that US domestic demand could continue to increase and sustain the exports of their own economies' (Brenner, 2009: 31).

So globalization was essentially the ideology under which, for a time, the United States was successful in engineering a situation in which the rest of the world was lending it more money than it had ever done before, doing so through its stock market, and even seeming happy to do so. In policy terms it denoted practices that systematically broke down barriers to the flow of capital across the world to enable this to happen, and it engaged in the rhetoric about productivity miracles and new gravity-defying economies that induced it to happen. These policies also involved justifying the declines in competitiveness, outflows of productive capital through US FDI, and yawning trade deficits that resulted, and the demand of bond markets that government deficits be kept low as the new normality of the new economy.

Outside the United States these practices prolonged the neoliberal growth stagnation and under-investment, increased inequality, and imposed income deflation on workers and peasants almost universally (Patnaik, 2008), although they were not able to prevent growth acceleration even under these conditions in some countries, as the 'BRICs thesis' (O'Neill, 2001) pointed out. Of course, given its origins in a US investment bank, the proponents of this thesis could hardly afford to mention that they were countries that remained wary of the charms of unrestrained economic integration, and were sufficiently powerful to resist US demands for it.

Within the United States, on the other hand, capital inflows powered an investment boom that misdirected capital into ICT without regard to profitability, and a consumer boom among those enjoying the 'wealth effect' of the rising stock market, increasing their dis-saving. At the other end of the income spectrum, working-class living standards partially kept up despite stagnating wages, thanks to the cheap prices of imports, produced by even more luckless workers abroad and sold cheaply thanks to the big-box retailing revolution. Unemployment was kept down by the proliferation of unattractive service-sector jobs, while the fabled low inflation of this era needed the hocus pocus of the Boskin Commission despite the effects of insecurity on the US workforce and the cheap consumer imports. Inequality rose to historic heights under the Democratic 'third way' president (Phillips, 2002). Finally, globalization was supposed to be the tide that lifted all boats, but in reality, during this period the United States grew at the expense of both Western Europe and Japan, as the more fundamental problem of the long downturn, the inability of all industrial centres to grow together, remained unresolved (Freeman, 2001).

Capital flowing into the US stock market was the key to this geopolitical economy. When the stock market bubble burst in March 2000 these flows dried up. This was the end of globalization.

8

EMPIRE?

The events of September 11, 2001 appeared to define the twenty-first century. The Bush administration invoked them to justify its unparalleled projection of US military power thereafter – in Afghanistan, Iraq and against 'terrorism' worldwide. The Fed and the administration also invoked 9/11 and the recession it allegedly caused to justify the economic policies, particularly the low interest rates, of the years that followed (ERP, 2002: 23, 30). Combined with the innovation of a financial sector now freed from the Glass-Steagall separation of commercial from investment banking, these policies attracted greater torrents of capital into the United States than even in the heyday of globalization, despite rock-bottom interest rates and a declining dollar. Capital from abroad flowed into the market for real-estate-backed securities, which swelled alongside real estate prices, seemingly unstoppably, opening a new phase of US- and dollar-centred financialization. It not only financed more gargantuan fiscal and current account deficits than ever before, but also sustained the liquidity the dollar needed for its status as a reserve currency despite its relentless slide. These military and economic responses to 9/11 were credited with repositioning the United States as the world's leader, inaugurating the new American century that the Project for the New American Century (PNAC) had called for.

A new genre of writing about the United States's 'empire' and 'new imperialism' emerged alongside obituaries of 'globalization' (*Economist*, 2001a; Ferguson, 2005). Advocates enjoined imperialism on the 'reluctant' United States as a historic duty, and cast imperialism in a positive light – as characteristic of the peaks of human civilization – for the first time since the First World War (Boot, 2003; Ferguson, 2004; Maier, 2006; Mallaby, 2002; Ignatieff, 2003, 2004). The United States was a New Rome with 'the classical architecture of its capital and the republican structure of its constitution' (Ferguson, 2004: 14; see also Maier, 2006). Accompanying economic discourses extolled the resilience, stability and rising wealth of the US economy. Of course, the empire had many critics, but too many assumed that it was militarily and economically successful and sustainable (e.g. Panitch and Gindin, 2004). A minority of critics did, however, recall how imperium had unravelled the Roman republic, and warned that the Tigris and Euphrates could be the modern Rubicons (Johnson, 2004: 15–17). They exposed yawning gaps between the rhetoric of freedom and justice and the reality of power and interests, and pointed to the growth of unsustainable deficits and international imbalances (Mann, 2004, Johnson, 2004; Bacevich, 2002). But few predicted how soon the empire would unravel. Arrighi, whose prescient 2005 verdict was quoted at length in Chapter 1, was a brilliant exception.

In the event, the project met its demise in the events of another September, a mere seven years later. The Fed began to raise interest rates in 2004 to counteract downward pressure on the dollar, and less than two years later, the US real estate bubble, which had relied on low interest rates, burst. As house prices declined, mortgage defaults and repossessions increased from those who had relied on continuing price increases rather than their incomes to pay their mortgages. Given the reliance of US growth on the consumption of those enjoying the wealth effects of the real estate bubble, a recession began in 2007. Eventually the credit bubble based on mortgage-backed securities (MBSs) burst too. The highly leveraged investment bank Bear Stearns collapsed in early 2008 and was bailed out by the government. But when another such bank, Lehman Brothers, was allowed to collapse in September, the US-centred international financial system, which funnelled capital into the US economy and undergirded the dollar's world role, teetered on the brink. Contrary to official rhetoric, the US economy and its storied financial system turned out to have been powered by little more than credit-fuelled consumption and a housing bubble which was even more destructive than the stock market bubble. Worse, though capital inflows financed a military budget that rose, both relative to other countries and absolutely, to unprecedented levels (Stiglitz and Bilmes, 2008), as early as 2005 the US occupations of Iraq and Afghanistan were faltering.

History's most massive bailout appeared to save the US-centred world financial system, but it would never be the same again. Dollar-denominated international capital flows collapsed in 2008, with only a very modest recovery thereafter (Borio and Disyatat, 2011: 14). The crisis raised questions about which national financial authority was responsible for which international operation, and cautioned banks against reckless international activity. New webs of predominantly national regulations, including the United States's own Dodd–Frank bill, made financial sectors even more national. The dollar resumed its decade-long decline after a brief and spectacular rally in the autumn of 2008, as panicked US international investors flew home to safety. Questions about its status as the world's money (Zhou, 2009; United Nations, 2009; Subbachi and Driffill, 2010) that rose immediately after the crisis were put in abeyance by the Eurozone crisis that erupted in 2010. However, it is doubtful that they can remain there for very long. Around the world, especially among emerging economies, a host of alternatives to using the dollar were springing up (Grabel, 2011; Wade, 2011). And the United States remained mired in the Great Recession, or very weak recovery, for years.

Thus empire proved to be the United States's final and most swaggering attempt to emulate British-style world dominance and it was, fittingly, brought down by defiant combined development elsewhere. Consequent increases in commodity prices, especially oil prices, put pressure on the already downward-sliding dollar and necessitated the monetary tightening that triggered the crisis. As financial crisis compounded recession, the ongoing shift in the world's economic centre of gravity away from the United States, Western Europe and Japan accelerated. In post-crisis summitry, the G-20 replaced the G-7 as the relevant body for informal multilateral management of the world economy. Barack Obama, who won the US presidency only because the financial crisis moved enough white workers to vote for him (Davis, 2009), admitted that the United States was 'living beyond its means', began to scale down the wars in Iraq and Afghanistan, and hailed the 'multipolar' world. Some argued that US world power remained substantially undiminished because there was no successor 'hegemon' in sight. This was, however, beside the point if the ideas of hegemony generally, and of US hegemony, were merely never-realized US desires in theoretical drag, and the unfolding of uneven and combined development (UCD) had now closed the door on even attempts to realize them.

The events of the two Septembers seven years apart bookend the final attempt at US world dominance, and this chapter retraces it. It begins by discussing how 'empire' differed from 'globalization', going on to place Bush Jr's 'imperial' strategy in a historical perspective on postwar US security policy. The three sections that follow trace the intensifying contradiction between power projection and economic debility. As the unquestioned manager of the economy, the Fed kept interest rates low to keep the housing bubble inflating because the credit-fuelled consumption generated by its wealth effect was the only source of growth. At the same time, the housing bubble itself rested on another bubble, a credit bubble, which relied critically on international capital inflows. Keeping these up required the United States to generate a new series of tall tales to assure investors that its economy was a fitting destination for them, despite its feeble economic performance and low interest rates.

These sections also correct our understanding of the causes of the 2008 financial crisis in a critical manner. Analysts and policy makers have debated whether the banks or their regulators had erred. To be sure, without deregulation, which the commercial banks sought and the Greenspan Fed encouraged, the housing bubble and the accompanying inflation of the market in MBSs would not have been possible. But deregulation was merely the sufficient condition. The necessary condition was provided by the Fed when it systematically inflated the housing and credit bubbles as the only growth motor of the US economy, and in turn, the only support for the dollar's international role. Indeed, the intensified competition that the Fed's actions created in the financial sector turned financial institutions into its creatures. The culmination of these processes in the crisis, and the Bush and Obama administrations' responses, are discussed in the final two sections.

THE IMPERIAL ECONOMY

While Clinton's 'globalization' presidency was hardly averse to unilateralist militarism, and many pointed to the continuities in the geopolitical economy of globalization and empire when the housing bubble replaced the stock market bubble, there were also important differences between the two. Clinton at least started out with a diagnosis of, and prescription for, US economic problems, even if he soon handed over the reins of economic policy to the Fed and bond markets. Whether Bush's economic policies ever went beyond cutting taxes, which he did in spades, can be doubted. Certainly his economic reports were even more devoid of ambition or analysis than Reagan's. Inclining to a sanguine view of economic prospects ('The New Economy is alive and well': ERP, 2002: 60), the Bush CEA let the Fed and the financial markets get on with it.

What they got on with was inflating a historic housing bubble which powered consumption and residential investment-led growth, with business investment bumping along the bottom, in contrast to the (albeit misdirected) investment boom of the previous decade's stock market bubble. The administration and the Fed, while expressing the pious hope that increased consumption would eventually revive business investment, concentrated on ensuring the economy could do without it: and that meant keeping the housing bubble growing. While the stock market bubble had also increased employment, the housing boom created so little employment that economists wondered what happened to the so recently celebrated Great American Jobs Machine (Baily and Lawrence, 2004). With the misdirected investment boom having exacerbated overcapacity and overinvestment, and lowered profitability, manufacturing shrank further, import penetration increased, and the trade deficit widened despite relatively slow growth.

Finally, whereas the stock market bubble had swelled amid historically high interest rates, the housing bubble needed ever-lower interest rates to grow. Low interest rates were always justified in terms of getting productive growth going, but with the productive economy in no shape to respond to their stimulus, low rates could only inflate asset prices. Even as the administration and the Fed congratulated themselves that housing wealth was spread more widely than stock market wealth, as was the credit based on it, private dis-saving spread farther down the social scale. As the government's pursuit of tax cuts and the war on terrorism widened the federal deficit, US savings rates dipped even lower than in the previous decade. Although consumption's share of the US economy grew to historic heights, the economy had grown so weak that even under the Fed's determined credit Keynesianism it grew more slowly than in earlier postwar decades.

This was the economy on whose back the Bush administration took the United States's share of world military expenditure to over half, while cutting taxes. The resulting twin deficits were left to the rest of the world to finance. Whereas in the 1990s, Clinton had closed the fiscal deficit and the current account deficit was financed by private capital inflows into US equity markets, in the 2000s capital inflows took the form of investments in US Treasury and agency debt, and in housing-related securities. While the Clinton Administration had justified the current account deficit by pointing to the investment boom it generated, under Bush, net capital inflows mainly financed consumption and were part of gross inflows that swelled to between two and three times the current account deficit (Borio and Disyatat, 2011: 14).

These inflows rested on confidence, in the US securities market and in the US economy. In the 1990s, with faster growth, rising employment and investment, maintaining such confidence had required high interest rates and economic tall tales. Now with the lowest growth rates ever, confidence had to be created with even less to work with. But Greenspan's creativity, now supplemented by that of Ben Bernanke, who was appointed a member of the Fed's Board of Governors in 2002 and chairman in 2006, was up to the challenge. Between them they produced a series of even taller tales to explain away the US economy's various debilities.

First, when it became clear that consumption based on credit extended on rising house prices was the only force for growth out of the 2000–01 recession, and that it relied on low interest rates, Bernanke raised the 'danger of deflation', which could only be averted by ever-lower interest rates (Bernanke, 2002), while Greenspan cheered the boost that mortgage markets gave to consumption (Greenspan, 2002a). After 2003, as the bubble entered its sub-prime phase, Bernanke extolled the 'great moderation' in the volatility of inflation and output, so as to draw attention away from the low economic growth and low employment growth that could spell disaster (Bernanke, 2004), and Greenspan told refinancing homeowners and lenders to be even more adventuresome (Greenspan, 2004). When, by the middle of the decade, the dollar came under pressure and required higher interest rates to keep funds flowing in, Bernanke explained away the inevitable questions about the sustainability of these financial flows by inventing the 'global savings glut' argument (Bernanke, 2005). While few could deny that a correction of this patently unsustainable situation was inevitable, the Fed breezily put it in far in the future. However, once the Fed had to begin to raise interest rates to prop up the dollar in July 2004, this sort of political economy, and geopolitical economy, were not long for this world.

THE BUBBLE OF MILITARIST HUBRIS

Most critics of Bush's militarism focused on his 'intractable provincialism, religious zealotry, and ... reckless temperament of a gunslinger' (Bacevich, 2006: 4). Many scholars (e.g. Johnson, 2004; Mann, 2003) pointed to his neoconservative lieutenants, 'the cabal of warmongers', who used 9/11 as a pretext for the invasion of Afghanistan and Iraq (Bacevich, 2006: 4). Certainly the neoconservatives had, as we have seen, been exerting growing influence over US defence policy since the 1980s. While Bush's military expenditure increases followed reductions by previous post-cold-war presidents, even under them, US military expenditures had continued to increase relative to those of other powers.

So the Bush Administration's aggressive militarism was not 'a conspiracy foisted on a malleable president and an unsuspecting people by a handful of wild-eyed ideologues'. If it were, Michael Mann's remedy to '[t]hrow the militarists out of office' (Bacevich, 2006: 4) would have worked. Rather, like the economic slowdown blamed on 9/11, US military actions, which were allegedly in response to it, had deeper roots in the United States's 'militaristic disposition'. This rested on four 'core convictions': that history is an onward march of freedom; that the United States embodies, exemplifies and advocates freedom; that the United States is the agent of liberty; and that 'for the American way of life to endure, freedom must prevail everywhere' (Bacevich, 2008: 74–5). Such convictions, modern versions of the formative US expansionism detailed in Chapter 3, issued 'an infinitely expansible grant of authority, empowering the United States to assert its influence anywhere it chooses since, by definition, it acts on freedom's behalf' (2008: 75). The continuity of Bacevich's critique with that of Williams and Beard (reviewed in Chapter 3) was conscious. That it was, more remarkably, also credible, testifies to the long-term continuity of US purposes.

The Bush Administration's foreign policy used 9/11 as a rationale for the wars that followed in a pattern going back to Paul Nitze, who 'seized upon the Soviet bomb, the Chinese Revolution and later the Korean War to argue for rebuilding American military power' (Bacevich, 2008: 116) after the Second World War. And, as with those events, the official version is contested on many critical points. It is widely known that the Bush Administration, ably assisted by the United Kingdom's Blair government, concocted evidence about weapons of mass destruction (WMD) in Iraq to justify war. What is perhaps less well appreciated is that the links between 9/11, al-Qaeda and the war in Afghanistan, were also far from clear (MacGregor and Zarembka, 2010: 157–8).

The rhetoric accompanying the Iraq war – whether about WMD or regime change unleashing democracy in the Islamic world – worked 'to lift any and all restrictions on the use of armed force by the United States' (Bacevich, 2004: 117). The doctrine of anticipatory self-defence, which even Nitze had found 'morally repugnant' (and which the United States was, in any case, in no position to pursue as long as the USSR existed), now came to life. With the United States no longer willing to 'confin[e] its actions to those directly involved in the terrorist conspiracy' and eager to 'end ... states who support terrorism', it was conducting 'open-ended global war' (Bacevich, 2008: 118–19).

Hitherto justified as advancing freedom worldwide, US military actions abroad were now justified unabashedly as advancing Americans' freedom. This was, moreover, increasingly equated with material comfort and indulgence (just when the US economy was decreasingly able to provide them). Within US society, the human costs of war were radically maldistributed. The draft had been out of the question since Vietnam, and additions to armed forces personnel were considered unnecessary in waging capital-intensive warfare. So 'the 0.5 percent of the population that made up the all-volunteer force would bear the brunt of any sacrifice', with repeated tours of duty (2008: 61). Domestic political opposition to the war remained confined to a small, vocal minority. On the whole, 'while soldiers fought, people consumed', and 'most Americans subscribed to a limited-liability version of patriotism' in which bumper stickers replaced fatigues (2008: 62–3). The costs of this militarism could be kept off the political agenda as long as the US-centred world financial system financed them. It kept the wars grinding on, and US enemies multiplying.

However, even the most expensive military in the world could not prevail in Iraq or Afghanistan, because the policy was built on 'three great illusions'. The first was that the United States had reinvented war through technology capable of 'surgical strikes' against 'regimes not nations', and through 'full spectrum dominance – unambiguous supremacy in all forms of warfare', it had achieved the military version of the 'end of history' (2008: 127–8). The second illusion, the so-called Weinberger–Powell doctrine, was that defeat in Vietnam had been caused by the recklessness of civilian leaders, and the problems encountered there could be corrected by fighting wars with 'concrete and attainable objectives' by mobilizing the resources necessary for a prompt and decisive victory' (2008: 129). The third illusion was that the Gulf War had restored the bond between the people and the US army. In the 2000s the three illusions were compounded by the 'Bush doctrine' – an inchoate amalgam of unilateralism and aggression – which took leave of reality to an even greater extent. Journalist Ron Suskind's widely cited conversation with 'a senior advisor to Bush' is worth recalling. He dismissed 'the reality-based community' which believed that 'solutions emerge from your judicious study of discernible reality':

'That's not the way the world really works anymore,' he

continued. 'We're an empire now, and when we act, we create our own reality. And while you're studying that reality – judiciously, as you will – we'll act again, creating other new realities, which you can study too, and that's how things will sort out. We're history's actors ... and you, all of you, will be left to just study what we do.'

(Suskind, 2004)

In fact, although US military power sufficed to dominate small and isolated nations, it had singularly failed to prevail in any major military confrontation, including Korea and Vietnam. And three decades after the defeat in Vietnam, during which in the United States had professionalized its army and built up military capacity in a 'never again' spirit by spending unimaginable amounts, the United States faced an even more ignominious defeat:

> In purely military terms, the Iraqi insurgents, unlike the Vietnamese, do not field heavily-armoured vehicles, nor do they have long experience of guerrilla warfare in a favourable natural environment, or enjoy the support of a superpower like the USSR. ... This is why the Bush Administration hoped the invasion of Iraq would reverse the Vietnam verdict; but it is also the reason why failure to do so would constitute a far greater blow to the credibility of US military might than defeat in Indo-China.
>
> (Arrighi, 2005a: 57)

Not only would Bush's militarism prove futile, its fiscal outlays relied on the unlikeliest yet of the geopolitical economies of US imperial attempts.

THE REAL ESTATE BUBBLE: SECOND TIME AS FARCE?

Greenspan had his eye on the tightening labour market when he began raising interest rates in July 1999. Since all his talk about the real economy was aimed only at sustaining the stock market's rise, he did not react when, by July 2000, 'the economy entered into a frightening free fall', and he did not begin to lower interest rates until stock markets faltered in January 2001. By then, however, growth, investment and real aggregate wages and salaries were falling faster than in any previous postwar recession (Brenner, 2009: 34). Greenspan followed the 0.5 per cent cut of January 2001 with four more cuts by May, and two further cuts of 0.25 per cent each over the summer. Thus, not only was the economy weakening well before 9/11, the stock market decline had frightened Greenspan enough that he had begun to cut rates massively well before then too. After 9/11, three further cuts of 0.5 per cent and one of 0.25 per cent followed before the year ended. The rate cuts would continue until they took the Federal funds rate from 6.5 per cent in 2001 to 1 per cent by June 2003. It remained there for the next year.

Plane crash or investment crash?

Although the data clearly showed that the economy had been slowing since mid-2000, the Fed and the administration created the myth that 9/11 'and the subsequent precipitous decline in consumer and business confidence late in 2001 were sufficient to tip the Nation into ... recession' (ERP, 2002: 36), citing the National Bureau of Economic Research (NBER) Business Cycle Dating Committee's tentative surmise that the attacks might have turned a mild contraction into a recession (2002: 42). However, the NBER's considered opinion was that the recession had started in March 2001 (ERP, 2004: 30–1). The administration disingenuously expressed anxiety about consumers' retrenchment after 9/11 'as they mourned the loss of life and revaluated the risks inherent in even the most mundane activities, such as shopping at malls and travelling by air' (2004: 31). In fact, consumer confidence bounced back rather smartly even before 2001 ended. However, so eager were the Bush administration and the Fed to milk 9/11 as the cause of any and all economic bad news and to justify their policies, that the administration even went so far as to make the economically illiterate suggestion that expected increases in security spending would reduce GDP growth, because 'more labor and capital will be diverted toward the production of an intermediate product – security – and away from the production of final demand' (ERP, 2002: 56).

Lower rates failed to revive business investment, which had slumped after the mis-directed investment boom of the 1990s. Conditions were simply unpropitious. Capacity utilization in the ICT sector went from 85.9 per cent in 1999–2000 to 59.7 per cent two years later (Brenner, 2009: 34). The administration blamed a 'capital overhang' (ERP, 2002: 39–40). It could say that again: businesses 'had every incentive to slow down capital accumulation and reduce costs by way of cutbacks on jobs and plant and machinery, while availing themselves of falling interest rates to pay down their debt. And that is what they did' (Brenner, 2009: 35).

Unable to boost productive investment, the continually falling cost of borrowing now fed the housing bubble. It had begun to inflate in the mid-1990s, and during the recession, with stock prices falling, rising house prices and their wealth effect propped up consumption and residential investment, and powered such recovery as there was. Residential investment, investment in multi-family structures and in residential building improvements rose at annual rates of 5.6 per cent, 15.3 per cent and 3.2 per cent respectively, while investment in single-family structures rose 6 per cent after declining for most of 2000 (ERP, 2002: 29). The Fed too recognized this, and noted the role of low interests rates in it: 'Through much of last year's slowdown ... spending by the household sector held up well and proved to be a major stabilizing force', mainly because 'low mortgage rates had boosted the building of new homes, sales of existing homes, and extraction of capital gains through sales as well as refinancing' (Greenspan, 2002b). Now the Fed would set about fanning this single economic spark in the US economy's dying embers. Having initially lowered interest rates to prop up the falling stock market, the Fed would now lower them further and keep them low as long as it could to keep house prices, and borrowing based on these prices, rising. They fed consumption and, in turn, the only kind of growth that was now possible.

After house prices had remained essentially flat through the postwar period, their rise in the mid-1990s was initially boosted by the rising stock market, and after 1999 by expanded mortgage lending by the government-sponsored enterprises Fannie Mae and Freddie Mac, because the Clinton Administration pressured them to lend to low and moderate-income borrowers. And real estate prices continued to rise after the stock market bubble burst mainly because of the decline in international long-term interest rates, over which the Fed, which was only able to set short-term US rates, had little control (Brenner, 2009: 37–8). House prices rose 51 per cent and household wealth by 64 per cent between 2000 and 2005. Growth in personal consumption and residential investment, at annual rates of 2.9 per cent and 6.0 per cent respectively, accounted for 98 per cent of the increase in GDP between 2001 and 2005 (Brenner, 2009: 40).

As we have seen, US consumption patterns had been becoming more unequal since the Reagan era, and the consumption boom of the Clinton era, resting as it did on the wealth effects of the stock market bubble, continued this trend. As falling stock prices passed the baton of wealth-effect-generated consumption to rising house prices, Greenspan celebrated its broader basis: while upper-income households who had most benefited from the wealth effects of rising stock prices were restraining their spending, the rise in house prices was boosting consumption among '[m]oderate-income households [which] have a much larger proportion of their assets in homes' (Greenspan, 2002a). However, the consumption that was leading recovery was hardly more demotic. Indeed it had an unusual trait. Normally the consumption of non-durables, like food, clothing and footwear, held up better in recessions and increased first during recoveries. Instead, furniture, household equipment and motor vehicles were now particularly robust (ERP, 2002: 27).

Boosting consumption was now the main priority, and reviving business fixed investment was to be, at best, its result. Inventory cycle upswings would be 'short-lived unless sustained increases in final demand kick in before the positive effects of the swing from inventory liquidation dissipate' (Greenspan 2002a). Consumption was already robust, and so these increases would have to be unprecedented. Whether or not Greenspan really believed in, or even cared about, business investment revival, he was lowering expectations and exaggerating difficulties so that the inevitably unspectacular recovery, with or without business investment recovery, would look as good as possible. If it got under way, Greenspan argued, investment recovery would testify to 'a truly remarkable performance for the American economy in the face of so severe a decline in equity asset values and an unprecedented blow from terrorists to the foundations of our market systems', and to a 'significantly milder downturn than the long history of business cycles would have led us to expect'. And, he added, it would show that something had changed in 'our economy in recent decades to provide such resilience'.

Greenspan identified three changes. The information revolution gave businesses 'real time information', reducing economic imbalances. Deregulation increased flexibility ('the collapse of Enron barely registered in the ... markets for natural gas and electric power'). And deregulation and innovation in the financial sector created '[n]ew financial products – including derivatives, asset-backed securities, collateralized loan obligations, and collateralized mortgage obligations' to disperse risk toward those able and willing to bear it, and ensure that economic shocks did not lead to 'cascading credit failure' (Greenspan, 2002c). The latter had helped keep consumption resilient, facilitating home equity extraction even without sales to finance consumption expenditures and home modernization. Without this activity, 'economic activity would have been notably weaker' after the stock market crash (Greenspan, 2002b).

The danger of deflation

Though, as we have seen, Greenspan's attention was usually more focused on capital and labour markets than the real economy, he had claimed that interest rates were cut after 9/11 because 'the risks of weaker economic activity outweighed the risks of higher inflation' (ERP, 2002: 46). As this justification began to wear thin, 'helicopter Ben' Bernanke provided a rationale for keeping rates low even as the economy strengthened and potentially risked inflation. Having vanquished inflation in recent decades, the United States now faced the opposite danger – deflation. Although this would be unlikely given the economy's 'resilience and structural stability' and the Fed's commitment to avoiding deflation, 1990s Japan stood as a warning that the risk was 'not purely hypothetical'. An inflation buffer – a higher than zero inflation rate – and a willingness to back a 'healthy, well capitalized banking system and smoothly functioning capital markets' were necessary. If the economy deteriorated when inflation was already low, 'the central bank should act more preemptively and more aggressively than usual in cutting rates' (Bernanke, 2002). And if this proved ineffective, 'under a fiat money system' deflation was 'always reversible', '[b]y increasing the number of U.S. dollars in circulation, or even by credibly threatening to do so' (2002).

Even when short-term interest rates reached zero, the Fed could counter deflation by committing to keep short-term rates at zero for a time to put downward pressure on long-term rates. It could also announce 'explicit ceilings for yields on longer-maturity Treasury debt', and enforce them through 'unlimited purchases of securities up to two years from maturity at prices consistent with the targeted yields'. It could also buy foreign government debt to inject money into the economy. And finally, the government could cut taxes and the Fed could monetize the resulting fiscal deficits to stimulate consumption or the acquisition of real or financial assets which would, by increasing asset values, lower the cost of capital and increase the credit-worthiness of borrowers. Such an act would be equivalent to Milton Friedman's famous 'helicopter drop' of money (Bernanke, 2002). Ostensibly a plan for dealing with non-hypothetical deflation, Bernanke's speech was a justification of low interest rates and the expanding federal deficit.

To effectively inflate the housing bubble and keep up consumption and growth, the Fed's interest rates had to be lower than the already low international long-term rates, which ruled in the mortgage market. Only this would allow US banks to borrow in the short term more cheaply than they lent in the long term. International long-term rates – for instance 10-year Treasury bond rates and 30-year fixed mortgage rates – had been on a downward curve since the Volcker shock. The resulting search for higher, riskier returns underlay the widely noticed increase in financial crises during this period (Bordo and Eichengreen, 2002). Rates would tick upwards when the search appeared successfully concluded – in the stock market bubbles of the mid-1980s and the late 1990s, for instance. Rates would resume the downward slide after these bubbles burst. By the beginning of the new century low long-term interest rates, a symptom of the long downturn, would send investors into the MBSs that the US financial system was producing.

Financial innovation

The infamous financial innovations on which the housing bubble was built were largely the product of the 2000s. In 1999, after long years when executive deregulation under Greenspan's chairmanship of the Fed ate away at its edges, the Glass–Steagall separation of commercial and investment banking was repealed (Hendrickson, 2001). Commercial banks could now engage in securities trading and underwriting.

Regulation in the wake of the 1929 stock market crash and the subsequent Great Depression had made the US financial system one of the most regulated in the world: it separated investment and commercial banking, protected savers though the Federal Deposit Insurance Corporation (FIDC) and prevented over-competition between commercial banks through Regulation Q ceilings on the interest rates they could offer. Rising inflation and interest in the 1970s had made these regulatory structures obsolete, and financial institutions began to erode them at their edges. Commercial banks successfully lobbied to enter the municipal bond market (Frontline, n.d.) while investment banks encroached on the former's depository territory by offering money market mutual (MMM) funds invested in government bonds and commercial paper as effectively higher-interest bank deposits. The favourable response from depositors expanded these funds, increasing the demand for commercial paper so that more and more businesses issued it (ERP, 1991: 162–7).

With no attempt being made to update the regulatory structure so as to preserve the original aims of preventing excessive build-up of risk and shaping the financial sector to mobilize savings and finance productive investment, the bias was toward deregulation. With low demand for productive investment in the long downturn, creeping deregulation could only increase the possibilities for speculation. It would also increase competition and narrow profit margins, forcing banks into increasingly risky practices.

An early casualty was the savings and loans (S&L) sector. It was particularly hard hit by increased inflation and nominal interest rates in the 1980s because its assets were 20–30 year mortgages, whose rates had been fixed when interest rates were lower. S&L assets were devalued as rates rose, and the sector faced competition from MMM funds for depositors. Congress responded with deregulation while leaving the fundamental asset–liability mismatch unaddressed. By 1989 almost half the S&Ls were gone.

Banks experienced similar pressures, but being larger, they were less vulnerable. Between Carter's 1980 termination of Regulation Q ceilings on savings account interest rates, which became effective in 1986, and the 1999 repeal of Glass–Steagall, deregulation took place outside Congress. While Paul Volcker, who opposed banking deregulation, remained Fed chairman it was minimal. Capital requirements were lowered in 1981 (resulting, in cooperation with the Bank of England, in the 1988 Basle Accord on international capital requirements). And commercial banks were permitted to obtain up to 5 per cent of gross revenue from investment banking for existing clients.

Of course, banks exploited limits and loopholes in the regulations to pursue securities activities overseas, trade in currencies and, increasingly, in over-the-counter (OTC) derivatives which were not technically securities. Over the 1980s and 1990s, such activities became more important to commercial banks even as they continued to profit from deposit insurance and membership of the Fed, and they began to lobby for the repeal of Glass–Steagall. By combining investment banking and insurance with their sprawling depository operations, they hoped to dominate banking as veritable financial supermarkets.

After Greenspan, a former director of the commercial bank J. P. Morgan, became Fed chairman in 1987, a strong deregulatory trend set in. The Reagan Administration's 1983 Task Group on Regulation of Financial Services had supported repealing Glass–Steagall, and an initial attempt was made in 1988. After it failed, the Fed, aided now and then by the courts and the Comptroller of Currency, the other two main agencies involved in financial regulation, issued a series of 'piecemeal decisions'. So already before Glass–Steagall was repealed, the separation of commercial and investment banking had been considerably weakened (Hendrickson, 2001: 860–3). The percentage of revenue commercial banks could earn through securities activities for existing clients was progressively increased, as were the sorts of securities they could deal in. Greenspan's former employer, J. P. Morgan, was the first beneficiary (Frontline, n.d.). Commercial banks were also permitted to acquire investment bank subsidiaries that could deal with all forms of securities. Finally, the courts issued other deregulatory judgements, including allowing banks to sell insurance and accepting that annuities were a banking product (Hendrickson, 2001: 862).

Investment banks, for their part, sought deregulation on their terms. Their influence on the Clinton Administration meant that while the Fed and the courts drove an ever-wider deregulatory wedge into Glass–Steagall, various attempts to repeal it in 1988, 1991 and then every year in the four years preceding 1999 could never produce a stable compromise between them and commercial banks, small and large banks, and non-bank institutions (Hendrickson, 2001). Only the 1998 merger of Citicorp, a commercial bank, and Travellers Group, an investment bank with insurance interests, to create Citigroup forced Congress's hand. Instead of blocking the move, the Fed supported it. The merged entity had between two and five years under Glass–Steagall to divest disqualifying assets, but it banked on, and won, repeal instead. The stage was now set for US- and dollar-centred financialization to scale heights not even imagined in the 1980s and 1990s.

After 1999, legislators once again withdrew from the regulatory field. What ensued could be seen as a form of regulatory capture, a situation in which the regulated regulate the regulators. In reality, as the Fed sought to feed the housing bubble with low interest rates, increased competition drove financial institutions and actors into the insane build-up of credit that was the only motor of growth in the US economy. Rather than anything so furtive as regulatory capture, the next decade witnessed regulators brazenly advertising and advocating the results of 'light touch' (read 'no') regulation by propagating beliefs in the efficiency, indeed, the wonder, of markets and innovation, as well as a raft of other beliefs which justified capital inflows.

THE HOUSING BUBBLE GETS INTO ITS STRIDE

For all the talk of the economic shock of 9/11, the economy actually resumed its consumption-led growth before 2001 ended.

The administration attributed it to monetary and fiscal stimulus: low interest rates, tax cuts and tax incentives in the Job Creation and Worker Assistance Act (JCWAA). However, the wealth effect of rising house prices did not yet completely offset the negative wealth effect of the stock price decline – $7 trillion was lost between early 2000 and the end of 2002, with the Enron and World Com scandals making their contribution – and this growth remained weak (ERP, 2003: 28).

Through 2002, Greenspan continued to profess confidence that the 1990s investment boom had permanently increased productivity and would eventually drive increases in business investment, though he had to admit that recent productivity increases resulted from work intensification and were unlikely to be sustained (Greenspan, 2002a, 2002b). By 2003, however, he had lighted on a new boosterism – that of the ingenuity and efficiency of financial markets and innovation in banking.

As banks and securities markets displaced the stock market from its centrality to the US economy, the administration admitted an important truth: the strong statistical correlation between stock prices and business investment since 1995 had been no more than that, and the investment boom of the late 1990s had been financed largely through debt, not equity. The admission was made because it was now convenient: stock prices might be dropping but they need not affect investment. What mattered now was whether corporate debt markets functioned well to assess risk, whether the inflexibility of interest payments relative to dividend payments would cause a liquidity crisis and/or a credit crunch, and whether problems in either could cause another recession (ERP, 2003: 36–9).

Of course, as with the stock market, Greenspan refused to admit that rising house prices might constitute a bubble. He could no longer feign ignorance about detecting bubbles for fear that would appear, after the stock market rise had turned out to be a bubble, to be not sophisticated but garden-variety ignorance of a kind no Fed chairman could afford to display. So Greenspan took to adducing reasons why housing was especially unsuited to bubbles. He told Congress's Joint Economic Committee how the stock and real estate markets were different: how sales in the latter 'incur substantial transactions costs' such as 'the financial and emotional costs' of moving; how the stock markets turned over 'more than 100 percent annually' and real estate markets only 10 per cent, 'scarcely tinder for speculative conflagration'; and how in the latter, arbitrage opportunities were more limited – 'A home in Portland,

Oregon is not a close substitute for a home in Portland, Maine, and the "national" housing market is better understood as a collection of small, local housing markets' (Greenspan, 2002a). At worst, there might be local housing bubbles. Of course, Greenspan hedged all this. Housing bubbles were not impossible, he conceded; only, given the differences between the two markets and because the underlying demand for homes was revised very gradually, 'the speed and magnitude of price rises and declines ... are more difficult to create in markets for homes' (Greenspan, 2002a). This new wisdom was repeated by the CEA (ERP, 2003: 44).

Employment remained low, with manufacturing employment faring worst. Long-term unemployment rose, and an increasing proportion of job losers reported permanent rather than temporary separation in 2002. The administration clutched at what straws it could find. Though productivity growth was rooted in intensified work, rather than investment, it could be considered 'lasting' because it had 'stayed high since 1995' (2003: 49). Of course, in fact inflation remained low only because rising imports were cheap and wages low (and because post-Boskin measures reduced the measured CPI), while throughout 2003,

> three years into the business cycle, the levels of private employ-
> ment, investment, and net exports, as well as nonfinancial
> corporate profits, all remained significantly *below* their levels of
> 2000, while ... the S&P500 stock index still languished about
> 500 points, or one-third, off its boom-time peak.
>
> (Brenner, 2009: 41)

And the current account deficit widened despite slow growth. In the 1990s its increase had been accompanied with an increase in national saving thanks to deficit reduction. In the 2000s not only did the US trade deficit, the largest component of the current account deficit, continue to rise, national dis-saving, private and public, rose steeply (ERP, 2003: 60).

While the administration admitted that the United States was 'consuming and investing [in real estate, that is] more than it is producing' (2003: 60), that the country's net international investment position had 'moved from an accumulated surplus of slightly less than 10 percent of GDP in the late 1970s to a deficit of almost 20 percent of GDP in 2001' (2003: 61), and that the debt could not 'increase without limit' (2003: 61), it was now scraping the bottom of the barrel of ways to make such an economy seem a fit destination of international capital flows. The United States, it claimed, was 'far from the point at which servicing its international debt becomes an onerous burden', not least because *'until last year* more investment income was generated by U.S. investment in foreign countries than by foreign investments inside the United States'. So since 'the rates of return on U.S. investment abroad were higher than the returns enjoyed by foreign investors in the United States', 'debt service is unlikely to amount to a significant portion of US output in the foreseeable future' (2003: 61–2, emphasis added). It neglected to mention, of course, that the rest of the world was lending it money more cheaply than vice versa because, for lack of an alternative, the rest of the world had to hold reserves substantially in dollars. The hobbled US economy was now reliant on this compulsion just to produce the perverse, credit-fuelled and consumption-led growth.

The great moderation

That the Bush Administration stopped hoping, let alone trying, for a better growth pattern was confirmed in two documents of early 2004: ERP, 2004, which sought to normalize this pattern of economic growth, and Ben Bernanke's speech to the Eastern Economic Association meeting in Washington DC extolling 'the Great Moderation' – the reduction in the volatility of output and inflation that US economic mangers had engineered.

The CEA took heart because the recovery's reliance on consumption meant that GDP declined less than usual in the recession, while the recovery left the labour market even weaker relative to output than in previous 'jobless recoveries' as a result of the continued productivity growth. And it drew five lessons designed to allay any fears about the state of the economy. First, structural imbalances like the capital overhang took time to resolve. Business investment had dropped 9 per cent in 2001 and risen just 2 per cent the following year but, the report claimed, '[b]y late 2003 ... depreciation, rising demand and falling cost of capital goods and reductions in taxes were finally leading to higher business investment' (ERP, 2004: 35–6). Second, uncertainty – as a result of 9/11, recent corporate scandals, the impending war in Iraq and declining stock markets – could hold back business investment and consumption. Third, aggressive monetary policy could help reduce the depth of the recession. Fourth, fiscal stimuli in the form of tax cuts could raise after-tax incomes and thus incentives to work, save and invest. Finally, the low employment performance was to be expected in a recovery with strong productivity growth, and was necessary for future growth and employment. The loss of manufacturing jobs was due to an entirely salutary shift to higher-value manufacturing and services (2004: 76).

A month later Fed governor Bernanke traced the decline in variability of quarterly real output growth since the mid-1980s to better monetary policy, at once allaying concerns about US economic performance and establishing the Fed's credentials to be the best arbiter of its fate. In the high-volatility 1960s and 1970s, monetary policy was premised on two related and faulty perspectives: 'output optimism', that monetary policy could exploit the trade-off between inflation and unemployment through 'fine-tuning' to eliminate short-term fluctuations and deliver a permanently low level of unemployment and that the NAIRU lay below 4 per cent; and 'inflation pessimism', that inflation arose from cost-push shocks and could not be controlled through monetary policy. It was only when policy makers, beginning with Paul Volcker, 'were finally persuaded by the evidence that sustained anti-inflationary monetary policies would actually work' that the great moderation set in. Now the US economy was unlikely to experience sharp fluctuations in either output or inflation, mainly because the Fed had found the formula to keep it humming along. The US economy might not be growing fast but it would not tank either.

Growth clocked in at 2.8 per cent in 2002 and 4.4 per cent in the first three quarters of 2003, 'supported by robust gains in consumption, residential investment and defense spending' (ERP, 2004: 84), and 'core consumer inflation declined to its lowest level in decades' (2004: 83). With consumer spending growing at 3 per cent in the first two quarters of 2003 and 6.9 per cent in the third, the administration claimed to see signs of business fixed investment reviving, led by purchases of equipment and software (2004: 90), and claimed that it would play a greater role in growth in the future (2004: 84), and consumption a lesser one (2004: 85). That certainly needed to happen: with the largest number of housing starts since 1978 and fixed-rate 30-year mortgage rates at 5.75 per cent, the lowest level in 32 years, the administration had to admit that residential investment could not keep up such a hectic pace forever.

The US current account deficit reached 5 per cent of GDP in 2003. The administration claimed that adjustments could come from decreased capital inflows, increased demand for exports or increases in national saving. Since decreases in investment, largely residential, were undesirable, adjustment through involuntary decreases in capital flows was to be avoided at all costs (2004: 264).

THE SUB-PRIME PHASE

By 2003, house prices were peaking as homes became less affordable. Prices could only keep rising, and delivering economic growth, if the Fed managed 'not only to [keep] short term rates down for as long as possible, but also to somehow enable ever less qualified borrowers-purchasers to buy homes at ever higher prices' (Brenner, 2009: 42). And it did. As prime mortgage originations peaked in 2003, various forms of non-conforming mortgage originations shot up. Had they not done so,

> the housing bubble would likely have quickly expired, endangering the cyclical upturn, as US households had insufficient funds to keep both housing sales and housing prices rising, not least because, over the length of the business cycle, US real median family income failed to rise for the first time during the postwar epoch, while real wages for production and non-supervisory workers, about 80 per cent of the labor force, remained essentially flat.
>
> (Brenner, 2009: 43)

Sub-prime mortgages paradoxically made house prices and credit rise even more steeply and precariously. Extended to those long excluded from home ownership, with low or even no down payments, they made borrowers willing and able to pay even higher prices. The gap between what buyers agreed to pay and their ability to do so from their income widened. They stood to lose their homes if and when house prices stopped rising and they could not refinance or secure a capital gain. House prices had increased 17 per cent between the end of 2000 and the middle of 2003. They increased 29 per cent from then to the end of 2005 (Brenner, 2009: 45).

The Fed and the Bush Administration even invoked a nineteenth-century law to prevent states legislating against predatory lending (2009: 43) to keep the housing bubble inflating. Instead, Greenspan extolled the virtues of US financial innovation. '[I]ncreased efficiency and scale' and innovation in US consumer finance had a long history of making credit popular, and now 'brought about a multitude of new products such as subprime loans and niche credit programmes for immigrants'. It was harnessing technological advances such as credit scoring models that

> reduced the costs of evaluating the creditworthiness of borrowers,

and in competitive markets cost reductions tend to be passed through to borrowers. Where once more-marginal applicants would simply have been denied credit, lenders are now able to quite efficiently judge the risk posed by individual applicants and to price that risk appropriately.

(Greenspan, 2005)

The year before, Greenspan had praised derivatives for permitting 'financial risks to be unbundled in ways that have facilitated both their measurement and their management', making both individual financial institutions 'less vulnerable' and the system 'more resilient'. Derivatives also enabled risks to be shifted from 'an admittedly few large U.S. banks' to other financial institutions and insurance companies at home and abroad 'with diffuse long-term liabilities or no liabilities at all'. When increased competition decreased margins, they helped banks to calibrate their risk portfolios carefully to their risk appetites. Such innovation created a veritable 'new paradigm of active credit management' (Greenspan, 2004).

And sub-prime mortgages were critically reliant on that paradigm. The only way they could grow was by being securitized into MBSs and taken off originating banks' balance sheets in the 'originate and distribute' model. And the only way they could be securitized successfully, with the high credit ratings necessary to permit their main buyers, the highly regulated pension and mutual funds, to acquire them, was by bundling them with safe, conforming mortgages and ensuring those bundles were given the requisite credit ratings. But neither such creative bundling nor the ever more complex derivatives succeeded in managing the resulting risk structure. There were 'misaligned incentives' and 'information deficits', whether between sub-prime borrowers and lenders, between originators of mortgages and the buyers of MBSs based on them, or between the infamous credit ratings agencies and securitizers who paid them to rate their securities. However, these factors do not entirely explain how such MBSs, which would later be termed 'toxic', came to be marketed so successfully. After all, as Brenner noted, those buying them were 'highly-paid and presumably well-trained professionals representing giant institutions and managing billions of dollars whose very job it was to assess the quality of assets such as these and who possessed the best information that money could buy'. Any explanation of what made them so credulous had to lie in the 'the other bubble', the credit bubble (Brenner, 2009: 50).

While the Fed's low interest rate policy created opportunities for profiting by borrowing cheap short term and lending at higher rates long term, intense competition in the deregulated financial sector sent the demand for mortgage-backed assets so high that yields dropped and the search for higher yields drove investors into ever more risky assets. High demand for MBSs drove four key processes. It kept mortgage originations high, and eventually brought investment banks themselves into the origination business, as they bought lending and finance companies (2009: 55). It ensured that, as ever more risky borrowers were reached, interest rates, rather than rising, fell. It drove the process of resecuritization of high- and low-risk MBSs as banks attempted to calibrate their risk portfolios ever more finely to somehow lower risk and increase returns. And finally, banks sought to insure their securities through complex and 'absurdly underpriced' derivatives (2009: 55–6).

The consumption-fuelled growth this housing boom created widened the current account deficit, which now peaked at 6 per cent. It was accompanied by a widening budget deficit, and an ever-lowering dollar. Such an explosion of debt – personal and government – and the consumption it was fuelling caused widespread concern. Paul Volcker was representative:

> As a nation we are consuming and investing about 6 percent more than we are producing. What holds it all together is a massive and growing flow of capital from abroad, running to more than $2 billion every working day, and growing. ... I don't know of any country that has managed to consume and invest 6 percent more than it produces for long. The United States is absorbing about 80 percent of the net flow of international capital. And at some point, both central banks and private institutions will have their fill of dollars.
>
> (Volcker, 2005)

That this limit might be reached at any time was now the danger facing the precarious geopolitical economy of Bush Jr's empire, resting on the housing and credit bubbles. As with all bubbles, it would be reached when confidence cracked. The only people who thought this process was sustainable were those who managed to subscribe to some version of HST that exempted the United States from the constraints of being just another national economy. Certainly Volcker was not one of them.

The global savings glut

So now a new argument appeared to naturalize even this scary geopolitical economy. The US current account deficit, US debt, public and private, and the capital inflows financing them were, Ben Bernanke informed the world, the result of a 'global savings glut' (GSG), 'a significant increase in the global supply of saving'. This explained the rising US current account deficit and 'the relatively low level of long-term interest rates in the world today' (Bernanke, 2005). It, rather than US competitiveness problems, foreign military expenditures, or the Fed's encouragement of the housing and credit bubbles, explained the US current account deficit and its recent rise. The latter was 'the tail of the dog … passively determined by foreign and domestic incomes, asset prices, interest rates, and exchange rates' (2005).

Bernanke's argument relied on the accounting identity between national savings and investment, in which the two were deemed to be equal in national accounts, and the excess of the one over the other was financed by capital outflows or inflows. In this model, 'investment' included inventories as well as residential and unproductive investment, and it was not a reliable measure of productive investment at all, let alone a factor that caused shortfalls in 'savings'. Nevertheless, Bernanke argued that the United States's 'current account deficit … was caused by neither personal indebtedness nor federal deficits'. The current account deficits had expanded both with and without federal deficits (as in the late 1990s). Instead, the low national saving rate was just a reflection of the GSG. Though he cautioned that his arguments relied on 'realized patterns of investment and saving rather than changes in the rates of investment and saving desired from an ex ante perspective' (Bernanke, 2005), he blithely went on to assume that realized and desired savings were one and the same (Chandrashekhar and Ghosh, 2005).

Bernanke admitted that the GSG was a curious phenomenon. It should have emerged among rich countries with low returns on domestic investment and rising savings by ageing populations. Instead the developing world had 'metamorphosed' from 'a net user to a net supplier of funds to international capital markets' (Bernanke, 2005) because it had rectified the mismanagement of international capital flows that the East Asian financial crisis exposed by accumulating larger reserves. They were 'war chests … to be used as a buffer against potential capital outflows', and, in some cases (a reference to China), to undervalue the national currency through market interventions. In so far as they were the former, Bernanke was blaming the developing world's financial mismanagement, not the unreliable, speculative and unproductive character of short-term funds that flowed from the West into it and to which the United States insisted the developing world remain open. In this view, developing-country governments were essentially acting as 'financial intermediaries, channelling domestic saving away from local uses and into international capital markets'. The sharp rise in oil prices and the resulting revenue accumulation among its exporters had also added to the GSG (Bernanke, 2005).

These developments led to 'adjustments in asset prices and exchange rates'. Whereas between 1996 and 2000, international investors attracted to US equities had delivered wealth effects to US nationals and lowered their saving, now the low international interest rates, and thus low mortgage rates in the United States combined with 'low real interest rates' caused by demand for US Treasury securities, supported 'record levels of home construction and strong gains in housing prices' in the United States. Combined with recovery in the stock market, the rise in house prices had restored 'the wealth-to-income ratio of U.S. households to 5.4, not far from its peak value of 6.2 in 1999 and above its long-run (1960–2003) average of 4.8'. On the one hand, with this wealth being tapped by US households through equity withdrawals and the like and with the expanding government deficits, US national saving was plummeting. On the other, '[a]s U.S. business investment has recently begun a cyclical recovery while residential investment has remained strong, the domestic saving shortfall has continued to widen, implying a rise in the current account deficit and increasing dependence of the United States on capital inflows' (2005).

Bernanke could not credibly ignore the problematic aspects of the GSG – the undesirability of developing countries with more scope for growth lending to rich countries; the dearth of productive investment opportunities in these rich countries; the adverse effects of the inflows on US export competitiveness; and the possibility of disorderly adjustment if the inflow of foreign funds were disrupted. However, while reducing the federal deficit and increasing private saving were in themselves good things, they would not, by themselves, affect the current account deficit and the GSG. Resolving them would require 'developing countries to re-enter international capital markets in their more natural role as borrowers, rather than as lenders' by working to 'improve their investment climates by continuing to increase macroeconomic stability, strengthen property rights, reduce corruption, and remove barriers to the free flow of financial capital' (2005).

The reasons that the world's savings were flowing into the United States in particular included the 'attractiveness of the United States as an investment destination during the technology boom of the 1990s', 'the depth and sophistication of the country's financial markets' which 'allowed households easy access to housing wealth', and 'the special status of the dollar as the leading international reserve currency' (Bernanke, 2005).

Bush's CEA joined Bernanke in attempting to bolster confidence in the US economy and postpone the breaking point that otherwise seemed so near. It relabelled the current account deficit a 'capital account surplus' (ERP, 2006: 125–47) which was a result of low and declining US saving, its high growth compared with other advanced industrial countries, including high productivity growth, a more favourable investment climate, financial market size and efficiency, and finally, the dollar's international role. The world's export of capital had gone up 160 per cent since 1995, thanks largely to reserve accumulation, and the United States had imported 70 per cent of it, up from 33 per cent in 1995. Capital inflows on this historically unprecedented scale were not, contrary to the opinions of many, necessarily a problem, and they could continue indefinitely provided they 'promote strong US investment, productivity and growth' (2006: 144).

Moreover, the CEA argued, the United States earned net foreign income despite its net debt, and the former made the latter less burdensome. This was a short step from Hausmann and Sturzenegger's theory of 'dark matter', which appeared at this time, arguing that the US international investment position of minus $2.5 trillion must, in reality, be a positive $600 billion since the United States had been earning a net foreign income of $30 billion over recent years. The modest assumption of a 5 per cent rate of return on assets suggested that US foreign assets were worth more. This additional worth was the 'dark matter' because 'it corresponds to assets that we know exist, since they generate revenue but cannot be seen (or, better said, cannot be properly measured)'. Hausmann and Sturzenegger suggested that they included the knowledge transfer value of US FDI, the liquidity services of the US dollar and the insurance provided by the safety value of US assets (Hausmann and Sturzenegger, 2005). This reasoning was much like Greenspan's when he claimed that the 'productivity miracle' had to exist because investor behaviour required it to do so.

DESCENT INTO CRISIS

While the Fed and the administration sought to conjure away the inherent problems of the geopolitical economy of the housing and credit bubbles, developments that would prick both these bubbles were already in train. Demand from fast-growing emerging economies was already pushing oil prices up when the invasion of Iraq, rather than succeeding quickly and increasing the supply of oil under US control, ran aground and pushed oil prices up even further (Sarkis, 2004). The Fed had to address the resulting inflation fears and downward pressure on the dollar so as to maintain the inflow of foreign funds on which the economy had become so critically dependent. The long era of low short-term US interest rates ended in July 2004 with the first of a series of rate hikes which would take interest rates from their year-long low at 1 per cent to 5.25 per cent in January 2006. They would remain there until July 2007. Growth, which had been accelerating through the recovery (at 1.1 per cent, 1.8 per cent, 2.5 per cent and 3.6 per cent between 2001 and 2004), slowed immediately to 3.1 per cent in 2005.

The credit bubble at the centre of US- and dollar-dominated financialization that attracted funds into the United States had been based on the difference between low long-term international rates and the even lower short-term US rates the Fed set. The difference had allowed the financial institutions generating the credit and the securities based on it to borrow short term at rates lower than the low long-term rates they were offering to their borrowers. And, of course, these low mortgage rates ensured that house prices kept rising. So as the Fed started to raise short-term rates, it became 'excruciatingly difficult for banks and other financiers to profit in the traditional manner by borrowing short cheap and lending long dear' (Brenner, 2009: 58). This made the desperate search for returns even more desperate, and sent banks competing for ever riskier assets. As competition narrowed margins even for these assets, only greater leverage could muster the financial throw-weight necessary to make the desired returns.

As banks bought more and more MBSs with money borrowed on the short-term paper market, the unregulated 'shadow banking system' expanded. It had existed since MMM funds emerged in the 1970s as an unregulated form of credit, and consisted of investment conduits that did not show up on banks' balance sheets but nonetheless constituted claims on them. In the 2000s such conduits held the mortgage loans temporarily while banks were securitizing them. However, these banks 'could not resist investing in and holding on to the dubious products' (Brenner, 2009: 59), and as they did so, they concentrated risk in themselves, rather than dispersing it along the lines of the 'originate and distribute' model. Unregulated and unprotected by deposit insurance, these conduits operated on 'razor thin margins', and were

> profoundly vulnerable, not just to a fall in price of the ever more dubious non-conforming mortgages that underpinned their securities but also to a rise in the cost of short term borrowing – neither of which eventuality they had any reason to consider at all unlikely.
>
> (Brenner, 2009: 60)

This shadow banking system was critical to keeping the bubble in MBSs expanding (2009: 60). As short-term interest rates started to rise, it was only a matter of time before it led to the unravelling of the now vast and precarious financial structure that rested on the MBS bubble.

With interest rates rising, the housing market peaked in 2006. Now 'the film of housing-driven expansion [ran] backward even faster' (2009: 70). As house prices fell, so did residential investment, credit based on rising house prices, and consumption fuelled by credit while incomes stagnated. Declining consumption and residential investment slowed growth. Increasing foreclosures decreased the value of the portfolios of MBSs that the financial institutions had produced to distribute but had held on to instead, increasing their vulnerability.

House-price-dependent US growth had already peaked in 2004 at a mere 3.6 per cent, and it slowed in each successive year. The administration nevertheless congratulated itself because in 2005 growth was still 'above the historical average' and higher than in other advanced countries (ERP, 2006: 3), while the even poorer performance in 2006 was explained away by talk of the lingering cost of Hurricanes Katrina and Rita, inflation in non-energy prices, and higher interest rates. It took comfort that falling residential investment was offset by investment in mining and oil fields, replacement of destroyed facilities in the Gulf of Mexico, trucking (thanks to new environmental regulations) and in 'office buildings, multi-merchandise centers, lodging facilities, and recreational structures' as well as in 'petroleum and natural gas structures' (ERP, 2007: 30–1) and by exports thanks to a falling dollar and faster growth elsewhere.

Residential investment contracted by 7.3 per cent in 2006 and 18.5 per cent in 2007, growth slowed to 2.5 per cent (later revised to 2.1 per cent), and house prices fell even more sharply (ERP, 2008: 29). For the first time in 16 years, disposable income rose faster than nominal consumer spending, increasing personal saving slightly. The wealth-to-income ratio stopped rising, unemployment stopped falling, and such resilience as consumer spending still showed arose from higher energy costs (2008: 27). Housing stopped accounting for increases in household wealth by mid-2007, when the still rising stock market took over.

Only now did the president admit that the economy was 'undergoing a period of uncertainty' (2008: 3), although it was also a 'period of rebalancing', a 'reorientation of the U.S. economy away from housing investment and toward exports and investment'. Not only did this investment still steer clear of productive plant and machinery (2008: 32), it had risen at a slower pace than the year before, and it was feared that the turmoil in financial markets might affect investment rates (2008: 32–3). Exports had grown thanks to strong growth among US trading partners and the low dollar (2008: 79–98), and both the trade and current account deficits had fallen for the first time since 2001.

In 2007, moreover, international long-term interest rates were finally, and quite unexpectedly, pushed upward. At root was a combination of developments. To continued demand for capital to drive growth in the United States were added a surge in Chinese consumption, as the country's breakneck productive expansion of recent decades began to lift mass consumption despite its export orientation; food and energy price inflation; the requirements of Chinese intervention in currency markets to counteract the upward pressure on the yuan; and finally, an increase in risk appetite moving money away from safe, low-yielding US Treasuries (Makin, 2007). As the long-term interest rates to which mortgages were tied went up, house prices stopped rising, setting off foreclosures and bankruptcies, beginning among sub-prime mortgage originators and moving up the financial food chain. Bear Stearns was the first headline grabber among them. A credit crunch resulted, and finally, in autumn 2008, the US government ended up rescuing a number of financial institutions except, fatefully, Lehman Brothers.

With rising interest rates and falling house prices, by 2007 defaults not only affected sub-prime mortgages, by then 20 per cent of mortgage originations (ERP, 2008: 53), but also extended beyond them, particularly to adjustable-rate mortgages. Moreover, the tightening of credit standards that came with the credit crunch 'raise[d] the possibility that spending by businesses and consumers could be restrained in the future' beyond residential investment, while 'declines in housing wealth may also limit consumer spending' (2008: 51). By mid-2007, as sub-prime lenders filed for bankruptcy and money poured out of secondary credit markets in a 'flight to quality' that sent US Treasury yields down, the long-term debt market contracted more generally (2008: 63). The conduits in the shadow banking system owned by mainline banks now issued 'short-term debt to finance long-term assets', or in other words, 'new commercial paper to repay maturing commercial paper (a process called rolling)'. However, they now faced

> greater investor scrutiny and investor reluctance to purchase commercial paper issued by entities with limited or no backstop liquidity [and] the volume of outstanding ABCP [asset backed commercial paper] shrank more than 35 percent, from $1,180 billion in early August to about $750 billion in late December 2007.
>
> (ERP, 2008: 65?)

Banks were forced to 'either bring the underlying assets (and their associated liabilities) back onto their balance sheets or to sell them, further depressing their value' (2008: 65). Other leveraged financial activities, such as mergers and acquisitions, were also affected by these developments, and they induced stock market volatility.

The Bush Administration and the Fed approached the gathering crisis by affirming their faith in 'market based reforms' and 'fair and open trade and investment policies' (2008: 17). The administration cut taxes further, and announced programmes to help families refinance their homes and avoid foreclosure (2008: 3–5). The Fed, which had kept rates steady at their plateau of 5.25 per cent for more than a year, began to decrease them rapidly, beginning with a 50 basis point reduction in September 2007, followed by two 25 basis point cuts in October and December. It also took other measures to ensure liquidity in the financial system, including open market transactions to inject liquidity into the financial markets. The Federal funds rate was now below its target rate, and the discount rate at which it lent to banks at its discount window was reduced by 1 per cent in two stages in August and September 2007. The Fed also lengthened the terms of its loans and broadened the range of collateral it accepted for loans at its discount window to include home mortgages and related assets. By the end of the year it also resorted to a new device – term fund auctions – to lend money to depository institutions and make dollars available to European and Swiss authorities for their liquidity provision operations for their own financial institutions. These institutions were more exposed to the calamity unfolding in the United States than financial institutions anywhere else.

For the rest, however, the administration believed that

> [p]articipants in the credit and housing markets are actively addressing challenges that were revealed during the summer of 2007. Markets are generally better suited than government to adapting to changes in the economic environment; markets can respond quickly to new information, while government policy often reacts with a lag or has a delayed impact.
>
> (ERP, 2008: 52)

The Bush Administration admitted that the financial innovations of the recent past had entailed 'some costs', but still insisted that '[o]ver time, markets tend to retain valuable innovations and repair or eliminate flawed innovations' (2008: 52).

The departing Bush Jr Administration's last report looked back over the events of 2008, including 'the failure or near failure of several major financial institutions in September 2008' and the recession that had begun in 2007, which led to 'employment losses average[ing] 82,000 per-month during the first 8 months of 2008, before accelerating to a 420,000 per-month pace during the next three months' (ERP, 2009: 20–1). The administration sought refuge in the idea that the US economy was 'rebalancing'. It had been doing so since 2006, moving 'away from housing investment and consumer spending and toward exports and investment in business structures', although this process had been 'neither smooth nor graceful' because of the unravelling of the housing and credit bubbles (2009: 31). The administration's economic stimulus programme, amounting to $113 billion or 0.8 per cent of GDP, in tax rebates to low and middle-income taxpayers and generous investment allowances (21, 34), and the continuation of the Fed's series of interest rate cuts, had 'helped maintain positive real GDP growth in the first half of 2008 [but this] was not sufficient to prevent the steep falloff in employment, production, and aggregate spending' after mid-September (2009: 31–2). The recession was serious enough to have led to a decline in oil consumption. With declining stock and house prices, the ratio of household wealth to income had been lowered from 6.3 years of disposable income by 1 year of income in the first three quarters of 2008, and further decline was estimated to wipe out another half year in the final quarter. Naturally, consumer spending had fallen and savings had risen. Business fixed investment had also fallen, and although business investment in structures for manufacturing and oil and gas exploration and wells had grown, the tightening credit environment meant it was likely to decrease again in 2009. Exports, which had resumed growth in 2004, thanks to a low dollar, had decelerated sharply in 2008 (2009: 31–60).

Bush left office putting the central blame for the crisis on the GSG. This, he claimed, had resulted in 'a large influx of capital to the United States and other industrialized countries, driving down the return on safe assets' and encouraging 'investors to look for higher yields from riskier assets, whose yields also went down'. Overall,

> an underpricing of risk across a number of markets (housing, commercial real estate, and leveraged buyouts, among others) in the United States and abroad, and an uncertainty about how this risk was distributed throughout the global financial system, set the stage for subsequent financial distress.
>
> (ERP, 2009: 62)

In reality, the GSG, if such it was, had neither caused the bubble nor played a role in its crash. The GSG argument focused on net flows, on Asia, and on trade and financial imbalances. However, Asian governments had not, by and large, been the main investors in the burgeoning credit bubble that had been inflating in the United States (and they would not be its main victims when it burst in 2008). The gargantuan US current account deficit was being financed amid gross capital flows into and out of the United States which bore no relation to the current account deficit which net flows financed. These flows had grown fast in the late 1990s, reaching 10 per cent of US GDP when the US current account deficit was about 3 per cent, and decreased to about 5 per cent after the stock market decline. Thereafter, however, that they increased most spectacularly, and reached 20 per cent of GDP in 2007, with the current account deficit peaking at 6 per cent around 2006. The bulk of them constituted not official reserve accumulation by successful emerging economy exporters but the purchase by foreign banks and institutions of US non-Treasury securities originating in the exploding housing finance market. These investments were a 'telling sign of the strong global financial boom which saw the United States at its epicentre'. And these banks and institutions were not based in the East Asian or OPEC countries implicated in the GSG argument, but in other advanced countries, mainly Europe which 'accounted for around one-half of total inflows in 2007 .... Of this, more than half came from the United Kingdom, a country running a current account deficit, and roughly one-third from the euro area, a region roughly in balance' (Borio and Disyatat, 2011: 15).

OBAMA'S CHANGE

Although Barack Obama became president amidst and because of the crisis, as the candidate most likely to deliver 'change' and address the dire economic problems the United States faced, his electoral victory proved a false dawn. The Obama Administration blamed 'years of irresponsible risk-taking and debt-fuelled speculation – unchecked by sound oversight' for the financial crisis and the recession which, economists across the political spectrum feared, might 'sink into a second Great Depression'. It also traced the roots of the crisis far deeper into the history and structure of the US economy, and sought not only to 'rescue' but to 'rebalance and rebuild' it (ERP, 2010: 25).

Much was also said about the needs to replace lost jobs and deal with the problems of long-term unemployment with a jobs bill, and to address 'fundamental weaknesses in the economy: rising health care costs, growing dependence on foreign oil, an education system unable to prepare all of our children for the jobs of the future'. These tasks had to replace the 'spending bills and tax cuts for the very wealthiest [that] were approved without paying for any of it, leaving behind a mountain of debt', and an economy where, while 'Wall Street gambled without regard for the consequences, Washington looked the other way' (2010: 5). It was also necessary, the administration opined, to move 'beyond an economy that is fuelled by budget deficits and consumer demand' to one that could 'export more and borrow less from around the world' and could 'save more money and take on less debt here at home'. This would require 'policies that will promote innovation' and 'power new jobs, new businesses – and perhaps new industries'. Such policies included making the research and experimentation tax credit permanent, 'harnessing the growth potential of international trade', and reforming the financial system, which had decreased savings and increased debt (2010: 7–8). Ultimately, it was necessary to put the US economy on the 'path to full employment' (2010: 29).

However, Obama faced re-election in 2012 having failed to deliver on almost every count. This was fundamentally because success would have entailed forsaking the world role that the United States had so vainly tried to play for nearly a century. Such a role, this book has argued, was and remains structurally impossible, and the debility of the US economy, not to mention a multitude of other harms in and outside the United States, were its direct results. While the Obama Administration was forced to admit many things that demonstrated this – *inter alia*, that the United States was living beyond its means and that the world order had become multipolar – it never explicitly renounced US imperial ambitions, including the dollar's world role, let alone identified that role as the chief cause of US economic problems. For one thing, although Obama announced troop withdrawals from Iraq and Afghanistan, defence spending continued to mount during his administration.

Perhaps the most important indicator of things to come was the continuity of personnel with the Bush Administration. Tim Geithner, the president of the New York Federal Reserve who had worked closely with the Bush Administration Treasury secretary, Hank Paulson, in the design and implementation of the Bush Administration's financial bailout, became Treasury secretary. Robert Gates, Bush's secretary of defense, continued in the same position. And Ben Bernanke was reappointed Fed chairman in 2010. It was as though the reorientation of the Democratic Party engineered by the Democratic Leadership Council in the late 1980s and 1990s had been so thorough that Democratic presidents no longer had even a distinctive set of advisers and cabinet members, let alone a distinctive set of policies. The only possible exception to this was the appointment of former Fed chairman and deregulation opponent Paul Volcker as the chairman of the President's Economic Recovery Advisory Board, from where he influenced financial sector re-regulation legislation in Congress.

There were three key elements in the Obama Administration's response to the crisis: the bailout, the fiscal stimulus and the 2010 Dodd–Frank Wall Street Reform and Consumer Protection Act. And there was Fed policy. The Bush Administration's Troubled Asset Relief Program (TARP) had sought to stabilize financial markets through a capital infusion into financial institutions to the tune of $700 billion, and the Obama Administration continued this bailout of 'the very banks and institutions whose actions had helped precipitate this turmoil'. It also passed 'the most sweeping economic recovery package in history: the American Recovery and Reinvestment Act', which provided

> not only ... tax cuts to small businesses and 95 percent of working families and provided emergency relief to those out of work or without health insurance; it also began to lay a new foundation for long-term growth. With investments in health care, education, infrastructure, and clean energy, the Recovery Act has saved or created roughly two million jobs so far, and it has begun the hard work of transforming our economy to thrive in the modern, global era.
>
> (ERP, 2010: 4)

This stimulus played its part, alongside 'automatic stabilizers' such as unemployment compensation and other fiscal outlays that became necessary during economic downturns, in ensuring that Great Recession, as the economic downturn was now called, did not turn into another Great Depression. But it failed to ensure anything like robust recovery during Obama's first term. Finally, the Dodd–Frank Act that was signed into law in January 2010 was already marked by the lobbying efforts of the bailed-out financial institutions, which prevailed even over the wrath of Congress to ensure that the 'Volcker rule' would be a considerably weaker version of the Glass–Steagall separation of commercial and investment banking, particularly preventing commercial banks enjoying federal deposit insurance from engaging in proprietary trading. And the devil still lay in the detail of implementation, which had begun to be contested vigorously by financial institutions by early 2012.

In any case, the administration's fiscal and legislative measures remained on the back seat of economic management, where they had lain since Clinton's capitulation to the Fed and 'a bunch of fucking bond traders'. The Fed was the key manager of the economy. In the name of stimulating recovery, it poured money into the financial system via 'quantitative easing' (QE), effectively another, even more massive bailout to the tune of $2 trillion, dwarfing TARP. QE did not succeed in its stated goal of getting US banks to start lending to US businesses again. It could not because businesses were simply unwilling to borrow (Brenner, 2009: 73). But it did succeed in getting banks speculating abroad again, driving down the US dollar and flooding emerging economies and commodity markets (UNCTAD, 2011). Governments around the world attempted in various ways to restrict these inflows, including through the use of capital controls, which now regained a certain, albeit limited, respectability as a legitimate policy tool, even in the eyes of the IMF (Grabel, 2011).

QE also strengthened the world's aversion to valueless dollars. One clear sign was the rising price of gold. Another was the increase in bilateral trade arrangements to denominate trade in currencies other than the dollar, multilateral reserve pooling (Grabel, 2010) and calls for a new world currency, led by China (Zhou, 2009; Subacchi and Driffill, 2010; Stiglitz, 2009). Most importantly perhaps for the future of the dollar as the world's currency, however, US individuals and private and public institutions now held nearly 70 per cent of US debt (ERP, 2011: 93), largely as a result of QE, under which the Fed bought MBSs and other 'toxic' assets from US banks while allowing them to recapitalize with safer US Treasury securities, and bought and held Treasuries for this operation. Even more importantly, foreign investors held 11 per cent of the overall financial assets in the US economy (2011: 93) as dollars were repatriated. While in this situation any dollar depreciation was likely to hurt US private and public holders more than foreign holders, it was now no longer within US powers to prevent it. As Obama neared re-election, and the Eurozone appeared to stabilize, if not to resolve its crisis, the announcement of QE3, nicknamed QE infinity because the Fed made an indefinite commitment to purchase $40 billion of MBSs monthly until employment figures improved, seemed set to drive the dollar down further.

9

CONCLUSION:
THE MULTIPOLAR MOMENT

The multipolar moment of the twenty-first century closes the long chapter in the history of imperialism in which single powers could dominate, or attempt to dominate, the capitalist world order. Successive waves of contender development, of which that of the USSR and communism generally was the strongest, and that of the BRICs and the emerging economies is the latest, spread productive power ever more widely, and by the early twenty-first century had made such dominance impossible. Imperialism has not come to an end: the more powerful states, the poles of the multipolar capitalist world, will still attempt to stall further diminution of the unevenness that favours them by new bouts of contender development. However, their very multiplicity works against them, and accelerates instead an evolution towards ever more numerous and less powerful poles, and a world order in which unevenness becomes progressively less consequential. That it may be neither smooth nor graceful does not make it less inexorable.

The drivers of the geopolitical economy of capitalism are its contradictions, most critically the paucity of demand and the tendency of the rate of profit to fall (TRPF). As states attempt to manage them, including by externalizing their consequences, each according to its capabilities, they transmit them onto 'the grandest terrain where they appear ... in their grandest development, as the relations of producing nations' (Marx, 1858: 886–7). On this terrain too, other states, capitalist or not, attempt to resist such externalization of the consequences of other capitalisms' contradictions. The vectoral sum of these interactions forms the dynamic of geopolitical economy. It reacts back on domestic political economy, and both also change historically. For instance, as the option of managing demand deficits through colonial conquest and control faded in the postwar world, the expansion of domestic demand became necessary. This change in domestic political economy laid the basis of the very different geopolitical economy of postwar capitalism that Brenner outlined.

Therefore nations, as well as classes, are the agents of capitalism's history. The Bolsheviks understood their revolutionary historical conjuncture and their tasks in it in these terms, and similar understandings are once again necessary as world capitalism enters a new phase of its geopolitical economy. For, as ever, it contains the possibility that popular forces can wrest control of capitalist states, marking a transition from capitalism. On the one hand, while states' increasing economic roles do not amount to socialism, they do, as capitalist classes are all too uneasily aware, open wider the possibility that 'national capitalism would serve simply as a stopping point on the road to some type of socialism' (Block, 1977: 9). On the other hand, as the further unfolding of uneven and combined development (UCD) narrows the options for managing capitalism's contradictions by externalizing them, these states must increase their economic roles and become that much more vulnerable to popular challenge. That is why UCD, ultimately rooted in the insights of Marx and Engels and their account of capitalism's crisis tendencies, lies at the core of capitalism's inherently contradictory geopolitical economy. Reconstructing that understanding has required us to rescue these insights and the later traditions in which they were embodied from avowed Marxists and Marxist economists who take as free market a view of capitalism as any nineteenth-century free trader or contemporary globalist, as well as from the condescension of more than a century of bourgeois thought.

Of course, the theorists of combined capitalist development such as List and Hamilton have also contributed to geopolitical economy. Recently Reinert and Daastøl (2004) placed them centrally in a five-century-long 'other canon' of economics which understood the centrality of states' economic roles in development. However, the marginal position to which they relegated the other canon may be misleading. For the resources for geopolitical economy are greater than the dominance of the cosmopolitan ideologies hitherto might lead one to believe. Classical political economy even before Marx – whether of Smith or Malthus, as well as the most weighty twentieth-century thinking after him, pre-eminently Keynes – did not support the cosmopolitan outlook.

Indeed, something resembling geopolitical economy, perhaps as a further development of the classical theories of imperialism and UCD, would have prevailed after UK world dominance ended in the 30 years' crisis and free trade was dispelled. After all, state-centric understandings of the world economy prevailed in the form of economic nationalist, social democratic and developmental thinking after the Second World War. However, that catastrophe briefly enabled the United States to concentrate such overwhelming economic and political power in itself as to permit it to at least try to realize its ambition to replace the United Kingdom as the 'managing segment' of the world economy. That set in train the developments – historical and intellectual-historical – that would give imperialism the strange afterlife it lived in the repeatedly failing US attempts to sustain the dollar's world role, and the cosmopolitan ideologies – hegemonic stability theory (HST), and later globalization and empire – that accompanied them. Reviewing them in this book has pointed up the important truth that cosmopolitan ideologies – from free trade to 'empire' – were designed to obscure: that the capitalist world order, embodying as it does the contradictions of capitalism, has never been and cannot be a stable system of international economic and monetary governance.

THE LIFE AND STRANGE AFTERLIFE OF SINGLE-POWER DOMINANCE

The new account of the geopolitico-economic evolution of the capitalist world order that this book has rescued from cosmopolitan distortions, old and new, can now briefly be resumed.

Contrary to the image of free-trading Britain, which Gerschenkron's idea of 'late development' and debates on British industrial decline reinforced in different ways, the United Kingdom's industrial revolution was fostered through state measures, including protection and imperialism. They were necessary even in a largely pre-capitalist world. After the United Kingdom became the world's dominant industrial power, free trade ideology dissimulated its imperial efforts to keep markets open to its manufactured goods – the trade policy most favourable to the industrially dominant country – and to discourage, and in the case of its colonies prevent, the erection of barriers behind which contenders could industrialize. These efforts were, as Hobson and Luxemburg so clearly saw, rooted in capitalism's endemic demand deficiency.

By dominating the world industrially, the United Kingdom also dominated it commercially, financially and of course militarily. Within the Empire, the United Kingdom could impose one-way free trade on its colonies so they could serve as outlets for surplus UK goods and capital. British imperialism, ironically, created the closest thing the world has ever witnessed to a unified world market. However, large as the empire was, it was not coextensive with the world. Powerful states could and did emerge in territories outside British control to flout free trade and industrialize behind protectionist walls. Industrial development in the United States, Germany and Japan, in particular, fractured the unity of the world market, spread productive power more widely, and eroded the United Kingdom's industrial superiority. We could say that this was, in fact, the original multipolar moment. The world dominance of the first industrial capitalist country was inevitable as long as the world outside it remained pre-capitalist and pre-industrial. By the 1870s such a world had ceased to exist, and now such dominance became impossible. Though the United Kingdom's commercial and financial dominance persisted longer, it too ended in the First World War.

The period between 1870 and 1914 is best seen as an equipoise between the UK-dominated world and the trend toward multipolarity that had already appeared so powerfully in it. The period's distinctive geopolitical economy involved the industrial competition that undermined the United Kingdom's industrial superiority, as well as imperial competition for colonies which replaced the 'expansion of England' simply because the world still contained territories that could be easily acquired and held, because they were either stateless or had weak states. This combined industrial and imperial competition, not imperial competition alone, was the object of the classical theories of imperialism and UCD. It made the world economy even less liberal than it had been under the United Kingdom's unchallenged supremacy, thanks to protectionist contender development and industrial and imperial competition between 'nationalized', 'finance' or 'monopoly' capitalisms, as Bukharin, Hilferding and Lenin termed the distinctive new political economies of capitalism of their time. That this period is generally regarded as the heyday of free trade, when the United Kingdom successfully operated the gold standard with sterling as the world's money, is an illustration of how far cosmopolitan ideologies always lay from realities.

Another important development undermined liberalism even further. The political assertion of the working classes in the major capitalist states required those states to offer them material concessions and insulate employment and production levels from the vagaries of the world market. As states responded, they made economies more national and state roles in them more prominent. The allegedly 'automatic' gold standard already operated politically when competing contenders could accept its advantages and refuse its deflationary adjustment as they pleased. With working-class assertion, which made the preservation of minimum employment levels even more important, it was consigned it to the dustbin of history (Eichengreen, 1992).

It was probably inevitable that contender states challenging the United Kingdom's singular world dominance would nurture aspirations to emulate it, but equally inevitable that such ambitions would be thwarted. The first wave of contender development had already dispersed productive power too widely to permit any single power to dominate. Moreover, competition between the multiple contenders would expand possibilities for newer contender states' combined development, and further undermine the imperial possibilities available to any one of them. Of course, collusion between imperial states was also possible, as Lenin as well as Kautsky feared at different times. However, whether that would have been untinged by competition and have sufficed to contain further contender development in the way even UK dominance could not, is questionable. As contender development prevailed over attempts to maintain unevenness at each stage, the world would move toward ever-greater multipolarity.

What complicated such relatively simple unfolding of UCD was not merely that the United States aspired to replace the United Kingdom as the 'managing segment of the world economy', albeit only by making the dollar the world's money in place of sterling, but the wars that, twice, gave it the overwhelming economic and financial superiority which it deployed to the hilt in attempts to achieve that aspiration. Having established the Federal Reserve in 1913 and ensured international acceptance for the dollar, the United States was poised to exploit the opportunities the world wars provided. It entered the First World War to continue to benefit from the bonanza of allied orders, which its banks, backed by the state, also financed, transforming the United States from the world's debtor into its creditor. US insistence on repayment of allied war debts led, in turn, to allied insistence on German reparations payments, and they were then financed from New York. Thus, it was on that tangle of intergovernmental obligations that the dollar and New York rose to interwar prominence. If the United States had achieved its desire, it was only in a perverse sense, in that sterling and London had presided over private capital flows. The interwar financial merry-go-round was implicated in the Great Depression, which hit the United States the hardest.

However, the Second World War presented a 'second chance'. The boost it gave the US economy as the supplier of war materiel, and the devastation it caused in rival capitalist countries, were both greater, and the United States's economic and financial dominance at the war's end was more overwhelming. This would be the most promising opportunity the United States would have to establish the dollar as the world's money. It defeated proposals for multilateral world economic governance at the 1944 Bretton Woods conference, and insisted on making the gold-backed dollar the world's currency. However, realities would reassert themselves.

In postwar circumstances, running one national economy among others, however great its relative size, at high capacity – a requirement of political legitimacy in the age of mass politics as much as of international competition, not to mention the United States's imperial desire to maintain its productive dominance – clashed with the necessity of maintaining the dollar's value in two ways. First, the policy toolkit of combined development had to be put aside for fear it would reduce the United States to the status of a contender. The narrow range of measures it could take to foster growth – macro-economic policy, supplemented with an industrial policy for defence industries – handicapped the US pursuit of growth even as war-devastated rivals deployed the full range of policy tools and reduced the United States's relative economic weight and competitiveness. That was why the main event in the long boom or golden age of the 1950s and 1960s was the combined development of Western Europe, Japan and (to a lesser extent) the developing world.

Meanwhile, the United States could only produce inflationary growth, which widened the trade and current account deficits, and this undermined the dollar's world role, as Triffin predicted in 1959. Gold outflows had already necessitated the formation of the gold pool to back the dollar in 1961, and a decade later, Nixon accepted the obverse: that US economy could only grow if it gave up trying to maintain the gold-backed dollar's world role. In the interim, the Kennedy–Johnson attempt to finance imperialism through national economic growth had demonstrated the impossibility of the enterprise, as highly inflationary growth not only undermined the dollar further but also exhausted the patience of other capitalist powers with existing monetary arrangements.

The geopolitical economy of the twentieth century also made any attempt to emulate British nineteenth-century world dominance more difficult. UCD had already advanced far enough by the early twentieth century to whittle this emulation down to giving the dollar sterling's old role, a territorial empire being out of the question. However, the former was not possible without the latter. Britain's colonies had been critical to maintaining sterling's world role: they yielded the surpluses that allowed the United Kingdom to export capital and thus provide international liquidity in sterling, not to mention the soldiers to fight far-away colonial wars.

During the First World War, the United States had exported capital to finance its exports for an essentially destructive enterprise which actually decreased its debtors' capacity to pay it back, and in the inter-war period, forced repayments created financial havoc under New York's supervision. In the latter twentieth century, when maintaining high employment levels became a parameter of national economic policy, no national economy, no matter how large, could afford to export capital on anywhere near the scale necessary. Not only was the United States without any colonies to speak of, it wanted to maintain, if not increase, its relative economic size. Worse, capital exports would only finance contender development, as Marshall Plan funds did. And even that meagre capital export had necessitated 'scaring the hell out of the country' and launching the cold war before Congress would approve it.

Moreover, there was also all too much combined development going on in the postwar period. For one thing, communism in Russia, Eastern Europe and China took large swaths of the world out of the ambit of capitalism entirely. Posing a contender threat greater than combined capitalist development, it also forced the United States to encourage combined development among recovering and developing countries, if only to lure them away from communism. And as that proceeded, the United States was simply unable to sustain the gold-backed dollar's world role.

With neither capital exports not deficit-fuelled liquidity provision possible, the dollar could not function stably as the world's money even in the 1950s and 1960s, when it was allegedly 'hegemonic'. Indeed, the roots of the idea that it was, HST, lay in the mounting troubles of the dollar in the 1960s. The international financial intermediation hypothesis (IFIH) argued that the dollar's world role was secure because, contrary to economists like Triffin, who thought of the US economy as just another national economy, the United States was, in fact, the world's banker and its debts to the rest of the world were merely its liabilities. The problem lay not with US deficits or competitiveness, but with the inability of foreign governments and central bankers to appreciate this, as the IFIH claimed private investors did.

By the time the Nixon government closed the gold window in 1971, the combined development of the recovering economies had resulted in the overcapacity and overproduction to which Brenner attributed the long downturn. It would form the context for the further career of the dollar as the world's currency. The long downturn persisted thanks to the transformed dynamics of postwar geopolitical economy. With the end of formal colonialism, advanced capitalist economies had become much more dependent on demand generated domestically, and on such export markets as they could access though highly political trade negotiations. National economic managers proved unwilling to impose the sort of 'slaughter of capital values' that would be necessary to revive capitalist accumulation in their own economies. For if others did not follow suit, such efforts, rather than leading to a revival of the country's own industry, could end up benefiting capitalists in other countries. In any case, the economic costs of reduced production and the political costs of opposition from both capital and labour in an age of mass politics were too great. (The UK Thatcher government was the exception because manufacturing interests were uniquely disempowered in that country, but whether it could have imposed a 25 per cent contraction on UK manufacturing without the North Sea oil bonanza which it used to weaken the inevitable political opposition is questionable.)

In this context, one or more capitalist economies could only benefit at the expense of the others, depending on the relative value of currencies, in the 'hydraulic dynamic' of zero-sum growth Brenner described. While this required a measure of cooperation between the major capitalist powers, particularly as expressed in G-7 meetings, there were also antagonisms. The announcement of the 'snake' of currency coordination by the Europeans after the closing of the gold window, and its eventual development into the euro, was perhaps one of the most prominent forms of antagonism, though the US–Japanese trade and financial relationship was not without its tough reciprocities. It is not a coincidence, perhaps, that as competition with its own capitalist rivals intensified, the focus of US foreign policy shifted from anti-communism to the control of oil in the Middle East.

HST emerged after the closing of the gold window, and played a rather different role than free trade had played for the United Kingdom in the nineteenth century. First, since the political management of capitalism could hardly be denied, it was reserved for the 'hegemonic' state alone. Second, while free trade had accompanied UK industrial supremacy, HST emerged after the United States lost such supremacy. And whereas free trade lived on after 1870 to articulate the financial and commercial supremacy the United Kingdom could still exercise, thanks to its colonies, HST could only try to create the illusion that the dollar's world role was still intact after 1971, if only the rest of the world would see it. The IFIH had prefigured HST, and remained at its core. While there is no evidence that US policy makers actually followed their prescriptions, or that the health of the US economy ceased to be the central factor determining the dollar's value, since all further attempts to maintain the dollar's world role would now rest on a succession of dollar- and US-centred financializations, HST contributed to making each one credible before it failed, and another became necessary. All these financializations were accompanied by massive trade imbalances which needed to be financed.

The first of the financializations occurred when the United States arranged that OPEC oil surpluses would be recycled through dollar-denominated financial assets. It briefly stabilized the dollar's world role by making it indispensable for financing the major international trade and financial imbalance of the time, that between oil exporters and importers. To do so, it directed incoming capital outwards to the developing and communist world and, uniquely among the dollar-centred financializations since 1971, financed industrialization there. All later financializations would strangle growth in most parts of the world, and direct capital into the United States instead. Since thanks to the long downturn it could not be employed productively there, it could only result in asset-price bubbles: the stock market bubbles that burst in 1987 and 2000, and the housing and associated credit bubbles that burst in 2008.

Geopolitical Economy's account of the financializations that were necessary to undergird the dollar's world role sheds a special light on the broader phenonmenon of financialization. First, while financialization did affect all countries to some extent, it had a distinct geography and financial structure. The United States, and the United Kingdom which appeared in a special supporting role in each financialization, were the most financialized economies, and the financializations themselves were overwhelmingly US-driven and dollar-centred processes. They linked the US economy's increasingly perverse growth processes with the maintenance of the dollar's world role. The role ensured that the growth processes would remain perverse because underlying competitiveness problems would remain unresolved, and this perversity would eventually catch up with each financialization.

Second, neither any single financialization nor financialization in general occurred because money is inherently 'fungible' and uncontrollable. They occurred because successive US governments, aided by UK governments, pursued policies and strategies to create and maintain them. The key aim of these policies was to support the dollar by creating the level of dollar-denominated liquidity that would preserve its status of the dollar as a reserve currency. That is why debates about whether the 2008 financial crisis was caused by the errors of bankers or their regulators miss a critical point. While the financial institutions were hardly blameless, the unsustainable financial practices that they pursued were practically mandated by the policies pursued by US economic managers, pre-eminently the Fed, to keep capital flowing into the US economy, to maintain consumption- and credit-fuelled growth, and ensure international confidence in the dollar by keeping the house price and mortgage bubbles growing. The competitive processes they unleashed drove bankers to throw ever larger and ever more leveraged sums into increasingly risky investments to make ever-thinner profit margins.

Finally, the United Kingdom's supporting role also appears in a new light. As we saw in Chapter 2, Marx had expected that the relationship between financial and productive capital would, with the development of capitalism, lose the early, atavistic form where the former subordinated the latter, and take a modern form based on the reverse relationship. This modern form was first observed in what Hilferding called 'finance capital' in the 'protectionist countries', which he opposed to the British pattern, which continued in its atavistic form thanks to the dominance of financial capital within British capitalism and Britain's empire. This pattern would have been wound down along with British world dominance after the First World War had not the United States resurrected it on its own shores in pursuit of its desire to emulate British world dominance. The financialization that met its nemesis in the 2008 crisis was the culmination of this long historical development.

Though justified in terms of directing capital towards more productive investment, financialization functioned mainly to direct funds into the US economy, with the exception of two periods: first in the 1970s when, given the long downturn in the Western economies, the oil surpluses deposited in Western and US banks were channelled into productive investment in the developing world; and second in the mid-1990s, when largely short-term capital entered East Asian financial markets. Though the first was better than the second for the developing world while it lasted, increasing industrialization there, both ended disastrously, in the 1982 debt crisis and the 1997–98 Asian financial crisis respectively, exacting a great human and developmental cost. For the rest of the time the funds that financialization channelled into the United States could only fail to make the United States more competitive and blow up asset bubbles instead, given the overcapacity and overproduction in the system as a whole. This was further exacerbated in the US case because its governments would not permit themselves any industrial policy except in the perverse forms of military Keynesianism and military Schumpeterianism.

HST had emerged amid the declinism that gathered over the closing of the gold window, defeat in Vietnam and economic malaise, to retrospectively discern US hegemony and by the late 1980s renewalists began to argue that it has been restored. However, well into the 1990s the economy remained too troubled – dipping to historic lows in the late 1970s and early 1990s – for renewalism to take hold. In closing the gold window, the Nixon Administration had not assumed, per the IFIH, that private confidence would hold the dollar's value up. Rather it was acutely aware that the mercantilism of its actions could spell the end of the dollar's world role. Only a major currency intervention and then the agreement to recycle OPEC oil surpluses stabilized the dollar. But even so, by the late 1970s the United States needed the cooperation of other major industrial economies in regular G-7 meetings to stabilize exchange rates and maintain growth, and the second oil shock sent the dollar plunging again. The new Fed chairman, Paul Volcker, jacked up interest rates to double digits to shore up the dollar, and 'declinism' peaked with Jimmy Carter's 'malaise' speech, proposing to scale down the US world role and increase competitiveness so Americans could earn their keep.

Ronald Reagan's election set the United States back on the rocky path of maintaining the dollar's world role, but his neoliberal, monetarist and supply-side economics failed to do so. Amid high interest rates, the government generated growth through the massive fiscal stimuli of tax cuts for the wealthy, and recharged military Keynesianism and military Schumpeterianism. With the United States's fundamental competitiveness problems remaining unresolved, growth widened not only trade deficits but now also budget deficits. The dollar only remained strong because capital flowed into the United States thanks to Volcker's high interest rates, third-world debt repayments, capital flight from Europe, and Japanese financing of US deficits in return for access to US markets. These capital inflows constituted a second major burst of dollar-denominated financialization. They sent the dollar so high above its value that manufacturers pressured to bring it down, as did leading policy makers worried that it might suffer a catastrophic uncontrolled fall. The 1985 Plaza accord organized controlled dollar depreciation. The dollar's decade-long decline was helped along its way when the US stock market bubble burst in 1987. For despite Reagan's fiscal stimulus, the US economy could only absorb so much capital: the rest inflated the stock market bubble. After it burst, the new Fed chairman's 'Greenspan put' – the provision of extra liquidity to financial markets amid crises – was widely credited with averting a recession, though none actually occurred because the stock market bubble was unconnected with the productive economy.

As the dollar declined, it briefly indicated the direction US economic fundamentals could really sustain. Higher demand for US exports combined with slower growth limiting imports helped close the US trade deficit briefly in the early 1990s. If imperial aspirations were forsaken in favour of a determined state effort to revive productivity and competitiveness, prosperity could have been had. It was not to be. By the time communism collapsed, the US economy was in the doldrums and the president and party that 'won' the cold war were defeated in the 'It's the economy, stupid!' election.

The stage was now set for globalization's strange trajectory. During Clinton's campaign the word referred to competitive threats to be countered with a strategy for higher-value production and trade promotion aimed at the 'big emerging markets' (BEMs). This soberly productive Reichian vision gave way to the heady Stiglitzian financial brew focused on opening capital markets around the world, after Clinton was re-elected and his earlier programme was eclipsed by the deficit reduction, higher interest rates and the high dollar favoured by the financial interests that stood behind him. After briefly taking a centripetal form, with securitized short-term capital flowing outwards from the United States to BEMs which had been persuaded to lift capital controls, and causing the series of financial crises that culminated in the massive 1997–8 East Asian crisis, international capital flows turned centrifugal, pouring into the United States.

Only then did the geopolitical economy of globalization – in which the US-centred international financial system sucked in capital from around the world and poured it into the United States, particularly the US stock market – compose itself fully. The word acquired its more familiar meaning of the desirability and inevitability of a unified world economy, and in particular, a unified world capital market, which was fully expressed in ERP, 1997. These flows, particularly of private capital into the US stock market, were further encouraged by Greenspan's tall tales about the new economy and its 'productivity miracle'. The result, the real and intended result of globalization as it came into its own in the late 1990s, was the stock market bubble and associated consumption and investment booms. When the stock market bubble burst in 2000, the main motor of globalization fell silent.

Empire proved the last and most desperate form of US imperial mimesis, and the financialization that accompanied it was the biggest ever. Having taken office with something like the war on terrorism already on its agenda, the Bush Jr Administration used the cue of 9/11 to indulge in the greatest military spending spree ever, on the back of a US economy less prepared than ever to support it.

The Fed had become the main manager of the US economy since

Clinton's turn to deficit reduction, and the Bush Jr Administration with its one-point agenda of tax cuts was not about to change that. Amid the recession that accompanied the stock market crash, the Fed recognized that credit-fuelled consumption among the upper income groups who had been enjoying the wealth effects of a housing bubble inflating since the mid-1990s was the only source of growth. It committed itself to inflating it further as the only way to growth, and brought interest rates down to their 1 per cent floor of the early 2000s. Even so, this growth relied on foreign funds flowing in to finance the United States's ever-widening deficits and support the dollar.

A new series of discourses emerged to explain away the risky financial structure that was fuelling the housing bubble (the wonders of 'financial innovation'), the US economy's reliance on rock-bottom interest rates (the 'danger of deflation'), its inability to grow fast despite them (the 'great moderation'), and the manifest obscenity of the world's capital financing consumption, predominantly of the rich, in one of the world's richest societies, rather than much-needed developing world production (the 'global savings glut'). The capital inflows not only financed the United States's deficits cheaply, they also expanded the volume of dollar-denominated financial activity on which the downward-sliding dollar's liquidity depended. The bulk of these flows came from the rest of the advanced industrial world, particularly Europe: not East Asia, as commonly assumed.

Talk could, of course, postpone the inevitable only so long, and when it came, it did so in a form that vindicated UCD. For neither US power nor all the cosmopolitan discourses it could generate had succeeded in preventing further combined development and growth in the emerging economies, particularly China, which began to push commodity prices up and the dollar down. The high interest rates that were now necessary triggered the bursting of the housing bubble, thus ending the consumption-led growth and the international capital inflows it had supported.

Beginning in 2007, for the second time in less than a century, the United States led a massive economic downturn. For a second time financial networks centred on New York transmitted its effects around the world, and for a second time its causes were deeply intertwined with US imperial ambition and the impossibility of its realization in a world subject to UCD. But whereas the Great Depression was ended by a war that boosted US power enough to bring it closer to achieving its imperial ambition than it would ever be, the Great Recession happened because UCD forced certain policy decisions, critically the raising of interest rates beginning in 2004, and created certain conditions, most importantly the rise in long-term interest rates beginning in 2007. These brought down the last and most fragile financialization that sustained the dollar's world role. The 2008 financial crisis spelled its end. Whether it is long-drawn-out or rapid, it cannot be avoided. The dollar had never had a stable basis, and with the greater advance of UCD and multipolarity, the United States cannot furnish even another unstable and volatile one.

THE MULTIPOLAR FUTURE

Crises proverbially bring opportunities, and this one brings them in spades, although opportunities not seized also contain risks. The present multipolar moment contains more hopeful possibilities than even the end of the Second World War. Then the inordinate power that war gave the United States set the world on a long detour from the sort of international world of multilateral economic governance which contemporaries had looked forward to, and which Keynes's original proposals had sought to realize. When the 2008 financial crisis ended that detour, history finally caught up with Keynes's far-sighted vision (Desai, 2009a). That vision was of a world in which the economic roles of states have legitimacy and are reinforced by the institutions of international economic governance. Such a relegitimization of states' economic roles is necessary before they can be oriented toward popular interests and even socialism. During the decades when neoliberal and cosmopolitan ideologies undermined that legitimacy, states did not stop intervening in and shaping economies, they simply did so overwhelmingly in the interests of the propertied classes. Naturally they also became less democratic. They must now be made more so, and made to intervene in economies in the popular interest if the unequal and unproductive financialized economic patterns of recent decades that are so destructive of nature and second nature (culture) are to be transformed in egalitarian, productive, green and culturally dynamic directions.

Such a reinstatement of states' economic roles will mark the end of the long period when imperialism, accomplished or attempted, sought to write the economic role of states out of the script of geopolitical economy for reasons already discussed. No doubt the more powerful states will continue to attempt to influence less powerful ones to their own advantage, and imperialism is a term too loosely used to rule out the possibility that the ideas and concepts associated with it will shed light on such actions. However, if this book has been at all persuasive, the need to understand how historical circumstances expand or contract the scope of its operation and change its nature should also be clear.

States will have to play the economic roles that are critical for resolving the problems of the long downturn. The overcapacity and overproduction that have plagued it can be resolved in one of, or a combination of, two ways. The first is, as the Carter Administration along with the rest of the world had briefly glimpsed, an expansion of demand in the developing world. To a great extent, the state-led combined development in emerging economies is already creating it, and modelling it for the rest of the developing world. Early on in the crisis, some speculated that the emerging economies, especially China, would emerge as the new growth motor of the world economy. Such a view implies that the emerging economies would open themselves to absorbing goods and capital from elsewhere, as the United States did over recent decades. This is neither possible nor desirable. However, the expansion of demand within emerging economies, combined with more or less balanced trade with the rest of the world, does carry the most favourable prospect for productive and egalitarian growth patterns in these economies.

The other way is particularly applicable to the developed world, but by no means without relevance to the more successful and prosperous emerging economies. In societies that are prosperous in the aggregate, and where capitalism has only delivered financialization and inequality over the past three decades, growth patterns that increase egalitarianism and aim at 'sustainability and the full development of human creativity' (Chick and Freeman; 2012; see also Freeman, 2009; Bakshi, Desai and Freeman, 2009) combined with egalitarian redistribution can be prioritized. It would be based on the recognition that, in the rich countries at least, the resumption of growth on the pattern of the long boom is neither possible under capitalist conditions, nor desirable. There is also no reason to doubt that such a society and political economy based on expanding ecological and cultural activities which deliver value in new and desirable ways would be closer to, and provide a transition to, socialism.

The crisis has done considerable work: it has put old ideologies, policies and institutions into question. However, the destructive work of crises only takes us so far. The full realization of the possibilities outlined above depends on popular mobilizations that are organized to take and use state power, motivated to exercise it in the interests of the broadest possible constituencies, and informed by an analysis of the problems and possibilities of the current momentous historical conjuncture. Such mobilizations do not usually erupt, fully formed, on the morrow of crises.

It took more than a year after the financial crisis hit for major signs of popular unrest and mobilization to emerge. The Eurozone crisis that began in early 2010 generated considerable unrest, leading to a major electoral upset in Ireland in 2010, and 2011 opened with the wave of protests that inaugurated the Arab Spring (a sure sign that the United States had lost its grip in the Middle East). Protests then spread to the United Kingdom and elsewhere in Europe, and by autumn 2011, the Occupy protests had erupted in the United States. Powerful economic concerns underlay them all. However, the political organization necessary to translate popular concerns and interests into a viable national economic plan seemed more or less universally absent. That does not mean, however, that things are back to pre-crisis business as usual.

True, incumbent governments of the advanced industrial countries most severely affected by the crisis simply imposed costly burdens on ordinary people to give financial capital the aid it demanded for being too big to fail. This happened nowhere more than in the American epicentre of the crisis. However, it remained unclear whether this aid restored financial capital's former dominance. While international capital flows as a percentage of world GDP collapsed in 2008 and 2009 and then revived, they remained until 2010 at least at less than a third of their pre-crisis volumes (Borio and Disyatat, 2011: 14). The size of the bailouts financial institutions had received in affected countries naturally renationalized finance considerably, as did new financial regulation and tangled questions about the relevant lender of last resort for financial institutions' foreign operations.

In contrast to European banks which were asked to take sizeable 'haircuts' – to discount their assets substantially – amid the Eurozone crisis, US banks enjoyed considerably better treatment, but its price will yet be paid in a reduced role for the dollar as it drops in value thanks to the vast increase in US debt, and as some of the more attractive investment destinations become increasingly averse to US financial institutions pushing short-term funds into them and resort to capital controls. Financial institutions, especially the well-bailed-out US financial institutions, are once again engaged in speculation, particularly in commodity markets, raising the question of whether the next crisis will not find them too big to bail out by governments already laden down by debts incurred in previous bailouts, even if popular opinion did not already rule that out as an option. It is also unclear whether the policies of austerity dictated by finance can actually serve its interests if they merely prolong the great recession, as they appear set to do.

The emerging economies are growing strongly, but they will only continue to do so if they limit their reliance on stagnant Western markets by establishing alternative trading arrangements and expanding their internal markets. While there is considerable evidence that the Chinese government is aware of, and acting on, this front, other governments may still be trapped in yesteryear's growth-limiting models. Just as historically workers' struggles were central to expanding domestic markets in the advanced industrial countries, today they are necessary in emerging and developing economies. And if these economies are to construct an alternative and progressive political agenda, the dubious but still lingering cosmopolitan ideologies that created and supported today's discredited national and international structures of privilege and promise to prolong the crisis must be dispelled. This story told in this book should go a considerable way towards doing so.

For it shows that capitalism does not, cannot and has never relied on a strict demarcation between the state and market. Not only have states played central roles in capitalist economies, one could argue that their actions – such as imperialism or welfare states – have been critical to creating capitalist booms. What makes a given society capitalist is not that the state stays out of the economy, but that its economic role favours capital over labour on balance. However, this can last only as long as the capitalist class is better organized behind strategies that deliver relatively stable growth, or the working classes remain unorganized. Today, in the advanced countries at least, the policies that financialized capitalist classes favour are deeply contradictory, incapable of delivering even what they want.

In the past, working people have scored historic successes in exploiting the opportunities of mass politics to bend state action in their favour. Their gains may have given capitalism greater stability, for instance by expanding domestic markets, but they also changed national capitalisms into something much more tolerable. Moreover, the reforms that working classes won also resourced them better to demand more, leaving open the possibility that regulated national capitalisms might become transitions to socialisms. There is no inherent reason why working people should not match and surpass those historic achievements.

Therefore, the apparently radical idea that reforms are useless since the capitalist state cannot be reformed, only overthrown by 'revolution' in ways that are never specified, is actually profoundly conservative. Without a credible conception of how people might expect to achieve such a revolutionary overthrow, it simply derides the reforms they are able to achieve. Instead, we need to recognize that reforms enable working people to build more just societies, and through multilateral international action, for constructing a more just international order.

In recent decades left and progressive intellectuals agreed with the globalization and empire analyses, and even espoused them all the more ardently to demonstrate the power and exploitative nature of capitalism. In doing so, however, they too wrote the state's economic role out of the script of capitalism, and of any viable strategy for socialism. It is time to take stock of the real basis of these cosmopolitan ideologies, and appreciate once more that the state was and remains central to capitalism. This is capitalism's political Achilles' heel. A strategy of reforms forcing states to serve the interests of working people and democratizing them so they contribute to strengthening working people's power and organization is a viable strategy for meaningful reform and even, potentially, revolution leading beyond capitalism (Patnaik, 2009b). The distinction between the two does not rest on the nature of the demands: whether given demands are reformist or revolutionary depends on whether the ruling classes are willing and able to fulfil them, and if not, whether popular forces are sufficiently organized to realize the demands themselves and take on the inevitable opposition to their doing so.

It is true that, historically, combined development has tended to take authoritarian forms in both its capitalist and communist versions (on the latter see Lewin 1995's explanation of the authoritarianism of the Soviet state). However, in good part this was because of the persistence of the power of older landed elites, or imperialist machinations. The power of such forces has now waned, and moreover, working classes are simply a much larger social force throughout the world. The historical record is not without instances where democracy and developmental states have creatively intertwined (White, 2006; Robinson and White, 1998).

Nowhere is the need for mobilization for popular demands clearer than in the United States. In pursuit of imperial ambitions, US governments jettisoned the toolkit of combined development with the partial and rather perverse exceptions of military Keynesianism and military Schumpeterianism. So such attempts as it made to improve its economic performance were made, as it were, with one hand tied behind its back. They failed its manufacturing sector, its international competitiveness, the skills of its working people and the integration of its marginalized minorities, particularly black and Hispanic. There is a wide range of policy options available for addressing these problems, but to avail itself of them the US government will need to abandon the economically liberal ideological straitjacket of the vainly imperial decades. Ross Perot's surprisingly successful third candidacy in the 1992 presidential elections broke out of this straitjacket from the right. The left has yet to show that it can do so.

When it does, the United States will be better able to come to terms with its status as one national economy among many, albeit a large and potentially very dynamic one, and support rather than vainly trying to thwart the underlying trend towards ever greater multilateralism (Ruggie, 1992). The replacement of the G-7 by the G-20 was an important recent marker, and while it remains true that the G-20 is not the G-192, just as the enfranchisement of capitalist classes and their mutual competition made political openings for working-class political assertion in so many capitalist countries historically, this widening of the circle of countries involved in world economic governance beyond the formerly imperial powers cannot but open up spaces for the assertion of the interests of countries farther down the geopolitico-economic hierarchy.

While the rest of the world has long resented US imperial attempts, and done much to counteract and undermine them, Americans themselves have so far been slow to count the cost they themselves have paid for their governments' imperial pursuits, let alone those they inflicted on others. These costs were mainly not those of the military build-up and wars, although these costs were substantial. The greater price came from the neglect of the US economy's productivity and competitiveness, and the pursuit of financialization. Exactly how the United States's imperial pursuits – its military misadventures and support for dollar-denominated financial capital – will be wound down is impossible to predict. But if an upsurge of popular anger such as the 2011 Occupy Wall Street movement, but socially even wider and deeper, plays a central role, the American people will have reclaimed the respect and affection of the rest of the world that their governments have done so much to squander.

REFERENCES

Abrams, Eliot (and many others). 1998. Letter to President Clinton, January 28. www.newamericancentury.org/iraqclintonletter.htm (accessed September 21, 2012).

Adams, F. Gerard. 1992. 'Removing the impediments to economic recovery', *Current History* (Apr), 156–61.

Ahamed, Liaquat. 2009. *Lords of Finance: The bankers who broke the world*. New York: Penguin.

Ali, Tariq. 2000. 'Throttling Iraq', *New Left Review* 5 (Sept–Oct), 5–14.

Althusser, Louis. 1969. 'On the young Marx', trans. Ben Brewster, in *For Marx*. London: Verso.

Amsden, Alice H. 1992. *Asia's Next Giant: South Korea and late industrialization*. New York: Oxford University Press.

Amsden, Alice H. 2001. *The Rise of 'the Rest': Challenges to the West from late-industrializing economies*. Oxford: Oxford University Press.

Amsden, Alice H. 2007. *Escape from Empire: The developing world's journey through heaven and hell*. Cambridge, Mass: MIT Press.

Anderson, Perry. 1964. 'Origins of the present crisis', *New Left Review* 1(23) (Jan–Feb), 26–53.

Anderson, Perry. 1968. 'Components of the national culture', *New Left Review* 1(50) (Jul–Aug, 3–57.

Anderson, Perry. 1976. *Considerations on Western Marxism*. London: NLB.

Anderson, Perry. 1983. *In the Tracks of Historical Materialism*. Wellek Library Lectures. London: Verso.

Anderson, Perry. 1987. 'Figures of descent', *New Left Review* 1(161) (Jan–Feb), 20–77.

Angell, Norman. 1909. *The Great Illusion: A study of the relation of military power to national advantage*. London: William Heinemann.

Arnold, Thurman Wesley. 1937. *The Folklore of Capitalism*. New Haven, Conn.: Yale University Press.

Arrighi, Giovanni. 1978. *The Geometry of Imperialism: The limits of Hobson's paradigm*. London: New Left Books.

Arrighi, Giovanni. 1994. *The Long Twentieth Century: Money, power, and the origins of our times*. London: Verso.

Arrighi, Giovanni. 2003. 'The social and political economy of global turbulence', *New Left Review* 20 (March–April).

Arrighi, Giovanni. 2005a. 'Hegemony unravelling – I', *New Left Review* 32 (Mar–Apr), 23–80.

Arrighi, Giovanni. 2005b. 'Hegemony unravelling – II', *New Left Review* 33 (May–June), 80–116.

Bacevich, Andrew J. 2002. *American Empire: The realities and consequences of U.S. diplomacy*. Cambridge, Mass: Harvard University Press.

Bacevich, Andrew J. 2006. *The New American Militarism: How Americans are seduced by war*. Oxford: Oxford University Press.

Bacevich, Andrew J. 2008. *The Limits of Power: The end of American exceptionalism*, 1st edn. New York: Metropolitan Books.

Bagchi, Amiya Kumar. 1998. 'Growth miracle and its unravelling in East and South-East Asia: unregulated competitiveness and denouement of manipulation by international financial community', *Economic and Political Weekly* 33(18) (May 2), 1025–42.

Bagchi, Amiya Kumar. 2004. *The Developmental State in History and in the Twentieth Century*. New Delhi: Regency.

Bagchi, Amiya Kumar. 2005. *Perilous Passage: Mankind and the global ascendancy of capital*. Lanham, Md: Rowman & Littlefield.

Bagehot, Walter. 1978. *Lombard Street*. New York: Arno Press.

Baily, Martin and Lawrence, Robert Z. 2004. 'What happened to the Great US Jobs Machine?' *Brookings Papers on Economic Activity* 35(2), 211–84.

Bakshi, Hasan, Desai, Radhika and Freeman, Alan. 2009. 'Not rocket science: the case for public R&D in the arts'. London: Mission Money Models.

Banaji, Jairus. 1977. 'Modes of production in a materialist conception of history', *Capital and Class* 3 (Autumn).

Baran, Paul A. and Sweezy, Paul M. 1966. *Monopoly Capital: An essay on the American economic and social order*. Harmondsworth: Penguin.

Beard, Charles Austin. 1935. *The Open Door at Home: A trial philosophy of national interest*. New York: Macmillan.

Bello, Walden. 1998. 'The end of the Asian miracle'. Amsterdam: Translational Institute. www.tni.org/es/archives/act/597 (accessed September 21, 2012).

Berger, Suzanne and Dore, Ronald Philip (eds). 1996. *National Diversity and Global Capitalism*. Ithaca, N.Y.: Cornell University Press.

Bernanke, Ben. 2002. 'Deflation: making sure "it" doesn't happen here', speech to National Economists Club, Washington, DC, November 21. www.federalreserve.gov/boarddocs/speeches/2002/20021121/default. htm (accessed September 21, 2012).

Bernanke, Ben. 2004. 'The great moderation', speech to Eastern Economics Association, Washington DC, February 20. www.federalreserve.gov/ boarddocs/speeches/2004/20040220/default.htm (accessed September 21, 2012).

Bernanke, Ben. 2005. 'The global savings glut and the US current account deficit', speech at St Louis, Miss., March 10. US Federal Reserve. www. federalreserve.gov/boarddocs/speeches/2005/20050414/default.htm (accessed September 21, 2012).

Bernard, Mitchell. 1999. 'East Asia's tumbling dominoes: financial crises and the myth of the regional model', pp. 178–208 in L. Panitch and C. Leys (eds), *Socialist Register*. London: Merlin.

Bingham, Richard D. 1998. *Industrial Policy American Style: From Hamilton to HDTV*. Armonk, N.Y: M.E. Sharpe.

Block, Fred. 1977. *The Origins of International Economic Disorder: A study of United States international monetary policy from World War II to the Present*. Berkeley, Calif.: University of California Press.

Block, Fred. 2008. 'Swimming against the current: the rise of a hidden developmental state in the United States', *Politics & Society* 36(2) (June), 169–206.

Boot, Max. 2003. *The Savage Wars of Peace: Small wars and the rise of American power*, 1st edn. New York: Basic Books.

Bordo, Michael D. and Eichengreen, Barry. 2002. 'Crises now and then: what lessons from the last era of financial globalization?' NBER Working Paper 11383. Cambridge, Mass: National Bureau of Economic Research.

Borio, Claudio and Disyatat, Piti. 2011. 'Global imbalances and the financial crisis: link or no link?' Bank for International Settlements Working Paper no. 346, May.

Braudel, Fernand. 1992. *Civilization and Capitalism, 15th–18th Century*, 3 vols. Berkeley, Calif.: University of California Press.

Brenner, Robert. 1977. 'The origin of capitalist development: a critique of Neo-Smithian Marxism', *New Left Review* 1(104) (July–Aug), 25–92.

Brenner, Robert. 1998. 'The economics of global turbulence', *New Left Review* 1(229) (May–June), 1–265.

Brenner, Robert. 2001. 'The Low Countries in the transition to capitalism', pp. 275–338 in Peter Hoppenbrouwers and Jan Luiten van Zanden (eds), *Peasants into Farmers? The Transformation of rural economy and society in the Low Countries (Middle Ages–19th century) in light of the Brenner debate*. Turnhout, Belgium: Brepols.

Brenner, Robert. 2002. *The Boom and the Bubble: The U.S. in the world economy*. London: Verso.

Brenner, Robert. 2003. 'Towards the precipice', *London Review of Books*, February 6, pp. 18–23.

Brenner, Robert. 2006. *The Economics of Global Turbulence: The advanced capitalist economies from long boom to long downturn, 1945–2005*. London: Verso.

Brenner, Robert. 2009. 'What is good for Goldman Sachs is good for America: the origins of the current crisis', prologue to the Spanish edition of Brenner 2006, April 18. www.sscnet.ucla.edu/issr/cstch/papers/BrennerCrisisTodayOctober2009.pdf (accessed September 21, 2012).

Broz, J. Lawrence. 1997. *The International Origins of the Federal Reserve System*. Ithaca, N.Y: Cornell University Press.

Bukharin, Nikolai Ivanovich. 1917/2003. *Imperialism and World Economy*. London: Bookmarks.

Calleo, David P. 1982. *The Imperious Economy*. Cambridge, Mass: Harvard University Press.

Calleo, David P. 2009. *Follies of Power: America's unipolar fantasy*. New York: Cambridge University Press.

Callinicos, Alex. 2007. 'Does capitalism need the state system?' *Cambridge Review of International Affairs* 20(4), 534–49.

Callinicos, Alex. 2009. *Imperialism and Global Political Economy*. Cambridge, UK/Malden, Mass.: Polity.

Carnoy, Martin. 1984. *The State and Political Theory*. Princeton, N.J: Princeton University Press.

Carr, Edward Hallett. 1939/1989. *The Twenty Years' Crisis, 1919–1939*. London: Macmillan.

Catephores, George. 1994. 'The imperious Austrian: Schumpeter as a bourgeois Marxist', *New Left Review* 1(205) (May–June), 3–30.

Chandler, David. 2003. 'International justice', pp. 27–39 in D. Archibugi (ed.), *Debating Cosmopolitics*. London: Verso.

Chandrashekhar, C. P. 2007. 'Global finance today: déjà vu?', www.networkideas.org/news/jun2007/print/prnt140607_Global_Finance.htm (accessed September 21, 2012).

Chandrashekhar, C. P. and Ghosh, Jayati. 2005. 'The myth of the global savings glut', September 30. www.networkideas.org/focus/Sep2005/fo30_Bernanke.htm (accessed September 21, 2012).

Chang, Ha-Joon. 2002. *Kicking Away the Ladder: Development strategy in historical perspective*. London: Anthem.

Chernomas, Robert. 1984. 'Keynes on post-scarcity society', *Journal of Economic Issues* 17(4) (Dec), 1007–26.

Chick, Victoria. 1992. 'Inflation from a longer-term perspective', pp. 31–54 in Philip Arestis and Sheila Dow (eds), *On Money, Method and Keynes*. Basingstoke: Macmillan.

Chick, Victoria and Freeman, Alan. 2012. 'The economics of enough: a possible future for capitalism?' prepared for the *Cambridge Journal of Economics* special issue in honour of Geoff Harcourt: The Future of Capitalism.

Chick, Victoria and Freeman, Alan. 1983. *Macroeconomics After Keynes: A reconsideration of the* General Theory. Oxford: Philip Allan.

Clarke, P. F. 1978. *Liberals and Social Democrats*. Cambridge: Cambridge University Press.

Clarke, Simon. 1991. *Marx, Marginalism and Modern Sociology: From Adam Smith to Max Weber*, 2nd edn. Basingstoke: Macmillan.

Clarke, Stephen V. O. 1967. *Central Bank Cooperation: 1924–31*. New York: Federal Reserve Bank of New York.

Cohen, Benjamin J. 2008. *International Political Economy: An intellectual history*. Princeton, N.J.: Princeton University Press.

Cooper, Andrew Fenton, Higgott, Richard A. and Nossal, Kim Richard. 1991. 'Bound to follow? Leadership and followership in the Gulf conflict', *Political Science Quarterly* 106(3) (Oct), 391–410.

Cox, Robert W. 1996. *Approaches to World Order*. Cambridge: Cambridge University Press.

Crouch, Colin. 2011. *The Strange Non-Death of Neoliberalism*. Oxford: Polity.

Cumings, Bruce. 1998. 'The Korean crisis and the end of "late" development', *New Left Review* 1(231), 43–72.

Davidson, Paul. 1991. *Controversies in Post Keynesian Economics*. Aldershot: Edward Elgar.

Davis, Mike. 1985. 'Reaganomics magical mystery tour', *New Left Review* 1(148) (Jan–Feb), 45–65.

Davis, Mike. 1986. *Prisoners of the American Dream: Politics and economy in the history of the US working class*. London: Verso.

Davis, Mike. 2009. 'Obama at Manassas', *New Left Review* 56 (Mar–Apr), 5–40.

De Cecco, Marcello. 1984. *The International Gold Standard: Money and Empire*, 2nd edn. London: Pinter.

Desai, Radhika. 1994a. *Intellectuals and Socialism: 'Social Democrats' and the Labour Party*. London: Lawrence & Wishart.

Desai, Radhika. 1994b. 'Second hand dealers in ideas: think-tanks and Thatcherite hegemony', *New Left Review* 1(203) (Jan–Feb), 27–64.

Desai, Radhika. 2002. 'Tryst with fate: India and Pakistan in the war on terrorism', *Economic and Political Weekly* 37(33) (Aug 17), 3456–63.

Desai, Radhika. 2007a. 'Dreaming in technicolour: India as a BRIC economy', *International Journal* (Autumn), 779–803.

Desai, Radhika. 2007b. 'The last empire? From nation-building compulsion to nation-wrecking futility and beyond', *Third World Quarterly* 28(2), 435–56.

Desai, Radhika. 2009a. 'Keynes redux: from world money to international money at last?' pp. 123–43 in Wayne Anthony and Julie Guard (eds), *Bailouts and Bankruptcies*. Halifax: Fernwood.

Desai, Radhika. 2009b. 'The inadvertence of Benedict Anderson: engaging *Imagined Communities*', *Asia-Pacific Journal* 11 (March 16).

Desai, Radhika. 2010a. 'Consumption demand in Marx and in the current crisis', *Research in Political Economy* 26, 101–41.

Desai, Radhika. 2010b. 'Is India having a good crisis?' *Soundings* 48 (Winter), 132–45.

Desai, Radhika. 2010c. 'The absent geopolitics of pure capitalism', *World Review of Political Economy* 1/3, 463–84.

Desai, Radhika. 2012. 'Marx, List and the materiality of nations', *Rethinking Marxism* 24(1) (Jan), 47–67.

Desai, Radhika and Freeman, Alan. 2009. 'Keynes and the crisis: a case of mistaken identity', *Canadian Dimension* (Jul), 17–19.

Desai, Radhika and Freeman, Alan. 2011. 'Value and crisis theory in the Great Recession', *World Review of Political Economy* 2(1), 35–47.

Despres, Emile, Kindleberger, Charles P. and Salant, Walter S. 1966. 'The dollar and world liquidity: a minority view', *Economist* (Feb 5), 526–9.

Deyo, Frederic C. 1987. *The Political Economy of the New Asian Industrialism*. Ithaca, N.Y.: Cornell University Press.

Dillard, Dudley D. 1983. *The Economics of John Maynard Keynes: The theory of a monetary economy*. Westport, Conn: Greenwood.

Divine, Robert A. 1967. *Second Chance: The triumph of internationalism in America during World War II*, 1st edn. New York: Atheneum.

Dobbin, Frank. 1994. *Forging Industrial Policy: The United States, Britain, and France in the railway age*. Cambridge: Cambridge University Press.

Dore, Ronald Philip. 2000. *Stock Market Capitalism, Welfare Capitalism: Japan and Germany versus the Anglo-Saxons*. Oxford: Oxford University Press.

Dostaler, Gilles. 2007. *Keynes and His Battles*. Cheltenham: Edward Elgar.

Economist. 1943. 'The dollar problem I and II', *Economist,* Nov 27 and Dec 4.

Economist. 1966. Commentary on Despres, Emile, Charles P. Kindleberger and Walter S. Salant, 'The dollar and world liquidity: a minority view', *Economist* (Feb 5), 529.

Economist. 2001a. 'Is globalisation doomed?' *Economist* 360(8241), 14.

Economist. 2001b. 'Globalisation and its critics.' *Economist* 360(8241), 3–5.

Eichengreen, Barry. 1992. *Golden Fetters: The Gold Standard and the Great Depression, 1919–1939.* Oxford: Oxford University Press.

Elliott, William Yandell. 1955. *The Political Economy of American Foreign Policy: Its concepts, strategy, and limits.* New York: Holt.

Engels, Friedrich. 1880/1989. *Socialism: Utopian and Scientific,* pp. 281–325 in *The Collected Works of Marx and Engels,* Vol. 24. New York: International Publishers.

Engels, Friedrich. 1888/1990. 'Protection and free trade: preface to the Pamphlet Karl Marx, *Speech on the Question of Free Trade,*' pp. 521–36 in *The Collected Works of Marx and Engels,* Vol. 26. New York: International Publishers.

Evans, Trevor. 1988. 'The dollar is expected to rise, fall or stay steady, experts agree', *Capital and Class* 34, Spring, 10–15.

Federal Open Market Committee (FOMC). 1995. 'Meeting of the Federal Open Market Committee'. Washington: Federal Reserve Board, August 22.

FOMC. 1999. 'Meeting of the Federal Open Market Committee'. Washington: Federal Reserve Board, June 21–30.

Ferguson, Niall. 2004. *Colossus: The price of America's empire.* New York: Penguin.

Ferguson, Niall. 2005. 'Sinking globalization', *Foreign Affairs* (Mar–Apr), 64–77.

Ferguson, Thomas. 1995. *Golden Rule: The investment theory of party competition and the logic of money-driven political systems.* Chicago, Ill.: University of Chicago Press.

Fine, Ben. 2004. 'Examining the ideas of globalization and development critically: what role for political economy?' *New Political Economy* 9/2 (June), 213–31.

Fleckenstein, William A. 2008. *Greenspan's Bubbles: The age of ignorance at the Federal Reserve.* New York: McGraw-Hill.

Foreign Policy in Focus. 2000. 'Clinton's foreign policy', *Foreign Policy in Focus* (Nov), 18–28.

Freeland, Richard M. 1972. *The Truman Doctrine and the Origins of McCarthyism: Foreign policy, domestic politics, and internal security, 1946–1948,* 1st edn. New York: Knopf.

Freeman, Alan. 2001. 'Europe, the US and the world economy: Alan Greenspan's search for a fifth Kondradieff', paper for the Fifth International Conference in Economics organized by the Economic Research Center (ERC) of the Middle East Technical University (METU) in Ankara, September 11–13, 2001.

Freeman, Alan. 2009. 'Investing in civilization', pp. 145–66 in Wayne Anthony and Julie Guard (eds), *Bailouts and Bankruptcies*. Halifax: Fernwood.

Freeman, Alan. 2010. 'Marxism without Marx: a note towards a critique', *Capital and Class* 34(1) (Feb 1), 84–97.

Freeman, Alan, Kliman, Andrew and Wells, Julian (eds). 2004. *The New Value Controversy and the Foundations of Economics*. Cheltenham: Edward Elgar.

Freeman, Christopher. 1974. *The Economics of Industrial Innovation*. Harmondsworth: Penguin.

Frontline. n.d. 'The long demise of Glass Steagall'. www.pbs.org/wgbh/pages/frontline/shows/wallstreet/weill/demise.html (accessed September 21, 2012).

Gallagher, John, and Robinson, Ronald. 1953. 'The imperialism of free trade', *Economic History Review* 6(1) (New series), 1–15.

Gerschenkron, Alexander. 1962. *Economic Backwardness in Historical Perspective: A book of essays*. Cambridge, Mass.: Harvard University Press.

Gershman, Carl. 1980. 'The rise and fall of the foreign policy establishment', *Commentary* (July), 13–24.

Giddens, Anthony. 1994. *Beyond Right and Left*. Cambridge: Polity.

Gilpin, Robert. 1971. 'The politics of transnational economic relations', *International Organization* 25(3) (July 1), 398–419.

Gilpin, Robert. 1975. *U.S. Power and the Multinational Corporation: The political economy of foreign direct investment*. New York: Basic Books.

Gilpin, Robert. 1987. *The Political Economy of International Relations*. Princeton, N.J.: Princeton University Press.

Glyn, Andrew. 2006. *Capitalism Unleashed: Finance globalization and welfare*. Oxford: Oxford University Press.

Göçmen, Doğan. 2007. *The Adam Smith Problem: Human nature and society in* The Theory of Moral Sentiments *and* The Wealth of Nations. London: Tauris.

Gordon, Robert J. 2000. 'Does the "new economy" measure up to the great inventions of the past?' *Journal of Economic Perspectives* 14(4), 49–74.

Gordon, Robert J. 2002. 'Recent productivity puzzles in the context of Zvi Griliches' research', paper presented to meeting of the American Economic Association, 5 January. http://faculty-web.at.northwestern.edu/economics/gordon/Aeazg.pdf (accessed September 21, 2012).

Gordon, Robert J. 2004. 'Why was Europe left at the station when America's productivity locomotive departed?' Northwestern University and CEPR, March 31.

Gowa, Joanne S. 1983. *Closing the Gold Window: Domestic politics and the end of Bretton Woods*. Ithaca, N.Y.: Cornell University Press.

Gowan, Peter. 1999a. *The Global Gamble: Washington's Faustian bid for world dominance*. London: Verso.

Gowan, Peter. 1999b. 'NATO powers and the Balkan tragedy', *New Left Review* 1(234), 83–105.

Grabel, Ilene. 2010. 'Promising avenues, false starts and dead ends: global governance and developmental finance in the wake of the crisis'. Amherst, Mass.: Political Economy Research Institute

Grabel, Ilene. 2011. 'Not your grandfather's IMF: global crisis, "productive incoherence" and developmental policy-space', *Cambridge Journal of Economics* 35, 805–30.

Graham, Otis Jr. 1992. *Losing Time: The industrial policy debate.* Cambridge, Mass.: Harvard University Press.

Grahl, John. 1988. 'The stock market crash and the role of the dollar', *Capital and Class* 34 (Spring), 21–4.

Grandin, Greg. 2006. *Empire's Workshop: Latin America, the United States, and the rise of the new imperialism.* New York: Metropolitan Books.

Greenspan, Alan. 1996. 'The challenge of central banking in a democratic society', Francis Boyer lecture to the American Enterprise Institute for Public Policy Research, Washington DC, December 5. www.federalreserve.gov/boarddocs/speeches/1996/19961205.htm (accessed September 21, 2012).

Greenspan, Alan. 1998. 'Testimony of Chairman Alan Greenspan', *The Federal Reserve's semiannual monetary policy report.* Committee on Banking, Housing, and Urban Affairs, U.S. Senate, July 21. www.federalreserve.gov/boarddocs/hh/1998/july/testimony.htm (accessed September 21, 2012).

Greenspan, Alan. 2002a. 'Monetary policy and the economic outlook', testimony to the Joint Economic Committee, Washington DC, April 17. www.federalreserve.gov/boarddocs/testimony/2002/20020417/default.htm (accessed September 21, 2012).

Greenspan, Alan. 2002b. 'The economic outlook', testimony to the Joint Economic Committee, US Congress, November 13. www.federalreserve.gov/boarddocs/testimony/2002/20021113/default.htm (accessed September 21, 2012).

Greenspan, Alan. 2002c. Testimony of Chairman Alan Greenspan. Federal Reserve Board's semiannual monetary policy report to the Congress Committee on Financial Services, US House of Representatives, February 27.

Greenspan, Alan. 2004. 'Banking', speech to the American Bankers' Association Annual Convention, October 5.

Greenspan, Alan. 2005. 'Consumer finance', speech to the Federal Reserve System's Fourth Annual Community Affairs Research Conference, Washington DC, April 8.

Habib, Irfan. 2006. 'Introduction', in Iqbal Hussain (ed.), *Karl Marx on India.* New Delhi: Tulika.

Hale, Jon F. 1995. 'The making of the New Democrats', *Political Science Quarterly* 110(2) (July 1), 207–32.

Hamilton, Clive. 1986. *Capitalist Industrialization in Korea.* Boulder, Colo.: Westview Press.

Harvey, David. 2003. *The New Imperialism.* Oxford: Oxford University Press.

Hausmann, Ricardo and Sturzenegger, Federico. 2005. 'US and global imbalances: can dark matter prevent a big bang?', November 13. www.setav.org/ups/dosya/26346.pdf (accessed September 21, 2012).

Heilbrunn, Jacob. 2008. *They Knew They Were Right: The rise of the neocons*, 1st edn. New York: Doubleday.

Held, David and McGrew, Anthony. 1999. *Global Transformations: Politics, economics and culture*. Cambridge: Polity.

Helleiner, Eric. 1994. *States and the Reemergence of Global Finance: From Bretton Woods to the 1990s*. Ithaca, N.Y.: Cornell University Press.

Heller, Henry. 2011. *The Birth of Capitalism: A twenty-first century perspective*. London: Pluto.

Hendrickson, Jean. 2001. 'The long and bumpy road to Glass–Steagall reform', *American Journal of Economics and Sociology* 60(6).

Henning, C. Randall. 1994. *Currencies and Politics in the United States, Germany, and Japan*. Washington DC: Institute for International Economics.

Henwood, Doug. 2005. *After the New Economy*. New York: New Press.

Hilferding, Rudolf. 1910/1981. *Finance Capital: A study of the latest phase of capitalist development*. London: Routledge & Kegan Paul.

Hirsch, Fred. 1973. *An SDR Standard: Impetus, elements, and impediments*. Princeton, N.J: International Finance Section, Princeton University.

Hirsch, Fred and Oppenheimer, Peter. 1976. 'The trial of managed money: currency, credit and prices, 1920–70', in Carlo Cipolla (ed.), *Fontana Economic History of Europe: The twentieth century part 2*. London: Fontana.

Hirst, Paul Q., Thompson, Grahame and Bromley, Simon. 1996/2009. *Globalization in Question: The international economy and the possibilities of governance*, 2nd edn. Cambridge: Polity.

Historical Materialism. 1999. Special issue on Brenner's *The Economics of Global Turbulence*, 4(1).

Hobsbawm, E. J. 1964. 'The Fabians reconsidered', in *Labouring Men*. London: Weidenfeld & Nicholson.

Hobsbawm, E. J. 1968. *Industry and Empire: An economic history of Britain since 1750*. London: Weidenfeld & Nicolson.

Hobsbawm, E. J. 1994. *Age of Extremes: The short twentieth century, 1914–1991*. London: Michael Joseph.

Hobsbawm, E. J. 2008. *On Empire: America, war, and global supremacy*, 1st edn. New York: Pantheon.

Hobson, J. A. 1902/1965. *Imperialism: A study*. Ann Arbor, Mich.: University of Michigan Press.

Hoff Wilson, Joan. 1971. *American Business and Foreign Policy, 1920–1933*. Lexington, Ky.: University Press of Kentucky.

Hofstadter, Richard. 1955. *The Age of Reform: From Bryan to F.D.R.* New York: Vintage.

Hofstadter, Richard. 1959. *The American Political Tradition and the Men Who Made It*. New York: Vintage.

Hopenhayn, Benjamin and Vanoli, Alehandro. 2006. 'Capital flows in the twentieth century: from Pax Britannica to Pax Americana', in K. S. Jomo (ed.), *Globalization Under Hegemony: The changing world economy*. New Delhi: Oxford University Press.

Houthakker, H. S. and Magee, Stephen P. 1969. 'Income and price elasticities in world trade', *Review of Economics and Statistics* 51 (May), 111–25.

Howard, M. C. and King, J. E. 1989. *A History of Marxian Economics*, Vol. I. Basingstoke: Macmillan.

Howard, M. C. and King, J. E. 1992. *A History of Marxian Economics*, Vol. II. Basingstoke: Macmillan.

Hudson, Michael. 1972/2003. *Super Imperialism: The origin and fundamentals of U.S. world dominance*, 2nd edn. London: Pluto.

Hudson, Michael. 1977/2005. *Global Fracture: The new international economic order*. London: Pluto.

Hudson, Michael. 2010. 'From Marx to Goldman Sachs: the fictions of fictitious capital and the financialization of industry', *Critique* 38/3 (Jul), 419–44.

Huntington, Samuel. 1988. 'The US – decline or renewal?' *Foreign Affairs* (Winter), 76–96.

Huntington, Samuel. 1993. 'Why international primacy matters', *International Security* 17(4), 68–83.

Ignatieff, Michael. 2003. *Empire Lite: Nation-building in Bosnia, Kosovo, and Afghanistan*. Toronto: Penguin Canada.

Ignatieff, Michael. 2004. *The Lesser Evil: Political ethics in an age of terror, the Gifford Lectures*. Princeton, N.J: Princeton University Press.

Ingham, Geoffrey K. 1984. *Capitalism Divided? The City and industry in British social development*. Basingstoke: Macmillan.

Islam, F. 2002. 'Myth of the American boom is banished by the fall', *Observer*, July 7.

Jervis, Robert. 1993. 'International primacy: is the game worth the candle?' *International Security* 17(4), 52–67.

Johnson, Chalmers A. 2004. *The Sorrows of Empire: Militarism, secrecy, and the end of the republic*. New York: Metropolitan Books.

Joll, James. 1974. *The Second International, 1889–1914*. London: Routledge & Kegan Paul.

Jorgenson, Dale and Stiroh, Kevin. 2000. 'Raising the speed limit: U.S. economic growth in the information age', March 16. www.irpp.org/events/archive/may00/jorgenso.pdf (accessed September 21, 2012).

Judis, John B. 1996. 'Dollar foolish', *New Republic* (December 9), 23–4.

Kalecki, M. 1943. 'Political aspects of full employment', *Political Quarterly* 14(4), 322–31.

Kanburi, A. A. and Mansur, S. 1994. 'The political economy of Middle Eastern oil', pp. 313–27 in G. R. Underhill and R. Stubbs (eds), *Political Economy and the Changing Global Order*. Basingstoke: Macmillan.

Kautsky, Karl. 1914/1970. 'Ultra-imperialism', *New Left Review* 1(59), 41–6.

Kennan, George. 1948/1976. 'PPS/23: review of current trends in U.S. foreign policy', pp. 509–29 in *Foreign Relations of the United States*, Vol. 1, *part 2* (Washington DC: Government Printing Office.

Kennedy, Paul M. 1987. *The Rise and Fall of the Great Powers: Economic change and military conflict from 1500 to 2000*, 1st edn. New York: Random House.

Keohane, Robert O. 2005. *After Hegemony: Cooperation and discord in the world political economy*, 1st edn. Princeton, N.J: Princeton University Press.

Keynes, J. M. 1919/2004 *The Economic Consequences of the Peace*, repr. in *The End of Laissez Faire and the Economic Consequences of the Peace*. New York: Prometheus.

Keynes, J. M. 1931/1973. 'An economic analysis of unemployment', pp. 343–67 in *The Collected Works of John Maynard Keynes, Vol. XIII: The General Theory and After*. London: Macmillan.

Keynes, J. M. 1933. 'National self sufficiency', *Yale Review* (Summer), repr. in *New Statesman and Nation* (July 8, 1933).

Keynes, J. M. 1936/1967. *General Theory of Employment, Interest and Money*. London: Macmillan.

Keynes, J. M. 1963. *Essays in Persuasion*. New York: Norton.

Keynes, J. M. 1980. *The Collected Writings of John Maynard Keynes, Vol. XXV: Activities 1940–1944*. London: Macmillan and Cambridge University Press.

Kindleberger, Charles Poor. 1950. *The Dollar Shortage*. Cambridge, Mass.: Technology Press of Massachusetts Institute of Technology.

Kindleberger, Charles Poor. 1961. 'La fin du role dominant des Etats-Unis et l'avenir d'une politique économique mondiale', *Cahiers de l'Institut de Science Economique Appliquée*, Série P. (May 5), 91–105.

Kindleberger, Charles Poor. 1973. *The World in Depression, 1929–1939. History of the world economy in the twentieth century, Vol. 4*. Berkeley, Calif.: University of California Press.

Kindleberger, Charles Poor. 1981. 'Dominance and leadership in the international economy: exploitation, public goods, and free rides', *International Studies Quarterly* 25(2), 242–54.

Kindleberger, Charles Poor. 1986. *The World in Depression, 1929–1939*. Berkeley, Calif.: University of California Press.

Kliman, Andrew. 2007. *Reclaiming Marx's Capital: A refutation of the myth of inconsistency*. Lanham, Md.: Lexington.

Kotz, David M. 1997. *Revolution from Above: The demise of the Soviet system*. London: Routledge.

Krasner, Stephen D. (ed.). 1983. *International Regimes*. Ithaca, N.Y.: Cornell University Press.

Krasner, Stephen D. 1976. 'State power and the structure of international trade', *World Politics* 28(3) (Apr), 317–47.

Krause, Lawrence. 1970. 'A passive balance of payments strategy for the United States', *Brookings Papers on Economic Activity* 3, 339–60.

Krippner, Greta. 2005. 'The financialization of the American economy', *Socio-Economic Review* 3, 173–208.

Kristol, William and Kagan, Robert. 1996. 'Toward a neo-Reaganite foreign policy', *Foreign Affairs* (Jul), 18–32.

Laclau, Ernesto. 1977. 'Feudalism and capitalism in Latin America', in *Politics and Ideology in Marxist Theory*. London: Verso.

Lafeber, Walter Frederick. 1963. *The New Empire: An interpretation of American expansion, 1860–1898*. Ithaca, N.Y.: Cornell University Press.

Lary, Hal. 1943. *The United States in the World Economy: The international transactions of the United States during the interwar period.* Washington DC: Government Printing Office.

Lawrence, Robert Z. 1984. *Can America Compete?* Washington DC: Brookings Institution.

League of Nations. 1945. *Industrialization and Foreign Trade.* Geneva: League of Nations.

Lenin, Vladimir. 1916/1942. 'The socialist revolution and the right of nations to self-determination', pp. 143–6 in *Collected Works*, Vol. 22. Moscow: Progress.

Lenin, Vladimir. 1916/1970. *Imperialism, the Highest Stage of Capitalism: A popular outline.* Moscow: Progress.

Lens, Sidney. 2003. *The Forging of the American Empire.* London: Pluto.

Lewin, Moshe. 1995. *Russia–USSR–Russia: The drive and drift of a superstate.* New York: New Press.

Leys, Colin. 1985. 'Thatcherism and British manufacturing', *New Left Review* 1(151).

Leys, Colin. 1989. *Politics in Britain: From Labourism to Thatcherism*, rev. edn. London: Verso.

Leys, Colin. 1990. 'Still a question of hegemony', *New Left Review* 1(181).

Linden, van der, Marcel. 2007. 'The "law" of uneven and combined development: some underdeveloped thoughts', *Historical Materialism* 15, 135–45.

Lipietz, Alain. 1992. *Towards a New Economic Order: Postfordism, ecology, and democracy. Europe and the international order.* New York: Oxford University Press.

List, Fredrick. 1841/1856. *National System of Political Economy.* Philadelphia, Pa.: J. B. Lippincott.

Livingston, James. 1986. *Origins of the Federal Reserve System: Money, class, and corporate capitalism, 1890–1913.* Ithaca, N.Y.: Cornell University Press.

Löwy, Michael. 1981. *The Politics of Combined and Uneven Development: The theory of permanent revolution.* London: New Left Books.

Luce, Henry. 1941/1999. 'The American century', *Diplomatic History* 23(2) (Spring).

Luttwak, Edward. 1990. 'From geopolitics to geoeconomics', *The National Interest* 20 (Summer), 17–23.

Luttwak, Edward. 1993. *The Endangered American Dream: How to stop the United States from becoming a third world country and how to win the geo-economic struggle for industrial supremacy.* New York: Simon & Schuster.

Lynd, Staughton. 1970. 'Beyond Beard', in Barton J. Bernstein (ed.), *Towards a New Past.* New York: Pantheon.

Luxemburg, Rosa. 1913/1951. *The Accumulation of Capital.* New Haven, Conn.: Yale University Press.

Luxemburg, Rosa. 1913/2003. *The Accumulation of Capital.* London: Routledge.

MacGregor, David and Zarembka, Paul. 2010. 'Marxism, conspiracy and 9–11', *Socialism and Democracy* 24(2), 139–63.

Madrick, Jeff. 1998. 'Computers: waiting for the revolution', *New York Review of Books* (March 26).

Madrick, Jeff. 1999. 'How new is the new economy?' *New York Review of Books* (Sep 23).

Maier, Charles S. 2006. *Among Empires: American ascendancy and its predecessors*. Cambridge, Mass.: Harvard University Press.

Makin, John H. 2007. 'Why interest rates are rising', *AEI Online*, June 20. www.aei.org/outlook/26377 (accessed September 21, 2012).

Mallaby, Sebastian. 2002. 'The reluctant imperialist: terrorism, failed states, and the case for American empire', *Foreign Affairs* 81(2), 2–7.

Mandel, Ernest. 1969. 'Where is America going?' *New Left Review* 1(54), 3–15.

Mandel, Ernest. 1978. 'Introduction', pp. 11–79 in Karl Marx, *Capital*, Vol. II. London: Penguin.

Mann, James. 2004. *Rise of the Vulcans: The history of Bush's War Cabinet*. New York: Penguin.

Mann, Michael. 2003. *Incoherent Empire*. London: Verso.

Martin, Terry. 2001. *The Affirmative Action Empire: Nations and nationalism in the Soviet Union, 1923–1939*. Ithaca, N.Y.: Cornell University Press.

Marx, Karl. 1843/1974. 'Contribution to a critique of Hegel's *Philosophy of Right*: Introduction', repr. as pp. 243–58 in *Early Writings*. London: Penguin.

Marx, Karl. 1845/1975. 'Draft of an article on Friedrich List's book: *Das Nationale System der Politischen Oekonomie*', pp. 265–93 in *The Collected Works of Marx and Engels*, Vol. 4. New York: International Publishers.

Marx, Karl. 1847/1976. 'Speech of Dr Marx on protection, free trade, and the working class', in F. Engels, 'The Free Trade Congress at Brussels', pp. 282–90 in *The Collected Works of Marx and Engels*, Vol. 6. New York: International Publishers.

Marx, Karl. 1848/1976. 'Speech on the question of free trade delivered to the Democratic Association of Brussels at its public meeting of January 8, 1848', pp. 450–65 in *The Collected Works of Marx and Engels*, Vol. 6. New York: International Publishers.

Marx, Karl. 1858/1973. *Grundrisse*. London: Penguin.

Marx, Karl. 1867/1977. *Capital*, Vol. I. London: Penguin.

Marx, Karl. 1884/1978. *Capital*, Vol. II. London: Penguin.

Marx, Karl. 1894/1981. *Capital*, Vol. III. London: Penguin.

Marx, Karl. 1969. *Theories of Surplus Value*, Vol. I. London: Lawrence & Wishart

Marx, Karl. 1979. *Theories of Surplus Value*, Vol. III. London: Lawrence & Wishart.

Marx, Karl. 1974. *Political Writings II: Surveys from Exile*, New York: Vintage.

Marx, Karl and Engels, Friedrich. 1848/1967. *The Communist Manifesto* trans. Samuel Moore, intro. by A. J. P. Taylor. London: Penguin.

Mayer, Arno J. 1964. *Wilson vs. Lenin : Political origins of the new diplomacy, 1917–1918*. New York: H. Fertig.

Mayer, Arno J. 1981. *The Persistence of the Old Regime: Europe to the Great War*. New York: Pantheon.

McKinsey Global Institute (MGI). 2001. *US Productivity Growth 1995–2000: Understanding the contribution of information technology relative to other factors*. Washington DC: MGI.

Meek, Ronald L. 1977. *Smith, Marx, and After: Ten essays in the development of economic thought*. London/New York: Chapman & Hall/Wiley.

Mehringer, Hartmut. 1978. *Permanente Revolution und Russische Revolution. Die Entwicklung der Theorie der permanenten Revolution im Rahmen der marxistischen Revolutionskonzeption 1848–1907*. Frankfurt am Main: Peter Lang.

Melman, Seymour. 1974. *The Permanent War Economy: American capitalism in decline*. New York: Simon & Schuster.

Mokyr, Joel and Stein, Rebecca. 1997. 'Science, health and household technology: the effect of the Pasteur revolution on consumer demand', in Timothy Bresnahan and Robert Gordon (eds), *The Economics of New Products*. Chicago, Ill.: University of Chicago Press.

Morgan, Mary S. and Rutherford, Malcolm. 1998. 'American economics: the character of the transformation', pp. 2–26 in M. S. Morgan and M. Rutherford (eds), *From Interwar Pluralism to Postwar Neoclassicism*. Durham, N.C.: Duke University Press.

Murphy, R. Taggart. 1996. *The Weight of the Yen*. New York: W. W. Norton.

Murphy, R. Taggart. 2006. 'East Asia's dollars', *New Left Review* 40(Jul–Aug), 39–64.

Nicolaus, Martin. 1973. 'Foreword', pp. 7–63 in Karl Marx, *Grundrisse*. London: Penguin.

Nordhaus, William D. 2002. 'Productivity growth and the new economy', *Papers on Economic Activity*. Washington DC: Brookings Institution.

Nye, Joseph S. 1990. *Bound to Lead: The changing nature of American power*. New York: Basic Books.

O'Neill, Jim. 2001. 'Building better global economic BRICs', Global Economics Paper No. 66, New York: Goldman Sachs.

Okishio, N. 1961. 'Technical change and the rate of profit', *Kobe University Economic Review* 7, 86–98.

Oliner, Stephen D. and Sichel, Daniel E. 2000. 'The resurgence of growth in the late 1990s: is information technology the story?' *Journal of Economic Perspectives* 14(4), 3–22.

Ohmae, Kenichi. 1990. *The Borderless World: Power and strategy in the interlinked economy*. New York: HarperBusiness.

Oppenheim, V. H. 1976. 'Why did oil prices go up? The past: we pushed them', *Foreign Policy* 25 (Winter), 24–57.

Palan, Ronen. 2003. *The Offshore World: Sovereign markets, virtual places, and nomad millionaires*. Ithaca, N.Y.: Cornell University Press.

Panitch, Leo and Gindin, Sam. 2004. *Global Capitalism and American Empire*. London: Merlin.

Parboni, Riccardo. 1981. *Dollar and Its Rivals: Recession, inflation, and international finance*. London: NLB.

Parboni, Riccardo. 1986. 'The dollar weapon: From Nixon to Reagan', *New Left Review* 1(158), 5–18.

Parrini, Carl P. 1969. *Heir to Empire: United States economic diplomacy, 1916–1923*. Pittsburgh, Pa.: University of Pittsburg Press.

Patnaik, Prabhat. 2007. 'Some reflections on China's economic performance'. International Development Economics Associates. www.networkideas. org/news/jan2007/news31_china_economy.htm (accessed September 21, 2012).

Patnaik, Prabhat. 2008. 'The accumulation process in the period of globalization', D. D. Kosambi Memorial Lecture, International Development Economics Association, May 28. http://www.networkideas. org/feathm/may2008/ft28_Globalization.htm_(accessed September 30, 2012).

Patnaik, Prabhat. 2009a. *The Value of Money*. New York: Columbia University Press.

Patnaik, Prabhat. 2009b. 'Socialism and welfarism', International Development Economics Associates. www.networkideas.org/news/ aug2009/print/prnt250809_Socialism.htm (accessed September 21, 2012).

Patnaik, Utsa. 2005. 'Ricardo's fallacy: mutual benefit from trade based on comparative costs and specialization?' in K. S. Jomo (ed.), *The Pioneers of Development Economics*. London: Zed.

Patnaik, Utsa. 2006. 'The free lunch – transfers from the tropical colonies and their role in capital formation in Britain during the industrial revolution', in K. S. Jomo (ed.), *Globalization under Hegemony*. Delhi: Oxford University Press.

Perelman, Michael. 2002. *The Pathology of the U.S. Economy Revisited: The intractable contradictions of economic policy*, 1st edn. New York: Palgrave.

Perroux, François. 1950. 'The domination effect and modern economic theory', *Social Research* 17(2) (June 1), 188–206.

Perroux, François.1988a. 'The pole of development's place in a general theory of economic activity', in Benjamin Higgins and D. Savoie (eds), *Regional Economic Development: Essays in honor of François Perroux*. Boston, Mass.: Allen & Unwin.

Perroux, François. 1988b. 'Peregrinations of an economist and the choice of his route', in Benjamin Higgins and D. Savoie (eds), *Regional Economic Development: Essays in honor of François Perroux*. Boston, Mass.: Allen & Unwin.

Phillips, Kevin. 2002. *Wealth and Democracy: A political history of the American rich*, 1st edn. New York: Broadway.

Polanyi, Karl. 1985. *The Great Transformation*. Boston, Mass.: Beacon Press.

Pollin, Robert. 2000. 'Anatomy of Clintonomics', *New Left Review* 3 (May–June), 17–46.

Pollin, Robert. 2003. *Contours of Descent: U.S. economic fractures and the landscape of global austerity*. London: Verso.

Poulantzas, Nicos A. 1978. *State, Power, Socialism*. London: New Left Books.

Project for a New American Century. 2006. Home page, as at 2006. www. newamericancentury.org/index.html

Reich, Robert B. 1991. *The Work of Nations: Preparing ourselves for 21st-century capitalism*. New York: A.A. Knopf.

Reich, Robert B. and Rohatyn, Felix G. 1984. 'Coping with Reagan's economic legacy', *World Policy Journal* 2(1), 1–32.

Reinert, Erik S. 2007. *How Rich Countries Got Rich and Why Poor Countries Stay Poor*. London: Constable.

Reinert, Erik S. 2008. 'Krugman and the vices of economists', *The Hindu*, December 10.

Reinert, Erik and Daastøl, Arno. 2004. 'The other canon', pp. 21–70 in Erik Reinert (ed.), *Globalization, Economic Development and Inequality*. Cheltenham: Edward Elgar.

Robinson, Joan. 1942. *An Essay on Marxian Economics*. London: Macmillan.

Robinson, Joan. 1951. 'Introduction' to Rosa Luxemburg, *The Accumulation of Capital*. New Haven, Conn.: Yale University Press.

Robinson, Mark and White, Gordon (eds). 1998. *The Democratic Developmental State: Politics and institutional design*, Oxford Studies in Democratization. New York: Oxford University Press.

Rohatyn, Felix. 1987a. 'On the brink', *New York Review of Books*, June 11.

Rohatyn, Felix. 1987b. 'What next?' *New York Review of Books*, December 3.

Rohatyn, Felix. 1994. 'World capital: the needs and the risks', *New York Review of Books*, July 14.

Roosa, Robert. 1970. 'Capital movements and balance of payments adjustment', *Business Review* (Sep), 21–38, Philadelphia, Pa.: Federal Reserve Bank.

Rosecrance, Richard N. (ed.). 1976. *America as an Ordinary Country: U.S. foreign policy and the future*. Ithaca, N.Y: Cornell University Press.

Rosenberg, Justin. 1994. *The Empire of Civil Society: A critique of the realist theory of international relations*. London: Verso.

Rosenberg, Justin. 2000. *The Follies of Globalisation Theory: Polemical essays*. London: Verso.

Rothkopf, David. 1998. 'Beyond manic mercantilism', in James Shinn (ed.), *Riding Tigers: American commercial diplomacy in Asia*. Washington DC: Council on Foreign Relations.

Rothermund, Dietmar. 1996. *The Global Impact of the Great Depression, 1929–1939*. London/New York: Routledge.

Ruggie, John Gerard. 1982. 'International regimes, transactions, and change: embedded liberalism in the postwar economic order', *International Organization* 36(2), 379–415.

Ruggie, John Gerard. 1992. 'Multilateralism: the anatomy of an institution', *International Organization* 46(3) (July 1), 561–98.

Salant, Walter S. 1963. *The United States Balance of Payments in 1968*. Washington DC: Brookings Institution.

Salant, Walter S. 1966. 'Capital markets and the balance of payments of a financial center', in William Fellner, Fritz Machlup, Robert Triffin et al. (eds), *Maintaining and Restoring Balance in International Payments.* Princeton, N.J.: Princeton University Press.

Sardoni, C. 1997. 'Keynes and Marx', in G. C. Harcourt and P. Riach (eds), *A 'Second Edition' of* The General Theory. London: Routledge.

Sarkis, Nicholas. 2004. 'Is there really a rise in oil prices?' *Le Monde Diplomatique*, July.

Saul, S. B. 1960. *Studies in British Overseas Trade, 1870–1914.* Liverpool: Liverpool University Press.

Schorske, Carl E. 1983. *German Social Democracy, 1905–1917: The development of the great schism.* Cambridge, Mass: Harvard University Press.

Schrag, Peter. 1975. 'America needs an establishment', *Harper's* 251(1507) (Dec), 51–8.

Schumpeter, Joseph Alois. 1951. *Imperialism and Social Classes.* Oxford: Basil Blackwell.

Semmel, Bernard. 1993. *The Liberal Ideal and the Demons of Empire: Theories of imperialism from Adam Smith to Lenin.* Baltimore, Md.: Johns Hopkins University Press.

Shaikh, Anwar. 1978. 'An introduction to the history of crisis theories', pp. 219–41 in *U.S. Capitalism in Crisis.* New York: URPE.

Shull, Bernard. 2005. *The Fourth Branch: The Federal Reserve's unlikely rise to power and influence.* Westport, Conn: Praeger.

Sichel, Daniel E. 1997. *The Computer Revolution: An economic perspective.* Washington DC: Brookings Institution Press.

Skidelsky, Robert. 2000. *John Maynard Keynes: Volume 3, Fighting for Britain 1937–1946.* London: Macmillan.

Smith, Adam. 1776/1976. *An Inquiry into the Nature and Causes of the Wealth of Nations.* Chicago, Ill.: University of Chicago Press.

Smith, Neil. 1990. *Uneven Development*, 2nd edn. Oxford: Basil Blackwell.

Smith, Neil. 2003. *American Empire: Roosevelt's geographer and the prelude to globalization.* Berkeley, Calif.: University of California Press.

Soros, George. 2008. 'The worst market crisis in 60 years', *Financial Times*, January 22.

Standage, Tom. 1998. *The Victorian Internet: The remarkable story of the telegraph and the nineteenth century s on-line pioneers.* New York: Walker.

Stedman-Jones, Gareth. 1970. 'The specificity of US imperialism', *New Left Review* 1(60) (Mar–Apr), 59–86.

Stiglitz, Joseph. 1989. *The Economic Role of the State*, ed. Arnold Heertje. Oxford: Basil Blackwell.

Stiglitz, Joseph. 2001. 'Autobiography', for the Sveriges Riksbank Prize in Economic Sciences in Memory of Alfred Nobel 2001. http://nobelprize.org/nobel_prizes/economics/laureates/2001/stiglitz-autobio.html (accessed September 21, 2012).

Stiglitz, Joseph. 2002. *Globalization and Its Discontents*, 1st edn. New York: W.W. Norton.

Stiglitz, Joseph E. and Bilmes, Linda. 2008. *The Three Trillion Dollar War: The true cost of the Iraq conflict.* New York: W.W. Norton.

Strange, Susan. 1970. 'International economics and international relations: a case of mutual neglect', *International Affairs* 46(2) (Apr), 304–15.

Strange, Susan. 1987. 'Persistent myth of lost hegemony', *International Organization* 41(4) (Autumn), 551–74.

Subacchi, Paola and Driffill, John (eds). 2010. *Beyond the Dollar: Rethinking the international monetary system*. London: Chatham House.

Suskind, Ron. 2004. 'Faith, certainty and the presidency of George W. Bush', *New York Times Magazine*, October 17.

Teschke, Benno. 2003. *The Myth of 1648: Class, geopolitics, and the making of modern international relations*. London: Verso.

Therborn, Göran. 2001. 'Into the 21st century: the new parameters of global politics', *New Left Review* 10 (Jul–Aug), 87–110.

Tily, Geoff. 2007. *Keynes's General Theory, the Rate of Interest and 'Keynesian' Economics: Keynes betrayed*. Basingstoke: Palgrave Macmillan.

Torr, C. S. W. 1980. 'The distinction between an entrepreneur and a co-operative economy', *South African Journal of Economics* 48, 429–34.

Triffin, Robert. 1961. *Gold and the Dollar Crisis: The future of convertibility.*, rev. edn. New Haven, Conn.: Yale University Press.

Triplett, Jack E. 1999. 'Economic statistics, the new economy, and the productivity slowdown', January. Washington DC: Brookings Institution. www.brookings.edu/~/media/Files/rc/articles/1999/04technology_triplett/199904b.pdf (accessed September 21, 2012).

Trotsky, Leon. 1934. *The History of the Russian Revolution*. London: Gollancz.

Trotsky, Leon. 1969. *The Permanent Revolution, and Results and Prospects*. New York: Merit.

Truman, Harry. 1947. 'President Harry S. Truman's address before a Joint Session of Congress', March 12. http://avalon.law.yale.edu/20th_century/trudoc.asp (accessed September 21, 2012).

Tugan-Baranowski, M. 1901/2000a. 'Chapter 1: The fundamental causes of crises in the capitalist economy', trans. Alejandro Ramos-Martınez. Repr. in *Research in Political Economy* 18, 53–80.

Tugan-Baranowski, M. 1901/2000b. 'Chapter 7: Marx's theory of crises', trans. Alejandro Ramos-Martınez. Repr. in *Research in Political Economy* 18, 81–110.

Turner, Frederick Jackson. 1893/1958. *The Frontier in American History*. New York: Henry Hold.

Uchitelle, Louis. 2000. 'The Solow computer paradox: what do computers do to productivity?' *Canadian Journal of Economics* 32(3) (Apr), 309–34.

United Nations. 2009. *Report of the Commission of Experts of the President of the United Nations General Assembly on Reforms of the International Monetary and Financial System*. New York: United Nations.

UN Conference on Trade and Development (UNCTAD). 2011. *Post-Crisis Policy Challenges in the World Economy*. New York/Geneva: United Nations.

US Department of State. 1950. *United States Objectives and Programs for National Security*, NSC-68. Policy Planning Staff, April 7.

US Task Group on Regulation of Financial Services. 1984. *Blueprint for Reform: The Report of the Task Group on Regulation of Financial*

Services. Washington DC: US Government Archive. www.archive.org/details/blueprintforrefo01unit (accessed September 21, 2012).

Van der Pijl, Kees. 1984. *The Making of the Atlantic Ruling Class.* London: Verso.

Van der Pijl, Kees. 2006a. *Global Rivalries from the Cold War to Iraq.* London: Pluto.

Van der Pijl, Kees. 2006b. 'A Lockean Europe', *New Left Review* 31 (Jan–Feb), 9–37.

Veblen, Thorstein. 1919. 'Peace', *The Dial* 46 (May 17), 485–7.

Vernon, Raymond. 1971. *Sovereignty at Bay: The multinational spread of U.S. enterprises.* London: Longman.

Volcker, Paul. 2005. 'An economy on thin ice', *Washington Post*, April 10.

Volcker, Paul A, and Gyohten, Toyoo. 1992. *Changing Fortunes: The world's money and the threat to American leadership*, 1st edn. New York: Times Books.

Wade, Robert. 1990. *Governing the Market: Economic theory and the role of government in East Asian industrialization.* Princeton N.J: Princeton University Press.

Wade, Robert. 1996a. 'Japan, the World Bank and the art of paradigm maintenance: the East Asian miracle in political perspective', *New Left Review* 1(217), 3–36.

Wade, Robert. 1996b. 'Globalization and its limits: reports of the death of the national economy are greatly exaggerated', pp. 60–88 in Ronald Dore and Suzanne Berger (eds), *National Diversity and Global Capitalism.* Ithaca, N.Y.: Cornell University Press.

Wade, Robert. 2011. 'Emerging world order? From multipolarity to multilateralism in the G20, the World Bank, and the IMF', *Politics and Society* 39(3), 347–78.

Wade, Robert and Veneroso, Frank. 1998a. 'The Asian crisis: the high debt model versus the Wall Street–Treasury–IMF Complex', *New Left Review* 1(228), 2–23.

Wade, Robert and Veneroso, Frank. 1998b. 'The gathering slump and the battle over capital controls', *New Left Review* 1(231), 13–42.

Wallerstein, Immanuel Maurice. 1974. *The Modern World-System: Studies in social discontinuity.* New York: Academic Press.

Wallerstein, Immanuel Maurice. 1976. *The Modern World-System: Capitalist agriculture and the origins of the European world-economy in the sixteenth century.* New York: Academic Press.

Wallerstein, Immanuel Maurice. 1980. *The Modern World System II: Mercantilism and the Consolidation of the European World Economy 1600–1750.* New York: Academic Press.

Wallerstein, Immanuel Maurice.1991. 'World system', in Tom Bottomore et al. (eds), *A Dictionary of Marxist Thought.* Oxford: Blackwell.

Wasshausen, D and Moulton, B. 2006. 'The role of hedonic adjustments in measuring real GDP in the United States', Washington DC: Bureau of Economic Analysis. www.bea.gov/papers/pdf/hedonicGDP.pdf (accessed September 21, 2012).

Warren, Bill. 1980. *Imperialism, Pioneer of Capitalism*, ed. John Sender. London: New Left Books.

Weiss, Linda. 1998. *The Myth of the Powerless State*. Ithaca, N.Y.: Cornell University Press.

White, Gordon (ed.) 1988. *Developmental States in East Asia*. Basingstoke: Macmillan Williams.

White, Gordon. 2006. 'Towards a democratic developmental state', *IDS Bulletin* 37(104) (Sep), 60–70.

Williams, William Appleman. 1972. *The Tragedy of American Diplomacy*, 2nd edn. New York: Dell.

Williamson, John. 1977. *The Failure of World Monetary Reform, 1971–74*. Sunbury-on-Thames: Nelson.

Wojnilower, Albert M. 1980. 'The central role of credit crunches in recent financial history', *Brookings Papers on Economic Activity* 2(1), 277–326.

Wolf, Martin. 2004. *Why Globalization Works*. New Haven, Conn.: Yale University Press.

Wolf, Martin. 2009. 'This crisis is a moment, but is it a defining one?' *Financial Times*, May 19.

Woo-Cumings, Meredith (ed.) 1999. *The Developmental State*. Ithaca, N.Y: Cornell University Press.

Wood, Ellen Meiksins. 1981. 'The separation of the political and the economic in capitalism', *New Left Review* 1(127), 66–95.

Wood, Ellen Meiksins. 1999. 'Unhappy families: global capitalism in a world of nation-states', *Monthly Review* (Jul–Aug), 1–12.

Woodward, Bob. 1994. *The Agenda: Inside the Clinton White House*. New York: Simon & Schuster.

Woodward, Bob. 2000. *Maestro: Greenspan's Fed and the American boom*. New York: Simon & Schuster.

World Bank. 1990. *World Development Report: Poverty*. Washington DC: World Bank.

World Bank. 2010. 'Old concept of "third world" is outdated', Zoellick says', press release no. 2010/347/EXC. Washington DC: World Bank.

Zarembka, P. 2003. 'Lenin as economist of production: a Ricardian step backwards'. *Science and Society* 67(3), 276–302.

Zhou, Xiaochuan. 2009. 'Reform the international monetary system'. Beijing: People's Bank of China.

INDEX

Printed and bound by CPI Group (UK) Ltd, Croydon, CR0 4YY

16/04/2025

14658481-0004